Criminal Procedure Systems in the European Community

# Criminal procedure systems in the European Community

Christine VAN DEN WYNGAERT
*Editor*

and
C.GANE
H.H.KÜHNE
F.MCAULEY
*Co-editors*

**Butterworths**
London, Brussels, Dublin, Edinburgh
1993

| United Kingdom | Butterworth & Co (Publishers) Ltd, 88 Kingsway, LONDON WC2B 6AB and 4 Hill Street, EDINBURGH EH2 3JZ |
| Australia | Butterworths, SYDNEY, MELBOURNE, BRISBANE, ADELAIDE, PERTH, CANBERRA and HOBART |
| Belgium | Butterworth & Co (Publishers) Ltd, BRUSSELS |
| Canada | Butterworths Canada Ltd, TORONTO and VANCOUVER |
| Ireland | Butterworth (Ireland) Ltd, DUBLIN |
| Malaysia | Malayan Law Journal Sdn Bhd, KUALA LUMPUR |
| New Zealand | Butterworths of New Zealand Ltd, WELLINGTON and AUCKLAND |
| Puerto Rico | Equity de Puerto Rico, Inc, SAN JUAN |
| Singapore | Butterworths Asia, SINGAPORE |
| USA | Butterworth Legal Publishers, CARLSBAD, California and SALEM, New Hampshire |

A CIP Catalogue record for this book is available from the British Library.

ISBN   0 406 02276 3

Printed and bound in Great Britain by Clays Limited, St Ives plc

# Foreword

Until recently, there was relatively little interest in comparative criminal procedure. This may be explained by the fact that criminal procedure, more than any other legal discipline, resists harmonisation. A political reason for this phenomenon may be that criminal procedure is essentially linked to State sovereignty and the rules of criminal procedure belong to those rules which set the limits of the powers of a State vis-a-vis its citizens. As such, they regulate the State's monopoly on the use of power, not only in respect of convicted criminals, but also in respect of suspects, who may be subjected to such measures as arrest, search and seizure and telephone surveillance. From this perspective, criminal procedure is a standard to measure the degree of democracy of a given society. It is hardly surprising that States have a tendency, not only to be chauvinistic about their own criminal justice systems, but also to be suspicious about foreign systems. Efforts towards harmonisation in this field are therefore very often considered as an unacceptable interference in their domestic affairs.

This phenomenon is very clear in the European Community, where criminal procedure has, so far, remained almost completely immune to the general pattern of integration that has affected most other legal disciplines. Within the Community, the most striking difference still is that between civil law countries and common law countries. The (real or perceived) gulf between these countries may be greatest in the field of criminal procedure. Notwithstanding the fact that, under the influence of the European Convention on Human Rights, the gap between the "inquisitorial systems" on one side of the Channel, and the "adversarial systems" on the other, is gradually being bridged, the differences remain great. And even within each group of States, there are considerable differences, despite their common legal heritage.

However, the problems States face nowadays are largely identical: a general increase in crime, particularly in such fields as organised crime, fraud and economic crime; an insufficiency of financial means for the different enforcement levels (police, prosecutors, courts, prisons, etc.); a lack of coordination between these enforcement levels; the complexity of the legislation; increasing demands in respect of the quality of criminal proceedings (mainly due to the requirements of the European Convention on Human Rights); slowness of the proceedings; miscarriages of justice; insufficient protection for victims of crime; and, last but not least, the fact that, for these reasons, the general public seems to be gradually loosing confidence in the criminal justice system.

States on either side of the Channel are now facing these problems and have started to question the merits of their criminal justice systems. In the course of this questioning, they have raised doubts about the very foundations on which these systems are based, both for fundamental and pragmatic reasons. For example, many of the "continental" countries have recently imported features of the anglo-american "adversarial system", whereas in England, changes are being proposed which are inspired by some of the inquisitorial features of the continental systems. Despite this, in many discussions underlying the debate in various European countries, there seems to be a lack of understanding about foreign criminal justice systems.

There is, however, a growing need for such an understanding within the European Community. Despite the fact that European integration, does not, so far, include criminal procedure, Member States of the European Community, whether they want it or not, will be obliged to cooperate with each other in this field in the future. Even though there is no real obligation on Member States in this respect, the Maastricht Treaty (art.K.1) clearly provides that crime suppression is henceforth to be considered as a matter of common concern for the Twelve. Even if they are not prepared to harmonise their legislation, they will have to cooperate through such procedures as extradition and, perhaps more important in the future, mutual assistance and transfer of proceedings and of the execution of sentences. Failure to do so may have grave consequences. Whereas economic borders have disappeared in the European Community, political borders have remained. Criminals are free to cross these borders, but not so the police or the judiciary. If the fight against criminality is not dealt with through increased cooperation amongst the Member States, the Community may become a paradise for criminals, especially for fraudsters who direct their fraudulent wits against the budgets of the Member States and of the European Community, and who benefit directly from the lack of a structured and centralised criminal justice system in the Community.

This book seeks to contribute to a greater knowledge and mutual understanding in this field, by offering a general introduction to the criminal procedure systems of the Member States of the European Community. The idea of publishing it grew out of the need of having a textbook for students of comparative criminal procedure. When I started teaching this course some years ago at the University of Antwerp, Belgium, I was surprised to find that there was no such textbook available. Later, in 1992-93, when I was part of a group of experts participating in a study project on E.C.-fraud, commissioned by UCLAF (the anti-fraud unit of the European Community) and the Directorate General for Financial Control of the E.C.-Commission, I was again surprised to find that there were no materials available explaining the criminal procedure systems in the Member States.

Lacking both the knowledge and the time to write a comprehensive book on comparative criminal procedure encompassing the entire European

Community myself, I asked a number of colleagues in other E.C.-countries, who, in their teachings, were obviously facing the same problem, to write the book together with me. It is intended as a first introduction to the different criminal justice systems in Europe. It consists of a collection of articles describing the criminal procedure systems of the twelve Member States of the European Community plus Scotland. The structure of each chapter follows a general scheme which encompasses the entire criminal justice process from police investigations until judgment and sentence.

The book is in the first place addressed to *students*, as more and more of them, under the influence of the Erasmus-programme (the E.C.-financed student mobility programme), have become interested in comparative courses, including comparative criminal procedure. It also addresses *practitioners*, who tend to be increasingly confronted with cases involving foreign criminal justice systems. Lawyers may have clients who are prosecuted abroad, or who, within the context of national criminal proceedings, are confronted with international elements which lead them to study aspects of foreign criminal justice systems. Also, the growing use of procedures such as extradition, international letters rogatory and the transfer of proceedings has created a need for a greater knowledge of other criminal justice systems. In addition, lawyers are becoming increasingly aware of the differences in procedural rights of defendants in criminal proceedings throughout Europe, without always having the necessary materials to guide them through the labyrinth of foreign systems.

I have hesitated about the language to be used for this book. The choice was between either French or English, or a combination of both. I finally chose English. I know that Jean Pradel of the University of Poitiers, one of the contributors to this book, will regret my decision. However, he is himself the cause of my choice: thanks to Jean Pradel, a number of excellent comparative studies have appeared in French, in the three volumes of the *Revue Internationale de Droit Pénal* that were published under his direction. As there is, so far, no English equivalent, I decided to publish this book in English. This was not the easiest option, as the majority of the contributions were by authors from civil law countries, describing criminal justice systems based on an underlying inquisitorial philosophy and terminology. Very often, translation was nearly impossible because there were no equivalent expressions in English to translate typically inquisitorial concepts. Struggling with the index, an even greater difficulty was that identical terms have different meanings in different systems, whereas identical ideas are often expressed in different terms.

I wish to express my gratitude to all those who have contributed to this book. In the first place, I wish to thank Stephan Trechsel of the University of St.Gallen, Switzerland, who, without realizing it himself, was the one who triggered the idea to publish a book of this kind, when he sent me a reprint of his chapter on Swiss criminal procedure, published as part of a collection of articles on Swiss law. This chapter, both in structure and in scope, happened to correspond exactly to what I had in mind for the purposes of this book. With his permission, I took it as a model for the common outline of the 13 chapters.

I discussed my project at an early stage with Finnbar McAuley of the University College of Dublin and Hans-Heiner Kühne of the University of Trier, whom I had met in the framework of the Erasmus-programme. They were both very enthusiastic and were the first two colleagues who agreed to contribute. They kindly advised me on the common outline which became the general structure of all the chapters, and promoted the book while I was editing it.

I am very indebted to Chris Gane of the University of Sussex, who helped me with the editing. He read the manuscripts after I had edited them, and corrected them linguistically and conceptually from his perspective as a common lawyer. He co-ordinated the "common law chapters" (England and Wales, Ireland and Scotland) and translated the Spanish and French chapters into English.

I also wish to express my gratitude to the other contributors to this book for the excellent chapters they have written. All have been extremely cooperative, especially when it came to respecting deadlines and to updating their contributions just before publication.

Finally, I wish to thank my collaborators at the University of Antwerp, Bart De Smet, Guy Stessens, Raf Janssens and Eric Verbert who helped with the proofreading.

Last but not least I wish to thank my husband, Francis Camerlinckx, for his constant moral and intellectual support.

Christine Van den Wyngaert
15 October 1993

# General Contents

# Common Scheme

1. **Sources**
   1.1. GENERAL OBSERVATIONS
   1.2. THE CONSTITUTION
   1.3. HUMAN RIGHTS INSTRUMENTS
   1.4. THE CODE OF CRIMINAL PROCEDURE
   1.5. OTHER STATUTES
   1.6. CASE-LAW AND LEGAL DOCTRINE
2. **Structure of the criminal justice system**
   2.1. INVESTIGATING AUTHORITIES
   2.2. PROSECUTING AUTHORITIES
   2.3. THE JUDICIARY
3. **Parties to criminal proceedings**
   3.1. THE PUBLIC PROSECUTOR
   3.2. THE DEFENCE
   3.3. THE VICTIM
4. **General principles concerning criminal procedure**
   4.1. GENERAL PRINCIPLES
   4.2. PRINCIPLES GOVERNING THE OPENING OF CRIMINAL PRO-
        CEEDINGS
   4.3. PRINCIPLES GOVERNING THE TAKING OF EVIDENCE
   4.4. PRINCIPLES GOVERNING THE TRIAL
5. **Coercive measures**
   5.1. ARREST AND DETENTION
   5.2. SEARCH AND SEIZURE
   5.3. EXAMINATION OF BODY AND MIND
   5.4. INTERFERENCE WITH THE RIGHT TO PRIVACY
6. **The ordinary course of criminal proceedings**
7. **Evidence**
8. **Special forms of procedure**
9. **Remedies**
10. **Other questions**
11. **Select bibliography**

# Detailed Contents

## Chapter 5 - Germany . . . . . . . . . . . . . . 137

# Chapter 8 - Italy . . . . . . . . . . . . . . . . 223

# Chapter 1 - Belgium

Prof. Christine **VAN DEN WYNGAERT**
Law Faculty
University of Antwerp

## 1. Sources

### 1.1. GENERAL OBSERVATIONS

Belgium was founded in 1830, after a short revolution against the Kingdom of the Netherlands, into which Belgium had been incorporated by the Vienna Congress (1815). During the period of the "Dutch rule" (1815-1830), most of the Napoleonic codes, including the Penal Code and the Code of Criminal Procedure (CCP) (except for the abolition of the jury), remained in force. The drafters of the Belgian Constitution (1830) announced their explicit intention to introduce a completely new set of Codes, pending which the Napoleonic codes would remain applicable (art.139 of the Constitution, abolished in 1971).

In the field of criminal procedure, however, this ambitious intention never materialised. Except for some minor modifications, the old *Code d'Instruction Criminelle* is still applicable in Belgium today. Many reform proposals have been made, but none has as yet been accepted. Meanwhile, whereas most states on the European continent have gradually abandoned (in whole or in part) the Napoleonic model, Belgian criminal procedure has retained most of the inquisitorial characteristics of the old code.

Despite the inertia of the legislator, the system has nevertheless evolved due to the *European Convention on Human Rights*, which Belgium ratified at an early stage. From 1955, Belgium has accepted the right of individual application, and from 1971, the Supreme Court (*Cour de Cassation*) has recognised the direct effect of the Convention, and concomitantly, its priority over domestic law. Through the direct application of the right to a fair trial (art.6) and the right to personal freedom (art.5), the European Convention has softened some of the harsh inquisitorial features of the Belgian system, and in doing so, has realised what the legislator has not been able to achieve since 1830: adapting criminal procedure to contemporary concepts of fairness and justice.

Another, more future-oriented element that may characterise Belgian criminal procedure in the next decades is the recent federalisation of the Belgian state. Whereas criminal law and criminal procedure were, until 1993, an exclusively federal competence, the constitutional revision of 1993 has left

1

room for departures from this principle. Accordingly, it is not excluded that, in some fields, the three economic *regions* (Flanders, Wallonia and Brussels) and the three cultural *communities* (the Flemish, French and German communities) will develop their own procedural rules in the future.

## 1.2. THE CONSTITUTION

The Belgian Constitution was one of the first liberal constitutions of the 19th Century, after the *Ancien Régime* had been restored by the Vienna Congress (1815).

The second title of the Constution contains an enumeration of a number of *fundamental rights and freedoms*, some of which relate to criminal procedure. These rights, which have nowadays become classic in constitutional law, were nevertheless quite modern in 1830. They include the right to personal freedom (art.7), the legality principle (art.9), the inviolability of the home (art.10) and of correspondence (art.22) and the freedom of the press (art.17).

The Chapter on *the Judiciary* sets out a number of fundamental principles, including the competence of the "natural judge" (art.94)[1], the principle that trials should be held in public and that judgments should be publicly pronounced (art.96), the principle that judges should give reasons for their judgments (art.97), and the principle of the independence of the judiciary (arts.99-104).

According to the Constitution, the most serious crimes should be judged by a jury (art.98). The same guarantee applies to *political crimes* and *"press crimes"*. The latter must be understood in their historical context: as most of the drafters of the Belgian constitution had themselves been political dissidents of the previous regime (some of them had even been prosecuted because of their critical comments in the press), they wanted to give a special constitutional protection to political and press offenders, who were given the right to trial by jury. This right was originally reserved for political and press offences only, but was later extended to the most serious common offences.

## 1.3. THE EUROPEAN CONVENTION ON HUMAN RIGHTS AND OTHER HUMAN RIGHTS INSTRUMENTS

Belgium became a party to the European Convention on Human Rights in 1955[2], and was one of the first states to accept the right of individual application. It has also ratified the International Covenant on Civil and

---

[1]Meaning that the competence of a judge in a particular case must be determined by law, not by the parties. In other words, "jurisdiction shopping" is excluded, and so are exceptional tribunals and ad hoc tribunals.

[2]*Moniteur belge*, 19 August 1955.

2

Political Rights[3].

These two international instruments, especially the European Convention, have had a very great impact on Belgian criminal procedure for two reasons: the right of individual application and the direct effect of the Convention in the Belgian legal order.

The early acceptance of the *right of individual application* has given rise to quite a large number of cases in which the European Commission and Court for Human Rights have had the opportunity to rule on the compatibility of parts of Belgian criminal law and procedure with the European Convention on Human Rights. Some of the "condemnations" in Strasbourg have prompted legislative changes in Belgium. For example, after the *Lamy* case[4], a totally new statute on detention on remand was passed.

However, far more important than the results of cases in which individuals avail themselves of their right to petition the European Commission is the fact that rules of international law have *direct effect* in Belgium. This principle, which was accepted by the *Cour de Cassation* in the early Seventies[5], allows courts in Belgium to set aside national laws that are contrary to the European Convention: in case of a conflict between a national rule and a directly applicably rule of international law, the latter prevails. In practice, this has allowed the courts in Belgium to soften somewhat the severe inquisitorial features of the Code of Criminal Procedure.

## 1.4. THE CODE OF CRIMINAL PROCEDURE

Belgium and Luxembourg are probably the last states in Europe to apply the Napoleonic *Code d'Instruction Criminelle* of 1808. However, unlike Luxembourg, Belgium has hardly modified the original code. Except for one chapter, that was introduced into the Code in 1878 (Preliminary title to the Code of Criminal Procedure), the original Napoleonic Code has remained almost intact. Taking into account the fact that, as far as pre-trial procedures are concerned, the Napoleonic code is, to a large extent, a copy of the *Grande Ordonnance Criminelle* of Colbert (1670), which, in turn, heavily draws from the *Constitutio Criminalis Carolina* (1530), criminal procedure in Belgium is probably one of the most conservative in Europe.

---

[3]*Moniteur belge*, 6 July 1983.

[4]LAMY v. Belgium, European Court of Human Rights, 30 March 1989, *Publ. E.C.H.R.*, Series A, vol. 151.

[5]*Cour de Cassation*, 27 May 1971, *Belgian State v. Fromagerie Franco-Suisse Le Ski*, *Pasicrisie*, 1971, 886, with the conclusions of *procureur général* Ganshof Van der Meersch.

### 1.5. OTHER STATUTES

There are a number of important codes and statutes which supplement the Code of Criminal Procedure. Amongst these codes and statutes are: the *Code of Civil Procedure* (1967), which sets out the rules on the composition and the competence of the courts, on the structure of the *ministère public* and which supplements the Code of Criminal Procedure on those matters which are not explicitly dealt with in that Code.

Detention on remand is not dealt with in the Code of Criminal Procedure, but has been regulated in a special *Statute on detention on remand* (1990), which replaces the old statute of 1874, after the "condemnation" of Belgium by the European Court of Human Rights in the *Lamy* case.

Other important statutes are: the Law on mitigating circumstances (1867), allowing for the procedure of correctionalisation (*infra*, 6.1.4.), and the 1969 Law on searches in private places.

Belgium still has a specialised military judiciary, though there are proposals to reduce or even abolish it. Procedure before the military courts is governed by a code which dates back to the Dutch period, the *Code of Procedure for the Land Army* (1814), which was supplemented by the *Code of Military Procedure* of 1899.

A special procedural regime exists for minors, *i.e.* persons below the age of 18. These rules are set out in the *Statute on the protection of minors* (1965), which has been recently regionalised. Mentally disabled offenders are judged by the ordinary courts, which, however, apply a special statute called *Statute on social defence* (1930), which contains a number of special substantive and procedural rules.

### 1.6. CASE-LAW AND LEGAL DOCTRINE

Case-law and legal doctrine are not formal sources of the law in Belgium. Even decisions of the *Cour de Cassation* are not binding upon the lower courts. However, *Cour de Cassation* decisions tend to have a great intellectual authority, and in practice, lower courts tend to follow the case-law of the *Cour de Cassation*.

## 2. Structure of the criminal justice system

### 2.1. INVESTIGATING AUTHORITIES

Crime investigation is a task of the State in Belgium. The so-called (in terms of the Napoleonic Code) *acts of judicial police* (*actes de police judiciaire*), basically acts of crime investigation, can, in principle, only be performed by sworn officers who have been invested by law with the capacity of investigation officer (*officier de police judiciaire*). These officers take an oath on the moment they assume their functions, and most of their investigation activities are deemed to be covered by this oath. For example, written records of investigation officers, *procès-verbaux*, have, by themselves, value as evidence in court, due to the mere fact that they have been made by sworn officers (*infra*, 7.1.).

Persons invested with the capacity of *officier de police judiciaire* are under the disciplinary supervision of the head of the *ministère public*, the *procureur général* at the Court of Appeal (art.279 CCP).

The Code of Criminal Procedure enumerates the persons which are invested with this capacity (art.9). In general terms, they are: the police, the public prosecutor and the investigating judge.

### 2.1.1. The police

There are three regular police forces in Belgium: the *gendarmerie*, the communal police and the judicial police.

The *gendarmerie* is organised on a national level. It comes under the authority of both the Ministries of Justice and the Interior. The *communal police* is organised on a local level, *i.e.* the level of towns and communes. The *judicial police* in theory has a national competence, but in practice it mainly operates at the level of the *arrondissement*, which is the territorial competence of the *parquet*. Whereas the gendarmerie and the communal police also have administrative tasks (*i.e.* monitoring the application of the law, and prevention of offences), the judicial police have no other duties than crime investigation.

Basically, there is no difference in competence *ratione materiae* between the three regular police forces: they all have a general competence, which means that they may investigate all offences, regardless of their nature or their seriousness. In practice, this overlapping competence creates problems: very often, there is no co-ordination at all between the police forces, or, worse, an unhealthy competition. The only difference, especially between the *gendarmerie* and the communal police, is *ratione loci*, because the former have national, the latter only local, jurisdiction.

In addition to the regular police forces, there are several civil servants who, in addition to their administrative responsibilities, are invested with the capacity of "investigating officer" (*officier de police judiciaire*), but only in respect of particular offences. For example, some inspectors of the Ministry of Agriculture have not only administrative tasks, *i.e.* monitoring the application of the agricultural legislation, but may also perform acts of investigation (*actes de police judiciaire*) and draw up *procès-verbaux*. The same applies to the inspectors of the Ministry of Economic affairs, who have been declared competent to investigate certain economic offences.

The police, whether it be members of the regular police forces or specialised police officers, are under an obligation to make written records of their findings (*procès-verbaux*). They must immediately report offences to the public prosecutor (art.29 CCP). They have no discretionary powers concerning the further action to be taken, and failing to record or to report an offence is a breach of duty, for which they may be reprimanded by the disciplinary authority, the *procureur général* at the Court of appeal. Beyond their initial report of the offence, (*procès-verbal initial*), which they are obliged to make *ex officio*, they have no investigative powers of their own. Once they have reported the crime, they must wait for further instructions from the public prosecutor.

### 2.1.2. The public prosecutor

The public prosecutor (*ministère public*, see *infra*, 2.2.) is the master of the investigations. He decides what action is to be taken after receiving the initial police report of the crime, and may, at any stage, decide not to proceed with the case.

The public prosecutor, being an *officier de police judiciaire* (art.9 CCP), has a general competence to investigate crimes. He has the same investigating powers as the police, and could, in theory, perform all the investigations himself. In practice, however, investigations are carried out by the police, on the instructions of the public prosecutor.

Despite the fact that the great majority of cases are investigated in this manner, this type of investigation is not regulated in the code. It is called *information*. In the *information*, the public prosecutor may order all investigations that are necessary to find the truth. The only limitation is that he must respect the law, and is not entitled to take coercive measures by which fundamental rights of the accused or of a third party would be infringed (*e.g.* detention on remand, or a search and seizure). These measures can only be taken by a judge. In such cases, investigations are led by a specialised judge, the investigating judge, in a procedure called preliminary judicial investigation or *instruction*.

### 2.1.3. The investigating judge (juge d'instruction)

According to the Code of Criminal Procedure, the normal course of pre-trial investigation is that conducted under the direction of the investigating judge following the procedure of the *instruction* (*infra*, 6.1.3.). However, in practice, this only occurs in very complex cases, or else when coercive measures must be taken. All other investigations are done by the public prosecutor, with the help of the police (*information*, see above, 2.1.2.).

Like the public prosecutor, the investigating judge is an *officier de police judiciaire*. There is, however, a great difference: unlike the public prosecutor, the investigating judge may not start an investigation *ex officio*: he can only proceed to an investigation if he has been formally requested to do so by the public prosecutor by means of a formal application called *investigation request* (*mandat d'instruction-vordering tot onderzoek*), or by the victim (*constitution de partie civile*, see *infra*, 3.3.2.), save in the exceptional case of an offender caught in *flagrante delicto*.

Moreover, the investigating judge is always limited by the terms of the investigation request (the *saisine)*: he may only investigate the offence of which he has been seized in the request, and may not extend his investigation to other, even related offences *(infra,* 6.1.3.).

The code does not regulate the powers of the investigating judge in great detail. It is generally accepted that the investigating judge has a general power to carry out whatever investigations he deems necessary to discover the truth. According to the *Cour de Cassation,* he may perform any act of investigation which is not forbidden by law and which is not incompatible with his professional dignity[6].

Like the public prosecutor, the investigating judge has, within the limits of his *saisine (i. e.* the investigation request of the public prosecutor), the same powers as the police. He too is an *officier de police judiciaire* (art.9 CCP). However, in practice, investigations are carried out by the police, under the instructions of the investigating judge.

In his capacity as an *officier de police judiciaire,* the investigating judge is subject to the disciplinary control of the public prosecutor, the *procureur général* at the Court of appeal (art.279 CCP). However, this control only relates to his activities as a police officer, not to his judicial acts *(i. e.* warrants of arrest or of search and seizure), about which he decides freely, with the independence and impartiality of a judge. In practice, however, the disciplinary control of the *parquet* creates tensions, as it is often perceived by investigating judges as an unwarranted interference in their judicial activities.

## 2.2. PROSECUTING AUTHORITIES

The prosecuting authority in Belgium is organised according to the ideas of the Napoleonic code: the prosecuting authority is the *public ministry (ministère public-openbaar ministerie)* which is the generic name designating the body of magistrates which performs the function of public prosecutors in the pre-trial investigations and in the courts. The term "public ministry" refers to the whole body of persons that are endowed, amongst others, with the function of public prosecutor. (They also have other functions, such as, for example, the execution of sentences).

The public ministry is a hierarchically organised body. At the top of the pyramid is the public prosecutor at the court of appeal (5 in number, one for each court of appeal), the *procureur général,* who is assisted by *advocates-general* and *substitutes-procureur général.* Then follows the public prosecutor at the court of first instance (27 in number, 1 for each court of first instance), the *procureur du Roi,* who is assisted by several *substitutes,* who vary in number according to the work-load of each court.

The name *parquet* refers to the body of public prosecutors in each

---

[6]*Cour de Cassation,* 2 May 1960, *Pasicrisie,* I, 1020

court. For example, the "*parquet* of Antwerp" includes the *procureur du Roi* of Antwerp and his 40 or so *substitutes*. The term *parquet général* refers to the public ministry at the level of the court of appeal. Thus, the *parquet général* of Brussels is the *procureur général* of Brussels, and his advocates general and substitutes.

One of the legacies of the Napoleonic code is the idea that the public ministry is said to be "*one and indivisible*". This means that, as far as concerns the outside world, the *parquet* acts as one single unit: individual members of one *parquet* do not act in their personal names but in name of the function. For example, official documents of the *parquet* are always signed on behalf of the procureur, regardless of the individual member of the parquet whose signature appears on the document. The "indivisibility" of the parquet also means that several members of one parquet can act for each other at any time. Hence, it may occur that, in one single case, one *substitute* directs the police inquiry, whereas a second takes the decision about whether or not to prosecute, while yet a third may plead the case when it is committed for trial.

A rather odd feature, also inherited from Napoleon (but not explicit in the Code), is that members of the parquet owe obedience to their hierarchical superiors only regarding written instructions, but not when they plead in court: " *La plume est serve, la parole est libre*". This basically means that members of the *parquet* are only bound by written instructions during the pre-trial stage of the proceedings; they resume their freedom when acting as a public prosecutor during the trial. For example, when the *procureur du roi* gives a written order to one of his substitutes to prosecute a particular case, the substitute cannot refuse to prosecute, even if he finds that, in the present case, prosecution is not appropriate. However, when the case is committed for trial, the same substitute would be free, at the hearing, to ask for the acquittal of the accused.

There is much discussion in Belgium regarding the nature of the function of the public ministry. According to some, the function is of a judicial nature, whereas others find that it is an executive, rather than a judicial function, while still others think that the public ministry, while not belonging to the executive state power, nevertheless represents the state before the courts. The question is especially relevant with respect to the wide discretionary powers of the *parquet* in respect of dropping the case or proposing *transactions* (see *infra*, 8.1. and 8.2.).

## 2.3. THE JUDICIARY

The organisation of the judiciary in penal matters reflects the dichotomy of criminal proceedings, which are divided in two stages: the pre-trial stage and the trial stage. The investigating judge and the courts of investigation are courts which do not render final judgments but which have various competences in the pre-trial stage (2.3.1.), the trial courts are those which decide on the merits during the trial stage of the proceedings (2.3.2.).

### 2.3.1. Courts in the pre-trial stage of the proceedings

The courts that have special competences in the pre-trial stage are: the investigating judge and the courts of investigation, *i.e.* the judicial council (*chambre du conseil-raadkamer* (first instance)) and the court of indictment (*chambre des mises en accusation-kamer van inbeschuldigingsstelling* (appeal)).

#### (i) The investigating judge
The *investigating judge (juge d'instruction-onderzoeksrechter)* is the feature *par excellence* of the inquisitorial system. He is a judge of the court of first instance (of which the *tribunal correctionnel* is a chamber), who is specially appointed for the purposes of the pre-trial investigation. The investigating judge does not take decisions about the merits of the case, *i.e.* he never delivers judgments or sentences. Instead, his task is to lead the *instruction*, *i.e.* the preliminary judicial investigation, and in doing so, he may perform essentially judicial tasks, such as the issuing of a warrant of arrest or a search warrant. Accordingly, the investigating judge combines two functions: the function of a police officer (*i.e.* an *officier de police judiciaire*, whose duty it is to investigate crimes, cfr *supra*, 2.1.) and that of a judge, whenever coercive measures must be taken.

There is, of course, nothing special in coercive measures being taken by a judge: the same principle also applies in common law systems. However, the essential difference with the inquisitorial system is that the investigating judge not only takes decisions about coercive measures, but, once he is seized, about the whole investigation. Accordingly, he not only decides on the legality of a coercive measure which the police or the *parquet* want him to take, but also about the appropriateness of the measure, in the given circumstances of the case.

Another striking difference is that the investigating judge, once he has been seized by an investigation request from the public prosecutor, acts *ex officio*: as from that moment, he becomes the master of the investigations. He must collect the evidence that is necessary to find the objective truth, in all objectivity. The essence of the investigating judge is that he is an impartial magistrate, whose duty it is to collect evidence both in favour of and against the accused.

Whereas, according to the *Code napoléon*, the investigating judge should conduct the great majority of investigations, his role has been considerably reduced in recent times (see *supra*, 2.1.). The majority of cases are now investigated by the public prosecutor by means of an *information* (*infra*, 6.1.2.), and the *instruction* (*infra*, 6.1.3.) is, in practice, limited to those cases in which judicial decisions (*i.e.* coercive measures) must be taken.

*(ii) The judicial council (chambre du conseil-raadkamer)*

The *judicial council* is a chamber of the court of first instance, which is competent to render decisions on various issues in respect of the pre-trial investigations. Like the investigating judge, the judicial council never, save in some exceptional cases, decides on the merits, but only gives orders *(ordonnances-beschikkingen)* relating to various aspects of the pre-trial investigations. These *ordonnances* are not judgments, in the sense of the Constitution, and hence reasons need not to be given for them, nor need they be publicly pronounced, like ordinary judgments (arts.96 and 97 of the Constitution).

The most important competences of the judicial council are: (a) periodic checks with respect to the further detention of persons who are detained on remand *(infra*, 5.2.); (b) the *règlement de procédure-regeling der rechtspleging*, which are basically committal proceedings *(infra*, 6.1.4.) and, (c), exceptionally, deciding about certain coercive measures during the *instruction* which cannot be taken by the investigating judge alone, namely some physical and mental examinations *(infra*, 5.3.).

*(iii) The court of indictment (chambre des mises en accusation-kamer van inbeschuldigingstelling)*

The court of indictment is a chamber of the court of appeal. It functions as an appellate court with respect to both decisions of the investigating judge *(ordonnances contraires*, *infra*, 6.1.3.) and orders *(ordonnances)* of the judicial council. Committals to the assize court can only be decided by the court of indictment. It has also a number of specific functions of its own, such as advising the government about the admissibility of an extradition request.

### 2.3.2. Trial courts

The organisation of the trial courts in Belgium, like in many other countries, is based on the division of offences in substantive criminal law. Following the French model, offences in Belgium are divided in three categories, *crimes*, *délits* and *contraventions*. *Crimes* are punishable with custodial sentences of 5 years and more, *délits* with sentences between 8 days and 5 years and/or a heavy fine, and *contraventions* with sentences of 7 days and less or with minor fines only.

As in Napoleonic times, the division corresponds to a tripartite court-system: *crimes* are judged by the assize court, a jury court, *délits* by the *tribunal correctionnel*, a chamber of the court of first instance composed of professional judges, and *contraventions* by a single judge, the police court. However, in the course of time this division has been blurred considerably.

Whereas, in principle, *crimes* should be judged by the *assize court*, most *crimes* are nowadays brought before the *tribunal correctionnel*. Only the most serious *crimes* (those which carry a sentence of 20 years and more) are brought before the assize court. Most other *crimes* are converted into *délits*, through a process called *correctionalisation*, and hence the *tribunal correctionnel* is competent (see *infra*, 6.1.4.). The assize court is not a permanent court: it only sits when there are cases which have been referred to it by the court of indictment. It is composed of three professional judges, borrowed from the court of appeal or the *tribunal correctionnel*, and of 12 lay judges appointed by lot. The assize court can pronounce sentences up to the death penalty (which, in practice, is always commuted into life imprisonment).

*Délits* are normally brought before the *tribunal correctionnel*, which is a chamber of the court of first instance. In theory, the *tribunal correctionnel* cannot pronounce sentences exceeding 5 years. *crimes* that have been "correctionalised", however, can be punished more severely (art.25 of the Penal Code).

*Contraventions* are judged by the police courts. However, many special statutes creating *délits* (which should normally be brought before the *tribunal correctionnel*), have attributed jurisdiction to the police courts. The most current example is that of road traffic offences, which, often being *délits*, are not judged by the *tribunal correctionnel* but by the police courts.

The jurisdiction of the courts mentioned above is based on the nature of the offence. This type of jurisdiction is referred to as jurisdiction *ratione materiae*. In addition, there are courts whose jurisdiction is based on criteria relating to the accused (jurisdiction *ratione personae*). They are: the *military courts*, who are competent vis-à-vis servicemen, the *juvenile courts*, who try cases against persons below the age of 18, and the *first civil chamber of the court of appeal*, which has an exclusive competence to try judges and public prosecutors who are accused of an offence.

### 2.3.3. The role of lay judges

The right to trial by jury was laid down in the Constitution as a reaction to the "Dutch rule" (1815-1830, *supra*, 1.1.), during which the jury had been abolished. Originally, its reintroduction was only proposed for political crimes and for "press crimes", a rather odd concept that can only be understood by reference to its historical origin (*supra*, 1.2.). Political crimes and press crimes are nowadays defined in such a restrictive manner that hardly any such crime has been submitted to the jury in the course of this Century.

In practice, it is mainly *crimes*, *i.e.* offences punishable by a custodial sentence of five years and more that are judged by the assize court. However, also in respect of *crimes*, the role of lay judges has been considerably reduced. Despite the fact that the right to trial by jury was laid down in the Constitution (art.98), the legislator has, since the second half of the last Century, gradually restricted the competence of the jury, by the process of *correctionalisation* (*infra*, 6.1.4.).

The question as to whether the jury system should be retained continues to be controversial in Belgium. In favour of the jury, it is argued that it is the only real democratic institution left, in which there is a direct participation by the people without interference of the state. Also, the jury has a great educational impact. Another advantage is that the jury is not bound by the rules of rational decision-making. Accordingly, the jury may acquit a person, even if his guilt has been established beyond reasonable doubt. The classic example in this respect is the famous thalidomide-trial in Liège in the Sixties, in which the jury acquitted the parents who had confessed to the murder of their deformed child.

Many, however, are in favour of abolishing the jury. They argue that, even in the Napoleonic code, the jury was considered as a rather odd institution, hardly reconcilable with the strong inquisitorial features of the code, "*un portail gothique sur un bâtiment moderne*", as it was said by Faustin Hélie, one of the great commentators on the Code. Against the jury, it is argued that assize procedures are often show trials that are not conducted with the necessary serenity. The possibility for the jury to return irrational verdicts is not an advantage, but a disgrace, according to these critics. Another point of criticism is that no appeal can be lodged against jury verdicts, which contrasts with the fact that judgments of professional judges, in less serious cases, are all subject to appeal. In addition, the selection of the cases that are submitted to the jury is rather arbitrary, as the technique of *correctionalisation* (*infra*, 6.1.4.) is employed for practical reasons only, that have nothing to do with concerns for justice or fairness. However, abolishing the jury would require a revision of the Constitution, and no political party has, so far, made concrete proposals in this respect.

### 2.3.4. Independence and impartiality

The Constitution contains a number of rules which guarantee the independence and impartiality of the judges. For example, judges are appointed for life. In addition, the Code of Civil Procedure, along with the traditional grounds for disqualification (*récusation*) of judges (art.828 CCP, see also art.542 CCP), provides a number of incompatibilities, also to guarantee independence and impartiality (art.292 CCP). For example, a person who has previously, in another judicial capacity, been involved in a particular case, cannot be a judge in the same case afterwards.

Until some time ago, courts tended to interpret this principle in a very restrictive way, limiting it to cases in which the same person was involved as a magistrate at first instance, and subsequently on appeal. The *Cour de Cassation* did not see any problems arising from the fact that, within one degree of jurisdiction, one person might discharge different functions consecutively in the same case. For example, it was accepted that a person could be first a judge in the judicial council, and subsequently a trial judge in the same case. In the same vein, it was held that an investigating judge could later act as a trial judge in the same case. The principle adopted by the *Cour de Cassation* was that judges were presumed to be impartial, until proof of the contrary was given.

This case-law was abandoned after the European Court of Human Rights, in a number of cases against Belgium[7], adopted a different approach, that of the *objective impartiality*: despite the fact that, in a particular case, there is no personal partiality on the part of the judge, *i.e.* there is no question of *subjective partiality*, certain judicial functions, if they are consecutively held by the same person in the same case, are *per se* incompatible, even though the magistrate in question may be totally impartial. What matters is not whether, in reality, the judge in question is impartial or not (subjective impartiality), but the impression that is created vis-à-vis the public: *justice must not only be done but must also be seen to be done.* Belgian courts have since complied with the ruling of the court of Strasbourg: a number of new incompatibilities are applied now, that are not based on domestic law, but on the case-law of the court of Strasbourg.

### 2.3.5. Nomination of the judges

According to the Constitution (art.100), judges are appointed for life by the King. In practice, nominations are done by the Minister of Justice. Candidates must have a law degree and a certain number of years of practice, either as a public prosecutor or as an advocate. Until recently, there were no examinations at all. This has given rise to severe criticisms, because the nomination of judges was often dictated by political considerations. This has now changed: according to the statute of 18 July 1991, persons who want to become a judge (or a public prosecutor), must pass a qualifying exam.

Most judges are in practice recruited from the ranks of the public prosecutor's office. Although this may seem rather shocking to common lawyers, this is a general practice. There is no incompatibility between the two functions, provided that there is no "objective" partiality, *i.e.* that a prosecutor who has become a judge does not deal with cases with which he has been involved in his previous capacity.

## 3. Parties to criminal proceedings

### 3.1. THE PUBLIC PROSECUTOR

The public prosecutor has the monopoly of prosecutions. He alone can decide whether or not to prosecute a case. The victim is only entitled to bring a civil claim (see *infra*, 3.3.).

---

[7]PIERSACK v. Belgium, European Court of Human Rights, 1 October 1982, *Publ. E.C.H.R.*, Series A, vol. 53; DE CUBBER v. Belgium, European Court of Human Rights, 26 Ovtober 1984, *Publ. E.C.H.R.*, Series A, vol. 86; BEN YAACOUB v. Belgium, European Court of Human Rights, 27 November 1987, *Publ. E.C.H.R.*, Series A, vol. 127.

As in most European countries that have inherited the institution of the *ministère public* from the Napoleonic code, the public prosecutor in Belgium has the duty to look for the material truth: he is obliged to look for evidence both against and in favour of the accused. For this reason, he is sometimes considered not to be a party to the proceedings, because his only mission/mandate is to protect the general interest, not to obtain a conviction. If he feels that the accused is not guilty, he must ask the judge to acquit him. Accordingly, the public prosecutor in theory does not have a partisan function, but performs his duties in full objectivity, in the sole interest of applying the law.

In practice, however, the dynamics of the proceedings usually put the *ministère public* in the role of a partisan prosecutor, and thus of a real party to the proceedings. It is the prosecutor who investigates the case, collects the evidence, applies, if necessary, for coercive measures to be taken by the investigating judge, formulates the indictment, and presents the evidence during the hearing. In case of an acquittal, or of any judgment that prejudices the prosecution, the prosecutor may file an appeal.

## 3.2. THE DEFENCE

### 3.2.1. *The accused*

The legal position of the accused varies in the course of the proceedings. During the pre-trial stage, he has almost no procedural rights, whereas, during the trial, he is a real party to the proceedings. As in many systems, there is a "terminological hesitation" about the term to be used to designate a person who is the subject of a criminal investigation, because the use of a particular term may trigger certain specific rights. The situation is rather confused in Belgium. There is no obligation on the part of the authorities to warn someone of the fact that he is under investigation, and hence, it is unclear as from what moment a person has the quality of a "suspect" or an "accused". Different terms exist to designate this person in the various stages of the proceedings: during the pre-trial stage, he is called *suspect (inculpé-verdachte)*, during the trial, he is called either *accusé-beschuldigde*, or *prévenu-beklaagde*, depending on whether he has been committed for trial to the assize court, or to another court. It is impossible to use all the appropriate nuances for the purposes of this contribution. Therefore, the term "accused" will be used throughout.

### (i) *The pre-trial stage*
During the pre-trial stage, which is inquisitorial, the accused is not a party to the proceedings. At this stage, there is a striking imbalance between his legal position and that of the public prosecutor. Unlike the *ministère public*, the accused has no right to consult the investigation *dossier*, he has no right to be present during investigations, he may not interfere, for example by opposing

certain investigations or by requesting the investigating judge to perform certain inquiries which may produce evidence in his favour. Whereas the public prosecutor may file appeals against decisions of the investigating judge, the accused has no right to do so. Interrogations of the accused (by the police, the public prosecutor or the investigating judge) are held without the presence of his counsel and he receives no copy of his statements. Although, in theory, the privilege against self-incrimination exists, there is no obligation on the part of the authorities to inform the accused of this right.

The question has arisen whether this difference in treatment is compatible with the *equality of arms-principle* in art.6 of the European Convention on Human Rights, and more specifically, with the procedural rights of the accused, enumerated in par.3 of article 6. So far, the European Commission and Court have held that the fair trial rights in art.6 are only applicable to the trial, not to the pre-trial stage. However, there is a tendency to soften this rigid position[8]. Firstly, even though art.6 does not apply to each and any stage of the pre-trial proceedings, the Commission and Court, when assessing the fairness of a particular trial, look at the case in its entirety: some elements of the pre-trial stage may indeed prejudice the position of the accused to such an extent that the trial as a whole becomes unfair and is therefore contrary to art.6. Secondly, there is at least one paragraph of art.6 that is applicable throughout all stages of the proceedings, namely art.6(2), on the presumption of innocence.

Following a "condemnation" of Belgium by the Court of Strasbourg in a case concerning a person who was detained on remand[9], the law has now been changed in respect of this particular situation: persons who are detained on remand have henceforth the right to consult the *investigation dossier* at regular intervals and they may, at certain moments, ask to be interrogated by the investigating judge in the presence of their defence counsel. However, as a result of this, discrimination now exists between two sorts of accused, those who are detained on remand, and those who are not: whereas the former have access to the *dossier*, the latter are not allowed to consult it.

*(ii) The trial stage*

During the trial stage, the accused is a real party to the proceedings. The Napoleonic Code of Criminal Procedure does not provide rules defining his legal position, nor does it contain a chapter on the rights of the defence in criminal proceedings. However, due to the direct effect of art.6 of the European Convention on Human Rights, the accused now has the benefit of

---

[8]See for example CAN v. Austria, European Commission of Human Rights, 12 July 1984, (report), European Court of Human Rights, 30 September 1985, *Publ. E.C.H.R.*, Series A, vol. 96. See also LUEDICKE, BELKACEM AND KOÇ v. Germany, European Court of Human Rights 26 November 1978, *Publ. E.C.H.R.*, Series A, vol 29.

[9]The *Lamy*-case, see *supra*, note 4.

all of the rights that are enumerated in that article.

The accused has the right to be present at his trial, but is under no obligation to do so. If he decides not to be present, the trial will be conducted in his absence (*par défaut-bij verstek*). Against convictions *par défaut*, a special remedy exists, namely *opposition* (*infra*, 9.1.). Different rules apply to the assize court: here, the accused must be present, failing which he will be judged *par contumace* (see *infra*, 8,7. and 9.1.).

### 3.2.2. Defence counsel

The accused has the right to be assisted by defence counsel of his own choice. The assistance of defence counsel, however, is not compulsory (except for the assize court). If the accused is indigent, he is entitled to defence counsel *pro deo*, which means that the fee is paid by the state. In practice, *pro deo* advocates tend to be young, inexperienced lawyers.

During the *pre-trial stage*, defence counsel has no right to be present when investigations are made. For example, he may not be present during the interrogation of his client, or when witnesses are examined, nor may he attend searches and seizure at his client's house or premises or at those of a third party. There are, however, two exceptions to the principle that defence counsel has no right to assist his client during the pre-trial stage: (a) he may be present during the committal proceedings before the judicial council (*infra*, 6.1.4.) and (b) when his client is detained on remand, he may be present during the hearing of the judicial council on the lawfulness of the detention. In those proceedings, he may assist, but not represent his client, *i.e.* the accused must be present.

During the trial, defence counsel may assist his client at any moment of the proceedings. In most cases, however, counsel may not represent his client: as a rule, the accused who chooses to be present, must attend his trial personally, failing which he will be tried in his absence (*par défaut*, see *supra,* 3.2.1. and *infra,* 8.7.). In other words, it is not sufficient for the accused to send his counsel to the trial: he has to appear personally. The only exception to this rule is when the sentence that can be imposed is not a custodial sentence, or when the court has expressly authorised his counsel to represent him (art.185 §2 and 3 CCP).

### 3.3. THE VICTIM

### 3.3.1. Private prosecution

Private prosecution is not possible in Belgium. Whereas victims can bring a civil action against an alleged accused (*infra*, the *partie civile*), they have no possibility of actually prosecuting a case, *i.e.* to seize a judge in order to have him impose a criminal sentence on a particular person. The latter is the privilege of the *ministère public*, who has the monopoly over prosecution (art.1 Preliminary Title Code of Criminal Procedure, *infra*, 4.1.2.).

There is however, a number of cases which cannot be prosecuted by the *ministère public* unless there has been a formal complaint by the victim of the offence (art.2 Preliminary Title Code of Criminal Procedure). In former times, there were several offences in this category. The classic example used to be adultery, but this has become obsolete since the abolition of this offence in 1987. Today, there are but few examples left. One remaining example is defamation *(calomnie et diffamation*, art.450 Penal Code).

But even in such cases, the public prosecutor is not obliged to prosecute. Nothing prevents him from deciding not to prosecute (*classement sans suite, sépot*, see *infra*, 8.1.), or, when the victim has seized the trial court, from requesting the acquittal of the accused.

### 3.3.2. The partie civile

While victims are not entitled to bring actual prosecutions before the courts in Belgium, they may, however, bring a civil action for compensation for the damage caused by the offence. They may ask for both material and moral damages. This procedure is called *constitution de partie civile*.

If the public prosecutor has decided to prosecute the case, the *constution de partie civile* will have the effect of the victim becoming a party to proceedings which are already pending. He will be involved in the committal proceedings (*règlement de la procédure*) before the judicial council (*infra*, 6.1.4.) and, of course, in the trial. If he looses his case, he will not have to pay the costs of the proceedings, which are born by the state, who started the case.

If, however, the public prosecutor has decided not to prosecute, or is still considering his position, the victim may, by constituting himself *partie civile*, actually seize the judge. This is a fundamental difference with the victim's mere complaint, which is little more than a denunciation of the crime: a complaint does not have any procedural consequences, it does not seize a court of law and the public prosecutor is free not to proceed with the case. In case of a *constitution de partie civile*, however, the case can only be closed with a formal judicial decision, either by the judicial council or by the trial court.

In the latter hypothesis, there are two ways for the victim to constitute himself *partie civile*. He can either summon the accused directly before the trial court (*citation directe-rechtstreekse dagvaarding*), or seize the investigating judge (art.63 CCP). Because, in both cases, the victim must bear the cost of the proceedings, in case of an acquittal or a dismissal, a *citation directe* will be appropriate only if the victim has enough evidence to obtain a conviction; otherwise, the wiser course is to seize the investigating judge, who will then be obliged to search for the evidence.

The *constitution de partie civile* is only open to the actual victim of the crime, or to his relatives, not to persons who have been indirectly damaged by the offence (art.3 Preliminary Title CCP). There is only one derogation from this rule: violations of the statute on the suppression of racism (1981) can give rise to *constitution de partie civile* by associations with legal personality that have existed for at least five years and whose statutory purpose is the protection of human rights or the fight against racism.

### 3.3.3. Civil claims before civil courts

The victim may also chose to bring his claim for damages before a civil court. If proceedings before the criminal court are still pending (or are started after the civil court has been seized), the civil court must postpone its decision until the criminal court has returned its verdict (art.4 Preliminary Title CCP). The decision of the criminal court is binding for the civil judge: according to the maxim *le criminel tient le civil en état*, the decision of the criminal court has priority over the decision of the civil court. This means that in practice, in the case of an acquittal of the accused by a criminal court, the chances of the victim obtaining compensation in civil proceedings are very faint.

### 3.4. THE CIVILLY RESPONSIBLE PARTY

Whereas the penal action, *i.e.* the prosecution, can only be brought against the accused, the civil action can also be brought against the person who, by virtue of the rules on civil liability, is civilly responsible for the damage caused by the accused. For example, parents can be held civilly responsible for damage caused by their children, and employers can be held civilly responsible for damages caused by their employees. The person thus summoned by the victim, *i.e.* the civilly responsible party, becomes a party to the proceedings, but only with respect to the civil claims.

## 4. General principles concerning criminal procedure

### 4.1. GENERAL PRINCIPLES

### 4.1.1. The two stages of the proceedings

Criminal proceedings in Belgium are conducted in two stages, the pre-trial stage, and the trial stage. The pre-trial stage is conducted either by the public prosecutor (*information*) or by the investigating judge (*instruction*), the trial by the trial courts. Whereas the pre-trial proceedings are inquisitorial, the trial is usually considered as accusatorial (*infra*, 6).

### 4.1.2. The principle of the search for the material truth

The purpose of criminal proceedings is to find the material truth. Everything is geared towards this end. All participants in the proceedings, whether it be during the pre-trial stage or during the trial, must contribute to this purpose. Accordingly, during the pre-trial stage, the police, parquet and investigating judge are under an obligation to collect all possible evidence, both in favour and against the accused. The trial judge is obliged to seek the material truth: if he deems that the evidence presented in front of him is not sufficient, he may ask the parties to produce additional evidence, and even collect evidence *ex officio*. The trial judge is not bound by strict rules of evidence (the principle of the free evaluation of the evidence, *infra*, 4.3.4..), and, in deciding on the merits, he must only rely on his *"intimate conviction"* (*infra*, ibid.). Even the accused and his counsel are, to some extent, involved in this process of searching for the material truth: the defence is supposed to help the judge in finding the truth.

### 4.1.3. The principle of the right to a fair trial

Under the influence of the European Convention on Human Rights, particularly art.6, the principle of the right to a fair trial is now fully accepted in Belgium, as least as far as the trial stage is concerned. Despite the fact that the Code does not regulate the position of the accused in great detail, art.6, which has direct effect in Belgium, is now the main source of the fair trial rights in criminal proceedings.

### 4.2. PRINCIPLES GOVERNING THE OPENING OF CRIMINAL PROCEEDINGS

### 4.2.1. The "ex officio" principle

The monopoly of prosecutions is with the *ministère public*, who is an official state authority (but whose exact constitutional status is debated, see *supra*, 2.2.). Accordingly, the *"public action" (l'action publique-de strafvordering)*, *i.e.* prosecution, is brought *ex officio*, by the state, in the name of the people, not in the name of the victim (art.1 Preliminary Title CCP). The victim may decide to join the case as a *partie civile* or may even start a case, but his claims are limited to civil damages (moral and material) only; he is not entitled to prosecute the accused penally (*supra*, 3.).

There are, however, a number of exceptions to the *ex officio* principle. Some offences can only be prosecuted if there has been a formal complaint by the victim (art.2 Preliminary Title CCP, *supra*, 3.3.1.). Other offences cannot be prosecuted by the public prosecutor, but by the administration. One noteworthy example is that of offences against the customs and excise legislation: these are not prosecuted by the public prosecutor, but by the customs officers themselves. A rather exceptional case is that of the prosecution of ministers: they can only be prosecuted on an indictment of the House of Representatives (arts.90 and 134 of the Constitution). In Belgian history, this has only happened once (in 1865, a Minister was prosecuted for having entered into a duel with a member of Parliament).

### 4.2.2. The principle of "opportunity"

The public prosecutor in Belgium has a wide measure of discretion whether or not to prosecute a case. This is not provided by law, but has grown from practice: it has become physically impossible to prosecute all the cases that are reported to the public prosecutor, and therefore, the prosecutor is given a discretionary power in this respect. Instead of prosecuting, he can drop the case, propose a *transaction*, etc. (see *infra*, 8.1.).

However, the decision not to proceed with the case is the monopoly of the public prosecutor. The police, when they find that a crime has been committed, are obliged to record the offence in a *procès-verbal* and to report it to the *parquet* (art.29 CCP). The police officer who decides not to do so would be in breach of his duty.

Similarly, an investigating judge who has been seized with an *instruction* (*infra*, 6.1.3.) by the public prosecutor, is obliged to proceed with the investigation; he may not drop the case.

However, once the public prosecutor has decided to prosecute, he loses his discretionary power, *i.e.* he no longer has the right to drop the case or to propose a *transaction*. If the prosecution has been launched, he must proceed with the case until it has been closed by a judicial decision, either by the judicial council (*infra*, 6.1.4.) or by the trial court (*infra*, 6.2.).

### 4.3. PRINCIPLES GOVERNING THE TAKING OF EVIDENCE

### 4.3.1. The principle that the means of evidence are free

In contrast with the civil law, the law of evidence is not regulated in penal matters. There are no special rules on the way evidence must be collected (*means of obtaining evidence, infra*, 7.2.), nor on the items that may qualify as evidence in court (*means of evidence-moyens de preuve-bewijsmiddelen infra*, 4.3.2. and 7.3.): in penal matters, the facts may be proven by all possible means. The law does not give an exhaustive list of these means (the enumeration in art.154 CCP is not exhaustive, but illustrative). The judge, when forming his "intimate conviction", may accept whatever element is produced in front of him as evidence, on condition that it has been lawfully obtained and that the accused has been given the opportunity to contradict it (*infra*, 4.3.4. and 7.2.).

### 4.3.2. The principle that the means of obtaining the evidence are free, but limited by the exclusionary rule

The law does not stipulate the way in which the evidence should be obtained. It obliges investigating officers (*officiers de police judiciaire*) to record all the evidence in a written record, the *procès-verbal*, but it does not systematically explain how these officers must proceed while collecting the evidence and

20

what means may be used.

This does not mean, however, that evidence may be obtained by whatever means. Evidence which has been obtained illegally is inadmissible in court. The concept of illegal obtained evidence is broadly interpreted: it covers not only evidence which was obtained in *violation of the law* (*e.g.*, evidence collected on the occasion of a search without a warrant, or evidence obtained by means of provocation), but also evidence obtained in *violation of the fair trial rights* of the accused (*e.g.*, evidence obtained in violation of the privilege against self-incrimination).

### 4.3.3. The burden of proof and the presumption of innocence

The burden of proof is on the public prosecutor. He must prove the accused's guilt beyond reasonable doubt. Although the latter concept is not, as such, used in Belgium, the rule that is applied in practice amounts to the same: there is a presumption of innocence in favour of the accused, and in case of doubt, he must be acquitted (*in dubio pro reo*).

The burden of proof is "indivisible" in criminal procedure. This means that, unlike in civil proceedings, the rule *excipiendo reus fit actor*, according to which he who raises an exception must prove it, is not applicable in a criminal trial. Accordingly, if the accused raises an exception, for example a justification (*e.g.* self-defence) or an excuse (*e.g.* duress, *force majeure* or mistake of law or of fact), it is for the public prosecutor to disprove the elements of law and of fact thus raised.

The principle of the presumption of innocence has been affected in respect of some, mainly technical, offences, in respect of which the burden of proof has been inverted by the technique of *proces verbaux that are "valid until disproven"*: for these offences, the law provides that the written police records are binding upon the trial court, unless the accused disproves them (*infra*, 7.1).

### 4.3.4. The privilege against self incrimination

The principle that the accused cannot be compelled to testify against himself is concomitant to the principle that the burden of proof lies with the prosecution. This principle is not explicit in the Napoleonic Code. However, it is now generally accepted, particularly under the influence of the International Covenant on Civil and Political Rights, which explicitly lays down the privilege against self-incrimination[10]. Belgian courts apply the exclusionary rule to evidence obtained in violation of this right. Accordingly, there has

---

[10]Altough this right is not explicitly contained in art.6 of the European Convention on Human Rights, the European Court has accepted that it forms part of it, see, for example, FUNKE v. France, European Court of Human Rights, 25 February 1993, *Publ. E.C.H.R.*, Series A, vol 256-A.

been a number cases in which the prosecution was declared inadmissible because the privilege of self-incrimination had been violated[11].

There is, however, no concomitant duty for police officers or judges to inform a suspect of his right to be silent. Accordingly, the police, when interrogating a suspect, are not obliged to caution him in advance, nor are the investigating judge or the trial judge.

### 4.3.5. The principle of the free evaluation of the evidence: the "intimate conviction" of the trial judge

There are no rules directing the judge about how he must asses the evidence. In other words, the judge deciding on the merits of the case is not bound by any other rule than his own "deep-seated conviction" (conviction intime-innerlijke overtuiging) about the guilt of the accused. This principle is only expressely formulated in respect of the jury, in art.342 CCP, but it is deemed to be applicable to other jurisdictions as well. It is a corrolary of the principle of the search for the material truth (supra, 4.3.1.): the judge must look for the truth and is bound by nothing else than his own appreciation of the evidence.

Accordingly, it is the "intimate conviction" of the judge which determines whether or not a given fact has been proven. He assesses the weight of the evidence that is put before him, and is not bound by a legal minimum (for example the rule unus testis nullus testis). The judge is not obliged to give reasons for his judgment on this point: he need not indicate on what evidence his judgment relies.

This, however, does not mean that judges may treat the evidence arbitrarily. The fact that they can freely assess the evidence does not imply that they are free to deny the evidentiary value of the evidence that is put in front of them. For example, if a procès-verbal states that a theft has been committed during the night, the judge cannot decide that the theft has been committed during the day, when there is no other evidence to sustain this finding.

Moreover, the assessment of the evidence may not contain internal contradictions. For example, a judge could not acquit an accused who has made a confession without explaining why he rejects the confession: a judgment which, on the one hand, acknowledges the confession of the accused and, on the other hand, ascertains that his innocence has been established would be tainted by internal contradiction and therefore susceptible to be reformed in appeal or quashed by the Cour de Cassation.

There are, however, a number of restrictions to the principle of the free assessment of the evidence: firstly, the judge is bound by certain procès-

---

[11]Cour de Cassation, 13 May 1986, Revue de droit pénal, 1987, 175, with the conclusions of advocate general Du Jardin.

*verbaux* (*infra*, 7.1.), and secondly, he may not rely on inadmissible evidence (exclusionary rule, see *supra*, 4.3.2.).

### 4.4. PRINCIPLES GOVERNING THE TRIAL

### 4.4.1. *The principle of publicity*

Trial proceedings are public (art.96 of the Constitution), as opposed to the pre-trial proceedings, which are secret.

However, the court may exclude the public from (part) of the *hearing* if it risks jeopardising public order or morality. In derogation of this rule, hearings before the juvenile courts are always held *in camera*. Another derogation exists in respect of the rare cases in which the judicial council *(chambre du conseil-raadkamer)* may judge the merits of the case, for example when imposing an *internement* on a mentally disabled accused (*infra*, 8.3.).

The *judgment*, however, must always be pronounced in public. In this respect, art.96 of the Belgian Constitution gives a wider protection than art.6 of the European Convention, which also allows derogations from the principle that judgments should be pronounced in public. Following art.60 of the European Convention, the Belgian Constitution prevails.

### 4.4.2. *The principle of orality*

Proceedings before the trial courts are oral, in contrast to in the pre-trial stage, where detailed written *procès-verbaux* are kept. The only written record of the trial is the *procès-verbal* of the hearing (*plumitif de l'audience- proces verbaal van de terechtzitting*), drawn up by the *greffier*, which is a general account of the trial, acknowledging who were the parties that appeared, who were the witnesses, etc.

### 4.4.3. *The principle of contradiction*

In principle, the accused has the right to "contradict" the evidence against him during the trial. However, in practice, this principle is seriously affected by the fact that the court relies heavily on the pre-trial *dossier*. Belgian courts, unlike courts in many other European states, are not bound by the principle of "immediateness", according to which all evidence must be produced "live" in court, in front of the judge(s). If the court finds that the elements, contained in the *dossier,* are sufficient to found its "intimate conviction", it may, for example, refuse to examine witnesses who have already been heard during the pre-trial stage. The defence, however, must be given the opportunity to present its arguments against the evidence in the *dossier*.

## 5. Coercive measures

### 5.1. ARREST AND DETENTION ON REMAND

### *5.1.1. Arrest*

Arrest has been very strictly regulated in the Statute on detention on remand (1990). A person can only be arrested if there are serious suspicions against him. The police may proceed to an arrest in respect of a person who is caught while committing an offence (*en flagrant délit-op heterdaad*). Likewise, any private person who catches a suspect who is committing an offence may proceed to his arrest, on the condition that public authorities are immediately informed. In all cases other than *flagrant délit*, the only authority competent to decide on arrest is the *public prosecutor*.

There is a constitutional time-limit on the duration of arrest, which may not last longer than 24 hours (art.7 of the Constitution). Any deprivation of liberty that goes beyond 24 hours must be decided by a judge.

### *5.1.2. Detention on remand*

Detention on remand can only be decided by a judge. In former times, the very fact that detention on remand was ordered by a judge was deemed sufficient as a guarantee for the protection of personal liberty. Hence, there were no further conditions except a duty for the judge to motivate, *i.e.* to give reasons for, his warrant. In the course of time, the margin of appreciation of the judge has been gradually restricted: today, according to the 1990 Statute on Detention on Remand, a warrant can only be issued under very strict conditions, which must be personally verified by the investigating judge in an interrogation of the accused, which must precede the warrant.

The following conditions must be present: (a) there must be serious suspicions that the person concerned has committed an offence; (b) the offence must be an *arrestable offence, i.e.* an offence carrying a sentence of 1 year in prison or more, and (c) detention on remand must be *absolutely necessary* in the interests of *public safety*, and (d) moreover (except for extremely serious crimes) one of the following four *reasons for the detention* must be present: there must be a risk that the suspect, if left free, will commit new offences, or that he will abscond, or that he will meddle with the evidence, or that there will be collusion with third parties.

Detention on remand can be ordered by the investigating judge, either *ex officio*, (which presupposes that he is already seized, see *supra* 2.3.1.), or on the request of the public prosecutor. No appeal lies against his decision, whether in case of refusal or where the warrant is delivered. However, if a warrant is issued, the matter will automatically be brought before the judicial council, who must, *ex officio*, check the lawfulness of the warrant within five days (see below).

Whereas, before the statute of 1990, the investigating judge had no other choice but to detain or release a suspect, he may now order *"alternative measures"*, such as house arrest, or a restriction order, or medical or other treatment. These alternatives are not enumerated in the law, but are freely decided by the investigating judge. They must, however, relate to one of the four reasons for which a detention warrant can be issued (re-offending, absconding, meddling with the evidence or collusion, see above). Moreover, alternative measures can only be imposed if the general conditions for detention on remand are met. This requirement is aimed at preventing the "netwidening effect" of alternative measures: alternatives should indeed be ordered as a substitute for detention on remand, and not be an additional possibility for the investigating judge to restrict the liberty of the suspect.

One such alternative measure is *bail*. Bail was already possible under the old legislation, but very seldom used in practice. There is a tendency nowadays to allow bail in a greater number of cases, but the instinctive reluctance against this measure, stemming from the feeling that bail discriminates against indigent offenders, is still very strong in Belgium.

The law provides for a periodic *review of the lawfulness of the detention* of persons who are detained on remand. Whereas there is no appeal against the original warrant of the investigating judge, there is an *ex officio* verification procedure before the judicial council, whenever a warrant has been issued. In this procedure, the judicial council not only verifies the legality of the warrant, but also verifies whether the continuation of the detention is still appropriate. In other words, the judicial council verifies the *lawfulness* of the detention, which covers both its legality and its appropriateness. These checks take place at regular intervals, first after 5 days, then each month. The hearing of the judicial council takes place *in camera*, in the presence of the accused and his lawyer, and of the public prosecutor and the investigating judge. The accused and his counsel may consult the investigation *dossier* prior to the hearing of the judicial council. If the judicial council decides to prolong detention, the accused may lodge an appeal against this decision with the court of indictment (*chambre des mises en accusation*).

A person who has been unjustly detained on remand may be entitled to compensation. The law distinguishes between two situations: either, the detention was unlawful, or it was not unlawful, but yet followed by the acquittal of the accused. In the first hypothesis, which is basically that of art.5(5) of the European Convention on Human Rights, the person who has been unlawfully detained may bring a compensation claim against the State, which is brought before the ordinary (civil) courts, and judged according to the general rules on civil responsibility (art.1382 Civil Code). If, however, there was no infringement of the law, but nevertheless an acquittal of the accused, the complaint can only give rise to partial compensation, which cannot be raised before the civil courts, but must be addressed to the Minister of Justice.

### 5.1.3. "Immediate arrest"

In Belgium, sentences can only be enforced when they have become final, *i.e.* when they are no longer subject to appeal. If a person lodges an appeal against his conviction, the execution of the sentence is suspended (*infra*, 9.2.). In order to bridge the period between the day on which the sentence was pronounced and the day on which it can enforced, the law provides for the possibility of arresting the defendant, according to a procedure called "immediate arrest" (*arrestation immediate-onmiddellijke aanhouding ter terechtzitting*). Immediate arrest cannot be ordered *ex officio*, but only on the request of the public prosecutor. In can only be ordered if the sentence is one year in prison or more, and if the general conditions for detention on remand (*supra*, 5.1.2. are fulfilled).

### 5.2. SEARCH AND SEIZURE

With respect to searches and seizures, a distinction must be made depending on whether they are carried out in private or in public places. If carried out in public places, they can be done by the police, *ex officio*, or on the instructions of the public prosecutor. If, however, they are carried out in private places, constitutional protections apply, and also the protection of the European Convention.

Searches and seizures, in the latter hypothesis, are infringements of the constitutional right to privacy (art.10, inviolability of the home) and of art.8 of the European Convention on Human Rights. Unlike restrictions on the right to personal liberty, restrictions on the right to privacy need not, *per se*, be ordered by a judge. The only conditions, spelled out in art.8 para.2 of the European Convention are that such restrictions must be based on law (*legality*), that they meet one of the purposes, enumerated in art.8 para.2, which includes the protection of public order and the prevention of crime (*legitimacy*) and that they must not go beyond what is necessary in a democratic society (*proportionality*).

In principle, searches and seizures in private places can only be done by virtue of a *warrant issued by the investigating judge*. There are, however, numerous exceptions to this rule, particularly in the field of economic crime, where specialised investigating officers often have far-reaching search powers, allowing them to enter private homes or premises, either without a warrant, or with a warrant of the police judge only. The normal rule, however, is that searches require a warrant from the investigating judge.

However, in case of suspects that are caught while committing an offence (*en flagrant délit*), searches can be carried out by the police or by the *parquet* without a search warrant from the investigating judge. Restrictions *ratione temporis* (see below) do not apply in those cases, not even to the investigating judge. The classical restrictions are likewise inapplicable if the owner of the house (or rather, the occupant, *i.e.* the person who actually exercises the right of privacy in the place to be searched) *consents to the search*. This consent must be given in writing, prior to the search.

The investigating judge is not required to be personally present during a search he has ordered. He can delegate the search to the police. However, in delicate cases, he will usually be present. For example, when premises are searched of persons that are protected by the *secret professionnel*, *i.e.* persons who are bound to respect professional secrets, this will usually happen in the presence of the investigating judge.

There are a number of *restrictions* ratione loci and temporis to the right to search private dwellings, even with a warrant of the investigating judge. *Ratione loci*, there is a restriction with respect to places that are covered by immunities flowing from public international law (*e.g.* embassies, consulates, premises of international organisations) and from constitutional law (*e.g.* houses of members of parliament). *Ratione temporis*, there is a restriction in time: searches are not permissible during the night, *i.e.* between 9 o'clock in the evening and 5 o'clock in the morning.

A general restriction, flowing from the *saisine* of the investigating judge and the principle that he can only investigate crimes of which he has been seized (*supra*, 2.3.1.), is the *speciality principle*: searches can only be made to discover evidence relating to the crimes in the investigation request. If, during the search, other offences are discovered, the investigating judge is not allowed to extend his investigation to those offences. He is under an obligation to report them to the *parquet* (art.29 CCP), in his capacity as investigating officer (*officier de police judiciaire*, art.9 CCP), but may take no further action in their respect.

Searches are often combined with seizure of items that may be used as evidence against the accused. All items that may be useful for the discovery of the truth may be seized, and also all the items that are subject to confiscation. The person whose property has been seized has no remedy against this, save perhaps a complaint to the *juge des référés*. There is only one category of items that are immune to seizure: those protected by professional privilege, *i.e.* items that are covered by the obligation of professional secrecy on the part of the person whose house or office is searched, *e.g.* in the case of a doctor, the files of his patients, or, in case of an advocate, the files of his clients. The foregoing does not apply, however, if the person protected by professional secrecy is himself suspected of an offence.

## 5.3. EXAMINATION OF BODY AND MIND

### 5.3.1. Examination of the body

Superficial body searches (*fouille-fouillering*) can be done by the police, without a warrant of a judge or a court. More invasive body searches require a special procedure, called *exploration corporelle-lichaamsonderzoek*. This is an examination which may affect the sexual integrity of the accused or the victim.

These searches require more than an ordinary warrant by the investigating judge: the warrant must be given by the judicial council, the court of indictment or the trial court (save in case of *flagrant délit*). In practice, however, this procedure is limited to those cases in which, literally, the sexual integrity of the person concerned is affected, *i.e.* when he or she is physically touched in these areas of his or her body. All other cases are considered as ordinary *fouilles*, for which no special court decision is necessary. Thus, obliging a person to stoop in order to discover drugs, concealed in his/her rectum or vagina do not require a court decision, but are deemed to be ordinary *fouilles*.

### 5.3.2. Examination of the mind

Examination of the mind can be done by an *expertise* that may be ordered by the investigating judge or by the trial court. Even the public prosecutor, in the course of the *information* (*infra*, 6.1.2.), may appoint a psychiatrist as a technical consultant.

However, if this expertise must be conducted in a mental institution, and thus involves the deprivation of the liberty of the accused without his consent, a special procedure must be followed, called the *mise en observation-inobservatiestelling*. This measure can only be ordered by the judicial council, the court of indictment or the trial judge, and is limited in time (art.1, Statute on social defence, 1930, amended in 1964).

### 5.4. INTERFERENCE WITH THE RIGHT TO PRIVACY

### 5.4.1. Telephones

Until the decisions of the European Court of Human Rights in the cases of Klass, Malone and Huvig/Kruslin[12], telephone surveillance was done without much problem in Belgium, even without judicial warrants. The prevailing opinion was that the investigating judge was competent to order telephone surveillance, by virtue of his general mission to discover the truth. However, the cases mentioned have put strict conditions on this very particular kind of invasion of the right to privacy. For example, in the Huvig/Kruslin case, the Court of Strasbourg rejected the idea that telephone taps can be justified by the mere fact that they are ordered by a judge. In order to be compatible with art.8 para.2, telephone surveillance must be regulated by law (legality), and must be legitimate and proportionate. Because there was no detailed

---

[12]KLASS v. Germany, European Court of Human Rights, 6 September 1978, *Publ. E.C.H.R.*, Series A, vol. 28; MALONE v. United Kingdom, European Court of Human Rights, 2 August 1984, *Publ. E.C.H.R.*, Series A, vol. 82; HUVIG and KRUSLIN v. France, European Court of Human Rights, 24 April 1990, *Publ. E.C.H.R.*, Series A, vol. 176.

legislation on the subject in France, the French situation was considered to be contrary to the Convention.

Following this case-law, courts in Belgium, after accepting telephone surveillance for years as admissible evidence, have declared such evidence inadmissible.

The legislator has resolved the issue in respect of *telephone registration* only, *i.e.* the recording of telephone numbers (not the content) that are dialled from or towards a certain telephone. Telephone registration can be ordered by the investigating judge (art.88bis CCP, introduced in 1991). However, *recording telephonic conversations*, which is not regulated by statute, is not permissible, not even with a warrant of the investigating judge. In 1993, the government (re)introduced a bill to allow for this type of investigation, under very strict conditions, *i.e.* with respect to certain crimes only, in the presence of a warrant of the investigating judge, which would be limited in time.

Meanwhile, courts in Belgium accept transcripts of telephonic conversations that are have been recorded in countries where this is permissible, provided that the foreign legislation complies with the requirements of art.8 para.2 of the European Convention of Human Rights. Thus, the courts have accepted telephone transcripts recorded in the Netherlands[13], but have refused French transcripts after the condemnation of France in the case of Huvig and Kruslin.

### 5.4.2. Letters

Letters are protected by art.22 of the Constitution, which guarantees *secrecy of correspondence*. It is an offence to open letters that have been put in the mail. However, it is usually accepted that letters may be opened by order of the investigating judge. It is doubtful, however, whether this practice, meets the standards of the Court of Strasbourg in the above-mentioned Huvig and Kruslin-case.

## 6. The ordinary course of criminal proceedings

### 6.1. THE PRE-TRIAL STAGE

There is a clear-cut distinction between the pre-trial stage, which is inquisitorial, and the trial stage, which is said to be adversarial.

### 6.1.1. The inquisitorial nature of the pre-trial stage

The pre-trial stage of proceedings is the stage during which the evidence against the accused is collected. The pre-trial stage starts with the initial

---

[13]*Cour de Cassation*, 24 May 1993, *Fundamentele Rechtspraak*, 1993, 3.

report of the offence to the public prosecutor, either by the police (the *procès-verbal* initial), or with a complaint by the victim, or by a denunciation by a third person. The inquisitorial features of the pre-trial stage are usually summarised by reference to three unwritten principles: the pre-trial stage is secret, written and non-contradictory.

It is *secret*, vis-à-vis both the public (*i.e.*, in practical terms, the press) and the accused, who are not informed about the proceedings. The investigation takes place outside the presence of the accused or his counsel (and of the victim), and court hearings are held *in camera* (usually, however, in the presence of the accused, and of his defence counsel).

It is *written*, in the sense that each investigation act must be recorded in writing, in a *procès-verbal*, which is put in a *dossier*, the dossier of the investigation. For example, when the accused is interrogated, or when witnesses are heard, their declarations are recorded in a *procès-verbal* which is added to the *dossier*. This *dossier,* which at the end of the pre-trial stage will contain all the evidence (theoretically both against and in favour of the accused), will be the basis upon which the trial will be conducted (*infra*, 6.2).

Above all, the pre-trial stage is *non-contradictory*. At this stage, the accused does not have the opportunity to participate in the proceedings, to present his evidence, to present arguments in his favour, etc. The rationale is that no decisions on the merits of the case are taken during this stage in the proceedings, which is only geared towards collecting the evidence supporting a prima facie case, not to establish the accused's guilt. The accused, according to this reasoning, will have ample opportunity to contradict the prosecution's case during the trial.

There are two possible scenarios for the pre-trial stage. The most current one is the so-called *information*, which is the investigation led by the public prosecutor. The second one is the preliminary judicial investigation or *instruction*, conducted by the investigating judge.

### 6.1.2. The "information"

The "information" (*information-opsporingsonderzoek*) is the procedure that is used in the great majority of the cases ($\pm$ 95%). It is not regulated in the code, but has developed on a totally *praetorian* basis, *i.e.* from the needs of day-to-day practice. Accordingly, the code does not detail the powers which the public prosecutor or the police have. The *Cour de Cassation* has held that the public prosecutor and the police may engage in all investigations that are necessary for the discovery of the truth, provided they do not breach the law in the course of their investigations, and that they do not violate the rights of the defence. Failing to respect this principle may result in the inadmissibility of the evidence thus collected.

The information is carried out by the police, under the direction of the public prosecutor. The public prosecutor also decides about the way in which the information will be concluded. There are several options:

- the public prosecutor may decide to drop the case (*classement sans suite - sepot*). He may do so at his discretion, and is not obliged to give reasons for his decision. A decision not to prosecute can always be revoked, *i.e.* it does not have the weight of an acquittal (see *infra*, 8.1.).

- the public prosecutor may decide to propose a *transaction*. Unlike the *classement sans suite*, a *transaction* is final: the case cannot be reopened (see further *infra*, 8.2.).

- if he finds that coercive measures must be taken, the public prosecutor can submit the case to the investigating judge, who will then further direct the case, according to a procedure called *instruction* (see *infra*, 6.1.3.). Once he has applied for an instruction, the public prosecutor is no longer free to drop the case or to propose a *transaction*.

- if there is enough evidence to commit the accused for trial, the public prosecutor may directly summon the accused before the trial court, by a *citation directe*. This *citation directe*, however, cannot be done in respect of the most serious crimes, which can only be committed for trial by the court of indictment (*chambre des mises en accusation*, see *infra*, 6.1.4.).

### 6.1.3. The preliminary judicial investigation ("instruction")

The "instruction" (*instruction-gerechtelijk onderzoek*) is the pre-trial investigation that takes place under the direction of the investigating judge, the *juge d'instruction*. Whereas, according to the Napoleonic code, this should be the normal way of conducting investigations, the *instruction* is, in practice, only used either in cases where coercive measures must be taken, or in very complicated cases. These cases represent only ± 5% of the total amount of investigation dossiers.

The investigating judge can be seized by either the public prosecutor (*mandat d'instruction*), or by the victim (*constitution de partie civile*, see *supra*, 3.4.). The investigating judge is limited by his *saisine*, *i.e.* he may only investigate the crimes of which he has been seized. Evidence collected beyond the limits of his mandate is inadmissible in court. It is generally accepted that the *saisine* of the investigating judge is *in rem*, not *in personam*: the investigating judge is seized with the offence, not with the person who is suspected of having committed the offence. Accordingly, he may investigate all potential authors and co-authors of the offence of which he is seized, but he may not extend his investigations to other, albeit related offences.

Like the *information*, the *instruction* is inquisitorial in nature: the investigating judge collects his evidence in *secret*, *i.e.* not in the presence of the parties, he must keep *written* records (*procès-verbaux*) of his investigations, which are added to the *dossier*. It is also *non -contradictorial*, *i.e.*

the accused has no right to make formal requests to him or to explain himself, nor can he appeal decisions of the investigating judge. Conversely, the procureur has the right to request specific investigations from the investigating judge, which the judge may grant or refuse, by giving a "contrary order" (*ordonnance contraire*), but the public prosecutor can lodge an appeal against this order with the court of indictment. The accused does not have these rights. Accordingly, there is *no equality of arms* before the investigating judge: the prosecutor is in a far more advantageous position than the accused.

The powers of the investigating judge are regulated in the Code, but very briefly. As in the case of the *information* by the parquet, the *Cour de Cassation* has held that the investigating judge is competent to carry out all investigations that are necessary to find the truth, provided he does not engage in activities that are forbidden by law or that are contrary to his professional dignity (*cfr.supra*, 2.1.3.).

It is usually held that the investigating judge is under a deontological obligation to hear the accused at least once during his *instruction*. In practice, however, this usually only occurs when the accused is detained on remand (in which case there is a legal duty to interrogate him). Because of their heavy workload, investigating judges frequently lack the time to interrogate the accused.

The investigating judge has no discretionary powers with respect to the prosecution. Unlike the public prosecutor who, after his *information*, may decide to drop the case, the investigating judge must report the results of his investigation to the public prosecutor, *i.e.* he must transmit the investigation *dossier* to the procureur, who will then further decide about the case. However, at that stage of the proceedings, the public prosecutor can no longer drop the case or propose a *transaction*: the *instruction* can only be formally terminated by an order (*ordonnance*) of the judicial council (or, in case of a serious crime, by the court of indictment).

### 6.1.4. Committal proceedings (règlement de procédure-regeling der rechtspleging)

Committal proceedings are the proceedings which formally end the *instruction*. They are conducted before the judicial council (first instance), or by the court of indictment (appeal), who sit *in camera*, in the presence of the *ministère public,* the accused and, if there is one, the *partie civile*.

If there is a *prima facie* case against the accused, he may be committed for trial to the trial court. Depending on the seriousness of the offence, the choice is between the police courts (petty offences-*contraventions*), the *tribunal correctionnel* (*délits*) and the assize court (*crimes*). Committals to the assize court can only be ordered by the court of indictment.

This distinction, however, has been blurred by the wide use of the technique of *correctionalisation*, which allows the judicial council and the

32

court of indictment to apply mitigating circumstances at the point of committal. Accordingly, crimes, which should normally be referred to the assize court can be referred to the *tribunal correctionnel*. This is done to reduce the workload of the assize courts, which proceed much more slowly than the other courts. Not all crimes, however, may be *correctionalised*: the most serious crimes, *i.e.* crimes that are punishable with 20 years or more in prison, can only be judged by the assize court.

A similar technique, called *contraventionalisation*, allows for the conversion of *délits* into *contraventions*, in order to reduce the workload of the *tribunal correctionnel*.

## 6.2. THE TRIAL STAGE

### 6.2.1. The adversarial character of the proceedings: still a reality?

The trial stage is the stage in which the decision on the merits is rendered, *i.e.* the decision concerning the guilt of the accused (*verdict*), and the *sentence*. Unlike the position in common law countries, both elements (verdict and sentence) are in principle decided in one single decision, the *judgment*, except for the assize court, where there is a clear-cut distinction between the two.

The trial is generally considered to be adversarial (syn. accusatorial) because its characteristics are directly opposed to those of the pre-trial stage: it is public, oral and contradictory (*supra*, **4.4.**).

Whereas these characteristics are usually sufficient to convince continental lawyers of the accusatorial nature of the trial proceedings, they are, however, less convincing than they may seem. Indeed, despite the public, oral and so-called contradictory character of the proceedings, the trial retains two very typically inquisitorial features, *i.e.* the active role of the judge(s), and the heavy reliance on the dossier of the pre-trial investigations.

Unlike their common law peers, judges in Belgium play an active role in the proceedings. Judges, not the parties, conduct the trial: the accused and the witnesses are heard, not by the parties, but by the court. Questions are put, not by the parties, but by the judge and the public prosecutor. Cross-examination does not exist. Witnesses are questioned by the accused through the judge, *i.e.* the accused or his defence counsel request the judge to ask the questions they want to be put. The judge may, at his discretion, decide to hear such and such a witness, depending on whether he thinks that the testimony will be relevant to discover the truth. Here, in fact, lies the crucial difference with common law judges: the judge in Belgium (and in many other continental countries) *has to find the material truth* (*supra*, **4.1.2.**). He is not a passive bystander, whose task is to assess the evidence which is presented in front of him by the parties; instead, his task is to discover the truth, *ex officio*, *i.e.* if necessary beyond the evidence that is revealed to him by the parties, *i.e.* the public prosecutor, the accused, and, where applicable, the *partie civile*.

The second inquisitorial feature of the trial in Belgium is that it is conducted, not "from scratch", *i.e.* from the *evidence* presented to the court by the parties, but *on the basis of the dossier* with the *procès-verbaux* of the pre-trial proceedings. In theory, according to the philosophy of the Napoleonic code, all the evidence collected in the pre-trial stage must be presented in court, and be open to a public, contradictory, debate between the parties. For example, witnesses who have been examined by the investigating judge, outside the presence of the accused, should, always according to the same philosophy, be examined again in court, in the presence of the accused. Even though the accused does not have a real right to cross examine witnesses, he will nevertheless have the opportunity to challenge the witnesses' declarations through the questions that he may ask the judge to be put to the witnesses.

However, in practice, this no longer occurs. Before the trial starts, the court will have studied the *dossier* and the case will be conducted on the basis of the *dossier*. The court will decide whether or not it is necessary to re-examine the witnesses who have already been heard by the police or by the investigating judge. Only if it is deemed necessary to discover the truth, will such witnesses be heard again, in the presence of the accused. As a result of this, the weight of the *dossier* on the proceedings has become much greater than in the Napoleonic scheme, and trial proceedings in Belgium have become probably more inquisitorial than the drafters of the code intended them to be. Even though, in theory, they are public, oral and contradictory, the reality is that, because of the preponderance of the pre-trial dossier, the conviction is often based on evidence that has been obtained during the pre-trial investigation, *i.e.* in a secret, written and noncontradictory manner.

The foregoing does not apply to the assize court, where the evidence has to be presented orally, in the presence of the jury. These proceedings are therefore usually considered to be really adversarial in Belgium. However, here too, inquisitorial features prevail: the presiding judge of the assize court has a discretionary power to discover the truth, *i.e.* he may do all that is necessary for this purpose. Whereas the jury may not read the written testimonies of the witnesses in advance, the president has carefully studied the *dossier* before the trial starts, and will conduct the hearing of the witnesses in court on the basis of what he has read in the records of their declarations to the police or to the investigating judge. His questions, which, according to anglo-saxon concepts, would be, for the greater part, "leading questions", are geared at having the witnesses repeat orally, in front of the jury, what they declared previously during the pre-trial proceedings.

This way of conducting trials permits a greater speed, at least as far as the trial itself is concerned (the pre-trial stage may last much longer than police enquiries in common law systems). It is not unusual for a court in Belgium to hear several cases in the course of one session only.

Reform proposals in Belgium do not aim at changing the way trials are conducted, but at the way the pre-trial investigations are done. Rather than proposing to render the hearing more adversarial, proposals aim at reinforcing the legal position of the accused during the pre-trial stage, *i.e.* by giving him access to the *dossier*, and by giving him a limited standing before the investigating judge, which would allow him, among other things, to apply for specific investigations and to lodge appeals against decisions of the investigating judge. These proposals stem from the concern of making the *dossier* reflect a more balanced version of the truth, whereas it is now often composed of records made on the request of the public prosecutor only. However, no proposal has been made so far to do away with the pre-trial *dossier*, as has been done in Italy, or to introduce the principle of immediacy into trial proceedings.

## 6.2.2. *The course of the proceedings*

### (i) Proceedings before the police courts and the tribunal correctionnel
Proceedings before the police courts and the *tribunal correctionnel* are largely identical, except for some minor differences. The scenario is laid down in art.153 (police court) and 190 (*tribunal correctionnel*) of the Code. It goes as follows:

In theory, the case should start with a short summary of the case by the public prosecutor or the *partie civile*. In practice, however, this seldom occurs, as all parties have read the *dossier* in advance.

Next comes, also in theory, the reading by the *greffier* of the *procès-verbaux* in the pre-trial *dossier*. This practice too has fallen in desuetude. The *Cour de Cassation* has decided that failure to read the dossier does not involve the nullity of the proceeding, and the result is that, in practice, this rule is no longer observed. It would, indeed, be very difficult and time consuming to read the whole dossier, which may contain hundreds, and, in complex cases, even thousands of pages. Moreover, prior to the hearing, the accused or his lawyer have had the opportunity of studying the dossier, and hence, they know the evidence that has been collected by the authorities which conducted the pre-trial investigations.

Thereafter, the presiding judge identifies the accused (if he is present).

After this, the witnesses are examined, starting with the witnesses against the accused, followed by the witnesses in his favour. The questions are put by the judge or the *ministère public*. The accused may not directly question the witnesses, but only through the judge. Hence, no cross examination exists.

The code says, both in art.153 and in art.190, that witnesses are examined "insofar as it is necessary" (*s'il y a lieu-zo daartoe grond bestaat*). It is for the judge to decide whether it is necessary to examine the witnesses. Often, witnesses have already been examined under oath by the investigating judge, and their testimonies are recorded in a *procès-verbal* which is in the *dossier*. The trial judge may consider that it is not necessary to hear the witness again, and rely on his declarations in the *procès-verbal*. In practice, this happens very frequently[14].

Witnesses are examined under oath. They are obliged to tell the truth, failing which they commit the crime of perjury. They are under a duty to testify, and may be compelled to appear in court if they fail to do so voluntarily. Some persons are exempted from the duty to testify (the spouse of the accused, and certain of his relatives, and the partie civile), whereas others can never testify (*i.e.* minors under the age of 15 and persons who have been deprived of their right to testify by a criminal sentence). All other persons are obliged to testify and to answer the questions put to them. Failure to do so is an offence, which is punished with a fine. It is also an offence for a witness not to appear in court after having been duly summoned (art. 80 CCP). There are only two exceptions to the rule that witnesses are under a duty to answer questions. Firstly, the *privilege against self-incrimination* allows them to refuse to testify against themselves (the judge, however, is not obliged to remind witnesses of their right to remain silent). Secondly, witnesses who are under an obligation of *professional secrecy* (*secret professionnel-beroepsgeheim*) may refuse to answer questions that relate to matters covered by professional secrecy, but are not under a duty to do so. In other words, whereas violating professional secrecy is an offence (art. 458 Penal Code), persons bound by secrecy may decide not to maintain it when they are required to testify in court. However, they cannot be *obliged* to reveal information covered by the obligation of secrecy. These persons are: lawyers, notaries, doctors, nurses, priests, policemen (in respect of, *e.g.* informers and undercover agents), but not journalists, bank directors and accountants (art. 458 Penal Code).

After the examination of the witnesses, comes the interrogation of the accused by the presiding judge. He is not heard under oath, and consequently failing to say the truth does not constitute the crime of perjury. The accused is not obliged to reply to the questions, and failing to do so may not be held against him. However, the judges are not under a duty to inform him of his right to remain silent.

After the interrogation of the accused, it is the turn of the *partie civile* (if there is one), to present his conclusions and to formulate his civil claim for compensation.

Then follows the *réquisitoire* of the public prosecutor, in which he summarises the case and presents his conclusions. Depending on the outcome

---

[14]This practice may be contrary to the European Convention on Human Rights, art. 6(3)d. In the *Cardot*-case, the European Comission held that art. 6(3)d imposes an obligation on the trial judge to hear *all* the witnesses that have previously been heard during the pretrial investigation (CARDOT v. France, European Commission of Human Rights, 3 April 1990, application n° 11069/84). There, is, however, no decision of the European Court on this point, as the application was declared inadmissible on technical grounds.

of the hearing, he may either plead that the accused be convicted, or acquitted (*cfr. supra*, 2.2. *la plume est serve, mais la parole est libre*).

After the réquisitoire, it is the turn of the accused (or his defence counsel), to plead his case. He may submit written conclusions to the court, to which the court will have to reply in detail in its judgment.

Then follow the answers (*répliques*) of the other parties, in the above-mentioned order. The accused always has the last word.

In contrast to anglo-saxon proceedings, there is no distinction between pleadings on the question of guilt, and pleadings concerning sentence. Both are done in one single argument and give rise to one judgment.

After this, the debates are closed, and the court withdraws *in camera* to deliberate about conviction and sentence. They decide by a simple majority. Dissenting opinions are never published in Belgium.

The *judgment* is then read out in court, in public. There are no possible exceptions to the publicity of the pronouncement of the judgment (art.96 of the Constitution). The judgment may be pronounced immediately after the deliberation, or at the next session.

The judgment can be either conviction, or acquittal, or dismissal (where the prosecution is inadmissible).

Judges must give reasons for their decisions (art.97 of the Constitution). The duty to give reasoned judgments, however, has been interpreted in a restrictive manner: it only means that judges are obliged to state the legal provisions that they apply in their judgments. The reasons must be consistent: a failure in this respect is deemed to be the same as failing to give reasons at all. In the late Eighties, the Penal Code was supplemented with a provision obliging judges to give reasons for their sentences: this justification goes beyond what is required by the Constitution, and obliges judges to say, why, in the individual case before them, they imposed a particular sentence, rather than another sentence, and they must also justify the measure of the sentence (arts.163 (police court), 195 (*tribunal correctionnel*) and 211 (Court of appeal) of the Penal Code).

*(ii) Proceedings before the assize court*
The proceedings before the assize court are comparable to those described above, with, however, a few important differences. In general, the assize procedure is much more formal than the procedure before the other jurisdictions. Unlike the trials described above, where the judges may rely on the pre-trial dossier, and, for example, decide not to examine witnesses again during the hearing, the assize procedure is strictly oral: the jurors do not receive copies of the *procès-verbaux* in the dossier, and hence, all the witnesses have to be examined again during the trial.

Another fundamental difference is the distinction between verdict and sentence: it is for the jurors to return the verdict, whereas the sentence is imposed by the jurors and the judges jointly.

Jury trial is conducted as follows. It starts with a "*preparatory proceed-*

*ing"* in which the accused is interrogated by the presiding judge, outside the presence of his counsel. Thereafter, the accused may see his counsel and consult the *dossier*. At least 24 hours before the hearing, the names of the witnesses are communicated to the parties.

The hearing starts with the identification of the accused by the president, after which he swears in the jurors. Then, the *greffier* reads out the committal order of the court of indictment, and thereafter the public prosecutor reads the indictment.

The next step is the reading of the names of the witnesses, whereupon the witnesses leave the courtroom, and are called in individually to testify. As it has been described above, witnesses are examined by the court, not by the parties, and no right to cross examine exists.

Then follow, as in ordinary proceedings, the conclusions of the *partie civile*, the *réquisitoire* of the public prosecutor, the pleadings of the defence, and the *répliques*, in the aforementioned order. The accused always has the last word.

After the closing of the debates, the president formulates the questions to which the jury must give an answer. These are questions that must be answered by yes or no. The jurors withdraw *in camera*, and deliberate without the presence of the professional judges. When they have reached their decision, the *verdict* is pronounced in public, but outwith the presence of the accused. In the event of a 6/6 verdict, the accused is acquitted. In case of a guilty verdict returned with a simple majority (7 against 5), the three professional judges decide whether or not to side with the majority. The final verdict is read by the *greffier*, in the presence of the accused.

When the verdict is "not guilty", the accused is immediately released. If, on the contrary, he is found guilty, the debates are resumed, and the arguments with respect to the sentence are developed. After the closing of these debates, the professional judges withdraw *in camera,* with the jurors, to decide on the sentence, which, once a decision has been reached, is pronounced in public.

## 7. Evidence

7.1. WRITTEN RECORDS OF THE PRE-TRIAL INVESTIGATION: THE *PROCÈS-VERBAUX*

A trial in Belgium is usually, at least in part, conducted on the basis of the evidence that has been collected during the pre-trial investigation, either by the *parquet* (*information*) or by the investigating judge (*instruction*): all the evidence that has been collected prior to the trial must be recorded in a *procès-verbal*, which is added to the *dossier* of the pre-trial investigation.

Not everybody is entitled to draw up a *procès-verbal*: only sworn officers who by law have been invested with the capacity of *officier de police judiciaire* are entitled to do so (*supra*, 2.1.). As such, they are privileged witnesses, whose declarations carry greater weight than those of other witnesses.

*Procès-verbaux* may be used as evidence in court. The officers who have made them are not usually heard as witnesses. The court may rely on their written records, which are covered by the oath that the officer has sworn when assuming his function. The accused and his defence counsel, who have, like the court, studied the dossier prior to the trial, may challenge the *procès-verbaux* during the hearing

A distinction is made between three different sorts of *procès-verbaux*: ordinary *procès-verbaux*, *procès-verbaux* that must be believed until proof of the contrary has been given and *procès-verbaux* that must be believed unless it has been formally established that they are false.

The facts acknowledged in ordinary *procès-verbaux*, like any other facts, must be established by the prosecuting party, the *ministère public*. The judge is not bound to believe what is stated by the ordinary *procès-verbal*. For example, if a *procès-verbal* states that a burglary has been committed during the night, the judge is free to deduce from other elements that it was committed during the day.

For some, mainly technical offences, however, the law has introduced *procès-verbaux* which have greater evidentiary value than ordinary police records: *procès-verbaux* recording such offences are deemed to be "valid until disproved" (*faisant foi jusqu'à la preuve du contraire-geldig tot tegenbewijs*), *i.e.* they must believed until proof to the contrary has been given. They bind the judge, but the accused may disprove the facts in the *procès-verbal* with all possible means. These *procès-verbaux* are used, for example, with respect to road traffic offences. *E.g.*, if a *procès-verbal* states that a person has jumped a traffic light, the judge will be bound to believe this statement, unless the accused proves that the statement is not true, for example by presenting witnesses in his favour.

*Procès-verbaux* that must be believed unless it has been established that they are false (*faisant foi jusqu'à inscription de faux-geldig tot inschrijving wegens valsheid*) have become exceptional today. These *procès-verbaux* may only be disproved by a special procedure, *inscription de faux*, which is aimed at formally establishing that they are false. One of the rare examples is the record of the trial (*plumitif de l'audience*), kept by the *greffier* (*supra*, 4.4.2.*): all that is stated in that record is presumed to be true, unless it has been established, in the special procedure of *inscription de faux*, that the greffier has made false statements.

## 7.2. MEANS OF COLLECTING THE EVIDENCE

The law does not regulate the way in which evidence should be gathered, nor does it deal in great detail with the powers of the officers whose duty it is to gather the evidence during the pre-trial stage of the proceedings. In general, courts apply the "*permissive rule*" in this respect: the police, the *parquet* and the investigating judge may use all possible means to discover the truth, provided they do not break the law and provided they respect the rights of the defence. In respect of the investigating judge, the *Cour de Cassation* adds that he must behave in conformity with the dignity of his profession (*supra*, 2.). Accordingly, the police and *parquet* are entitled to interrogate suspects and witnesses (not under oath), to visit and search places that are not protected by the right to privacy, to search houses with the consent of the occupants, to carry out bodily searches (see *supra*, 5.3.), etc. If coercive measures are necessary, they must be ordered by the investigating judge. Examples are: search and seizure, telephone registration, seizing mail, etc. Also, measures that are typically judicial, such as hearing a witness under oath, can only be performed by a judge. Evidence that has been obtained contrary to these rules is inadmissible, by virtue of the exclusionary rule (*supra*, 4.3.2.).

## 7.3. MEANS OF EVIDENCE

### 7.3.1. Confessions

Confessions are admissible evidence, provided they have been made freely, without violation of the privilege against self-incrimination. While the accused's silence cannot be held against him, there is, however, no obligation to inform the accused of his right to remain silent. Confessions, even if they are still *la reine des preuves*, do not relieve the public prosecutor of his duty to prove the facts.

The Belgian system does not know the plea of guilty. Even if the accused has confessed during the pre-trial stage, his guilt must still be proved during the hearing. This applies also in jury trials: the evidence against the accused will still have to be put before the jury, which, in exceptional cases, may even acquit the accused who has confessed the facts (see the example of the thalidomide-trial, *supra*, 2.3.2.).

### 7.3.2. Testimony

Witnesses may be heard both before the trial (by the investigating judge) or during the hearing. The rule *unus testis nullus testis* is not applicable in Belgium. Accordingly, a person may be convicted on the basis of the statements of only one witness, if the judge is "intimately convinced" of the accused's guilt (*supra*, 4.3.5.).

Witnesses are normally heard under oath. However, some persons cannot testify under oath: children under the age of 15 (art.79 CPP) and persons who have been deprived of their right to testify following a criminal conviction (art.31 Penal Code). These persons may give statements without an oath. Other persons who are not allowed to testify are: the accused's spouse and some of his relatives (art.156 CCP), and the *partie civile*.

As in many other countries, one of the great issues today is the question of the possibility of using statements of witnesses who, for various reasons, wish to remain anonymous. As far as the pre-trial stage is concerned, the *Cour de Cassation* has accepted that, failing to mention the identity of the witness in the *procès-verbal* of the interrogation, which is prescribed in the Code, does not entail the nullity of the *procès-verbal*. The question, however, remains whether declarations of anonymous witnesses can be used in court.

### 7.3.4. Investigations on the spot

Investigations on the spot, *i.e.* at the place where the crime was committed or at any other relevant place, are usually done by the police during the pre-trial investigation, and hence recorded in a *procès-verbal*. It is, however, possible for the trial court to do the same, *i.e.* to visit these places in the presence of all parties to the proceedings.

### 7.3.5. Expert witnesses

An expert witness is a person who, by reason of his expertise in a particular field, is appointed to perform certain specific investigations, called *expertise*. The mandate of the expert is clearly defined by the magistrate, ordering the expertise. The expert may only carry out the expertise in the mandate, he may not proceed to investigations *ex officio*. The accused may, at his own expenses, appoint an expert of his own choice.

The Code only mentions expert witnesses in passing, when dealing with the extraordinary powers of the *ministère public* in cases where the offender is caught while committing the offence (*in flagrante delicto*, art.43-44bis). However, it is generally accepted that both the investigating judge, during the *instruction* (*supra*, 6.1.3.) and the trial judge during the hearing, may appoint expert witnesses.

Before accepting his assignment, an expert witness must swear that he will perform his task faithfully and with due diligence (art.44 CCP), which is different from the oath of ordinary witnesses.

The expertise is always conducted privately, outside the presence of the accused or of the public. The results of the expertise are recorded in a report, the *expertise*, which is submitted to the investigating judge or to the court.

There are proposals to make the expertise adversarial, especially during the pre-trial stage, *i.e.* to allow the accused or the victim, or the experts they may want to appoint, to be present. There are good reasons for doing so: very often, by the time the case is committed for trial, it has become impossible to conduct a counter-expertise. How, for example, may an autopsy be repeated several months after the first *expertise*?

## 8. Special forms of procedure

### 8.1. PROSECUTORIAL DISCRETION (*CLASSEMENT SANS SUITE-SEPOT*)

The public prosecutor in Belgium has full discretion whether or not to proceed with a case. This is not explicit in the law, but it is generally accepted in practice. About 70% of the investigation *dossiers* are *classé sans suite*. There are no formalities to be fulfilled: when a public prosecutor decides not to proceed with the case, he simply files *the dossier*. He is not obliged to give reasons for his decision.

A decision not to prosecute is not binding: the prosecutor may reopen the case at any time. However, after a certain period of time has passed, the right of prosecution will lapse as a result of the effect of the statutes of limitation (see *infra*, 10.1.).

There are two types of *sepot*: technical *sepot* and policy *sepot*. *Technical sepot* means that the prosecutor drops the case because, for technical reasons, it would be impossible to proceed anyway. For example, when the accused cannot be traced, or when the statute of limitations has elapsed, or when the accused has died, the *dossier* will be *classé sans suite*.

*Policy sepot*, however, is a decision not to prosecute in a case where prosecution would be perfectly possible. *Policy sepot* has had a tendency to increase dramatically. It has become virtually impossible for the parquet to prosecute all the crimes that are reported to it by the police. Choices must be made. However, the parquet is very much criticised for the way in which these choices are made. "Policy" is often too flattering a word for very disparate, uncoordinated decisions by individual prosecution officers who manage the *dossiers*. Even though there are guidelines by the hierarchical superiors, prosecutorial discretion is often exercised on a highly individual or local basis. Crimes which are prosecuted in one *arrondissement* may be *classé sans suite* in another one, and vice versa.

More generally, the discussion with respect to policy *sepot* has given rise to a more fundamental debate about the role of the *parquet* in modern society, particularly the question whether it is acceptable for non-elected prosecutors to decide whether or not to enforce laws which have been passed by Parliament. Should not *the parquet* be bound by certain guidelines, given by Parliament, or even by the Minister of Justice? These questions, of course, are highly political, and have a direct link with the fundamentals of the organisation of society.

### 8.2. *TRANSACTION*

The Belgian system does not know the plea of guilty, and concomitantly, the concept of plea bargaining is unknown. However, *transactions* are widely applied. A *transaction* is an unilateral proposal by the public prosecutor to the accused, in which he proposes that the accused should pay a certain amount of money within a certain time-limit. If the accused should accept, the prosecution against him will be dropped (art.216bis CCP).

Until the early Eighties, *transactions* were only possible in respect of petty offences. Since then, however, *transactions* may be proposed in respect of all offences that carry sentences not exceeding 5 years, *i.e. contraventions* plus the whole middle-category of *délits* (*cfr. supra*, the tripartite division of offences between contraventions, délits and crimes).

Unlike *sepot*, which is not regulated by law, *transactions* can only be proposed if the criteria, set forth in art.216bis CCP are met. These are: the civil damages must have been paid; the offence may not carry a penalty exceeding 5 years in prison; there must be mitigating circumstances, which, should the prosecutor proceed with the case, would lead him to request only a fine, or a confiscation, but not a custodial sentence.

The consequences of *transaction* are also different from those of *sepot*: whereas *sepot* does not forfeit the prosecutor's right to prosecute, a *transaction*, once it has been accepted by the accused, formally ends the case. It will not be possible to reopen it at a later stage. As there is no conviction, there will be no mention on the criminal record of the accused, which is an important incentive for him to accept the *transaction*.

## 8.3. SUMMARY PROCEDURE

At this stage (October 1993), there are no summary proceedings in Belgium. All cases are conducted following the ordinary rules. The only techniques to reduce the work-load of the trial courts are the above mentioned *policy sepot* and the *transaction*.

However, *de lege ferenda*, proposals have been made to introduce summary proceedings, following the French and Italian examples. A bill is now pending before Parliament which would allow summary proceedings against persons who either confess or who are caught while committing the offence. Such persons would be directly summoned before the trial court and tried within a very short delay. It is by no means certain that these proposals will be accepted. They have been widely criticized by various sections in society.

## 8.4. MEDIATION

Another technique, for which legislative proposals have been made in order to reduce the work-load of the trial courts is the mediation between the accused and the victim. This mediation would be organised by the public prosecutor, in his chambers. The idea would be for the parties to agree on the compensation to be paid to the victim, and possibly also some services to be performed by the accused (*cfr.* community service). The agreement would be formally recorded by the public prosecutor in a *procès-verbal*. If the accused complies with the terms of this *procès-verbal*, the prosecution would be dropped, in the same manner as in case of a *transaction*.

This proposal too has been criticised, because of the large powers it attributes to the public prosecutor. Concern has been expressed for the rights of the victim, which may be less protected in mediation proceedings than in an ordinary trial.

## 8.5. PRIVATE PROSECUTION

Private prosecution is not possible in Belgium. The *ministère public* has the monopoly of prosecutions. However, the victim is entitled to bring civil claims before the criminal judge, which are dealt with, together with the penal aspects of the case (see *supra*, 3.4.).

## 8.6. JUVENILES

Juvenile offenders, *i.e.* persons under the age of 18, are not prosecuted before the ordinary courts but before juvenile courts, composed of a single judge. Juvenile courts do not impose criminal sanctions, but educative measures. Juvenile courts can be seized not only where a minor is suspected of having committed an offence, but also with respect to minors who are in a "problematic educational situation", often for reasons beyond their control, *e.g.* because of their living conditions, or because of the behaviour of their parents. The purpose of this latter competence is to allow juvenile courts to take preventive measures, in order to prevent minors from becoming criminal offenders.

A mixed regime is applicable to persons between 16 and 18 who, in principle, are referred to the juvenile court, but who can be brought before ordinary courts if the judge deems it more appropriate to have them tried according to ordinary procedure. Some offences committed by minors of that age are always prosecuted before the ordinary courts, for example road traffic offences and physical injury caused in connection with such offences.

## 8.7. MENTALLY ILL

There are no special proceedings for mentally disabled persons who have committed an offence. They are brought before the ordinary courts, judged according to the general rules of substantive criminal law. If, however, they are found guilty, no ordinary penal sanctions are imposed on them but compulsory psychiatric treatment in mental hospitals.

As this treatment is ordered for an indeterminate period of time, special supervision of the treatment has been organised by the law. An administrative commission called the social defence commission (*commission de défense sociale*), composed of a judge, a psychiatrist and an advocate, supervises the treatment and decides when it may come to an end, *i.e.* when the internee is apt to be released.

There have been proposals to confer the tasks of this administrative commission to a court of law, the "judge for the application of the sentences" (*juge de l'application des peines*), but none of these proposals has been accepted as yet.

As explained above, an accused is entitled, but not obliged, to attend his trial. If he chooses not to appear, he will be judged in his absence (*par défaut*). He may not be represented by his defence counsel, except in certain exceptional circumstances. A trial *par défaut* is conducted according to the normal rules of procedure. If the accused is convicted, a special remedy is available, *opposition* (*infra*, 9.1.).

Trials *in absentia* are quite common in civil law countries. They are not deemed *per se* to be contrary to art.6 of the European Convention on Human Rights, provided a person who has been convicted in his absence can reasonably oppose his conviction. For the same reason, the explicit provision in art.14 (3)d of the Covenant on Civil an Political Rights, which states that everyone has the right to be tried in his presence, is not considered to prevent trials *par défaut*, provided again that the convicted person is given a legal remedy to oppose his conviction, *i.e.* to be tried in his presence.

There may be a connection between trials *in absentia* and statutes of limitation. In Belgium, all crimes, even the most serious ones, prescribe after a certain amount of time. If the accused is not brought to trial within this time-limit, it is no longer possible to prosecute him. This may explain why the public prosecutor is given the right to prosecute contumacious defendants in their absence. It allows him to obtain a conviction before the time limit expires, whereas the person thus convicted always has a remedy against his conviction, namely *opposition*.

An accused who has been committed for trial to the assize court has no right to remain absent. If he does not appear, a special procedure is followed, which may lead to a conviction *par contumace*. These proceedings are conducted without a jury, and without the presence of a defence lawyer. Where an accused who has been convicted under this procedure is subsequently arrested, the conviction is automatically quashed and a new trial is held, this time with a jury.

# 9. Remedies

9.1. OPPOSITION

## *9.1.1. General principles*

Opposition is a remedy which submits the case for reconsideration by the same court as the one which has rendered the judgment. If the opposition is admissible, the original judgment is declared non existent and a new judgment is rendered instead.

This remedy is available to a person who has been judged in his absence. Accordingly, it is only available to those parties who are entitled to be absent during the trial, *i.e.* all parties (accused, partie civile, civilly responsible party) except the public prosecutor, whose presence is mandatory, failing which the trial will be null and void. It is possible to lodge both an opposition and an appeal against the same judgment.

Opposition is not possible against decisions *par contumace* rendered by the assize court: here, the judgment *in absentia* is automatically quashed if the convicted person is arrested, and a new trial is held.

The *requirements* for an opposition are: (a) that the decision of the first instance court was rendered in the absence of the party who opposes it and (b) that this party has an interest in using the remedy. For example, if the accused has been acquitted in his absence, he has no interest in opposing the judgment.

Opposition can only be used once: *opposition sur opposition ne vaut*. If the person, who was convicted in his absence, fails to appear again on the day which has been set for the reexamination of his case, the judgment *a quo* will be final.

### 9.2.2. Ordinary and extraordinary time-limit

The time-limit within which the accused must file *opposition* differs according to whether the judgment *in absentia* has been notified to him or not. In the first hypothesis, he has 15 days, starting from notification of the judgment. This is called the *ordinary time-limit*.

If the judgment cannot be notified (because, for example, the convicted person is abroad or has absconded), then the judgment will enter into force provisionally after fifteen days. The person will, however, get a new opportunity to file *opposition* as soon as he has knowledge of the conviction, in which case he has another, *extraordinary time-limit* of 15 days to file opposition. Thus, the person who was convicted *in absentia* and who returns to the country long after the judgment has entered into force, may be arrested upon his arrival, in execution of the judgment, but will always have the opportunity of *opposition* within a time limit of 15 days.

### 9.2. APPEAL

Appeal is a remedy which submits a case to a court which is hierarchically superior to the court which rendered the first instance decision. Appeal may cover both questions of law and of fact (*cfr. cassation*, which relates only to questions of law). The appellate court can either confirm the judgment *a quo* or reform it, as a whole or in part. The decision of the appellate court replaces the decision at first instance.

Appeal in Belgium is directed against the judgment of the first instance court as a whole, both conviction and sentence. It is not possible to restrict the appeal to one or the other only. This means that the appellate court will always have to re-examine the question of guilt, even though the accused, in fact, only contests his sentence.

When appeal is available, every party to the case can lodge it, the accused, the public prosecutor, and if there is one, the *partie civile* and the civilly responsible party. Appeals must be filed within strict deadlines, usually within 15 days after the judgment of the first instance court.

The following general principles apply to appeal: (a) it can only be used if the party has an *interest* in applying for an appeal. For example, an accused who has been acquitted cannot appeal against his acquittal; (b) appeal *cannot prejudice the party* who has applied for it, unless the other parties have also lodged an appeal. For example, if only the accused has appealed against his conviction, but not the public prosecutor, the appellate court cannot impose a more severe sentence; if, however, both parties have appealed against the judgment, the sentence can be increased, but only if there is an unanimous decision of the court of appeal; (c) the appeal court is seized only in respect of those questions against which the appeal was lodged (*tantum devolutum quantum appelatum*). For example, if a person has been convicted of theft and assault, and wants to contest the theft conviction only, he may restrict his appeal to the conviction for theft, and the appellate court will only be competent vis-à-vis the theft. Likewise, if two persons are convicted, and only one of them lodges an appeal, the appellate court is only seized of the appeal brought by the person who lodged the remedy; (d) in principle, the appeal *suspends the execution* of the judgment of first instance. There are, however, exceptions to this rule (art.203§3 CCP).

In general, most decisions of the trial courts are open to an appeal in Belgium. Conversely, decisions of the investigating judge and of the courts of investigation (judicial council) can usually only be appealed against by the public prosecutor. There are only a few exceptions to the rule that appeals are always possible against trial court judgments. The most noteworthy exception relates to decisions of the assize court, which cannot be the subject of an appeal (*vox populi vox dei*) but only of cassation.

## 9.3. CASSATION

Contrary to appeal and opposition, *cassation* can only be filed on legal questions. The application for cassation is brought before the *Cour de Cassation*. Grounds for cassation are: violation of the law or of a general principle of law; the non-observance of procedural rules that are either substantial or sanctioned with nullity.

A judgment can only be subject to *cassation* if it is rendered in last instance. Decisions, rendered in the pre-trial stage are, in principle, only open to cassation after the final judgment has been rendered by the trial court, in last instance.

If cassation is admissible, the *Cour de Cassation* can either confirm or quash the original decision, in whole or in part. The case will then be referred to another court at the same level (*e.g.* if a decision of the Court of Appeal of Antwerp has been quashed, the case may be referred for retrial to the Court of appeal of Ghent).

### 9.4. *CASSATION* TO REVISE A FINAL JUDGMENT (*REVISION-HERZIENING*)

Cassation to revise a final judgment is a special form of cassation, which is available in cases where there has been a miscarriage of justice. The convicted person may apply for a retrial, and also his family, if he is deceased, or the Minister of Justice.

Retrial can be applied for in the cases provided by law, including incompatibility between two judgments relating to the same fact, and the proof of innocence flows from the contradiction between the two, or when a witness, who testified against the accused, has been found guilty of perjury or when there is new evidence that proves the person's innocence (art.443).

## 10. Other questions

### 10.1. STATUTES OF LIMITATION

All offences, regardless of their seriousness[15], prescribe in Belgium. A difference exists between the prescription of the right to prosecute, and the prescription of the right to execute a sentence.

The public action, the *right to prosecute*, prescribes after 10 years (*crimes*), 3 years (*délits*) or 6 months (*contraventions*). These time-limits are very strict. They can be suspended, or prolonged, but only once (*i.e.* to a maximum of twice the original time-limit); once the period of limitations has elapsed, prosecution is no longer possible. In practice, this causes serious difficulties, especially with respect to *délits*, which make up the great majority of the offences that are put before the courts. Usually, the parquet has only 6 years to finish the case (2x 3 years), which means that, not only must the first instance judgment and the judgment at appelate level have been rendered and become final, but also, if the judgment has been subject to *cassation*, the decision of the court to which the case has been referred by the *Cour de Cassation* must have been rendered and become final. Especially in very complex cases, this is a strong impediment to prosecution. Many cases prescribe before the final judgment is rendered.

The sentence prescribes after respectively 20 years (*crimes*), 5 or 10 years (*délits*) and 1 year (*contraventions*) (art.93-95 Penal Code).

---

[15]However, an exception exists in respect of war crimes.

## 11. Select bibliography

*Books*

BRAAS, A., *Précis de procédure pénale*, Brussels, Bruylant, 1950 (vol. I) 1951 (vol. II), 1160p.

BEKAERT, H., *Handboek voor studie en praktijk van het Belgisch Strafrecht*, Brussel/Antwerpen, Universitaire Publikaties/Ontwikkeling, 1965, 359p.

CARNOT, M., *De l'instruction criminelle, considérée dans ses rapports généraux et particuliers, avec les lois nouvelles et la jurisprudence de la Cour de Cassation*, Brussels, 1830, 6 vols.

D'HAENENS, J., *Belgisch strafprocesrecht*, Ghent, Story-Scientia, 1985, 548p.

DUPONT, L. and FIJNAUT, C.(eds), *Criminal Law*, International Encyclopedia of Laws, Deventer, Kluwer, 1993.

FRANCHIMONT, M., JACOBS, A. and MASSET, A., *Manuel de procédure pénale*, Liège, Ed. Collection scientifique de la Faculté de Droit de Liège et ed. du Jeune barreau de Liège, 1989, 1157p.

HELIE, F., *Traité de l'instruction criminelle ou théorie de code d'instruction criminelle*, Brussels, Bruylant, 1863-69, 3 vols.

HOEFFLER, J., *Traité de l'instruction préparatoire en matière pénale*, Kortrijk-Heule, UGA, 1956.

TULKENS, F. and VAN DE KERCHOVE, M., *Introduction au droit pénal. Aspects juridiques et criminologiques*, Brussels, Story-Scientia, 2nd.ed.,1993, 462p.

TRAEST, P., *Het bewijs in strafzaken*, Ghent, Mys & Breesch, 1992.

VAN DEN WYNGAERT, C., *Strafrecht en strafprocesrecht in hoofdlijnen*, Antwerp, Maklu, 1991, 2 vols, 855p.

VERSTRAETEN, R., *Handboek Strafvordering*, Antwerp, Maklu, 1993, 566p.

X., *Les Novelles, Procédure pénale*, Brussels, Larcier, 3 vols.

X., *Les droits de la défense en matière pénale*, Actes du colloque des 30-31 mai-1er juin 1985, Liège, Ed. du jeune Barreau de Liège, 1985, 382p.

*Periodicals*

Panopticon
Revue de droit pénal et de criminologie
Journal des procès
Journal des tribunaux
Rechtskundig Weekblad

# Chapter 2 - Denmark

Prof. Vagn **GREVE**
Department of Criminal Law
University of Copenhagen

The State of Denmark consists of Denmark, the Faroe Islands and Greenland. The law of criminal procedure of the Faroe Islands is in almost all respects identical to the law of Denmark. The law of criminal procedure of Greenland is, however, different from the Danish as regards many essential points. The Faroe Islands and Greenland are not members of the European Community. This article deals exclusively with main principles of criminal procedure in Denmark proper. It is only possible to give an outline. Many exceptions and special rules will not be mentioned.

## 1. Sources

### 1.1. THE CONSTITUTION

The present Danish Constitution (*Grundloven*) was adopted in 1953. It contains a few rules relating to criminal procedure, for example Section 71 on arrest and detention on remand, and Section 72 on search and seizure. Most of the important principles in this area date back to the first democratic constitution of 1849.

According to the principle of checks and balances, the Danish courts have the power to declare an act of parliament unconstitutional. However, this power has never been exercised. Our Supreme Court has not delivered any expansive interpretations of individual constitutional guarantees. In general the Danish legal system accepts the supremacy of Parliament, also with regard to the interpretation of the constitution.

### 1.2. THE EUROPEAN CONVENTION ON HUMAN RIGHTS

The European Convention for the Protection of Human Rights and Fundamental Freedoms has been ratified by Denmark. In connection with considerations of ratification, the Government conducted a review of the relevant legislation. The Government deemed that Danish law was already in conformity with the Convention, and in the few cases where some doubts persisted, the necessary legal amendments were effected. Subsequent statutory amendments have also been adopted in the light of decisions made by the European Court of Human Rights. An example of this interaction is provided by amendment No.403 of the Danish Administration of Justice Act of 13 June 1990, designed to solve a possible conflict with the Convention with regard to the impartiality of judges after the European Court's decision in the Hauschildt case[1].

The European Convention has direct application and can be directly applied by the courts. Supreme Court decisions show that Danish courts of law and other authorities are under an obligation to base their interpretation of Danish national law, to the widest extent possible, upon the Convention[2].

If a person considers his rights to be violated Denmark accepts the individual's right to petition after exhaustion of domestic remedies, and the questions may finally be brought before the Commission and the Court in Strasbourg. One recent example in which aspects of Danish criminal procedure were put before the Court is the Hauschildt case.

### 1.3. LEGISLATION

There is no special code on criminal procedure. The relevant provisions are a part of the general *Administration of Justice Act* (*Retsplejeloven*, abbreviated *rpl.*). This Act was passed by Parliament in 1916, and implemented in 1919. It is currently under review by governmental committees, and it has been amended many times. The latest updated version of the Act can be found in *Lovtidende* (the official law gazette) No. 905, 10 November 1992. If nothing else is indicated, Sections quoted below refer to this Act. There is also a *Military Administration of Justice Act* (*Militær retsplejelov, Lovtidende* No. 643, 30 September 1987). This Act will not be taken into consideration hereafter.

We do not have a special system of administrative criminal law. Offences against customs laws, taxation laws *etc.* are in principle treated exactly like all other offences. Neither do we have an administrative fine-system, nor a ticket fine-system with immediate payment of the fines to a police officer. Therefore in some respects the Danish procedural system is rather simple compared to some others.

### 1.4. CASE-LAW

As the Administration of Justice Act is very detailed, case-law is of less importance in this area than it is in most other areas.

While in foreign literature, cases are often known by the names of the parties, in Denmark cases are simply referred to by their source. *U.f.R.* or *U* refers to the most important report, *Ugeskrift for Retsvæsen*. Cases from the

---

[1]HAUSCHILDT v. Denmark, European Court of Human Rights, 24 April 1989, *Publ. E.C.H.R.*, Series A, vol. 154.

[2]*Ugeskrift for Retsvæsen*, 1989, p.928 H; 1990, p.13 H and 181 H.

Supreme Court (*Højesteret*) are denoted by H. The High Court is now divided into two divisions, the Eastern High Court (*Østre Landsret*), denoted by Ø, and the Western High Court (*Vestre Landsret*) denoted by V. Thus a case referred to as *U.f.R. 1956 p. 31 H* is a Supreme Court case reported in *Ugeskrift for Retsvæsen* in 1956 on page 31.

## 2. Structure of the criminal justice system

### 2.1. INVESTIGATING AUTHORITIES

In Denmark, criminal investigations are conducted by the police. The Danish system does not know special investigating judges.

Denmark is divided into 54 police districts. The police comprise one single organisation; the former municipal police forces have by now for many years been integrated in the State police. The police are subdivided into plain-clothes criminal investigators, uniformed patrolmen, traffic police officers *etc.*. The subdivisions have no legal importance but are solely for administrative purposes.

Everybody has the *right* to report a *committed* crime to the police, but virtually no one has an *obligation* to report committed crimes. There are a few exceptions, for example, for some public servants, and a peculiar duty for hit-and-run drivers to report themselves (*cfr.* Section 9 of the Road Traffic Act). In addition, there is a general obligation to report some very serious *intended crimes*, if they cannot be prevented in any other way (for example, Section 141 of the Criminal Code).

The police act upon receiving a report from someone or after discovering the crimes themselves. It is their task to ascertain whether an offence has been committed, to secure evidence, and if possible to find the perpetrator (*efterforskning*, for example, Sections 108, 742 and 743).

While investigating a case, the police have to gather evidence irrespective of whether it be for the prosecution or for the defence (*objektivitetsprincippet*). Defence counsel is entitled to full discovery of the results of the police investigations as they appear. However, he may not always communicate the content of such material to the accused (Section 745). It is exceptional for the police to refuse to undertake steps requested by defence counsel during the investigation (Section 746). For this reason, it is very rare for the defence to engage in private investigation. Moreover, such activities may be illegal.

Some coercive measures can only be decided by the court (see further *infra, 5*). The use of *agents provocateurs* is limited by Sections 754 a-754 e. In case of dispute between the accused and the police with regard to the investigative measures, the court will decide the issue (Section 746, *infra, ibid.*). If the accused or someone else has complaints with respect to police behaviour in relation to the investigation, for example, in case of violent or rude behaviour, he may complain to a superior police officer or to a local Police Complaint Board (*cfr*. Sections 115, 115 a, and chapter 93 b of the Administration of Justice Act).

## 2.2. PROSECUTION AUTHORITIES

### 2.2.1. *The chief of police*

The local chief of police (*politimester*), has the authority to prosecute in nearly all cases (Section 104). When the investigation is finished, the chief of police or one of his deputies (*vicepolitimester, politiassessor, politifuldmægtig*) will decide whether the evidence warrants prosecution. The chief of police as well as the deputies always have a law degree. While investigating the police do not act as agents of the government but exercise their functions objectively (*objektivitetsprincippet*).

There is a distinction between abandonment of prosecution (*nolle prosequi - tiltaleopgivelse, henlæggelse*) and the omission to prosecute or withdrawal of charge (*tiltaleundladelse, tiltalefrafald*). The prosecutor has to consider whether there is enough evidence on each of the elements required to prove the offence, so that it can be said that there is a realistic prospect of conviction. *Nolle prosequi* refers to those cases in which the prosecuting authority concludes that the investigation cannot be expected to lead to the suspected perpetrator of a crime being found guilty and liable to punishment (Sections 749 and 721). (For the omission to prosecute or withdrawal of the charge, see *infra*, 2.2.2). Because of the weeding out of dubious cases, there are but relatively few contested trials (one third of the more serious cases), and acquittals still rarer.

The police have a general competence to accept compound fines (*bødeforelæg, cfr*. Section 931). In practice, the police send a letter with a very brief description of the crime and a reference to the provisions which allegedly have been violated. A postal check form is enclosed. If the amount is paid the case is closed. This is not a matter of plea-bargaining. Quite the contrary, the authorities endeavour to have the fine correspond precisely to the amount which would be the result of a court decision. If the compound fine is accepted but not paid and it is not possible to collect the sum by distraint, a replacement penalty is served in lieu.

### 2.2.2. *The public prosecutor*

The most serious cases are referred to the public prosecutor (*statsadvokat*) by the local police. He is also in charge of the cases for the High Court (jury cases and appeal cases).

Denmark is divided into six *stadsadvokat* districts. In addition to these regional prosecutors, there is a special attorney for the whole country who deals with serious economic crimes.

The public prosecutor may choose to omit prosecution. *"Omission to prosecute"* or "withdrawal of the charge"(*tiltaleundladelse, tiltalefrafald*) refers to cases where the prosecuting authority believes that it could well bring a case which would lead to conviction but for other reasons prefers to withdraw the charges. According to Section 722 of the Administration of Justice Act, the prosecuting authorities can omit to prosecute "in the light of special mitigating circumstances", as long as this can take place "without any harm being done to any public interest". Danish law has thereby adopted the "principle of opportunity" (*opportunitetsprincippet, princippet om den relative påtalepligt*) not the "principle of legality" (*legalitetsprincippet, princippet om den absolutte påtalepligt*). The principle of opportunity leaves a large amount of discretion to prosecuting authorities to drop a charge.

"Withdrawal of the charge" can be divided into two categories: withdrawal with conditions and withdrawal without conditions.

In practice, *withdrawal of the charge without conditions* is not used very often. For example, charges may be dropped in a case of a sober driver, who is blinded by the sun and runs into another car. If he himself is seriously injured, or if his children or spouse are killed, there is no reason for further punishment. In 1987 the provisions were modified to make it easier to handle very big cases, especially regarding corporate crime or serious white collar crimes. The public prosecutor may now reduce the case or withdraw charges if the prosecution will cause difficulties, costs, or a prolonged period in court out of proportion with the importance of the case or the sentence which may be expected (Section 722 (1)5). For example, in big fraud cases, where there is a large number of alleged frauds, the prosecution may decide only to prosecute a small number of frauds; likewise, in tax evasion cases, the prosecution may decide to limit the case to the most recent years, although there is reason to believe that a thorough investigation would make it possible to prove tax evasion over several more years.

*Withdrawal of the charge with conditions* can only take place, if, in court, the accused has made an unqualified confession, the correctness of which is supported by other circumstances that exist, and the conditions must be approved by the court (Section 723 (2) and (3) of the Administration of Justice Act). The same conditions may be laid down for withdrawal of the charges as for suspended sentences. A very important condition in this respect is that a young person is to be subject to welfare measures from the Children and Young Persons' Welfare Authorities and to comply with their instructions.

And of course: the prosecutor may indict.

## 2.2.3. The chief prosecutor

The Chief Prosecutor (*rigsadvokaten*) is head of the public prosecution. He appears before the Supreme Court in criminal cases, supervises other prosecutors and the police, and issues regulations of a general nature (circulars and the like, *meddelelser*) to the prosecutors and the police. In a limited number of cases, the decision to prosecute has to be made by him. For example, with respect to mass media offences.

## 2.2.4. The Minister of Justice

In some very limited areas, the decision to prosecute has to be made by the Minister of Justice (*justitsministeren*). For example, certain offences of a political character may only be prosecuted if the Minister so decides (see chapter 12 of the Criminal Code regarding offences against the independence and safety of the State).

### 2.3. THE JUDICIARY

The court system consists of the Supreme Court (*Højesteret*), the two high courts (*Vestre Landsret* and *Østre Landsret*), and 84 city courts. In the small circuits the same courts sit both in criminal and in civil cases. However, in most circuits the work is divided between the judges according to the nature of the case. In some instances an individual criminal law judge is appointed for life, in other jurisdictions there exists a sort of rotating division of the cases.

## 2.3.1. Competence

At *first instance*, three different possibilities exist.

### (i) A single judge in the city court
A single judge is competent to try petty crimes, the so-called "police cases" (*politisager*). This comprises all cases where the expected sanction is only a fine, and the case is of minor interest for the accused and for the public (Section 68).

The single judge is also competent to try any non-contested case (*tilståelsessag*) irrespective of its gravity, if in court the accused has made an unqualified confession, the truth of which is corroborated by other available evidence. However, the court, the prosecutor, the accused (and the guardian for minors) must all accept this simplified procedure. This happens in 30-40% of the more serious cases, although a guilty plea is not seen as a significant mitigating factor in sentencing. The accused, if under arrest or pre-trial detention, must be represented by a lawyer. If the accused is at liberty, he must be offered representation by defence counsel (Sections 925 and 686).

### (ii) A jury and three judges in the High Court
If all the conditions in Section 925 on non-contested cases are not fulfilled *and* if the prosecutor claims 4 years of imprisonment or more, a High Court jury will in most cases be the first instance (Section 687 (2)). Economic cases

such as fraud and forgery are excluded.

In a jury case (*nævningesag*) 3 judges and 12 jurors voting in separate chambers both have to find the accused guilty, otherwise he is acquitted (Sections 897 and 904). Among the jurors, at least 8 out of 12 have to vote for conviction, among the professional judges 2 out of the 3. This is the so-called "double guarantee"; on the other hand there is no appeal against these verdicts.

Then as a joint body they all pass the sentence. In this respect the jurors have one vote each, and the professional judges have four votes each. Thus the lay and the professional elements carry the same weight.

For some time there has been rather a widespread discontent with the jury system, and the applicable area has been reduced markedly. Today we only have around 60 cases a year. However, the constitution presupposes the jury system, so it has to be preserved, at least for a very limited number of cases (*cfr.* Section 65 (2) of the Constitution).

### (iii) Two lay judges and one judge in the city court

All other cases are heard in the city court by a mixed bench (*domsmandsret*) consisting of two lay judges (*domsmænd*) and one judge. They all have the same functions during trial, but the professional judge presides over the hearing. Their votes carry the same weight on all questions, whether fact, law or sentencing. It is possible to cast a dissenting vote.

The composition of the *appeal courts* will not be described.

### 2.3.2. The nomination of judges and jurors

*Judges* are appointed by the Government for life (*i.e.* until they reach 70 years of age) on recommendation by the courts. The office is restricted to persons with a qualified legal training.

*Lay judges and jurors* are appointed as follows: the municipal city councils select a list of respected ordinary citizens between 18 and 65 years of age every four years. On this basis, the courts make new lists by drawing lots. The lay judges and the jurors will be called to their respective courts in this random order for a specific case. On average, they serve four times a year.

### 2.3.3. Independence and impartiality

Judges are deemed to be independent *vis-à-vis* the Government and the Parliament. However, judges may be elected as members of parliament or appointed as ministers. In fact this rarely happens, and the person in question will apply for temporary leave from the courts.

Impartiality is protected. A judge must abstain *ex officio* from taking part in a decision as regards a case with which he has formerly dealt, for example, as a judge in a lower instance or in which he or a close relative has a personal interest (*inhabilitet*). A judge and a prosecutor or defence counsel may not be closely related by family. On the other hand it does not make the judge partial that he has expressed his opinion on a legal problem in a scholarly debate.

During recent years the area of illegal partiality has been broadened under influence from the European Court of Human Rights, after its decision in the Hauschildt case (*supra, 1.2.*). Today the limits are more narrow than they used to be with regard to judges who have presided in pre-trial hearings or in cases against the accused's accomplices.

## 3. Parties to criminal proceedings

### 3.1. THE PROSECUTOR

The public prosecutor (*anklageren*) is not supposed to actually "oppose" the accused, but it is his task objectively to intervene in the interests of law and justice and to find the objective truth (*objektivitetsprincippet*). Therefore, he may even file an appeal in the interest of the convicted person. See *supra*.

### 3.2. THE DEFENCE

By "defence" (*forsvar*) we refer to both the accused (*sigtede, tiltalte*) and his counsel (*forsvarer*). A distinction must also be made between the right to defence in the substantive sense, *i.e.* the right to answer the charge, and in the formal sense, *i.e.* the right to counsel.

### *3.2.1. The accused*

The accused's position in criminal proceedings is twofold. On the one hand he is to be regarded as an active subject, with the benefit of the presumption of innocence. He has the right to be heard, to present evidence, to put questions to witnesses, and to take remedies. On the other hand, he is also, to some extent, an object of investigatory measures such as finger-printing and blood test for alcohol (but possibly not for HIV-infection), and he may also have to submit to coercive measures such as arrest, search of his home and office or telephone-tapping.

Such interferences in a person's privacy must be based on law and respect the principle of proportionality, and they may not violate fundamental human rights. The accused is under no obligation actively to contribute to the prosecution and neither pressure nor cunning may be applied in view of obtaining statements (Section 752 and 754). Devices such as the lie-detector or methods like narco-analysis or hypnosis are inadmissible. Possibly, even if the person concerned consents.

## 3.2.2. Defence counsel

Everyone accused has the right to legal assistance by counsel of his own choice (Section 730). The accused has, at all times, the right to consult with his counsel in private. The only exception is with regard to the immediate answer to a specific question asked in court (Section 752 (5)).

However, it is not within the free discretion of the accused whether he wants legal assistance or not. In some cases it is mandatory (*nødvendigt forsvar*), such as in court hearings with a view to pre-trial detention, or in any case where the court regards defence counsel as desirable (Section 731). Thus, legal assistance is provided in all serious cases.

The police must inform the accused of his right to a publicly assigned defence counsel (*beskikket forsvarer*). The court regularly appoints the counsel wanted by the accused. The rights of the chosen and the appointed defenders are identical.

Defence counsel are private lawyers, who may be chosen freely by the accused or appointed to him by the court. There is no public defence office in Denmark. The "public defence lawyers" are private practising attorneys who belong to a pool of qualified lawyers selected by the Ministry of Justice upon application, on recommendations from the local judge and bar association. They are reputed as belonging to the better part of the profession. They take cases on a rotating basis in their circuit.

It is the right of the accused to have his defence counsel present during police interrogation and court hearings (Sections 745 and 748). Defence counsel's task is to act in the sole legitimate interest of his client by watching over the legality of the proceedings and taking all lawful steps with a view to obtaining the best result possible. If he behaves otherwise he may be liable to punishment under the Criminal Code or be rebuked by the Lawyers' Disciplinary Board (*cfr.* Sections 144, 150-152, and 154-157 of the Criminal Code, and chapter 15 b, and Section 739 of the Administration of Justice Act).

Defence counsel are assigned regardless of the financial situation of the accused. If the accused is convicted and unable to pay his defence counsel, the Treasury will in most cases provide the lawyer's fee and cover other costs, for example, with regard to an auditor's report. The courts will decide what amount is reasonable. If the accused is acquitted, the State will nearly always cover all costs.

### 3.3. THE VICTIM

## 3.3.1. Private prosecution

The victim has no right to be a party to the proceedings under the penal aspects of the case. He is notified of the action taken by the prosecution. If dissatisfied with the prosecution, he may complain up through the prosecutorial system, and eventually to the parliamentary ombudsman

(*Folketingets Ombudsmand*). In a very limited number of cases only, the victim is permitted to prosecute. The most important examples in this respect are offences against personal honour and certain individual rights, for example, libel and slander. In another very limited area the victim may prosecute, if the public prosecutor for some reason decides not to do so. Such cases of private prosecution will be regulated by the procedural rules regarding civil cases, not criminal cases. Also, a few offences are only prosecuted upon complaint.

The victim may be called as a witness under the normal rules regarding witnesses.

### 3.3.2. Civil claims

The victim may claim damages as a plaintiff in proceedings attached to the criminal prosecution (*adhæsion*).

## 4. General principles concerning criminal procedure

### 4.1. GENERAL PRINCIPLES OF PROCEDURE

### 4.1.1. The "principle of instruction"

The "principle of instruction" (*instruktionsmaximen*) as opposed to the "principle of negotiation" (*forhandlingsmaksimen*), imposes upon all authorities involved in criminal proceedings the duty to search for the true facts (*den materielle sandheds princip*). Even the courts are in no way bound by the evidence brought before them by the "parties". (See, however, *infra*, 4.2.3., the principles of "accusation" and "inquisition").

### 4.1.2. The principle of the right to be heard

No disadvantageous decision may be taken unless the person concerned is first given the opportunity to explain his point of view (*kontradiktion*).

### 4.1.3. The principle of acceleration

The right to a speedy trial imposes on the authorities a duty to avoid any unnecessary delay in criminal proceedings. Thus there are no court-holidays in criminal matters. The so-called constitutional court will sit at weekends and at night. Acceleration may not, however, impair the right to the necessary time for the preparation of the defence. Particular diligence is required in cases where the accused is detained on remand (Section 768).

## 4.2. PRINCIPLES GOVERNING THE OPENING OF CRIMINAL PROCEDURE

### 4.2.1. The ex officio principle

Since the beginning of the 19th century, the State has had a monopoly on criminal prosecution, and it has even assumed the right and duty to proceed *ex officio* (*officialprincippet*). This means that offences may be prosecuted irrespective of whether the victim so desires. (*Cfr. supra*, 3.3.).

### 4.2.1. The principles of "legality" and "opportunity"

See *supra*, 2.2.

### 4.2.3. The principles of "accusation" and "inquisition"

In an accusatorial system, the tasks of prosecuting and determining a case on the merits are separated, while in the inquisitorial system the judge also investigates the facts. In Denmark both the pre-trial proceedings and the trial itself follow the accusatorial system. However, this does not exclude the questioning of the witnesses and the accused by the presiding judge. On the contrary, it follows from the principle of material truth (*den materielle sandheds princip*) that the judge is obliged to elucidate all vague points (Section 873).

## 4.3. PRINCIPLES GOVERNING THE TAKING OF EVIDENCE

### 4.3.1. The principle of the free evaluation of the evidence

The principle of free evaluation of the evidence (*bevisbedømmelsens frihed*) is accepted (Section 896). This is a logical consequence of the duty to look for the substantive truth (see *supra*). The significance of this principle is partly a negative one: no formal rules of evidence - for example, that two witnesses can not be wrong, or that the spouse of the accused cannot be heard as a witness, or that hearsay evidence (Section 184) is inadmissible - may be applied. Also, the decisive element in the conviction is the firm belief of the court with regard to the actual facts. The court is in no way bound by a plea of guilty.

The defence has the right to be acquainted with all the police reports in which steps taken during the investigation are recorded.

Evidence produced or obtained in an illegal way is not necessarily inadmissible. Usually, it is taken into account by the court. In Denmark the "fruits of the poisonous tree" may be eaten. However, the police officer or the prosecutor who breaks the law to get evidence will be indicted for breach of duty. However, Danish law may be *en route* to a certain change in this respect. If the police, as a result of a lawful telephone tap, receive information about crimes other than the one under investigation (*tilfældighedsfund*), this so-called surplus information may be used for further police investigations but not as evidence in court (Section 789, as amended 1985).

### 4.3.2. The presumption of innocence

Everyone charged with a criminal offence shall be presumed innocent until proven guilty according to law. No one may be convicted unless the court is convinced on the basis of the evidence that he is guilty (*in dubio pro reo, favor defensionis*). The State is required to prove every element of a crime beyond reasonable doubt.

### 4.4. PRINCIPLES GOVERNING THE TRIAL

### 4.4.1. The principle of immediacy

The principle of immediacy or of "directness" (*bevisumiddelbarhed*) requires evidence to be presented "live" in court. For example, witnesses must be heard in person, no statements made during the preliminary investigation may be read out (Section 896).

There are a number of exceptions in Section 877. The principle of first-hand evidence is especially under discussion with regard to the issue of using police reports as part of the evidence. In practice, the prosecutor will confront the accused or a witness with their statements in the police reports, if he offers a different story during the examination in court.

### 4.4.2. The principle of orality

It follows from the principle of directness that the trial must be oral (*mundtlighedsprincippet*) (Section 148 (1)). However, written proceedings are common in appellate proceedings and with regard to complaints.

### 4.4.3. The principle of publicity

Both the preliminary investigations in court (for example, proceedings regarding detention on remand) and the trial on the merits are held in public (*offentlighedsprincippet*) (Section 29).

There are exceptions to this rule, in the interest of, for example, public morality or the preservation of specific public or private secrets (Section 29). Some cases may be heard *in camera* (*for lukkede døre*). This may be decided by the court, for example, if the accused is below 18 years of age. It is mandatory if requested by a victim in an incest or rape case.

There is a general right to publish what has taken place in court (*middelbar offentlighed*). However, television and radio are not permitted to make transmissions from the court room. Usually, if the hearing takes place *in camera*, no one is allowed to publish the proceedings etc. In some other cases the mass media will have access to the court room but be prohibited from reporting names, titles, and the like (*navneforbud*) (Section 31).

## 5. Coercive measures

As perpetrators and suspects often see their own interests in frustrating the course of justice, coercive measures are necessary to secure evidence and to prevent the accused from avoiding trial and, eventually, serving the sentence. Such coercive measures (*straffeprocessuelle tvangsindgreb*) must be based on law, they must respect the principle of proportionality, and they may not violate fundamental rights. Put in another way, there must exist a suspicion of some strength regarding a fairly gross offence; furthermore, there must exist a special reason for applying the measure. Some compulsory means may also be used in relation to a person against whom no charge has been made.

Arrests are made by the police on their own responsibility. The police are also authorized to use measures of minor proportions on their own. As a general rule other measures are decided by the court but carried out by the police. If the purpose makes it necessary to act with short notice (*periculum in mora*) the police may do what is necessary and later on inform the city court with a view to obtaining its approval. With regard to measures other than detention on remand, the suspect may consent and thus waive his right to a court decision.

### 5.1. ARREST AND DETENTION ON REMAND

The most serious coercive measures applied in criminal proceedings entail the deprivation of liberty.

### *5.1.1. Types of deprivation of liberty in criminal proceedings*

Arrests are authorized in a number of situations:

a. Persons found *in flagrante delicto* or immediately after having committed a crime (*fersk gerning, friske spor*) may be arrested by anyone, including private citizens (*anholdelse*). Private citizens are to proceed immediately to bring such an arrestee under the authority of the police. (Section 755).

b. The police may arrest any person, who is reasonably suspected of having committed a crime, if the arrest is considered necessary either to prevent further crimes, or to secure his presence, or to prevent his contact with other persons. A warrant is not needed. (Section 755).

c. The police may arrest a person if certain other circumstances are present, for example, when the suspect is unable to identify himself to the satisfaction of the police officer.

After having been brought to a police station and questioned, the person may be discharged. Even if formally charged, he may be set free. If taken into custody, the person concerned must be brought before a court of law within 24 hours after the arrest (the so-called constitutional hearing (*grundlovsforhør*, *cfr*. Section 71 of the Constitution)). According to Danish law a person cannot consent to be deprived of his liberty; thus, a person cannot subject himself to custody.

d. Arrest for a period of more than 24 hours has to be decided by the courts. The maximum for a prolonged arrest (*opretholdt anholdelse*) is 3 times 24 hours. (*cfr*. Section 71 of the Constitution).

e. Detention on remand (*varetægtsfængsel, varetægt*) can only be ordered by a court. (*cfr*. Section 71 of the Constitution). See further *infra*.

f. Persons who do not obey a summons to appear before a judicial authority can be ordered by the court to be brought by the police before such authority (*fremstilling*).

g. Detention pending execution of a sentence (*varetægtsfængsel*) consists of deprivation of liberty between the judgment in last instance and the beginning of the prison sentence or some other custodial sanction.

### 5.1.2. The prerequisites of detention on remand

A person against whom a criminal prosecution is initiated is not automatically subject to detention on remand. Detention on remand must be applied in accordance with the principle of proportionality. It cannot be used if the actual crime in practice carries only a fine or lenient imprisonment (*hæfte*). Beside these conditions, the *general rules* are:

Firstly, there must be reasonable suspicion that he has committed an arrestable offence, *i.e.* an offence which according to the law carries a maximum penalty of at least one year and six months. This is the maximum penalty for, *e.g.*, ordinary theft and burglary (Section 285 of the Criminal Code). Secondly, one or more of the following special grounds for detention (*fængslingsgrunde*) must be present: there are serious reasons to believe that the accused (a) will abscond (*flugtfare - unddragelsesarrest*); (b) might commit further offences of the same sort if left at large (*fare for gentagelse - uskadeliggørelsesarrest*); (c) will meddle with the evidence (*kollusionsarrest*).

In *specific cases* detention may also be used for other reasons: it is possible to use detention on remand to protect the public sense of justice (*retshåndhævelsesarrest*), if the *prima facie* evidence against the accused is very strong. In addition, the following conditions must be fulfilled: the crime in question must carry a maximum penalty of at least 6 years' imprisonment and there must be a special consideration to the enforcement of law, *or* the crime must be an assault (or some other violent crime), for which the expected punishment is at least an unconditional sentence of 60 days imprisonment (the standard penalty for assault), and consideration for the enforcement of the law demands that the accused is not at liberty. This last mentioned ground for detention has been especially heavily criticized since its introduction a few years ago. *Cfr*. Section 762 of the Administration of

Justice Act.

The court may decide that a person in detention on remand is to be *isolated* inside the prison (Section 770 a) (*isolation*). The decision has to be renewed at least every two weeks (Section 770 c). The use of this procedure in Denmark has attracted criticism from *Amnesty International*, among others.

### 5.1.3. The duration of detention on remand

Detention on remand must not exceed a reasonable time, but there is no fixed time limit. No one shall be detained for a period of more than four weeks without being produced in court to renew the remand. (Section 767). Thus, for example, an initial remand of 14 days may be ordered, followed by 4 weeks remand if necessary. Regard is to be had to the probable punishment and to the disturbance of the accused person's circumstances (Section 762 (3)).

### 5.1.4. Release on bail

The law provides for the possibility of release on bail (*kaution*, Section 765). However, this is regarded as an ill-founded privilege of the wealthy. In practise it is used extremely rarely, and it is an open question whether the rigid Danish practise is in accordance with the European Convention on Human Rights.

### 5.1.5. The control of legality

Decisions made by the city court relating to detention on remand can be appealed to the High Court and with special permission to the Supreme Court.

### 5.1.6. The right to compensation

Detention on remand is deducted from the sentence (*cfr.* Section 86 of the Criminal Code).

If acquitted, the person concerned has a right to compensation, unless specific circumstances prevail (*cfr.* chapters 93 a of the Administration of Justice Act).

### 5.2. SEARCH AND SEIZURE

Suspects and their homes or offices or any other place where relevant objects or wanted persons are presumably to be found may be searched (*ransagning*). The conditions for this measure depend on whether it is a public place (for example, a train) or the suspect's own house or a private house belonging to a third party, in addition to whether it is necessary to act with short notice and whether the person consents. Two independent witnesses will be summoned to the search unless the suspect waives his rights (*cfr*. chapter 73 and 75 b of the Administration of Justice Act). Compensation may be awarded for the infamy etc. caused by an improper search (Sections 1018 b and 1018 c). Objects of proof or loot may be seized wherever they are found (*beslaglæggelse*). If the seizure concerns documents, the papers will on request be sorted out by the court (Sections 829 and 794 (4)).

### 5.3. EXAMINATION OF BODY AND MIND

The accused must submit to an examination of his body, for example, to verify whether traces are found of a fight in connection with the crime of rape. Special rules in traffic law govern the breathalyser and blood tests (*cfr*. Section 55 of the Road Traffic Act).

The accused may be ordered to undergo a psychiatric examination (*mentalundersøgelse*), possibly in a mental hospital with a view to ascertaining criminal responsibility or of deciding whether measures of security or treatment ought to be applied (Section 809). The question of a defence of mental disorder is usually raised by the prosecutor during the police enquiry. However, Danish law presupposes that all persons are competent to stand trial, if assisted by defence counsel.

### 5.4. INTERFERENCE WITH THE RIGHT TO PRIVACY

Often, efficient investigation requires secret surveillance of a suspect's private life. The court may authorize the police to intercept, to read or to stop postal communications to and from a suspect (*brevåbning, brevstandsning*). Similarly, the police may be authorized to monitor telephone conversations (*telefonaflytning*) or to be informed of who has been connected to a suspect's telephone (*teleoplysning*). Recently, electronic eavesdropping of conversations by microphones and transmitters has been regulated (*rumaflytning, anden aflytning*). *Cfr*. Section 780 of the Administration of Justice Act.

## 6. The ordinary course of criminal proceedings

### 6.1. THE POLICE ENQUIRY

The first step is the enquiry carried out by the police. A formal investigation by the courts (*forundersøgelse*) no longer exists in Denmark.

### 6.2. THE INDICTMENT

At the end of an enquiry the case may be dropped, the charges may be withdrawn or the case may be brought before a court (*cfr*. supra). In the latter case, an indictment (*tiltale, anklage*) is drawn up. This indictment may be very summary, but at the very least it must contain a statement of the facts, the time and place of the crime, and the criminal code articles to be applied.

The indictment provides the framework within which the case is handled. Minor corrections regarding time, place etc. (*biomstændigheder*) can be made freely. Otherwise, the court is restricted by the contents of the indictment and may not deal with other facts unless the defence consents. The court is not bound by the prosecutor's legal description of the facts, but the defence must be given an opportunity to present its arguments on that question. (Sections 908 and 909). The court is not bound by the prosecutor's plea with regard to the sentence.

## 6.3. THE TRIAL

At the trial (*domsforhandlingen*), preliminary questions are dealt with first. Then the indictment is read out and the evidence is heard - questions will at least be put to the accused as to the facts and his personality. After the pleadings, the accused has the right to make a final statement. The court then deliberates *in camera*. Finally, the judgment is pronounced in open court. The operative parts are read out and the grounds are given orally. The full reasons will be supplied later in writing.

In a jury case the court will first rule on the conviction (*skyldspørgsmålet*). Then there are new pleadings as to the sanction, and finally the court decides on the sentence.

# 7. Evidence

Evidence is required to convince the court of the existence of the relevant facts related to the case and general scientific knowledge. Elements of proof are divided into two groups: personal evidence (*mundtlige* or *personlige bevismidler*) and objective proof (*reelle* or *tinglige bevismidler*).

The law itself is not subject to proof (*iura novit curia*) except the law of a foreign country.

## 7.1. PERSONAL EVIDENCE

### 7.1.1. *Questioning of the accused*

The right to be heard gives the accused the opportunity to state his point of view (*kontradiktion*), but he may also be questioned as a valuable and often the most reliable source of information (*afhøring*). No pressure may be exercised in order to obtain statements, and there is an obligation on the part of the authorities to inform the accused of his right to remain silent (Section 752 of the Administration of Justice Act). If the accused chooses to make a statement, he does not do so in the role of a witness. Lying is thus not an offense (*Cfr.* Section 159 of the Criminal Code). But if he aids and abets a witness with perjury, he will be liable to punishment as an accomplice (*Cfr.* Section 23 of the Criminal Code).

### 7.1.2. The hearing of witnesses

Witnesses (*vidner*) are persons obliged to testify under a threat of punishment should they lie (*cfr.* Section 158 of the Criminal Code). Everyone has the duty to be a witness in court but no one is obliged to take part in the police enquiry (Sections 168 and 750 of the Administration of Justice Act). If a witness refuses to testify in court, he faces coercive detention (*forvaring*) of up to six months or coercive day fines (*løbende bøde, tvangsbøde*) (Section 178).

Various reasons, however, may justify a refusal to testify (*vidneudelukkelsesgrunde, vidnefritagelsesgrunde*). Examples are: close family links to the accused, the risk of self-incrimination and professional secrecy (as in the case of clergymen, defence counsel, and mass media journalists). The rules on protection of professional secrecy differ with regard to the profession in question and the nature of the crime. (*cfr.* Section 170 and Section 171 of the Administration of Justice Act). If such persons are lying in the witness stand, depending on their profession, they may be acquitted or get a more lenient punishment than otherwise prescribed (*cfr.* Section 159 of the Criminal Code). The same restrictions apply with regard to a notice to produce a document (*edition*).

Witnesses are admonished to tell the truth and are reminded of the penalty for perjury; oaths are not used (Section 181 of the Administration of Justice Act). As a rule, witnesses are questioned by the prosecutor and defence counsel, but questions may also be asked by the presiding judge. The questioning is more informal and less elaborate than in the examination-in-chief and cross-examination "Anglo-Saxon style".

Witnesses are usually not assisted by a lawyer. If a victim of incest or rape requests a lawyer, the court shall assign one. In a number of other cases, such as, for example, murder, assault and robbery, the court may assign counsel to the witness. The request can also emanate from the police. (*cfr.* Section 741 a).

### 7.1.3. Experts

In some cases the testimony of an expert is required in order to ascertain the facts (for example, with regard to the degree of pollution in an environmental case). This statement may be given by a special authority, for example, the Medico-Legal Council (*Retslægerådet*) on forensic questions, or the University Institute of Forensic Medicine as to the amount of alcohol found in the blood. The statement may also be given by an *ad hoc* appointed expert; he is usually selected by the judicial authority. Experts usually give their evidence in writing, without subsequent cross-examinations. The courts are not bound by such evidence but as a rule they follow it.

It is very rare to have differing expert witnesses called by the prosecutor and the accused. Both parties nearly always depend on the supposedly neutral expert.

### 7.2. EVIDENCE *IN REM*

#### 7.2.1. Investigation on the spot

The term "investigation on the spot" (*besigtigelse*) is to be understood in a broad sense as including all forms of sensual confrontation with objects related to the offence - looking at localities, persons, weapons or pictures taken thereof as well as listening to tape recordings (Section 822). Incidental evidence is fully recognized as proof.

#### 7.2.2. Documents

Documents are also objects of *besigtigelse*, but differ in that they reveal the record of human thought, if read. Documents, the contents of which provide information regarding facts which can also be elucidated directly by testimony may only be submitted to a limited extent (Section 877).

### 7.3. INADMISSIBLE EVIDENCE

Evidence obtained in an illegal way is not automatically inadmissible evidence. See *supra*, 4.3.1., on the free evaluation of evidence.

## 8. Special forms of procedure

### 8.1. PRIVATE PROSECUTION

See *supra*, 3.3., the victim.

### 8.2. SUMMARY PROCEDURE

The most common form of summary procedure is that of compound fines imposed by the police (see *supra*, 2.2.1). Identical rules exist in relation to the tax authorities, the custom office, and the Ministry of Agriculture's administration of the European Community Market Organisations. If the person disagrees with the proposed solution, a simple declaration to that effect or merely his passivity will transfer the case to ordinary proceedings.

### 8.3. TRIAL *IN ABSENTIA*

If an accused is absent without justification, a warrant may be issued for his arrest and he may be picked up by the police.

In minor cases, judgment may be passed in his absence (*udeblivelsesdom*, Section 934). If he later appears in court and presents a reasonable explanation for the absence he may obtain a retrial (*genoptagelse*) (Section 987).

### 8.4. PROCEEDINGS AGAINST CHILDREN AND JUVENILES

Children under 15 years of age are not punishable (Section 15 of the Criminal Code). Therefore they cannot be prosecuted, remanded in custody etc. But they may be interrogated by the police (Section 752 (2) of the Administration of Justice Act). If intervention is necessary, the child in question must be handed over to the welfare authorities. This is an administrative body, and its decisions are subject to judicial review in civil proceedings.

Juveniles above the age of criminal responsibility can be prosecuted in accordance with the ordinary rules for adults, but the majority of 15-17 year olds are transferred to the social welfare authorities as a condition of the prosecutors' waiver of prosecution.

## 9. Remedies

Normally, there is the possibility of having a case tried at two and only two instances. A *complete appeal* refers to an entire review of the case, i.e. the appeal court has the power to try the case in law and fact (*fuldstændig anke*). A *revising appeal* only refers to the correct application of the law of procedure and/or the criminal law. A third kind of appeal does not question the conviction (the guilt), but only the sentence (the sanction) (*strafudmålingsanke*). (Sections 943 and 963).

Legal remedies in criminal matters are in principle subject to the prohibition of *reformatio in peius*. This means that in cases in which the accused alone has availed himself of a remedy, the previous decision may not be altered to his disadvantage (Section 960 (3)). However, there is nothing to prevent that outcome if the public prosecutor has lodged an appeal or presented a counter appeal. And this is nearly always done.

### 9.1. APPEAL

Appeal (*anke*) is the most comprehensive ordinary remedy. In principle, all judgments of the court of first instance are subject to appeal. However, appeal is excluded in petty cases having resulted in a minor fine and in jury cases with regard to the question of guilt (the verdict).

As a rule, no ground for appeal has to be filed, it is sufficient that the appeal be declared within the legal time-limit, usually 14 days. If the appeal is filed too late, the appeal court decides whether it will admit it; the decisive factor being whether the delay was caused by "reasons which are not imputable to him" (Section 949 (2) of the Administration of Justice Act).

A city court judgment can be appealed to the High Court. To bring the decision of this appellate court further to the Supreme Court, it is necessary to have special permission. At present, the permit must be granted by the Minister of Justice. But in the near future it will probably be given by the Supreme Court itself.

The High Court is the first instance in jury cases. The conviction as such is not subject to appeal. But there is free appeal to the Supreme Court with regard to the sentence and to legal mistakes committed by the High Court.

If the competent appeal court rules that there has been a mistake with regard to the interpretation of the law, it may quash the lower court decision and return the case. It will only quash the lower court conviction if there is sufficient reason to believe that following the rule in question would have produced a different judgment in the present case. It may also decide on the case and give judgment in accordance with the correct interpretation, and this is usually done. Numerous decisions suffering from minor flaws are not quashed.

## 9.2. COMPLAINT

The complaint or interlocutory appeal (*kære*) is a remedy aimed at the control of procedural activities and inactivities. This is normally based on written pleadings.

## 9.3. REVISING A FINAL JUDGMENT

The remedies mentioned above are subject to time-limits. If all remedies have been used or the time-limits have expired, a petition for retrial (*genoptagelse*) may be filed to a special Court of Revision (*klageretten*, literally the court of complaints). It is composed of 5 judges appointed for a 10 year-period. There is one judge from the Supreme Court, one from the high courts, one from the city courts, one defence counsel, and one university professor of law.

A retrial in favour of a convicted person is admitted if relevant new facts or proof have been found which were not known to the court when it convicted the applicant. The provision is applied very rarely in practice. A retrial will not be permitted simply because the courts later have taken another stand regarding interpretation of the law.

A petition for retrial may also be filed against an acquitted person. In this case, however, much stricter rules apply.

## 9.4. THE EUROPEAN COMMISSION ON HUMAN RIGHTS

See *supra*, 1.2.

# 10. Other questions

## 10.1. STATUTES OF LIMITATION

The period during which an offence can be prosecuted is limited in time, depending on the seriousness of the offence. The limitation periods are set out in Section 93 of the Penal Code. They vary between two years (where the offence is punishable with a penalty not exceeding one year's imprisonment) and fifteen years (when the offence carries an indeterminate sentence). Special time limits are set for certain economic offences, such as breaches of the provisions regarding companies and accounts (where the limitation period is 5 years), and tax fraud (limitation period of 10 years).

The limitation period is calculated from the day when the punishable act or omission ceased (Section 94 Penal Code). When liability depends on or is influenced by a consequence of the offence that has occured or by any later event, the period shall be calculated from the occurrence of such consequence or later event.

The limitation period can be suspended and prolonged. Prolongation results from acts of "interruption", *i.e.* any legal proceedings by which the person concerned is charged with the offence. An interruption results in the renewal of the prescriptive period.

# 11. Select bibliography

## *Books*

GOMARD, B., *Studier i den Danske straffeproces,* Copenhagen 1976.
GOMARD, B., MØLLER, J. and NILAS, C., *Kommenteret retsplejelov*, 4th ed, Copenhagen, 1989.
HURWITZ, S., *Den Danske strafferetspleje,* 2nd ed, Copenhagen 1949.
KOKTVEDGAARD, M. and GAMMELTOFT-HANSEN, H., *Lærebog i Strafferetspleje,* Copenhagen, 1978.
SMITH, E., *Straffeproces,* Copenhagen 1988.

## *Periodicals*

Nordisk Tidskrift for Kriminalvidenskab (Copenhagen)
Lov og Rett (Oslo)
Tidskrift for Rettsvitenskap (Oslo)
Svensk Juristtidning (Stockholm)

# Chapter 3 - England and Wales

Dr.A.T.H.**SMITH**
Gonville & Caius College
University of Cambridge

## 1. Sources

### 1.1. GENERAL OBSERVATIONS: LEGISLATION AND OTHER SOURCES

The law regulating English[1] criminal procedure and evidence, like its substantive criminal law, has never been the subject of systematic legislative attention. Consequently, the relevant law is be to be found scattered throughout an enormous range of sources including statutes, the common law (in judicial decisions), administrative guidelines[2] and directions[3]. Matters relating to the appointment and organisation of the judiciary, for example, are variously dealt with in the Supreme Court Acts and the Magistrates'Courts Act 1980.

Other relevant statutes include the Powers of Criminal Courts Act 1973, the Juries Act 1974, the Bail Act 1976, the Criminal Justice Acts 1982, 1987, 1988 and 1991, and the Drug Trafficking Offences Act 1986.

Lord Lane, a recently retired Lord Chief Justice, developed the institution of Sentencing Guideline judgments, but even this operated within an enormously complex statutory sentencing framework, recently supplemented

---

[1]England includes Wales for these purposes, but not Scotland, which has its own system. See *infra*, Chapter 12.

[2]E.g on making available to the defence so-called "unused material". These Guidelines are reproduced in (1982) 74 *Cr.App.R.* 302; [1982] 1 *All E.R.* 734. The Guidelines are sufficiently important that a failure to follow them might give rise to the quashing of a conviction, as in *Lawson* (1990) 90 *Cr.App.R.* 107. See also the Mode of Trial Guidelines, which give guidance to Magistrates as to the factors to be taken in to account in deciding whether a trial should be held summarily, or on indictment; these are reported [1990] 1 *W.L.R.* 1439. There are also guidelines on the use of the caution rather than the use of the prosecution process, which are considered in [1991] *Crim. L.R.* 591.

[3]Perhaps the most important of these are the Codes of Practice issued under Section 66 of PACE. These deal with the exercise by poolice officers of statutory powers of stop and search; the searching of premises by police officers and the seizure of property found by police officers on persons or premises; the detention, treatment and questioning of persons by police officers; the identification of persons. The are contained in an HMSO publication, *Police and Criminal Evidence Act 1984 (s.66): CODES OF PRACTICE* (1991).

by the Criminal Justice Act 1991[4]. The Police And Criminal Evidence Act 1984 (known colloquially as "PACE"), which was the end-product of a Royal Commission on Criminal Procedure (established 1977), now regulates in considerable detail the conduct of the police in the exercise of their powers[5]. It is plain that the work accomplished by that Commission has not wholly allayed public fears about the English Criminal Justice system. The appointment of another Royal Commission on Criminal Justice, established in June 1991[6] is evidence that confidence in the criminal justice process remains one of immense public interest and concern. The Commission reported in 1993[7], and its recommendations are expected to have considerable impact on the shape of the English criminal justice process.

## 1.2. THE POSSIBILITY OF A CRIMINAL CODE

For nearly a century and a half, the possibility has existed that Parliament might be persuaded to enact a criminal code[8]. Despite the best efforts of reformers such as Jeremy Bentham and Sir James Fitzjames Stephen in the nineteenth century, this has yet to be achieved. It is a long-cherished hope of the Law Commission that this will one day be accomplished, but that day is a long way off. In the meantime, the courts continue to claim a residual power to "declare" the law[9]. although that power is exercised only very rarely and in perhaps quite exceptional conditions, and the House of Lords (which is the highest Criminal court in the land) has on occasions said that it no longer enjoys such a power[10].

---

[4]For commentary, see the various articles in the [1992] *Crim. L.R.* 232-287, and LENG R. and MANCHESTER, C., *A Guide to the Criminal Justice Act 1991* (1991); ASHWORTH, A.J., *Sentencing and Criminal Justice* (1992).

[5]*Royal Commission on Criminal Procedure Report* Cmnd 8092 (1981).

[6]Because they disclose contemporary concerns about the state of the Criminal Justice process in England, the terms of reference of the Commission are set out in an appendix to this Chapter. The recommendations of the Commission are noted at appropriate points throughout this chapter.

[7]*Report* of the Royal Commission on Criminal Justice, Cm 2263, July 1993.

[8]On the historical aspects, see in particular Sir R. Cross, "The Making of English Criminal Law" [1978] *Crim. L.R.* 519 and 652. For more modern developments, see SMITH, A.T.H., "Judicial Law Making in the Criminal Law", (1984) 100 *L.Q.R.*,46 -76 ; SMITH, A.T.H., "The Case for a Code", [1986] *Crim. L.R.*, 285.

[9]Most recently in *R* [1991] 3 *W.L.R.* 767 (H.L.), where the House of Lords held that there is no longer to be any spousal immunity for the husband in the case of marital rape. See GILES, M. "Judicial Law-Making in the Criminal Courts: The Case of Marital Rape", [1992] *Crim. L.R.* 407.

[10]*Knuller* [1973] A.C. 435.

## 1.3. THE CONSTITUTIONAL FRAMEWORK

It is a well-known feature of the British constitution that there is no written constitution or Bill of Rights, and that in consequence Parliament is constitutionally virtually untrammelled in what it can do. In the field of criminal procedure, it has, for example, abolished the privilege against self-incrimination for certain purposes[11]. The European Convention on Human Rights is not directly applicable in English law[12], but there is a right of individual petition, and its indirect impact in the protection of civil liberties is considerable[13]. Britain is a signatory to the International Covenant of Civil and Political Rights[14]. but there is no right of individual petition, and perhaps in consequence, the impact of that instrument is not as considerable.

# 2. Structure of the criminal justice system

## 2.1. INVESTIGATING AUTHORITIES

Most of the initial investigation of criminal offences in England is conducted by the police[15]. The proceedings are in no way judicially supervised, although if it should be necessary to arrest a suspect, his detention is subject to some judicial scrutiny. There are, for historical reasons, some 43 different police forces in England and Wales[16]. There has never been a national police force. A considerable degree of local autonomy is allowed to the Chief

---

[11]The consequences of its having done so have only recently become fully apparent: *A.T.&T. Istel Ltd and Another* v. *Tully* [1992] 2 WLR 112; *Seelig and Spens* [1991] 4 *All E.R.* 429, [1992] 1 *WLR* 148; *In re Jeffrey S. Levitt Ltd* [1992] 2 W.L.R. 975. See also *In re London United Investments plc* [1992] BCLC 91 (Chancery Division); [1992] 2 W.L.R.850; *Sociedade Nacional* v. *Lundquist* [1991] 2 *W.L.R.* 280; *Bank of England* v. *Riley* [1992] 1 *All E.R.* 769; *Tate Access Floors Inc* v. *Boswell* [1991] 2 *W.L.R.* 304, [1990] 3 *All E.R.* 303; *R* v. *Director of the Serious Fraud Office, ex p Smith* [1992] 1 *All E.R.* 730; *Re A E Farr Ltd; Staverton Construction Ltd; Farr Securities Ltd; Farr PLC* Judgment delivered 29 Nov., 1991; *Re Arrows Ltd* [1992] BCLC 126; *Price Waterhouse* v. *BCCI Holdings (Luxembourg) SA* (1991) The Times, October 30th. *Bishopsgate Investment Management Ltd (in provisional liquidation)* v. *Maxwell and another* [1992] 2 W.L.R. 991.

[12]*R* v.*Secretary for the Home Department, ex parte Brind* [1991] A.C. 696; *Derbyshire County Council* v. *Times Newspapers* [1993] A.C. 534is the most important recent case in which the House of Lords has considered the jurisprudential status of the European Convention.

[13]For a recent account, see GEARTY, C. "The European Court of Human Rights and the Protection of Civil Liberties: An Overview", (1993) *Camb. L.J.*, 89.

[14]The status of the Covenant so far as English law is concerned is considered by MCGOLDRICK, *The Human Rights Committee* (1991), p.20.

[15]The leading works on the police and their powers are: V. Bevan and K. Lidstone, *The Investigation of Crime: A Guide to Police Powers* (1991); ZANDER, M. *The Police and Criminal Evidence Act 1984* 2nd edn (1991).

[16]See MARSHALL, G., *Constitutional Conventions,* (1984). REINER, R., *The Politics of the Police* (1985).

Constable in each district as to how he will deploy his resources, although also in practice a great deal of national uniformity is achieved. The forces are all subject to the same laws (such as the Police and Criminal Evidence Act 1984), and where there is a degree of discretion involved (as with the use of cautioning, rather than prosecutions, for example), these are frequently the subject of national guidelines issued by the Home Office[17]. Sometimes too national policies can be implemented through the use of the prerogative powers that are still residually available to the national Government, such as the prerogative power to preserve the peace[18].

In addition, there are other public detection agencies, particularly for example the Inland Revenue or the Customs and Excise and, in cases of serious fraud, the Serious Fraud Office[19] which, as its name implies, investigates and then prosecutes cases of particularly serious fraud. In cases of fraud against the European Community, the Ministry of Agriculture, Food and Fisheries both detects and brings prosecutions on behalf of the state.

The suspect is under no obligation to co-operate with these proceedings in any way as for example by answering questions. There is a right to remain silent, and the jury are prohibited from drawing adverse inferences from a failure to speak. Nor can prosecution counsel or the judge make adverse remarks in relation to the suspect's exercise of his right. This is subject to the remarkable exception of some powers given in the investigation of serious fraud offences, where investigations are conducted by inspectors appointed by the Secretary of State for Trade and Industry and the Serious Fraud Office[20].

## 2.2. PROSECUTING AUTHORITIES

Until the Prosecution of Offences Act 1985, the decision to prosecute was in the hands of the police, and the conduct of a subsequent prosecution was undertaken by or on behalf of the police. Acting on the recommendations of a Royal Commission[21], Parliament created the Crown Prosecution Service, whose role was to take over the conduct of all prosecutions in England and

---

[17]The Home Office circular issued to all police forces which urges the wider use of cautions, and setting out basic principles which should be followed is Circular 14/1985, printed (1985) 149 *J.P.* 173, 190.

[18]*R.v.Secretary of State for the Home Department ex parte Northumbria Police Authority* [1989] Q.B. 26.

[19]Established by the Criminal Justice Act 1987. For a discussion of its operation, see J. Wood, [1989] Crim. L.R. 175. See also KIRK D. and WOODCOCK, A., *The Investigation and Prosecution of Serious Fraud* (1992). See also STAPLE, G., "Serious and Complex Fraud: A New Perspective" (1993) 56 M.L.R. 127 - the author being the head of the Serious Fraud Office.

[20]See the court decisions referred to in note 11, which concern these powers.

[21]*Report of the Royal Commission on Criminal Procedure*, Cmnd 8092, 1979 (the Philips Commission).

Wales. It was felt that there was a potential in the previous system for miscarriages of justice; the police, it was thought, did not bring a sufficiently independent eye to the question whether or not there was sufficient evidence to charge a suspect, and the introduction of the Crown Prosecution Service was to screen weak cases before they were ever brought to court.

The Crown Prosecution Service is headed by the Director of Public Prosecutions, who is in turn politically answerable to the Attorney-General, a Member of Parliament and a member of the Government of the day. By strong constitutional convention, however, the Attorney-General makes decisions about prosecution entirely free of party political considerations[22].

In cases of particular sensitivity, the consent of one of the Law Officers of the Crown (the Attorney-General and the Solicitor General, or the Director of Public Prosecutions) is specifically required by statute. Prosecutions for incitement to racial hatred under the Public Order Act 1986, for example fall in to this category, or prosecutions for breaches of the Official Secrets Acts 1989.

## 2.3. THE JUDICIARY

### 2.3.1. Courts of criminal jurisdiction

Criminal jurisdiction in England is exercised for the most part (i.e. in the greatest number of cases) in the Magistrates' Courts. These courts consist of three lay magistrates[23] sitting together, advised by[24] a legally trained Clerk. In the major cities, there are legally qualified Stipendiary Magistrates (some 55 in number throughout the country), 40 of whom operate in London. Their jurisdiction is to hear summary offences and indictable offences which can, at the election of the defendant, be tried summarily. Their powers of imprisonment are limited to 6 months'.

There is also Crown Court trial, where cases are heard by judges sitting with a jury composed of twelve lay members of the public, chosen more or less at random. The Crown Court is part of the Supreme Court, and is governed by the Supreme Court Act 1981. In practice, the gravest cases are heard by a High Court judge, and the lesser offences are tried by Circuit Judges or (slightly down the scale of seniority) Recorders and Assistant Recorders who are specially appointed barristers (and now sometimes solicitors) of several years practising experience.

---

[22]The leading work on the role of the Attorney-General is EDWARDS, J.LL, *The Attorney-General, Politics and Public Interest* (1984).

[23]Appointed by the Lord Chancellor acting under the Justices of the Peace Act 1979, and advised by various local advisory committees. The office is an unpaid one.

[24]The reality of this in practice is questionable, since the advice will frequently be offered by an assistant clerk who lacks any real legal training. Complaints about this unsatisfactory situation have not given rise to any changes in the rules. See (1987) 151 *J.P.N.* 1.

Appeals against conviction are heard by the Divisional Court of the Queen's Bench Division of the High Court, which hears appeals on points of law by way of case stated from the Magistrates' Courts. The Court of Appeal (Criminal Division) hears appeals against conviction and sentence from the Crown Court. On matters of law alone, there is the possibility of a further appeal to the House of Lords, but this can be done only with leave (either of the Court of Appeal or of the House of Lords itself), and then in relation to a matter of general public importance.

The Crown (in whose name prosecutions are brought) has no right of appeal against acquittal, although there has recently been established a right of appeal against what are thought to be unduly lenient sentences[25]. Technically, when an appeal by the defendant succeeds, there is a power of re-trial, but it is very rarely exercised by the Court of Appeal. Until recently, this was because the power existed only where the appeal had been allowed after the reception of fresh evidence, which was (and is) a process that the English courts were extremely reluctant to permit. More recently, however, the Court of Appeal has been granted a much wider power of retrial. As yet, there is no real jurisprudence as to the sorts of circumstances in which such a power will be employed, but it may be expected that such factors as the seriousness of the offence, the age of the proceedings and similar considerations will have a bearing on whether or not the courts will exercise what is, in some respects, still a somewhat controversial power.

### 2.3.2. *The role of lay judges*

Serious criminal offences (indictable offences, and those triable either way which are tried upon indictment) are heard before a judge who acts with the assistance of a jury. The jury (of twelve) must, with some exceptions reach a unanimous verdict.

Qualifications for jury service were reduced significantly in 1972[26] when the property qualification was abolished. Now the Juries Act 1974 provides that any person between the ages of 18 and 65 who is eligible to vote in an election is eligible for jury service, unless he or she is ineligible, disqualified or exempted from service. People who have some legal qualification are generally ineligible. A person who has had a conviction for a serious offence is disqualified, and many people who are eligible can nevertheless claim exemption; MP's, members of the Armed Forces, doctors and members of allied professions. A jury of 12 is empanelled from a larger group who may be challenged without cause by the Crown (a process known as

---

[25]Criminal Justice Act 1987.
[26]By the Criminal Justice Act 1972.

"standing by"), but no longer by the person to be tried, the defendant[27]. Defendants retain a challenge "for cause", although it may be difficult to say what constitutes such a cause[28]. Juries are now "vetted" by the police who can advise the prosecution when to challenge an eligible but "unsuitable" juror, but only within strict guidelines, established by the Attorney-General[29]. The dominant principle is one of random selection but this can be varied, especially for cases involving terrorism or national security[30].

The role of the jury is as the trier of fact. The jury is subject to the direction of the judge as to matters of law but, in trials on indictment, the members of the jury are the sole arbiters of fact. The decision of the jury is regarded as being something sacrosanct, which in turn can sometimes make it very difficult for a person who believes that he has been wrongly convicted to persuade the appeal courts to interfere with a verdict. The view taken by the courts is that the jury had the benefit of seeing the defendant (who may or may not have testified) and the other witnesses, and seeing the other evidence given and being as a result in the best position to evaluate that evidence.

### 2.3.3. The court system and the classification of offences

There are three categories of criminal offence:
(a) summary offences which are tried in the Magistrates'Court;
(b) indictable offences. These are the most serious crimes (murder and rape, and serious offences against the person), which are tried in the Crown Court before a judge and jury. The defendant has no option of selecting summary trial.
(c) offences triable either way, a category that includes virtually all criminal offences, where the defendant can elect whether or not to have the case tried before a jury of his peers in the Crown Court. It is, however, open to the magistrates to decline jurisdiction of they take the view that the offence is beyond their sentencing competence[31].

---

[27]Until 1977, the defendant was entitled to make seven peremptory challenges. This was reduced to three in 1977 and abolished entirely in 1988, Criminal Justice Act 1988, s.118(1).

[28]In a *Practice Direction* [1988] 1 *W.L.R.* 1162, it is said that a juror should be excused for service "where he or she is personally concerned in the facts of the case or is closely connected with a party or prospective witness". How these connections can be established if the juror does not volunteer them is unclear.

[29]The Attorney-General's official statement is contained in (1980) 71 Cr. App. R. 30, and the text of the present guidelines (which were amended in December 1988) is to be found in (1989) 88 *Cr.App.R.* 123.

[30]The constitutionality of the practice was challenged and considered by the court in *McCann* (1990) 92 *Cr.App.R.* 239. The Guidelines on jury checks are published in [1988] 3 *All E.R.* 1086.

[31]The maximum sentence that magistrates may impose on any occasion is six month's imprisonment; Magistrates Courts' Act 1980, s.33.

The decision as to which process should be selected is the subject of extensive guidelines issued by the judges, indicating in particular, which aggravating features of the alleged incident make the offence inappropriate for summary trial[32].

The right of a person charged with an offence triable either way was considered by the Royal Commission on Criminal Justice[33] who found that most defendants who opted for trial in the Crown court as opposed to the magistrates'court did so "in the belief that they would stand a better chance of acquittal after a fairer trial"[34]. For reasons which appear to be largely related to administrative efficiency in the distribution of case-loads between the Crown Court and the magistrates'court, the Commission recommended that in cases involving "either way" offences, the defendant should no longer have the right to insist on a trial by a jury. The procedure recommended by the Commission would be as follows: where the Crown Prosecution Service and the defendant agree that the case is suitable for summary trial, it should proceed to trial in the magistrates'court. Similarly, if both the Crown Prosecution Service and the defendant agree that the case should be tried on indictment it would be tried in the Crown Court. But where the defence do not agree with the prosecutor's proposals on which court should try the case, the matter should be referred to the magistrates for a decision[35].

## 3. Parties to criminal proceedings

### 3.1. THE PROSECUTOR

In trials on indictment, the prosecutor will ordinarily be a barrister instructed (briefed) by the Crown Prosecution Service. The barrister is a self-employed man (or woman) who operates according to the Bar's Code of Conduct. His function is to place before the court the case against the defendant as fairly as the facts permit. He has very little say at the sentencing phase, although increasingly as the Crown is exercising powers to appeal against unduly lenient sentences, there is a tendency for the Courts to expect guidance from counsel as to the sorts of sentences that might be appropriate.

In the lower courts, the prosecutions were, until relatively recently, conducted by the police or on their behalf. This is no longer the case, and most prosecutions are conducted by members of the Crown Prosecution Service.

The subject of rights of audience before the courts is a matter of considerable debate and contention. The Courts and Legal Services Act 1990

---

[32]*Practice Note: Mode of Trial Guidelines* [1990] 1 *W.L.R.* 1439.

[33] Royal Commission, *Report*, Chapter 6 and Recommendation 114.

[34] *Ibid.*, par. 7.

[35] Royal Commission, *Report*, Recommendation 114.

opened the possibility that Solicitors and members of the Crown Prosecution Service might be granted rights of appearance in the Crown Court.

## 3.2. THE DEFENCE

Most defences are conducted, on indictment by barristers and in summary proceedings by solicitors, very often supported financially by the state through legal aid[36]. Barristers are also sometimes to be found in the Magistrates courts either prosecuting or defending.

Joint trials are a regular feature of the English process. Particular rules govern the question whether a co-defendant might be able to have his participation in the trial severed. There is perceived to be a risk of prejudice where the evidence against one of the co-defendants is considerably greater than that of his associates, but this will not always persuade the judge that the trials should be severed.

## 3.3. THE VICTIM

Technically, the victim has no locus standi in criminal proceedings. A compensation order can be made in his favour in relatively minor cases. Otherwise, however, a sharp distinction is drawn between civil and criminal proceedings, and if the victim wishes to pursue justice further, he must generally take proceedings in his own name in the civil courts.

Increased awareness of the interests of the victim has been shown in recent years. Thus the code of practice for Crown Prosecutors, in setting out the public interest criteria which may result in a decision not to prosecute states that while the public interest must be the paramount consideration, the interests of the victim are an important factor in determining the public interest and should be taken into account.

The Royal Commission on Criminal Justice, in considering the situation of "victims and other witnesses"[37] stated their broad agreement with this approach. At the same time, the Commission made several recommendations directed towards improving the sensitivity of the criminal justice system to the needs and interests of victims. Thus the Commission has recommended that, so far as practicable, "victims should be kept informed of the progress and outcome of cases, including decisions not to prosecute and, in some cases, the results of bail applications or successful appeals" by the accused[38].

---

[36]The Legal Aid Act 1988 regulates the granting of financial assistance to those accused of offending.

[37] Royal Commission, *Report,* Chapter 5, paras. 44 *et seq.*

[38] *Ibid.*

## 4. General principles concerning criminal procedure

### 4.1. GENERAL PRINCIPLES

#### 4.1.1. The adversarial nature of criminal proceedings

The criminal process is overwhelmingly adversarial in character, so that the trial is not so much a search for the truth as a test of the evidence that is presented before the court by the parties.

#### 4.1.2. The presumption of innocence and the burden of proof

It is an essential principle that a person is innocent until he is proven guilty, and that the burden of proving that guilt is upon the prosecution, beyond reasonable doubt[39]. It follows from the presumption of innocence that a person who is accused of criminal misconduct should generally be permitted his liberty on bail[40].

The English system also subscribes to the principle that nobody should be tried twice for the same offence, through the operation of the defences (really, procedural bars) of *autrefois acquit* or *autrefois convict*.

#### 4.1.3. Publicity

There is an overriding principle that justice must be done in the open and proceedings (including the names of the participants and victims) freely reported. This principle is enshrined in the Contempt of Court Act 1981. However the courts possess inherent and statutory powers to hear cases in camera and otherwise to restrict the publication of matters when this is thought to be necessary in the interests of, for example, national security.

#### 4.1.4. The right to silence

The suspect has a right to silence. This means that he cannot be obliged in any way to answer questions under police interrogation, that his silence cannot be made the subject of adverse comment either by the judge or by the prosecution lawyer, and the suspect is under no obligation to give evidence on his own behalf. If he does decide to give evidence, however, he loses the shield that the privilege would otherwise afford him.

The right of silence is frequently criticised on the ground that it is exercised by professional criminals in order to escape conviction. It was considered by the Royal Commission on Criminal Justice which examined the

---

[39]*Woolmington* v. *DPP* [1935] A.C. 462.

[40]For a recent account, see CORRE, N., *Bail in Criminal Proceedings* (1990) London, Fourmat.

research carried out in this area and, indeed, commissioned a research study of its own on this issue[41]. The Commission summarised the research findings as follows[42]:

> "The research evidence may be summarised as follows. The right of silence is exercised only in a minority of cases. It may tend to be exercised more often in the more serious cases and where legal advice is given. There is no evidence which shows conclusively that silence is used disproportionately by professional criminals. Nor is there evidence to support the belief that silence in the police station leads to improved chances of an acquittal. Most of those who are silent in the police station either plead guilty later or are subsequently found guilty. Nevertheless it is possible that some defendants who are silent and who are now acquitted might rightly or wrongly be convicted if the prosecution and the judge were permitted to suggest to the jury that silence can amount to supporting evidence of guilt."

The Commission's conclusion was that there should be no general departure from the right to silence, and that the current practice of advising suspects by means of the caution that they are not obliged to answer questions put to them by the police should be retained[43] and that adverse inferences should not be drawn from silence in the police station. The Commission did, however, recommend that once the prosecution's case was fully disclosed to the defendant, the latter should be required to offer an answer to the charges made against him, at the risk of adverse comment at trial on any new defence he may then disclose or any departure from a defence which he has previously disclosed[44]. It also recommended that investigators in serious fraud cases should retain their existing powers to require answers to questions[45].

### 4.1.5. The obligation of disclosure

The defendant is under no obligation to give any advance warning of the defence that he intends to put forward, with the exception of an alibi defence[46], or a defence of mental incapacity, or where he proposes to rely on the production of expert evidence.

Whereas the defence is under no obligation to give advance notice of the case that it proposes to advance by way of defence, subject to certain exceptions, the prosecution must disclose in advance the material that it intends to place before the court, and must in addition make available any "unused material" upon which it does not propose to rely. This latter practice is subject to guidelines, indicating the circumstances in which it might

---

[41] Royal Commission on Criminal Justice Research Study No.10, *The right to silence in police interrogation: a study of some of the underlying issues*, R. LENG.

[42] Royal Commission, *Report*, par. 19.

[43] Royal Commission, *Report*, par. 22 and Recommendations 82 *et seq.*

[44] Royal Commision, *Report*, Recommendation 83.

[45] *Ibid.*, Recommendation 84.

[46] Criminal Justice Act 1967, s.11.

sometimes be proper to withhold evidence from the defence where it is particularly sensitive. There has comparatively recently been some difficulty experienced where Ministers of the Crown have certified that material is so sensitive that it should be subject to the claim to "Public Interest Immunity", by virtue of which the Crown is entitled to prevent the defence from having access to particular material[47].

The issue of defence disclosure was considered by the Royal Commission on Criminal Justice, who have recommended[48] that the obligation of the defence to disclose its case should be extended. The Commission's view was that where it was the intention of the defendant to contest the charges, he should be obliged to disclose the substance of his defence in advance of the trial or to indicate that he will not be calling any evidence but will simply be arguing that the prosecution has failed to make out its case. Should the defendant present a defence at the trial without making advance disclosure of its substance, or if he presents a defence which differs substantially from that previously disclosed, the Commission recommended that the prosecution should be able, with the leave of the presiding judge, to invite the jury to draw inferences adverse to the accused[49].

## 4.2. PRINCIPLES GOVERNING THE OPENING OF CRIMINAL PROCEEDINGS

### 4.2.1. Proceedings in the magistrates'court

If the matter is to be dealt with in the lower court, the "information" is prepared and laid before the local Magistrates'Court. The attendance of the defendant is often secured by summons, although it may be by way of arrest. The information sets out the allegation which the defendant will have to answer and the summons calls for him to appear before the Court and answer to the information. These papers are then served on the Defendant or his legal advisers. The case is fixed for trial by the Magistrates'Court and the prosecution lawyer appears to present the case.

### 4.2.2. Proceedings in the Crown Court

In proceedings in the superior courts, the indictment is the formal statement of charge of which the defendant stands accused. It is subject to a number of technical requirements[50], but the general effect of these is that the indictment must contain sufficient detail to let the defendant know in advance what charge he has to face. The indictment can if necessary be amended at various

---

[47]See SMITH, A.T.H., "Public interest immunity in criminal cases", [1993] 52 *Camb. L.J.* 1

[48]Royal Commission, *Report*, Recommendations 132 *et seq.*

[49]*Ibid.*, Recommendation 136.

[50]Under the Indictments Act 1915, and the Rules made thereunder.

stages in the proceedings.

In cases of serious fraud that are destined to be tried upon indictment, there are mechanisms whereby the trial can be moved straight in to the Crown Court and under the directions of the trial judge.

4.3. PRINCIPLES GOVERNING THE TAKING OF EVIDENCE

Evidence is normally collected by the police, if verbal, in the form of written witness statements. Where there is a possible dispute about the identity of a suspect, there is detailed provision for the conduct of identity parades[51]. So far as interviews with the defendant himself are concerned, there has been a long history of allegations that the police have fabricated confessions ("verbals"), and the recent thrust of much reform is to prevent this from occurring or being alleged. The principal change has involved the tape recording of all interviews with suspects, a practice that is now universal in police stations. The practice of making video recordings of interviews is also being experimented with.

A suspect is entitled to have access to legal advice[52]. As a result of relatively recent changes, he must now be told of this right at regular intervals throughout an interview.

4.4. PRINCIPLES GOVERNING THE TRIAL

The defendant is placed in a dock throughout the trial which is regarded by some as at variance with the presumption of innocence. The judge should not interfere in the questioning of witnesses. His role is that of an impartial referee as between the parties. He has an inherent jurisdiction to ensure fairness to the defendant.

Witnesses cannot be assisted by counsel in the British system (apart from objections as to e.g. the propriety of a particular question on grounds of, for example relevance or that a question is leading). With some exceptions, evidence must be given by the witness in person, so that he can be cross-examined on it. Recent exceptions have been made in the case of certain documentary evidence[53].

# 5. Coercive measures

5.1. ARREST AND DETENTION ON REMAND

The coercive powers of the state are in general exercised by the police, whose powers in these respects have largely been codified in PACE 1984,

---

[51]Code D, Annex A of the PACE Codes of Practice.
[52]PACE, section 56.
[53]Criminal Justice Act 1988, sections 23 and 24.

and the Codes of Practice made pursuant to that Act. This legislation and delegated legislation has generated a vast amount of case-law[54].

### 5.1.1. Arrestable offences

Police powers of arrest underwent a transformation in England and Wales as a result of the Police and Criminal Evidence Act 1984[55], which creates three categories of powers of arrest. Some specified offences are made arrestable either by PACE itself, or by virtue of the fact that they satisfy the conditions stipulated for being arrestable offences. The most important of these is section 24 (1) (b), which provides that an offence is arrestable if it is such that a person over 21 who has not previously been convicted could be liable to imprisonment for a period of five years or more.

### 5.1.2. Non-arrestable offences, for which specific provision is made

Where offences are not arrestable by virtue of PACE, they may nevertheless be made specifically arrestable by virtue of some other Parliamentary enactment. It should be noted that most instances, the power of arrest is available to the constable only where he reasonably suspects that a person "is committing" the offence concerned, and this means that there is no power of arrest when the offence has completed. It may also be noted that there may still be a power of arrest under the general arrest conditions provided for by PACE where the summons procedure is for one reason or another inadequate. These powers are considered in the following section.

### 5.1.3. General arrest conditions

Section 25 of PACE creates the so-called "general arrest conditions". The gist of the section is that if a person is seen by a constable committing a non-arrestable offence, or one for which he has no express statutory power of arrest, and the police officer comes to the conclusion that the service of a summons would be an impracticable means of getting the offender before a court, he may rely upon the general arrest conditions. The relevant part of the section reads:

---

[54]A valuable source for keeping track of recent developments is the loose-leaf volume edited by COUSENS M. and BLAIR, R. *Butterworths Police and Criminal Evidence Act Cases*.

[55]The leading commentaries on PACE are ZANDER, M., *The Police and Criminal Evidence Act 1984* (1991) 2nd edn; BEVAN V. and LIDSTONE, K.W., *The Investigation of Crime: A Guide to Police Powers* (1991). See also LEIGH, L.H., *Police Powers in England and Wales* (1985) 2nd edn Chs 2,3 and 10; ROBILLIARD, St.J. and MACEWAN, J., *Police Powers and the Individual* (1986).

"(3) The general arrest conditions are
 (a) that the name of the relevant person is unknown to, and cannot be readily ascertained by, the constable;
 (b) that the constable has reasonable grounds for doubting whether a name furnished by the relevant person as his name is his real name;
 (c) that
  (i) the relevant person has failed to furnish a satisfactory address for service; or
  (ii) the constable has reasonable grounds for doubting whether an address furnished by the relevant person is a satisfactory address for service;
 (d) that the constable has reasonable grounds for believing that arrest is necessary to prevent the relevant person
  (i) causing physical harm to himself or any other person;
  (ii) suffering physical injury;
  (iii) causing loss of or damage to property;
  (iv) committing an offence against public decency; or
  (v) causing an unlawful obstruction of the highway;
 (e) that the constable has reasonable grounds for believing that arrest is necessary to protect a child or some other vulnerable person from the relevant person."

The conditions specified in para (d) do not necessarily require a belief on the constable's part that the person to be arrested is about to commit an offence. Thus, for example, it would be enough that he is about to damage his own property (in the course of a matrimonial dispute, for example). The phraseology "suffering physical injury" clearly covers a great deal more than the infliction of harm upon oneself, and the section does not say (cf. Para (d) (iv)) "committing an offence" of unlawful obstruction of the highway, although an unlawful obstruction will usually amount to such an offence.

## 5.1.4. Arrest for breach of the peace

In addition to the foregoing powers, the police (and citizens) have a somewhat uncertain power to arrest for breach of the peace[56], a concept recently refined by the courts in *Howell*[57] by Watkins L.J. in the Court of Appeal, who defined that slippery notion as follows:

"we cannot accept that there can be a breach of the peace unless there has been an act done or threatened to be done which either actually harms a person, or in his presence his property, or is likely to cause such harm, or which puts someone in fear of such harm being done".

Using that as a working definition, the powers of arrest may be stated as follows: any person may arrest for a breach of the peace committed in his presence. He may also arrest where, although no breach has actually taken place, he fears and has reasonable cause to believe that a breach of the peace

---

[56]Glanville WILLIAMS, "Arrest for Breach of the Peace" [1954] Crim. L.R. 578; "Dealing With Breaches of the Peace" (1982) 146 J.P. Jo. 199, 217; ROBILLIARD St. J. and MCEWAN, J. *Police Powers and the Individual* (1986) p. 37; LEIGH, L.H. *Police Powers in England and Wales* (1985) 2nd edn Ch. IX.

[57][1982] Q.B. 416, at 426.

will be committed in the immediate future. He may also arrest where a breach of the peace has been committed, and where he has reasonable grounds to believe that it will be renewed if no arrest is made. No power of arrest is available where the breach of the peace has taken place, and there is no reason to believe that it will be renewed.

The power is a preventive one, and the appropriate course for the arrester where no offence has been committed is to take is to bring the person arrested before the magistrates to have him bound over[58] to keep the peace in future. A person "bound over" to keep the peace must enter into an undertaking to be a future good behaviour, and may be required to find sureties to guarantee this. Failure to comply with a binding over order may result in the individual being brought before the court again and committed to prison.

5.2. STOP, SEARCH AND SEIZURE

### 5.2.1. General powers

The power of the police to search and seize is also minutely regulated by PACE, which makes separate provision for the rights to stop and search in the streets (on the one hand), and to enter premises and search them on the other. Each of these different areas is the subject of a separate Code of Practice issued under PACE. In addition, PACE enacts separate rules regulating the seizure of so-called "excluded material," "special procedure material" and items subjects to legal privilege. The effect of these categories is that it becomes more difficult and subject to an increasing range of safeguards in terms of judicial oversight of such information as personal records, samples of human tissue or tissue fluid taken for the purposes of diagnosis or medical treatment and which are held in confidence and journalistic material. "Special procedure material" is material (not being journalistic material) which is held subject to an express or implied undertaking of confidentiality or a statutory restriction on disclosure or obligation of secrecy, by someone who acquired the material in the course of a trade, business, profession or other occupation. This might include such things as company accounts in the possession of banks, solicitors or accountants.

### 5.2.2. Particular powers

There are additional powers to stop and search for firearms[59] and for drugs[60]. Where these powers are exercised, their use must generally be

---

[58]The power to bind over is an ancient one. see generally, SMITH, A.T.H. *The Offences Against Public Order* (1987) para 2.10 et *seq.*

[59]Firearms Act 1968, ss.47(3), 49(1)(2).

[60]Misuse of Drugs Act 1971, s.23(2).

recorded by the searching constable[61], so that their use can be regularly monitored. The various powers to search are generally subject to a requirement of reasonable suspicion on the part of the would-be searcher, and this should not be found in personal factors alone, such as a person's hairstyle or dress, colour or age. A person driving a motor vehicle on a road must stop the vehicle on being required to do so by a constable in uniform[62]. Although it is not police practice to carry out random breath testing of motorists, this could be done in effect, using this power, if there was reasonable cause to suspect that a person randomly stopped had been drinking.

How far the strict limits of police powers in these matters are observed, it is difficult to say, since the police are always entitled to police by consent. Citizens who voluntarily stop and answer questions, permit the police to inspect baggage that they are carrying are not the subject of regulatory monitoring, and it is difficult to assess the extent to which the police rely upon this to assist them in policing.

## 5.3. EXAMINATION OF BODY AND MIND

### 5.3.1. Intimate physical searches

PACE makes special provision for intimate searches, which may only be conducted under carefully controlled conditions, sometimes by police on the authorization of senior police officers, but more usually by a "suitably qualified person"[63], who will be a registered medical practitioner or a registered nurse. The senior police officer must have reasonable grounds for believing that a person may have concealed on him anything which he could use to cause physical injury to himself or others and that he might so use it, or that he has a Class A drug.

### 5.3.2. Blood Samples, etc.

Section 62 of PACE sets out the conditions under which an "intimate sample" (that is, a sample of blood, semen or any other issue fluid, saliva or pubic hair, or a swab taken from a person's body orifice[64]) may be taken from a suspect, or from a person in order to eliminate him from the category of suspect. (There are no legal provisions governing the conditions under which such samples may be taken from the alleged victim).

An intimate sample may only be taken from a person in police detention if a police officer of at least the rank of superintendent authorises it to be

---

[61]PACE, s.2.
[62]Road Traffic Act 1988, s.163(1). For a cyclist, s.163(2).
[63]PACE, section 55.
[64]PACE, s.65.

taken and if the "appropriate consent" is given[65]. "Appropriate consent" means, in relation to a person who has reached the age of 17, that person's consent; in relation to a person between the ages of 14 and 17, the consent of that person and his parent or guardian, and in relation to a person under the age of 14, the consent of his parent or guardian.[66] If such consent is withheld without good cause this may result in adverse inferences being drawn by the court or the jury in subsequent proceedings[67].

A police officer may only authorise the taking of an intimate sample if he has reasonable grounds for suspecting that the person from whom the sample is to be taken has been involved in a "serious arrestable offence"[68], and for believing that the sample will tend to confirm or disprove his involvement[69].

An intimate sample other than a sample of urine or saliva may only be taken from a person by a medical practitioners[70].

As with fingerprints, where an intimate sample has been taken, and no proceedings are instigated against the suspect, or if instigated result in his acquittal, the sample must be destroyed as quickly as practicable after the decision is taken not to proceed, or the conclusion of the proceedings, as the case may be[71].

### 5.3.3. Mental examination

A person who is accused of an offence punishable with imprisonment may be detained under the Mental Health Act 1983 for a report on his mental condition if a Magistrates' Court or Crown Court so orders[72]. The court must be satisfied on written or oral evidence of a registered medical practitioner that the accused person is suffering from mental illness before it can make such an order.

---

[65]PACE, S.62(1).

[66]PACE, S.65.

[67]PACE, s.62(10).

[68]According to PACE, s.116, the offences listed in Part I of Schedule 5 to that Act and offences under the enactments listed under Part II of that Schedule are always's serious arrestable offences'. These offences include Treason, murder, manslaughter, rape, kidnapping, incest with a girl under 13 and buggery without consent or with a boy under 16, possession of firearms with intent to injure, hostage taking and aircraft hijacking. All other arrestable offences are "serous" only if their commission has led to, or is intended or likely to lead to certain consequences, including serious harm to the security of the state or public order, the death of any person, serious injury to any person, serious interference with the administration of justice or with the investigation of crime: PACE, s.116(1)(3) and (6).

[69]PACE, s.62(2).

[70]PACE, s.62(9).

[71]PACE, s.64.

[72]Mental Health Act 1983, s.35.

## 5.4. OTHER FORMS OF INTERFERENCE WITH THE RIGHT TO PRIVACY

There is no right to privacy recognised by the English common law[73]. In consequence, when the police were discovered to have been wrongfully tapping a citizen's telephone, no remedy was available to him. As a result of a challenge to English law before the European Court[74], Parliament was forced to enact the Interception of Communications Act 1985, which sets this matter on a statutory footing. Even now, however, evidence wrongfully obtained will not necessarily be excluded by the courts[75].

# 6. The ordinary course of criminal proceedings

### 6.1. COMMITTAL FOR TRIAL

Where the matter is of a serious nature and is to be tried in the Crown Court, the case will initially go before the Magistrates' Court where the magistrates will decide whether there is sufficient evidence to commit the case to the Crown Court for a hearing by a judge and jury. They are in this procedure acting as examining magistrates. If the magistrates decide that there is such a case, the defendant will then be remanded either in custody (and there are time limits as to how long he can be kept in custody before the trial must begin), or on bail. The trial of the defendant in the Crown Court normally takes place several months later.

### 6.2. TRIAL IN THE CROWN COURT

### 6.2.1. *The arraignment*

Trial in the Crown court begins with the *arraignment* of the defendant. The defendant is brought to the bar of the Court, the indictment is read out to him and he is asked how he pleads to the charge, or charges, in the indictment. The answer will normally be a simple "not guilty" or "guilty", but exceptionally some other plea, such as an objection to the jurisdiction of the Court, or that the accused has already been tried on and acquitted (or convicted) (*autrefois acquit* and *autrefois convict*) of the offence with which he is now charged. If the accused refuses to plead a jury is empanelled in order to determine whether this is due to a deliberate decision on his part (the old term is *mute of malice*) or whether this is due to some other cause, such as, for example, mental incapacity (*mute by visitation of God*). In the former case a plea of not guilty is entered on behalf of the accused. In the

---

[73]*Malone* v. *MPC* [1979] Ch. 344.

[74]MALONE v. United Kingdom, European Court of Human Rights, 2 August 1984, *Publ.E.C.H.R.*, Series A, vol 82.

[75]For a brief summary of the 1985 Act, see *infra*, Chapter 12, par.5.4.

latter there may be a further inquiry into whether the accused is fit to plead (stand trial) at all.

### 6.2.2. The plea of guilty

It is always open to the accused to plead guilty to the charge(s) in the indictment. Were this not the case than the courts at all levels would be seriously over-loaded, and it is fair to say that the English criminal justice system depends to a large extent on the efficiencies and economies to be derived from the guilty plea. In some cases it is open to the accused to plead guilty to a lesser offence not expressly charged in the indictment where it would be competent for the jury to return a verdict of guilty of that offence. So, for example, an accused charged with murder may plead not guilty to that charge, but be willing to plead guilty to the lesser offence of manslaughter. An accused charged with rape may deny that charge but be prepared to plead guilty to indecent assault. A plea of guilty must be unequivocal. It must be made freely, without any pressure from counsel or the court, and it must be made in the knowledge and understanding of the elements of the offence[76].

The decision whether to accept a guilty plea or not is primarily one for prosecuting counsel, but if counsel seeks the approval of the judge, then he is bound by the judge's decision, and the court may take the view that it is not in the public interest to allow the accused to plead guilty to a lesser charge.

If the plea of guilty is accepted, there is no trial. There may be a brief, modified, inquiry into the facts of the case, for the purpose of determining sentence, but this is largely non-adversarial, and is conducted before the judge alone. The incentive for the accused to plead guilty, especially at an early stage in the proceedings (for example when he first appears for committal) is that it is well-established that a guilty plea will attract a 'discounted' sentence. That is, a sentence which is lower than would be applied for the same offence following conviction by the jury.

### 6.2.3. The leading of evidence

Where the accused pleads not guilty, a jury is empanelled, the prosecutor outlines the case that he intends to bring in some detail and then presents the case through the examination of the witnesses for the prosecution, by question and answer (examination-in-chief). The defence are given the opportunity to put questions to the witness to "cross-examine" him, and he may then be re-examined by the prosecutor.

It is not uncommon for the defence, after the prosecution has presented its case, to move that the proceedings be halted on the grounds that there is

---

[76]*Golathan* (1915) 11 Cr. App. R. 79; *Turner* [1970] 2 QB.321.

no case to answer because, for example, the witnesses adduced for the prosecutor did not "come up to proof", i.e. establish the case that the prosecutor believed in advance they would establish on behalf of the Crown. Equally, it may be that the defence can claim that the prosecutor has not made out his case because of some misunderstanding about the state of the substantive law. Should that plea fail, it is then for the defence to answer the charge, again through the process of asking questions of the witnesses that it produces, sometimes the defendant himself.

During examination-in-chief, a party is not permitted to ask "leading" questions, that is, a question which either suggests the answer which the questioner is seeking, or assumes the existence of a material fact which has not yet been formally established by the evidence in the case. For example, in a case of assault, if the prosecutor wishes to establish that the accused struck the victim, it would not be permissible to ask the victim "Where did he hit you?" before asking some question such as "Did the accused do anything to you? In practice, where the evidence is of a largely formal nature, or is not a matter of dispute between the parties, it is acceptable to counsel to lead a witness through his evidence.

The witnesses are examined by counsel for the prosecution and defence, and while the judge may ask questions of a witness, such questions should be limited to clarification of the witness's testimony.

Witnesses are under an obligation to testify, having been called to give evidence, and act under pain of a conviction for contempt of court for failure to do so, and for perjury if they can be proved to have given false testimony. In this respect the accused, if he chooses to give evidence (since he cannot be compelled to do so) is treated like any other witness. In particular, the accused cannot refuse to answer questions directed towards establishing that he is guilty of the offence with which he is presently charged[77]. In *DPP v Humphrys*[78] an accused person gave evidence at his trial (which resulted in an acquittal) which was subsequently shown to be false. The House of Lords held that there was no bar to his subsequently being tried on a charge of perjury in respect of the allegedly false evidence he gave at his first trial.

Expert witnesses are seen as being part of the adversarial process; they are not court witnesses, but those of the parties. This is controversial, and has recently been challenged[79].

At the conclusion of the evidence, the barristers for the prosecution and defence give their closing addresses (in that order) and the trial judge then sums up. He gives the jury advice as to the applicable law (making use of a series of model directions issues to the judges centrally, by the Judicial Studies Board), and instructs the jury as to how the law should be applied to

---

[77]Criminal Evidence Act 1989, s.I.(f).

[78][1976] 2 A11 E.R. 497.

[79]SPENCER, J.R., "The Neutral Expert: An Implausible Bogey" [1991] *Crim. L.R.* 106.

the facts. The jury must accept and apply the law as stated by the judge. The judge will highlight the evidence, but make it clear that they are the final arbiters of the facts. The jury then retires to the jury-room where they are kept incommunicado until they have arrived at a verdict.

The verdict (whether guilty or not guilty) must normally be unanimous. Until 1967[80] if a jury failed to reach a verdict this meant that the jury was discharged but that the accused could be re-tried at the option of the prosecution. However, since 1967 is has been possible for the court to accept a majority verdict (usually of not less than 10 to 2). The jury should nonetheless be told that they should attempt to reach a unanimous verdict, and they will not be given instructions on reaching a majority verdict until the court is satisfied that they cannot reach unanimity. The jury must have deliberated for at least two hours before a majority verdict can be taken[81]

If the jury convict then the judge will sentence the defendant according to the penalty laid down. At no time do the prosecution suggest what the appropriate penalty might be, the matter is left entirely to the judge.

There is no appeal by the prosecutor from an acquittal. The prosecutor may appeal on the question of the sentence imposed. The defendant may appeal against both the conviction and the sentence. From the Magistrates' Court the appeal is to the Crown Court. From the Crown Court it is to the Court of Appeal.

### 6.3. TRIAL IN THE MAGISTRATES'COURT

Trial in the magistrates'court broadly follows the order of proceedings in the Crown court, except, of course, that since there is no jury in the magistrates'court those elements of the procedure which relate to the jury are absent.

In the magistrates'court the magistrates are judges of fact, and are advised by a clerk on points of law, procedure and sentencing. The clerk takes no part in the magistrates'deliberations on the question of guilt or punishment, except to the extent of advising the magistrates on the law.

## 7. Evidence

### 7.1. GENERAL

The fundamental test of admissibility of evidence is that of relevance. However, not all evidence that is relevant is admissible and in many ways the English law of evidence in criminal cases can be seen as a body of rules relating to the exclusion of evidence. The best-known grounds on which

---

[80]Criminal Justice Act 1967.

[81]See Juries Act 1974, s.17 and *Practice Directions* at [1967] 1 WLR 1198 AND [1970] 1 WLR 916.

evidence may be excluded are that it constitutes hearsay, or that it has been unfairly or unlawfully obtained. There is an important difference between these reasons for excluding evidence in that while evidence which is hearsay is for that reason excluded (at least as evidence of the truth of what is reported) while evidence which is unfairly or even illegally obtained is not, in general, automatically excluded for that reason.

## 7.2. ILLEGALLY OBTAINED EVIDENCE

Evidence illegally obtained may be excluded at the discretion of the court, but is not automatically excluded. In a leading case in the House of Lords[82], the court took a very restricted view of its discretion to exclude improperly obtained evidence. It explicitly rejected any role for the courts in disciplining or otherwise superintending the police in their collection of evidence, and held that only where the evidence was unreliable was it proper to exclude it, although there existed a residual discretion to exclude evidence where this would prejudice the defendant at his trial. This has been supplemented by section 78 of PACE, which permits a judge to exclude evidence:

"if it appears to the court that, having regard to all the circumstances, including the circumstances in which the evidence was obtained, the admission of the evidence would have such an adverse effect on the fairness of the proceedings that the court ought not to admit it".

## 7.3. CONFESSIONS

While confessions may be excluded by the court in the exercise of its discretion under s.78 of PACE[83], they are subject to a specific exclusionary regime under section 76 of PACE. Again, the basic principle as to admissibility is one of reliability, so that a confession cannot be admitted unless the prosecution establish beyond reasonable doubt that the confession was not improperly obtained, and it will be so obtained if it was

"or may have been obtained - (a) by oppression of the person who made it; or (b) in consequence of anything said or done which was likely, in the circumstances existing at the time, to render unreliable any confession which might be made by him in consequence thereof."

For these purposes, "oppression" "includes torture, inhuman or degrading treatment, and the use or threat of violence (whether or not amounting to torture)" (PACE, s. 76(8)).

Where a challenge is made to the admissibility of a confession, an

---

[82]*Sang* [1980] A.C. 402. See now *Samuel* (1987) 87 Cr.App.L., 232. The courts have been very slow to give guidance as to the application of section 78. But see *Bryce*, [1992] *Crim.L.R.* 728.

[83]*Mason* [1987] 3 All E.R. 481.

examination of the circumstances in which the alleged confession was made will be carried out by the court by means of a so-called "trial-within-a-trial". In the Crown court this is done outwith the hearing of the jury. If the confession is held to be inadmissible, then the jury are not told of its contents, and in the magistrates' court the justices are required to disregard the confession in reaching their verdict.

# 8. Special forms of procedure

## 8.1. PROSECUTORIAL DISCRETION

The discretion to prosecute once the investigation is complete rests with the Crown Prosecution Service and not (as previously) with the police. This is supposed to ensure that there is a sufficiency of evidence so that weak cases are screened out at an early stage. The decision whether or not to prosecute is subject to detailed guidelines to Crown Prosecutors[84].

These guidelines emphasise that prosecutors at every level have great scope for the exercise of discretion, and point out that while the "judicious use" of this direction, based on "clear principles" can better serve justice, "the misuse of discretionary powers ... can have severe consequences not only for those suspected of crime, but also for the public at large and the reputation of justice and the [Crown Prosecution] Service itself"[85].

Amongst the issues which must be considered by prosecutors when considering the institution or continuation of proceedings are the sufficiency of the evidence, and whether the public interest requires a prosecution. So far as concerns the former, the *Code for Crown Prosecutors* states that a bare *prima facie* case is not sufficient to justify brining proceedings. The test which should be applied is 'whether there is a realistic prospect of a conviction'[86]. So far as concerns the question of the public interest, the *Code* emphasises that "it has never been the rule in England that suspected criminal offences must automatically be the subject of prosecution", and that regard must always be had to the effect which a prosecution (whether successful or not) would have upon public morale and order, and any other considerations affecting public policy[87]. The interests of the victim should also be taken into account, as should, *inter alia*, the fact that in the event of conviction it is likely that only a nominal penalty would be imposed, the lapse of time between the offence and the likely date of trial, the age of the

---

[84]The Code is issued under the Prosecution of Offences Act 1985, s.10, is included in the D.P.P's annual report to the Attorney-General and laid before Parliament and published. Its purpose is to promote efficient and consistent decision making.

[85]*Code for Crown Prosecutors*, par. 3.

[86]*Ibid.*, par. 4.

[87]*See Hansard*, House of Commons Deb., vol. 483, col. 681, January 29 1951 (statement by the Attorney-General Sir Hartley Shawcross).

accused (both youthfulness and old age and infirmity tending to count against prosecution), mental disorder on the part of the accused, the fact that the complainant has expressed a wish that no action be taken and the fact that the accused did not play a central part in the commission of the offence[88].

Decisions taken by the Crown Prosecution Service, and other prosecutors such as the Inland Revenue Commissioners in the exercise of their prosecutorial discretion are subject to judicial review in the High Court. In *R v Chief Constable of Kent and another, ex parte L (a minor), R v Director of Public Prosecutions, ex parte B (a minor)*[89], it was held that the discretion of the Crown Prosecution Service to continue or to discontinue criminal proceedings against a juvenile offender was subject to judicial review, but only where it could be shown that the decision had been made regardless of, or contrary to, a settled policy of the Director of Public Prosecutions which had been formulated in the public interest. In *R v Inland Revenue Commissioners, ex parte Mead and another*[90], it was held that the decision to prosecute and adult was in principle subject to judicial review in the High Court, but that the circumstances in which the supervisory jurisdiction of the High Court could be successfully invoked in this respect would be "rare in the extreme"[91].

## 8.2. PRIVATE PROSECUTION

Although it is not a widely used facility, there remains the possibility of an aggrieved citizen bringing a private prosecution. This is frequently done by large stores in cases of shoplifting, and by pressure groups, often in connection with motoring offences (especially drunken driving). The Director of Public Prosecutions retains a power to take over and conduct (which includes discontinuance of) any proceedings.

## 8.3. SUMMARY PROCEDURE

Most prosecutions in England are summary in nature, so that they hardly fit the description of "special forms of procedure" which is the general heading of this chapter. The truth is that most criminal justice in England, some 90% of it, is administered in the Magistrates'Courts, using summary procedures and guilty pleas. A great many cases, the majority in fact, are disposed of within the English system by way of guilty pleas. These are relatively informal, in the sense that although the defendant himself must plead guilty, there is no obligation on the prosecutor to give any evidence that corroborates the guilt of the defendant.

---

[88]*Code for Crown Prosecutors*, paras. 7 to 9.
[89][1993] 1 A11 E.R. 756.
[90][1993] 1 A11 E.R. 772.
[91]*Ibid., per* Stuart-Smith L.J. at p. 782.

## 8.4. TRANSACTION (PLEA BARGAINING)

Strictly speaking, the courts frown on the process of plea-bargaining, Lord Scarman having once said that "plea bargaining has no place in the English Criminal Law"[92].

There are, nevertheless, informal ways in which bargains can be struck within the English system. Discussions frequently take place between the prosecution and the defence in relation to the charge or charges made against the accused. The defence may offer to plead guilty to a lesser charge than the one brought by the prosecution, or, conversely, the prosecution may offer to accept a plea of guilty to a lesser charge, or to withdraw some of the charges. The practice of charging in the alternative is a clear invitation to the defendant to plead guilty to the lesser of the two offences.

The outcome of such 'bargains' is not, however, wholly within the control of the parties. While it is plain that a guilty plea can be met with a reduced sentence[93], a guilty plea offered by an accused may not be accepted by the court (in which case the prosecution must then proceed with the original charge, or, if it is strongly opposed to doing so, offer no evidence) and the length of a sentence is entirely in the hands of the court, and can scarcely be influenced by the prosecutor, so that there is little or no scope for a bargain as to sentence to be struck. Furthermore, the Court of Appeal has made it plain that it disapproves of discussions between counsel and the judge that might possibly give the appearance that the judge has given an undertakings as to matters of sentence which can in some sense be binding on him when he learns all the facts[94].

The Royal Commission on Criminal Procedure, expressing concern about the problem of "late" guilty pleas (that is to say a late change of plea to "guilty" when the accused is arraigned for trial) has recommended that the issue of sentence should be open to discussion between the parties and the Court and that the present system of sentence discounts for pleas of guilty "should be more clearly articulated, with earlier pleas attracting higher discounts"[95]

## 8.5. JUVENILES

Young offenders are dealt with in a separate regime. The rules of criminal responsibility are that no person under the age of 10 can be guilty of a criminal offence, and between the ages of 10 and 14, he or she can be guilty only if the prosecution can establish that the young person knows the differ-

---

[92]*Atkinson* [1978] 1 W.L.R. 425. See also Lord Widgery C.J. in *Wise* [1979] R.T.R. 57.

[93]*Haan* [1968] 2 Q.B. 108; *Cain* [1976] *Crim. L.R.* 464.

[94]The leading judgment is *Turner* [1970] 2 Q.B. 321.

[95]Royal Commission, *Report*, Recommendation 156.

ence between right and wrong, or has a "mischievous discretion". With the exception of really serious offences, the young offender was dealt with by magistrates in "Juvenile Courts", whose jurisdiction also extended to care proceedings in respect of children in need of care rather than correction. Recent legislation has changed this, so that the care aspect of the Magistrates'courts will be dealt with in family proceedings courts with the criminal jurisdiction being exercised in courts renamed "youth courts", youths being persons of 17 years and below.

### 8.6. MENTALLY ILL

Until recently, the English law regulating the disposition of the mentally ill suffered from the fact that, upon a finding of not guilty on the grounds of insanity, the trial judge had no sentencing discretion but was required to send the acquitted person to a mental institution, whether his condition really required this or not. In 1991, Parliament enacted the Criminal Procedure (Insanity and Unfitness to Plead) Act. This Act enables the court to accept a verdict of not guilty without necessarily having to make a restriction order, if it is inappropriate to do so. This change does not, however, apply to situations where the verdict is fixed by law, as murder is. Whether this change will make a great deal of difference to practice is, therefore, a matter of some doubt.

The other change effect by the 1991 legislation is that the question of whether or not the person accused is fit to plead to a charge (i.e. whether he understands the nature of the legal proceedings by which he is confronted) is to be determined only at the end of the case for the prosecution. This obviates the possible danger that a person might be detained for an offence that he or she cannot be proved to have committed, which the previous procedure might possibly have permitted.

### 8.7. TRIAL *IN ABSENTIA*

In summary trials, the defendant is frequently given the option of pleading guilty by letter, in which case his appearance is not required. Otherwise, if the suspect is absent without good explanation, a warrant will be issued for his arrest. It appears that there is no absolute rule in English law against a person being tried in his absence, but "there must be very exceptional circumstances to justify proceeding with the trial in the absence of the accused. The reason why the accused should be present at the trial is that he must hear the case against him and have the opportunity ... of answering it."[96]

---

[96] *R v. Lee Kun* (1916) 11 Cr. App. R. 293, *per* Lord Reading C.J.at p. 300.

## 9. Remedies

### 9.1. GENERAL

The English system permits a large range of appeals against both conviction and sentence. These are designed to ensure that the defendant's trial was a fair one, and that there was no irregularity in its conduct, and that there is some consistency in the process.

For the most part only the defendant (and not the prosecutor) may appeal. The prosecutor may appeal on a point of law from the magistrates'court, and he may bring an Attorney-General's reference after an acquittal by the jury in cases where the prosecution takes the view that the judge has misrepresented the law[97].

### 9.2. APPEAL IN SUMMARY PROCEEDINGS

Appeals against summary conviction can take three forms: on the merits, to the Crown Court; by way of case stated to the High Court or (more rarely) by an application to the High Court for judicial review. The first of these involves a rehearing, and may be brought as of right, without any need for leave[98]. Appeals are heard without a jury by a Circuit Judge or Recorder sitting with Justices. An application to appeal must be made within 21 days of the determination of guilt. The hearing is in effect not so much an appeal as a complete re-determination of guilt. Technically, the Crown Court has the power to increase sentences in cases that come before it in this fashion.

Appeal by case stated is open to the accused against conviction and to the prosecutor against acquittal. In this procedure the magistrates (in practice the Clerk) states a case for the opinion of the High Court. The case must state the facts found by the trial court and the questions of law on which the opinion of the High Court is sought. In determining an appeal by case stated, the High Court may uphold, reverse or amend the decision of the magistrates, or remit the case to them for reconsideration in the light of the Court's opinion[99].

### 9.3. APPEAL IN PROCEEDINGS ON INDICTMENT

#### 9.3.1. Appeal to the Court of Appeal

It is significantly more difficult to appeal against a conviction on indictment, partly because it involves questioning the verdict of a jury. There was no

---

[97]Criminal Justice Act 1972, s.36.

[98]Magistrates Courts Act 1980, s.108.

[99]*Cfr.* the similar Scottish procedure of appeal be stated case, *infra*, chapter 12, par. 9.1.2.

right of appeal until the Criminal Appeal Act 1907, which established the Court of Criminal Appeal, which was reconstituted as the Criminal Division of the Court of Appeal in 1966[100]. The Court is now composed of a Lord Justice of Appeal sitting with two High Court judges.

Persons who are legally aided (most defendants) who are convicted on indictment are automatically advised as to their prospects of appeal. There is an appeal as of right where a question of law is involved. On an appeal relating to a mixture of law and fact, the trial judge must grant a certificate of leave or leave given by the Court of Appeal. Applications are considered by one judge acting alone who makes his determination on the papers alone. Most applications for leave to appeal (75%) fail to pass this hurdle. The appeal must be based on the grounds that the conviction is, in all the circumstances, unsafe or unsatisfactory, that the trial judge made a wrong decision on a question of law or that there was a material irregularity in the course of the trial[101]. The Court is notoriously reluctant to interfere on the first of these grounds. If one of the other errors has occurred, the Court must allow the appeal, unless it can take that view that in all the circumstances, there has been no miscarriage of justice, in which case it can "apply the proviso" and uphold the conviction notwithstanding the error.

Technically, the Court has the power to allow the appeal and quash the conviction, to admit fresh evidence, to order a retrial and to convict of an alternative offence that was implicit in the juries'verdict. It will not admit fresh evidence unless the evidence appears likely to be credible, would have been admissible at the trial and (most importantly of all) there is a reasonable explanation for the failure to adduce it at trial[102].

The Court of Appeal has long possessed the power to send a defendant for a retrial if it allowed an appeal on the grounds of the admission of fresh evidence. This was not a power that it was particularly ready to exercise, perhaps on the grounds that it was of the view that the granting of a retrial offended in some fundamental way against the double jeopardy principle. Instead, it made a judgment for itself about the effect that it believed the evidence would have had were the first jury to have seen and heard what was being adduced for the first time in the Court of Appeal. More recently, the Court has been given a much wider power to grant retrials[103], but the evidence to date appears to be that the Court is proving no readier to use these extended powers either.

The manner in which the Court exercises these various powers has been

---

[100]Criminal Appeal Act 1966, consolidated in the Criminal Appeal Act 1968, which remains the principal source of the law regulating this area.

[101]Criminal Appeal Act 1968, s.2(1).

[102]Criminal Appeal Act 1968, s.23.

[103]Criminal Justice Act 1988, s.43. The power was exercised in *Toner* [1991] *Crim. L.R.* 627, where the trial judge had wrongly failed to permit a jury to consider admissible evidence.

the subject of a great deal of public concern, and was one of the matters under serious consideration by the Royal Commission[104] and the Commission has made a number of potentially far-reaching recommendations. These include[105]:

- replacement of the current grounds of appeal with a single broad ground of appeal which would give the Court greater flexibility to consider all categories of appeal. The suggested approach for the future would be for the Court to decide whether, in all the circumstances, the conviction "is or may be unsafe";
- in considering whether to receive fresh evidence, the Court of Appeal should take a broad approach to the question whether such evidence was available at the time of the trial, and if it was whether there is a reasonable explanation for the failure to adduce it then. The test for receiving such evidence should be whether it is "capable of belief";
- the power of the Home Secretary to refer cases to the Court of Appeal under section 17 of the Criminal Appeal Act 1968 should be removed and a new body (referred to by the Commission simply as "the Authority") should be set up to consider allegations that a miscarriage of justice may have occurred, to ensure that any further investigation that is called for is launched, to supervise that investigation, and, where there are reasons for supposing that a miscarriage of justice might have occurred, to refer the case to the Court of Appeal.

### 9.3.2. Appeal to the House of Lords

There is a further appeal to the House of Lords where leave has been obtained, either from the Court of Appeal (which is rarely given) or from the House itself, if the Court of Appeal certifies that there is a point of law of general public importance to be determined arising from the case[106].

### 9.4. THE PREROGATIVE OF MERCY[107]

Where a person convicted feels that even after the appeals procedure has been exhausted, he may appeal to the Crown for the exercise of the prerogative of Mercy. This is in practice decided by the Home Office. It is, understandably, extremely difficult to persuade the Executive branch of the Government to interfere in this way.

---

[104]See Appendix.

[105]Royal Commission, *Report*, Recommendations 316 *et seq.*

[106]See SMITH, A.T.H.,"Criminal Appeals in the House of Lords" (1984) 47 *M.L.R.* 133.

[107]See SMITH, A.T.H., "The Prerogative of Mercy, the Power of Pardon and Criminal Justice" [1983] *P.L.* 398.

## 10. Other questions

### 10.1. STATUTES OF LIMITATION

In summary trials, there is a time limit of 6 months from the date of the offence for issuing the summons. In more serious cases, however, there is no limit, although the courts possess an inherent jurisdiction to stop a prosecution on the grounds of abuse of process[108] if the time lapse is too great.

There are limits on the time for which a person can be kept in custody prior to trial.

## 11. Select bibliography

### Books

ARCHBOLD, *Criminal Pleading, Evidence and Practice* (1993)
BLACKSTONE's *Criminal Practice 1992*
SPENCER, J.R., *Jackson's Machinery of Justice* (1989)
WHITE, R.C., *The Administration of Justice* (1991) 2nd edn
THOMAS, D.A., *Current Sentencing Practice* (an encyclopaedia, regularly updated).
*STONE's Justices Manual* (an annual publication in 3 large volumes)
GUNN, M. and BAILEY, S.H. (eds), *Smith and Bailey on the Modern English Legal System* 2nd edn (1991).

### Periodicals

The leading periodical in the field of Criminal Law and Procedure is the *Criminal Law Review* (Crim.L.R.), which is produced monthly. See also the *Criminal Law Journal*, and such weekly publications as *Justice of the Peace* and *The Magistrate*. Important decisions of the Criminal Courts are reported in the *Criminal Appeal Reports* and in sentencing matters the Criminal Appeal Reports (Sentencing).

---

[108]*R* v. *Randle and Pottle* [1991] 1 *W.L.R.* 1087.

## 12. Appendix: Royal commission on criminal justice. Terms of reference

To examine the effectiveness of the criminal justice system in England and Wales in securing the conviction of those guilty of criminal offences and the acquittal of those who are innocent, having regard to the efficient use of resources, and in particular to consider whether changes are needed in:

i. the conduct of police investigations and their supervision by senior police officers, and in particular the degree of control that is exercised by those officers over the conduct of the investigation and the gathering and preparation of evidence;

ii. the role of the prosecutor in supervising the gathering of evidence and deciding whether to proceed with a case, and the arrangements for the disclosure of material, including unused material, to the defence;

iii. the role of experts in criminal proceedings, their responsibilities to the court, prosecution, and defence, and the relationship between the forensic science services and the police;

iv. the arrangements for the defence of accused persons, access to legal advice, and access to expert evidence;

v. the opportunities available for an accused person to state his position on the matters charged and the extent to which the courts might draw proper inferences from primary facts, the conduct of the accused, and any failure on his part to take advantage of an opportunity to state his position;

vi. the powers of the courts in directing proceedings, the possibility of their having an investigative role both before and during the trial, and the role of pre-trial reviews; the courts duty in considering evidence, including uncorroborated confession evidence;

vii. the role of the Court of Appeal in considering new evidence on appeal, including directing the investigation of allegations;

viii. the arrangements for considering and investigating allegations of miscarriages of justice when appeal rights have been exhausted.

# Chapter 4 - France

Prof.Jean **PRADEL**
Director of the *Institut de sciences criminelles*
Law Faculty
University of Poitiers

## 1. Sources

### 1.1. GENERAL OBSERVATIONS

Rules relating to criminal procedure are to be found at every level of the hierarchy of sources of law: every type of text has given rise to rules in this discipline, whether it be the Constitution, the European Convention on Human Rights, statute or regulatory texts. At the same time, the importance of case-law and practice should not be underestimated, despite the principle of legality which, in the field of criminal law, governs procedure as much as it does the substantive law[1].

### 1.2. THE CONSTITUTION

The supreme source of the law, the Constitution of 4 October 1958 influences criminal procedure through its preamble. The latter, whilst fairly brief, refers us back to the preamble of the Constitution of 1946 and the Declaration of the Rights of Man and of the Citizen of August 1789. These two texts thus form part of our constitutional law, as the *Conseil Constitutionnel* reminded us on 16th July 1971. Moreover, the Declaration of 1789 contains several principles relating to criminal procedure which are binding on the legislator, and any departure from them may be invalidated by the *Conseil Constitutionnel*. Thus the latter has invalidated laws which violated principles based on its interpretation of the Declaration, such as the principles of

---

[1] MERLE R. and VITU, A., *Traité de droit criminel*, I. n° 203 et *seq*, Cujas, 1988; STÉFANI, G., LEVASSEUR, G. and BOULOC, B., *Droit pénal général* , n° 118 *et seq*, Dalloz, 1990, 2d. Dalloz; RASSAT, M.L., *Procedure pénale*, Presses Universitaires France, 1991; PRADEL, J., *Droit pénal*, vol 1, n° 145 *et seq.*, Cujas, 8th ed., 1992; PRADEL, J. and VARIMARD, A, "*Les grands arrêts du droit criminel*, I, 3 *et seq*, Sirey, 1993.

inviolability of the home[2], freedom of the individual[3], and respect for the rights of the defence[4].

## 1.3. THE EUROPEAN CONVENTION ON HUMAN RIGHTS

Signed in Strasbourg in 1950, and ratified by France by the law of 31 December 1973, the European Convention is of interest for two reasons which combine with each other. On the one hand, it contains a certain number of guiding principles, the restrictive interpretation of denying liberty before judgment, the necessity of an independent and impartial court, and the right to defend oneself by questioning prosecution witnesses. On the other hand, since by virtue of art.55 of the Constitution, international conventions, and therefore the European convention, take precedence over domestic legislation and thus, for example, the code of criminal procedure (see *infra*, 1.4.), judges must ensure that the provisions of the convention prevail over domestic law in cases where there is conflict. This is why applications to the *Cour de Cassation* are increasingly based upon violations of the Convention, even if, indeed, its provisions are not contrary to the letter or spirit of French domestic law. It is true the *Cour de Cassation* still displays a certain caution with regard to the Convention and the decisions of the European Court in Strasbourg. For example, it held that telephone tapping ordered by a *juge d'instruction* was not contrary to art.8 of the Convention which asserts the right to privacy (nor, one might, add the case-law of the court in Strasbourg which lays down the conditions for this type of investigation)[5]. However, following the condemnation of France by the Court of Human Rights in Strasbourg[6], the *Cour de Cassation* has been lead to change its position.

## 1.4. LEGISLATION

Whatever one may say, legislation constitutes the principal source of criminal procedure in France. The most important statute is the Code of Criminal Procedure of 1959 with its 802 articles (*Code de procédure pénale*, hereafter CCP), which replaced the old *Code d'instruction criminelle* of 1808). This Code has been revised several times, notably in 1960, 1970, 1972, 1983,

---

[2]*Conseil constitutionnel*, 29 December 1983, *J.C.P.*, 1984-II, 20160, note DRAGO and DECOCQ.

[3]*Conseil Constitutionnel*, 12 January 1977, Dalloz 1978, 173, note HAMON and LÉAUTÉ.

[4]*Conseil Constitutionnel*, 20 January 1981, *Dalloz*, 1982, 441, note DE KEUWER; *Conseil Constitutionnel*, 3 September 1986, *Journal officiel*, 5 September, 10788.

[5]*Cassation criminelle*, 23 July 1985, *Dalloz*, 1986., IR. 117 and observ.

[6]HUVIG & KRUSLIN v. France, European Court of Human Rights, 24 April 1990, *Publ. E.C.H.R.*, Series A, vol. 176. See further *infra* 5.4.

1986, 1989 and 1991. In 1993, two important revisions have been made, one by the law of 4 January 1993, the second by the law of 28 August 1993.

Meanwhile, proposals have been made to redraft the code entirely. For example, the *Commission Justice pénale et droits de l'homme*, presided by Mme Delmas-Marty, has proposed radical changes, which would reduce the investigative powers of the *juge d'instruction* (investigating judge) and reinforce his judicial powers. These proposals have not, as yet, been accepted.

In addition to the Code of Criminal Procedure, reference should be made to the *Code de justice militaire* of 1982, which contains not only substantive but also procedural rules, and to a number of special statutes which, often very broad in scope, contain procedural provisions. Two good examples of this are the Statutes of 29th July 1881 on the freedom of the press, which provides for special rules relating to the prosecution and punishment of offences such as defamation, and of 1st August 1903 on fraud and deception, which also provides for special rules, notably concerning the evidence of experts.

Formerly, the *Cour de Cassation* had accepted that provisions of the *Code de procédure civile* of a general nature, could, exceptionally, be a source of criminal procedure. This is no longer the case today, since the 1958 Constitution places criminal procedure under the legislator's authority whereas the provisions of civil procedure come within the executive power[7].

## 1.5. REGULATORY TEXTS

The *Code de Procédure Pénale*, after its statutory part, which is composed of 802 articles, contains an extensive section made up of regulatory texts. These are: decrees of the Conseil d'Etat (*décrets en Conseil d'Etat*, art.R1-R250); ordinary decrees (*décrets simples*, art.D1-D600); orders (*arrêtés*, art.A1-A57) and administrative circulars on the application of the law (*circulaires d'application*).

These texts do little more than clarify the legislative provisions, having due regard to the principle of legality. Yet they contain provisions of some practical interest and which are applied every day by the judges, such as those relating to legal costs.

## 1.6. CASE-LAW AND GENERAL PRACTICE (*USAGES*)

In a legal system primarily based on legislation, such as the French one, case-law should not have any role to play. And yet, judicial decisions, notably those of the criminal division (*chambre criminelle*) of the *Cour de Cassation*, make an important contribution to criminal procedure. Sometimes the Court will interpret a rather vaguely defined concept. For example, it has

---

[7]*Cassation criminelle*, 19 January 1982, *Bull. crim*, n° 18.

decided that tests to determine the level of alcohol in a victim's blood were not an expert evaluation (*expertise*) within the meaning of art.156 *et seq.* of the CCP[8]. Sometimes, going further, case-law will create an important rule which it describes as a general principle of law, such as respect for the rights of the defence[9] or the principle of publicity[10].

Matters of general practice (*usages*) are only of interest if they contradict a law or fill in a lacuna. The former are the most interesting, and one can cite the example of *correctionalisation*. This consists of the judges treating an offence as a misdemeanour (*délit*) whereas, according to the strict letter of the law, it is a crime. The consequence is that the charge is referred to the *tribunal correctionnel* and not the *Cour d'assises,* which effects a simplification in the procedure.

## 2. The structure of the criminal justice system

### 2.1. INVESTIGATING AUTHORITIES

According to art.14 CCP the *police judiciaire* are under a duty to record breaches of the criminal law, to gather evidence of such breaches, and to find the perpetrators, as long as a preliminary inquiry (*information*) has not been opened. When an *information* has been commenced, they act on the instructions of the *juridictions d'instruction*, which, in practice, means that they act on the instructions (*commissions rogatoires*) of the investigating judge, the *juge d'instruction.* According to this text, responsibility for the investigation of crime rests with two main authorities: the "*police judiciaire*" and the "*juge d'instruction*". However other authorities must be mentioned, although on a secondary basis.

### 2.1.1. The police judiciaire

Often simply called "the police" in everyday language, the *police judiciaire* is made up of two distinct bodies: the *police nationale* attached to the Ministry of the Interior and the *gendarmerie nationale* attached to the Ministry of Defence. Whichever of these two great bodies they belong to, the members of the "*police judiciaire*" have the same powers and are subject to the same rules.

### (i) powers
The powers of the *police judiciaire* are only briefly set out in art.14 CPP. An important distinction exists between judicial police officers (*officiers de police*

---

[8]*Cassation criminelle*, 2 September 1986, *Dalloz*, 1987, Somm. 83 with observations.
[9]*Cassation criminelle*, 12 June 1952, *J.C.P.*, 1952, II, 7241, note BROUCHOT.
[10]*Cassation criminelle*, 10 July 1974. *Bull. crim.*, n°253.

*judiciaire* (OPJ)) and judicial police agents (*agents de police judiciaire* (APJ)).

The OPJ must have been personally commissioned by the *procureur général* of the court of appeal in whose jurisdiction they exercise their powers, and have by far the more important role. They receive complaints, conduct investigations, hear individuals and carry out searches and seizures. Their most significant prerogative is their power to detain a person in police custody for up to twenty four hours (*garde à vue*).

The APJ have more limited powers. They do not have the authority to detain a person in custody, and can only "assist the OPJ". Nevertheless, they may draw up official records (*procès-verbaux*) in respect of all offences (*crimes, délits et contraventions*), and record statements of individuals (art.20 CCP).

Evidentiary techniques offered by modern science have led to some distinctions being made. For example, the OPJ and the APJ may breathalyse those who commit certain offences such as driving under the influence of alcohol, and, even if the test is positive, they can order further biological and chemical analysis and a medical examination of that person by means of an instrument designed to determine the alcohol level in exhaled air (art.L(1)7 *Code de la route*). However, following recent and clear-cut case-law, they cannot organise the tapping of a suspect's telephone line[11].

A noteworthy statute, the Law of 19 December 1991, allows OPJ-officers to acquire, possess, transport and deliver narcotics in order to allow them to capture drug dealers *in flagrante delicto*. These practices, however, can only be used with the authorization of the public prosecutor or the investigating judge. This statute in fact authorises police officers (including customs officers) to participate in the commission of drug offences.

The OPJ, and under their authority, the APJ, are allowed to carry out identity checks and controls in their capacity of judicial officers (*officier de police judiciaire*), *i.e.* where an offence has already been committed. However, they may also proceed to identity checks in their capacity of administrative police officers (*officier de police administrative*), with a view to preventing the commission of an offence. These checks are carried out on the spot. Verification happens in cases where the person concerned has refused to, or cannot, establish his identity, and can give rise to his detention on police premises for a maximum of 4 hours with a view to his identification. This sensitive and ever changing question is now dealt with in great detail in arts.78-1 to 78-5 CCP.

*(ii) supervision*
The OPJ and the APJ are subject to control by the *procureur de la République* (art.12 CCP) and are under the general supervision of the

---

[11]*Cour de Cassation*, plenary session, 24 November 1989, *Dalloz*, 1990, Chronique, 15 *and seq.*(Baribeau case).

*procureur général* (art.13 CCP). Furthermore, provision is made for various procedures in the event of misconduct on their part: (a) internal disciplinary checks by hierarchical superiors which may lead to disciplinary sanctions such as a reprimand or temporary suspension; (b) criminal sanctions if the misconduct constitutes a criminal offence and proceedings have been brought by either the public prosecutor or by the victim *(partie civile)* [12]; (c) quasi-disciplinary sanctions imposed either by the *chambre d'accusation* or in the case of an OPJ by the *procureur général* (art.224 *et seq* CCP). The courts accept that the same official may be punished simultaneously by the *chambre d'accusation* and the *procureur général*[13].

## 2.1.2. The investigating judge (juge d'instruction)

Following the inquiry conducted by the OPJ and the APJ, the *juge d'instruction* enters the proceedings if the case is formally submitted to him by the public prosecutor or by the victim. The investigation by the investigating judge is called preliminary judicial investigation or *instruction préparatoire (infra,* 6.1.1.). The submission of the case to the investigating judge is mandatory in relation to *crimes*, but optional in relation to *délits*. There are around 500 *juges d'instruction*. There is at least one in each judicial region, and there are about sixty in Paris.

The *juge d'instruction* is a Janus-like figure: he has two types of power at his disposal.

On the one hand, he has powers of investigation, which he either carries out himself or which he may delegate to the *police judiciaire* by means of a formal instruction, called *commission rogatoire*. His powers in this respect are considerable, because "within the limits laid down by the law, the investigating judge may make whatever enquiries he considers necessary in order to discover the truth" (art.81(1) CCP).

On the other hand, he exercises judicial powers: he may decide to deprive the suspect of his liberty, to conduct searches, and, at the end of his *instruction*, he decides on how the matter is to proceed thereafter.

The powers of the *juge d'instruction* are not, however, unlimited. Each if his judicial decisions are subject to review by the court of indictment, the *chambre d'accusation*, which is a chamber of the court of appeal, made up of three judges.

---

[12]See the famous case of the Bordeaux police, *Cassation criminelle*, 18 February 1954, *J.C.P.* 1954-II 8036, note PATIN.

[13]*Cassation criminelle*, 4 May 1988, *Dalloz,* 1988, Somm. 357 with observations.

## 2.1.3. Other authorities

The *chambre d'accusation* may round off the preliminary judicial investigation (*instruction*) conducted by the investigating judge by ordering any further investigation that it considers useful (art.201 CCP), and may even order a supplementary inquiry (*supplément d'information*) (art.205 *CCP*).

The *préfet*, has judicial powers in respect of matters of national security or in cases of emergency (art.30 CCP). Issue has been taken over this prerogative of the *préfet*, which originates from Napoleon I himself, on the grounds that judicial and executive powers should be separated. It progressively falling into disuse in modern times in view of the conditions to which it is subjected.

Attention must also be drawn to the legions of civil servants who are invested with "*police judiciaire*-powers" in certain specific areas. In very general terms, art.28 CCP states that "civil servants, administrative and public service staff, on whom special laws confer certain powers of "police judiciaire", exercise those powers under the conditions and within the limits fixed by those laws". These special laws relate to road traffic, the railway police, the prevention of fraud, hunting, fishing, the misuse of drugs, employment, the general protection of public health, land management, forestry offences, the exploitation of marine and other natural resources, marine pollution, shipwrecks, *etc.*

### 2.2. PROSECUTING AUTHORITIES

The principal prosecuting authority is the public prosecutor, the *procureur de la République*. According to art.31 CCP, the public prosecutor exercises the "public action"[14] and requires the application of the law. The public prosecutor forms part of a body known as the *ministère public* (or *parquet*) the dominant characteristic of which is its hierarchical nature[15].

The *ministère public* is made up of the following ranks:
- At the level of the *tribunaux de grande instance*, the function of public prosecutor is held by the *procureur de la République*, who is assisted by *premiers substituts* and *substituts*.
- At the level of the police courts (*tribunaux d'instance*), the *procureur de la République*, is represented by a *substitut* or by a police superintendent.
- At the level of the Court of appeal, the function of public prosecutor is held by *procureur général* who is assisted by an *avocat général* and a number of *substituts généraux*.
- Before the *Cour de Cassation*, the *parquet* comprises a *procureur*

---

[14]With respect to this term, see *supra*, Chapter 1, par.4.2.1.
[15]See further *ibidem*, 2.2. On the term *parquet*, see *supra*, Chapter 1, 2.2.

*général* assisted by a number of *premiers avocats généraux* and *avocats généraux*.

The supreme head of the *parquet* is the Minister of Justice, the *Garde des Sceaux*. According to art.36 CCP, the Minister of Justice may "formally notify breaches of the criminal law of which he is aware to the *procureur général* of the court of appeal, and instruct him to commence proceedings or to cause them to be commenced".

This brief outline shows the place and the role of the *procureur de la République* in the instigation of criminal proceedings. He may certainly initiate proceedings in the public interest, but he may also receive instructions from the *procureur général,* the latter acting on his own initiative or on orders from the *Garde des Sceaux*.

In some exceptional cases, administrative authorities may, within their own sphere of competence, initiate criminal proceedings. Examples are the authorities responsible for Water Supplies and Forests, the Customs service, Posts and Telecommunications. These agencies may act alone or in conjunction with the public prosecutor in accordance with complex rules which are to a certain extent the product of history.

## 2.3. THE JUDICIARY[16]

There are numerous classifications of the courts which are competent in criminal matters. Accordingly, a distinction is made between courts of general and of special jurisdiction. Among the courts of special jurisdiction are the juvenile courts (*juge des enfants, tribunal des enfants, cour d'assises de mineurs*). Another distinction is between courts of first and second instance, without forgetting, of course, the *chambre criminelle* of the *Cour de Cassation* which hears appeals on points of law against the decisions of the courts of appeal. The most important distinction is that between courts which are competent in the pre-trial stage of the proceedings, and courts which are competent to pass judgments on the merits.

### 2.3.1. Courts in the pre-trial stage of the proceedings

These consist of the investigating judge (*juge d'instruction)* and the court of indictment (*chambre d'accusation*).

### (i) The investigating judge (juge d'instruction)
The investigating judge is appointed by presidential decree. Three aspects of his powers require consideration: (a) competence *ratione materiae*: the investigating judge must be involved in the investigation of *crimes*, whereas

---

[16]All judges and the members of the *parquet* have a common training undertaken by the *Ecole Nationale de la Magistrature* located in Bordeaux, with a large branch in Paris.

his involvement is only optional in the case of *délits* and *contraventions* (the latter are only very rarely investigated by an investigating judge); (b) competence *ratione loci*: the territorial competence of the investigating judge is determined by the place where the offence was committed, the place of residence of the suspect(s) or the place of arrest, even if the arrest was effected for some other reason (art.52 CCP ); (c) competence *ratione personae*: the investigating judge is competent to investigate charges against any person, except in those cases where he must share his competence with the *juge des enfants, i.e.* where the suspect was under eighteen when the offence was committed.

One fundamental rule is set out in art.49 CCP. This relates to the separation of the investigative and trial functions: a judge who has been involved at the investigative stage cannot participate in the judgment of matters which he has investigated, under penalty of nullity of the judgment.

### (ii) The court of indictment (chambre d'accusation)

The *chambre d'accusation* is a section of the *Cour d'appel*, and is made up of a president (appointed in the same way as the investigating judge) and two assessors (appointed each year by the general assembly of the court)[17]. It has the same competence as the investigating judge whose activities it supervises, except that, territorially, its jurisdiction coincides with that of the court to which it is attached.

### 2.3.2. Trial courts

### (i) Courts of first instance

At first instance there are three types of courts, reflecting the division of criminal offences into *contraventions*, *délits* and *crimes*. *Contraventions* are dealt with by the *'juge de police"* who is a single judge.

*Délits* are judged by the *tribunal correctionnel* which is part of the *tribunal de grande instance*. The *tribunal correctionnel*'s competence is the same as that of the *investigating judge*. This court is, in principle, composed of three judges. However, it may be joined by a fourth judge in complex matters. This judge will only intervene if one of the three judges making up the court cannot follow the proceedings to their conclusion. Conversely, the *tribunal correctionnel* may sit as a single judge for a long list of minor *délits* such as offences in connection with hunting and fishing and certain traffic offences (art.398-1 CCP).

*Crimes* are brought before the assize court (*cour d'assises*). The territorial jurisdiction of this court is based on the *département*. It does not

---

[17]The *chambre d'accusation* was formerly called *chambre des mises en accusation*, because one of its main functions is to decide about the committal of cases to the assize court. The old term is still used in Belgium, where de Code d'instruction criminelle of 1808 is still in force. See *supra*, Chapter 1, par.2.3.1.(ii).

sit permanently: assize sessions are, in principle, held every three months (art.236 CCP). The assize court consists of three professional judges (whose president must be a judge in the court of appeal (art.244 CCP) and nine jurors who are ordinary citizens drawn by lots using a fairly complex system of successive filters. These twelve people deliberate together, firstly on the question of guilt and then on the sentence. French law thus differs from the English system which separates the jurors (who determine the question of guilt) from the judge (who afterwards determines the sentence).

The jury system is currently the target of criticism. Moreover, it is in considerable demise: the judges often engage in *correctionalisations* as the legislator has also done. Additionally the latter created assize court without jurors in 1982 and 1986 to hear certain sensitive matters such as terrorist offences.

### (ii) Appeal courts

At the appellate level, decisions of the *juges de police* and the *tribunal correctionel* are taken, in the case of an appeal, before the *chambre des appels correctionnels*, a division of the court of appeal composed of three judges.

In contrast, there is no appeal against the decisions of the assize court. Two arguments can be presented in favour of this: firstly, the fact that the investigation phase has two obligatory stages to it (before the *juge d'instruction*, then before the *chambre d'arrestation*) and secondly, the fact that the jurors, who form the majority in the assize court, represent the voice of the people (*vox populi, vox dei*). It is, however, clear that decisions of the assize court can be referred to the *chambre criminelle* of the *Cour de cassation*.

## 3. Parties to criminal proceedings

Every criminal case has at least one party, the public prosecutor, but usually there are two parties, the public prosecutor and the person being prosecuted. Sometimes a there is a third party, the victim who has intervened in the proceedings as a civil party (*partie civile*), and even a fourth party, the civilly responsible party[18].

### 3.1. THE PUBLIC PROSECUTOR

The importance of the public prosecutor as a party to criminal proceedings is considerable, both from a statistical and a legal point of view. From the statistical viewpoint this is because it is he who most frequently initiates criminal proceedings, the victim only intervening, on average, in one case

---

[18]See on the civilly responsible party *supra*, Chapter 1,par. 3.4.

out of five. From the legal point of view, his rights are, during the proceedings, the most wide-ranging: thus he can lodge an appeal against all the decisions of the *juge d'instruction,* whilst the victim who has joined the proceedings as a civil party can only appeal against a limited number of rulings.

## 3.2. THE ACCUSED

The person suspected of having committed the offence is without doubt a party to the proceedings. Yet, he only becomes a formal party after the investigation is completed, *i.e.* from the moment when the public prosecutor (or the victim) sets in motion the prosecution.

Once a party to the proceedings, the accused is known as *la personne mise en examen*[19] during the pre-trial stage of the proceedings, and as *prévenu* during the trial. If he has been referred to the assize court, he is called *accusé.*

The defence is supported by the presence of a defence counsel who may assist him as from the stage of the preliminary judicial investigation (*instruction, infra,* 6.1.2.) .

## 3.3. THE VICTIM

The victim is not automatically a party to the proceedings. In order to become one, it is not sufficient for the victim to lodge a complaint. The victim must have formally demonstrated his intention of becoming a party to the proceedings by "constituting himself" as a *partie civile.* The *partie civile is* a private party to the proceedings, in contrast to the public litigant in the shape of the *ministère public.*

The intention of becoming a party to the proceedings is demonstrated by by the victim taking certain procedural steps: they may take the form either of initiating an independent action before the *juge d'instruction* (*constitution de partie civile*) or issuing a summons to bring the accused directly before the trial court (*citation directe*).

A very important rule, first acknowledged by case-law, allows for the victim to start proceedings if the public prosecutor, in the exercise of his discretion, declines to do so: in reality, by issuing a summons, or by initiating an independent action before the *juge d'instruction*, the victim sets in motion not only the civil action (thus becoming a party), but also the public proceedings[20]. Today, this rule is embodied in art.1 al.2 CCP, according to

---

[19]This is a new term, which was introduced by the Law of 4 January 1993, to replace the term *inculpé*, which was the traditional term that was previously used to designate the accused in the pre-trial stage. *Cfr. supra*, Chapter 1, 3.2.1.

[20]*Cassation criminelle*, 8 December 1906, *Dalloz*, 1907, I, 207, rapport LAURENT - ATTHALIN.

which the public action "may also be set in motion by the injured party ...". However, even in cases where the proceedings have been started by the victim, the public prosecutor remains the principal party, despite being embroiled in proceedings which, *ex hypothesi*, he did not wish to bring. For example, it is the prosecutor who will set the day on which the case will be heard by the trial court.

If the victim can thus activate the whole penal process, he may also be content to associate himself with proceedings already begun: this is known as *intervention*.

## 4. General principles concerning criminal procedure

### 4.1. PRINCIPLES GOVERNING ALL ASPECTS OF PROCEDURE

The debate between the two major ideas concerning systems of criminal procedure, that is to say the inquisitorial and the accusatorial, will always remain open. As far as French law is concerned, it endeavours to maintain the balance between the two systems by having numerous rules "with two faces": the public prosecutor normally instigating proceedings while preserving the victim's right to do so in case of inertia on the part of the public prosecutor; the secret nature of the preliminary judicial investigation (*instruction préparatoire*), but a public hearing at the trial (*instruction définitive*); extensive investigative powers afforded to the judge, but the right of the private parties to counsel, to acquaint themselves with the contents of the *dossier*, and thus with the charges, to attend proceedings and suggest certain action; presumptions in favour of the *ministère public*, but the overriding general principle of the presumption of innocence; comparative swiftness of justice guaranteed by numerous detailed provisions, but with a right to a hearing at appellate level as well as first instance; considerable authority being attached to the decisions of the courts, but with the obligation for the judges to give reasons for their decisions and the right of the person convicted to seek a review of the decision in case of an error of fact; the acceptance of measures restricting or removing the liberty of the defendant before judgment, but submitting these to strict regulation and control. Thus, alongside the considerable powers granted to the judge and the public prosecutor, the principle of the 'rights of the defence' has developed, to strike a subtle balance[21].

---

[21]This principle is, as such, confirmed by case-law, *Cassation criminelle*, 12 June 1952, see above note 9.

## 4.2. PRINCIPLES GOVERNING THE OPENING OF CRIMINAL PROCEEDINGS

### 4.2.1. The role of the police judiciaire

The first principle is that it is the *police judiciaire* who collect the first pieces of evidence, liaising with the public prosecutor who directs their actions. He is kept up to date with important developments in the investigations and notably any detention in police custody (*garde à vue*).

### 4.2.2. The principle of "opportunity"

The second principle is that of *l'opportunité des poursuites*: the public prosecutor is never obliged to initiate a prosecution. According to art.40 al.1 CCP: "the public prosecutor receives complaints and accusations and assesses how they should be followed up". This is an essential principle yet it needs clarification and has obvious exceptions.

Clarification first: this rule of *opportunité* only applies in relation to the commencement of a prosecution. Once criminal proceedings have been launched, the prosecutor no longer has a choice in the matter. Since it is crucial to preserve the independence of the courts, pressure, in the form of a threat to withdraw the accusation, should not be exerted on either the *juridictions d'instruction* or the *juridictions de jugement*.

Next, the obvious exceptions: at times the public prosecutor cannot act unless certain formalities have been observed (a complaint from the victim for certain offences, a complaint from administrative authorities, *e.g.* in a case of tax evasion, and if a member of parliament is to be prosecuted, his parliamentary immunity has to be lifted by the chamber in which he sits, *etc.*). At other times, the public prosecutor may be "obliged" to bring proceedings because of orders from a superior or because the victim has brought an independent action before the *juge d'instruction*.

## 4.3. PRINCIPLES COVERING THE TAKING OF EVIDENCE

### 4.3.1. Principles concerning the onus of proof

The burden of gathering the evidence falls on the party bringing the proceedings (the public prosecutor and, if there is one, the *partie civile*). In principle, therefore, the accused simply has to wait until the prosecutor proves he is guilty - as required by the principle of the presumption of innocence which is affirmed by both the Declaration of the Rights of Man 1789 (art.9) and the European Convention on Human Rights (art.6). Case-law has frequently reaffirmed this essential axiom.

The rule relating to the presumption of innocence thus has very important consequences. According to case-law, the prosecutor must adduce evidence of four elements:

- the legal prerequisites for the existence of an offence, such as the absence of an amnesty or the legal validity of the regulation on which the charges are based;
- the material element of the offence, particularly the commission of the *actus reus* and the factual responsibility of the accused *i.e.* his participation in the act.
- the mental element of the offence, *i.e.* the state of mind of the accused (intent or negligence)
- that prosecution is not barred by statutory limitations.

At the same time, the burden of proof resting on the prosecution is reduced in three ways. Firstly, there are certain presumptions in favour of the prosecution. The majority of these presumptions relates to the mental element of the offence (l'*élément moral* de l'infraction). For some offences, the accused's guilt is presumed, as soon as it has been established that he committed the material element of the offence. Some of these offences have been created by statute. For example, in respect of the offence of *abandon de famille* (*i.e.* failing to pay certain alimonies), non-payment is presumed to be voluntary (art.257-2 CCP). Others have been established by case-law. For example, the famous doctrine of the "*délit matériel*", according to which *mens rea* is to be presumed in relation to a *contravention* and even a *délit* in the absence of express legislation.

In the second place, the burden is lightened by the obligation on the accused to prove certain facts. For example, it is for the latter to prove the existence of facts giving rise to justifications and excuses (e.g. insanity and *contrainte*).

Finally, it is lightened by the role of the *juge d'instruction* who plays a very active role in the search for evidence. Yet it must not be thought that this magistrate is an assistant to the public prosecutor; since the investigating judge must look for evidence both against and in favour of the accused, he therefore "assists" both the public prosecutor and the accused.

### 4.3.2. The principle of that the means of evidence are free (la liberté de la preuve)

The second principle is that of freedom of the forms of proof. All forms of evidence are admissible as long as they do not conflict with the ethics of our system of criminal procedure. It is true that the legislator sometimes provides for special means of proving certain facts. This is the case, for example, in relation to driving under the influence of alcohol (art.L 1e Code de la route). However case-law has no hesitation in reminding us that a judge may use all means of proof[22].

---

[22]*Cassation criminelle*, 24 January 1973, *Gazette du Palais*, 1973, 1, 419.

However, *contraventions* may only be proved by a *procès-verbal* or police report, or, failing which, by the evidence of witnesses (art.537 CCP). Other forms of evidence such as "indications" (*indices*) are therefore excluded (see also *infra*, 7.).

### 4.3.3. Respect for the law

The third principle relates to the administration of evidence in accordance with the law. If indeed means of proof are unrestricted, very strict rules govern the search for evidence and its administration. For example, a search in a private dwelling (*perquisition*) cannot be started after 9 pm; the accused cannot be questioned without his lawyer being summoned and given the opportunity to consult the *dossier*.

### 4.4. PRINCIPLES GOVERNING THE TRIAL

If one considers the trial to be the last phase in the criminal process, and leaves to one side the *enquête* and the *instruction* (*infra*, 6.1.1. and 6.2.2.), the following are the governing principles:

### 4.4.1. The principle of orality

The first is that of orality, which flows from the rule of *intime conviction* according to which the judge is free to determine the weight to be given to any piece of evidence. The judge may only reach his decision on the basis of the evidence which has been directly laid before the court during the course of the trial. In application of the principle of orality, the accused, witnesses and experts are all heard. Any objects which have been seized are presented to the judge.

Yet the rule is not absolute. Exceptionally, in the *tribunaux correctionnels* and the *tribunaux de police*, the president of the court can authorise the use of documents by a witness (art.452 and 536 *CCP*) and experts can consult their notes (art.108 *CCP*).

### 4.4.2. The principle of publicity

The second principle concerns the public nature of proceedings. This is an important safeguard for the accused and has two aspects.

Firstly, the public are admitted to hearings, but subject to certain exceptions: the court can order the proceedings to be held *in camera* if there is reason to fear "that publicity would endanger public order or morals" (arts 306 and 400 CCP). Yet, case-law expects little by way of justification for such an order: in practice it is enough for the court to formally justify holding the trial *in camera* by invoking a threat to public order or morality but without having to indicate precise events since "the law leaves (a revealing word) it to the judge's discretion to assess the facts and circumstances necessitating a hearing in camera"[23].

Next, the principle of publicity is ensured by the presence of the press, who may report about court proceedings. This is indirectly made lawful by art.41 al.3 of the law of 29 July 1881 concerning the freedom of the press which makes "an accurate account of judicial proceedings made in good faith" immune from proceedings for defamation.

### 4.4.3. The principle of contradiction

The third principle concerns the obligation to hear all parties to the case, which is translated into the presence of the parties and of counsel for the defence. The presence of counsel is mandatory in the assize court.

As far as concerns attendance of the parties, this has two purposes according to recent French case-law. Firstly, it has been held that the principle of *contradiction* requires full disclosure to the person accused who must know the exact nature and cause of the allegations against him so that he is in a position to defend himself. Secondly, this principle allows the accused to benefit from interrogation of the prosecution witnesses and to call his own witnesses. The *Cour de Cassation* ensures that this right, which is, moreover, enshrined in art.6 of the European Convention on Human Rights, is respected and requires judges painstakingly to justify any refusal to hear a witness whose presence is requested by the defence[24].

## 5. Coercive measures

### 5.1. ARREST, *GARDE A VUE* AND DETENTION ON REMAND

### 5.1.1. Arrest

Arrest is always possible, whatever the type of procedure that is used. In the context of a preliminary enquiry (*enquête préliminaire*, see *infra*, 6.1.1.), a person can only be arrested by order of the public prosecutor, unless he gives himself up voluntarily to the police.

In the case of *enquête flagrante*, *i.e.* an enquiry relating to an offender caught *in flagrante delicto* (*infra, ibid.*), "any person may apprehend the perpetrator and take him to the nearest officer of the *police judiciaire*" (art.73 CCP), provided that the *crime* or *délit* in question is punishable by imprisonment.

Finally, during a preliminary judicial investigation (*instruction préparatoire*, *infra*, 6.1.2.), the investigating judge can order the arrest of a

---

[23]*Cassation criminelle*, 5 December 1978, *Dalloz*, 1979, 50, note KOERIG.

[24]*Cassation criminelle*, 22 March 1989, *Bull. crim.* No. 144; *Cassation criminelle*, 8 February 1990, *Bull. crim.* No. 70.

suspect either by issuing a summons called *mandat d'amener* (in cases where the suspect has not absconded), or by issuing a warrant for arrest called a *mandat d'arrêt* (where he has done so).

## 5.1.2. Garde à vue

Arrest, at least where it arises in the context of an *enquête préliminaire*, may be followed by "police arrest" (*garde à vue*), *i.e.* the situation in which a person is detained in custody by an OPJ for the purposes of interrogation, for a period of 24 hours. At the end of this period, the public prosecutor can grant an extension of equal length if there is evidence of guilt against the suspect. The *procès-verbal* drawn up following the questioning of any person in custody must state the length of the interrogations, the rest periods separating them, and date and time of his release or of his appearance before the *juge d'instruction* (arts 63, 64 and 78 CCP).

The same type of regime, but with longer time limits, has been laid down in two areas: firstly, in drug-trafficking cases, the initial time limit is 24 hours which can be extended first by 48 hours and then by a further 24 hours, making a total of 4 days (art.627-1 Code de santé publique). Next, in the case of terrorist offences, an extension of 48 hours, over and above the total time limit of 48 hours under the ordinary law, is possible with the agreement of a judge, which brings us to a total of 4 days (art.706-23 CCP).

Let us finally indicate that, since the law is silent on this matter, defence lawyers are not permitted to be present during the period of police interrogation (*garde à vue*). However, two recent statutes (of 4 January and 24 August 1993) have considerably improved the legal position of the suspect during the *garde à vue*. Firstly, any person who is under *garde à vue* must be immediately informed, in a language that he understands, of a number of rights: these rights include the right to have a family member informed by telephone of his arrest, the right to ask medical examination. Secondly, the suspect may, after 20 hours, ask to see a defence counsel. The police are obliged to inform the defence counsel about the nature of the alleged offence. The time limit is extended to 36 hours in case of *proxénétisme aggravé* (procuring sexual acts when aggravated *e.g.* by the minority of the individual or the use of violence) and in case of extortion of funds. The legislator originally intended to add drug trafficking and terrorism to this list, but the *Conseil Constitutionnel* in its decision of 11 August 1993 has nullified the relevant provisions in the bill.

## 5.1.3. Detention on remand (détention provisoire)

Detention on remand is governed by a more complex regime, which has been dealt with in ten different statutes since 1970. It exists in two different procedural contexts.

Firstly, detention on remand be ordered in the framework of the *comparution immédiate*, which is a special procedure used in respect of offenders caught *in flagrante delicto*. In this procedure, detention on remand is ordered by the president of the *tribunal* (or his delegate), on the request of the public prosecutor. It can only last five days, after which the offender must be brought before the trial court.

Secondly, detention on remand can be ordered in the framework of a preliminary judicial investigation (*instruction préparatoire, infra,* 6.2.2.), in which case the suspect can be detained for a longer period: one year in case of *a crime* and 4 months in case of *a délit* (with, however, in both cases, the possibility to extend the time limit, subject to the conditions laid down by statute). This form of detention can only be decided by a judge, the investigating judge, after a contradictory debate in the presence of the accused, his lawyer and the public prosecutor. The accused may appeal against the decision of the investigating judge. This appeal is brought before the *Chambre d'accusation.*

### 5.2. SEARCH AND SEIZURE (*PERQUISITIONS ET SAISIES*)

Search and seizure are regulated in great detail by the *Code de procédure pénale* because of the obvious threat which they pose to the right of privacy.

Who may carry out these acts? In the course of a preliminary enquiry (*enquête préliminaire*), search and seizure may be carried out by the OPJ, on the condition that the person whose house is searched consents. During a preliminary judicial investigation *(instruction préparatoire),* search and seizure are carried out by the *juge d'instruction*, or the OPJ acting on his orders. Some statutes derogate from these principles by attributing search powers to certain other public officials. For example, customs officers can open safety deposit boxes or search someone's home. Likewise, fraud and competition officers can perform searches for evidence of fraud.

Although there is no restriction on the places in which search and seizures may be conducted, they may not start before 6 am or after 9 pm. However, a few exceptions must be noted. For example the OPJ can carry out their duties at night in brothels or in places where drugs are misused or manufactured.

When any search or seizure is carried out, the law requires the presence of a witness who can testify as to the legality of the operation, and in particular the presence of the person on whose premises it is being effected. If the property being searched belongs to a person under a duty of professional secrecy, for example an advocate or a medical doctor, the officer conducting the search must previously inform the president of the local bar or the president of the medical association of the *département*, who is entitled to attend. The correspondence between the lawyer being searched and the accused can never be seized.

Any objects removed must have been seized in the interest of discovering the truth. Also, as soon as the custody of these items is no longer necessary for the investigation, restitution can be effected by the judge either on his own initiative or following the request of the owner.

## 5.3. EXAMINATION OF BODY AND MIND

In general these examinations are carried out by an expert (even if expert reports can also concern objects, such as a document, a machine or any other object).

It is the judge, in effect the *juge d'instruction*, who nominates the experts. In principle, he names one, except that he may nominate two or more if circumstances justify it. There are two particular situations where different rules apply: where fraud is being investigated, the accused nominates one expert, the judge nominating the other (the system of contradictory expert reports); in cases of urgency, where observation or examination cannot be delayed, the OPJ can appoint any qualified person as an expert.

The expert has fairly important powers at his disposal. He may hear anyone apart from the accused. He can even hear from the latter, but with certain differences. The expert can hear him if it is a matter of a psychiatric report. In all other cases, the expert must ask the authorization of the judge before hearing the accused. The general principle in French law indeed is that a suspect can only be questioned by a judge, and not by an OPJ or an expert. In any case, the expert has to liaise with the judge. Once he has finished the *expertise*, the expert submits his report to the judge who must notify the various parties of its conclusions.

## 5.4. INTERFERENCE WITH THE RIGHT TO PRIVACY

Two questions, which do not create the same degree of difficulty, arise: the seizure of letters and telephone tapping.

### 5.4.1. Letters

The seizure of letters was contested over a lengthy period because of the scope of the right to privacy. Finally, it was admitted by case-law in 1959, and the *Code de procédure pénale* confirmed the solution by recognising that the practice of seizure could apply to "papers, documents or other objects (art.56 al 1 CCP) and to "objects and documents useful in the discovery of the truth" (art.97 al 3 CCP).

In practice, the *juge d'instruction* who wishes to seize someone's post, sends a requisition to the postal service. We must, however remember that correspondence addressed to, or sent by, a lawyer or escapes all seizure.

### 5.4.2. Telephones

The question of telephone tapping is more delicate in the absence of express regulation of the matter in French law. Yet, such tapping occurs daily in

France on the basis of art.81 al.1 CCP on the authority of which, the *juge d'instruction* "carries out, in accordance with the law, any investigation which he considers necessary to discover the truth."

The decision which allowed telephone tapping in principle dates back to 1980[25]. It was a very clear decision which imposed two conditions at the most: an absence of fraud and no violation of the rights of the accused. Other decisions followed, but the question revived. Firstly, the *Cour de Cassation* held that telephone tapping by the OPJ was forbidden, only the *juge d'instruction* being able to order it[26]. Thereafter, the European Court in Strasbourg condemned France, not for its absence of legislation, since according to the European Court, case-law is a source of positive law, and France has plenty of it, but because the decisions of the *Cour de Cassation* do not deal with every aspect of telephone tapping, such as, for example, the question as to what has to be done with the tapes after the trial, *etc.*[27].

French *doctrine* was unanimous in calling for a law to be passed. In fact, France was one of the few countries in Europe without such legislation. The Statute of 10 July 1991, integrated in arts.100 et 101 CPP, allows telephone tapping, on the condition that it is decided by a *juge d'instruction* and then only if the sentence for the offence in question is at least 2 years' imprisonment. The telephone tap is limited to a period of 4 months (renewable) and the recordings must be destroyed when the public prosecutor's right to initiate proceedings becomes time-barred.

## 6. The ordinary course of criminal proceedings

Doctrine traditionally draws a distinction between two stages in the criminal proceedings: the pre-trial stage and the trial stage.

### 6.1. THE PRE-TRIAL STAGE

#### 6.1.1. The "enquête"

The procedure starts after a complaint by the victim, after a *dénonciation* (*i.e.* when a third person other than the victim reports a crime to the police) or even, very rarely, after an action by the *police judiciaire* itself. The latter open an investigation. There are two types of investigation - a preliminary enquiry (*enquête préliminaire*) and an enquiry in case of an offence *in flagrante delicto* (*enquête de flagrance*).

---

[25]*Cassation criminelle*, 9 October 1980, Dalloz, 1981, 333 and DI MARINO in *JCP* 1981-II, 18578.

[26]*Cour de Cassation*, plenary session, 24 November 1989, *Bull. crim.*, n°440 *Dalloz*, 1990, Chronique, 15.

[27]HUVIG & KRUSLIN v. France, European Court of Human Rights, 24 April 1990, supra, note 6 and *Dalloz*, 1990, 353 and note.

The dominant characteristic of the preliminary enquiry (*enquête préliminaire*) is that no coercive measures can be taken. Searches and seizures can only be carried out with the consent of the person whose home or premises are searched. For this purpose, the OPJ must obtain consent in writing prior to the search.

Larger and better-organised powers are conferred on the *police judiciaire* for enquiries *in flagrante delicto, i.e.* in cases where the offender has been caught while committing the offence (*l'enquête de flagrance*). *Flagrance* is not limited to the situation in which the offence is discovered in the course of being committed, but also extends to cases where the suspect is being pursued by "public clamour" (*la clameur publique*) or that he is found in possession of weapons or that signs of having participated in the offence are found on his person. Any OPJ who has been informed of the commission of such an offence must notify the public prosecutor and proceed to the scene of the crime to record (*constater*) the facts and to conduct the initial investigations. The OPJ can be joined at the scene by the public prosecutor who, by his mere presence, removes the case from the former's control and takes over the investigation.

The formal police records (*procès-verbaux*) drawn up during an enquiry are sent to the public prosecutor who can at this stage decide either to drop the case (*classement sans suite*) or to prosecute. If he decides to pursue the matter, he has the following options: he may apply for an *ordonnance pénale* (see *infra,* 8.2.1.); he may summon the suspect directly before the trial court (*citation directe*), but only if the offences in the charge are either *délits* or *contraventions*; he may refer the matter to an investigating judge for a preliminary judicial investigation , called *"instruction préparatoire",* see *infra,* 6.1.2.) if it concerns a *crime* or a *délit*. The direct summons is most frequently used (80%) and only about 8% of cases are referred to the investigating judge.

### 6.1.2. The preliminary judicial investigation ("instruction préparatoire")

When a case is referred to a *juge d'instruction*, a preparatory judicial investigation (*instruction préparatoire*) is opened. Invested with significant powers, the *juge d'instruction* questions the suspect, hears the witnesses and the *partie civile*, searches and seizes, designates experts, goes to the scene of the crime (investigation on the spot), the latter particularly to stage a reconstruction of the offence. In fulfilling his function of gathering evidence, the investigating judge may delegate matters to the *police judiciaire* by means of a *commission rogatoire, i.e.* a formal instruction to the police, ordering them to conduct certain investigations.

In conducting his investigations, the investigating judge is subject to the control of counsel for the accused and the *partie civile*. The latter must be summoned prior to each interrogation of their clients, to which they may be present. They must be given the opportunity to consult the *dossier* four days prior to each interrogation. After the first summons, they may consult the *dossier* at any moment, subject to the condition that they do not interfere with the work of the investigating judge (*"sous réserve du bon fonctionnement du cabinet d'instruction"*, art.114 al.3 CPP), which allows the investigating judge to refuse the communication of certain documents in particular circumstances.

The investigating judge may order the detention on remand of the accused, or place him under *contrôle judiciaire,* which is an alternative to detention on remand, created in 1970. *Contrôle judiciaire* may consist of a restriction order (prohibiting the accused to leave his house or the *département* where he lives, ordering him to hand over his passport, or to pay a sum of money as a surety bond, *etc.* (art.138 CPP).

Once he has completed his investigations, the investigating judge decides about the further course of the proceedings: dismissal of the case, transfer to the *tribunal de police* or the *tribunal correctionnel* (depending on whether the charge relates to a *contravention* or a *délit*), or, in the case of a *crime,* referral of the *dossier* to the *procureur général* who in turn refers the matter to the *chambre d'accusation* of the court of appeal.

The *chambre d'accusation*, the second level of the investigating jurisdictions, is necessarily involved where *crimes* are concerned. If it finds that there is a preliminary case against the accused, the case is referred to the assize court. The *chambre d'accusation* is also competent to hear appeals against the orders of the investigating judge, especially those which concern the freedom of the accused, and petitions for annulment presented by the investigating judge and the public prosecutor.

## 6.2. THE TRIAL

More straightforward than the pre-trial proceedings, the complexity of this second procedural stage depends on whether the case is dealt with in the assize court or in another court. In the *cour d'assises*, the hearing effectively starts with the selection of the jury (9 jurors with 1 or 2 supplementary jurors). This formality is made cumbersome by the fact that the prosecution can object to four jurors and the defence to five. Objections are discretionary and the parties may not reveal the reasons for the objection.

The following rules are common to all the trial courts. The accused may present *conclusions* in which he claims that the proceedings are null on the ground of earlier irregularities.

The president of the court the proceeds to the questioning of the accused, and thereafter of the witnesses and experts. The witnesses and experts, having been called at the beginning of the hearing, are excluded from the court room to be called later one after the other to give evidence. This system of separation prevents witnesses who testify towards the end of the hearing from acquainting themselves with the testimony of those who gave evidence before them.

This questioning and examination constitute the final investigation which can be quite long especially in cases involving *crimes*. If difficulties in relation to the evidence arise in the assize court, the judge must resolve them as they arise. To this end, the law has given him a discretionary power which permits him to "take every step which he believes to be necessary to discover the truth" (art.310 CCP) such as the summoning of a witness or an expert. Unique to the assize court, this special power is explained by the fact that to adjourn the hearing for additional enquiries would be prejudicial because of the presence of jurors who would need to be summoned again to the reconvened hearing.

Once the evidence has been taken, the *partie civile* pleads its case, whereupon the public prosecutor presents his *réquisitoire*. Thereafter comes the plea (*plaidoirie*) of the defence who, on pain of nullity of the proceedings, must be given the last word.

Finally, once the evidence has been taken and the closing speeches heard, the court delivers its judgment. In the *tribunal correctional* and the *tribunal de police* the judgment is either delivered immediately, from the bench , or after deliberation *in camera*, on the same day or on a subsequent date. The judgment will decide both on the "public action", *i.e.* the acquittal or the punishment of the accused, and on the "civil action", *i.e.* the claims for damages by the *partie civile*.

As far as *crimes* are concerned, the situation is a little more complex. First, the bench (3 judges) and the jurors (9 citizens) retire to chambers to deliberate on the public action together, deciding the question of guilt first and then the sentence. Once the decision has been made, they return to the court room and the president of the court reads out the judgment. Thereupon, the judges return alone to chambers to determine the civil action.

## 7. Evidence

### 7.1. GATHERING THE EVIDENCE

Searches and seizures have already been dealt with (*supra*, 5.2) as have expert reports (*supra*, 5.3). The testimony of witnesses and confessions still have to be considered. French law, contrary to Anglo-American law, draws a distinction between the evidence of ordinary witnesses and that of the accused.

### *7.1.1. The examination of witnesses*

As regards ordinary witnesses, the first question is that of determining who can be called upon to testify in court. The principle is that anyone can be a witness except persons who can avail themselves of professional secrecy. Yet in striking the delicate balance between the obligation of professional secrecy and the obligation to testify, case-law draws a distinction between various professions. Two categories appear:

*Les confidents nécessaires* are under an absolute obligation to remain silent. This category includes lawyers, priests and doctors. For these persons, the obligation of confidentiality is imposed as an obligation deriving from their status. It is general and absolute, nobody can free them of it[28].

The other category is comprised of professionals who, although under a duty of professional confidentiality, must nonetheless testify. For them, the duty of confidentiality is relative. This category includes bankers, civil servants and specialist teachers[29].

Once summoned, the witnesses are required to appear in court, take the oath (except for witnesses under the age of sixteen) and to give evidence. Refusal to fulfil these three obligations is punishable by a fine of 10,000 francs. To give false testimony constitutes the criminal offence of perjury for which the penalty varies according to whether it was committed in the assize court or before another court. In any case, a charge of perjury cannot be brought until the testimony in question becomes irrevocable *i.e.* when it has been maintained until closing of evidence at the trial. This means that witnesses can lie with impunity to police officers and even to the investigating judge.

### 7.1.2. The interrogation of the accused

The accused, both during the pre-trial investigations (*la personne mise en examen*[30]) and during the trial (*prévenu*) may make declarations and, in particular, may admit all or part of the facts in the indictment.

A confession (*aveu*) is obtained by means of an interrogation. According to case-law, interrogation is a crucial act in the proceedings, because it is both a means of investigation and of defence.

As a means of investigation, the interrogation must be carried out fairly: all directly coercive measures are forbidden as are scientific procedures which may infringe the integrity of the person, such as narco-analysis. The use of ruse and tricks gives rise to more subtle questions. The general idea is that the procedure will be fair if the interrogator restricts himself to the mere observing of the suspect's attitude. It will, however, cease to be fair if the interrogator is a real *agent provocateur* who plays an active role. Such criteria are, however, more strictly applied in the context of a preliminary judicial investigation by the investigating judge (*instruction préparatoire*, *supra*, 6.1.2.) than in the preliminary enquiry (*enquête préliminaire*, *supra*, 6.1.1.).

As a means of defence, the interrogation of the accused has several

---

[28]*Cassation criminelle*, 5 July 1985, *Bull Crim* n° 218, *Dalloz* 1986, IR 120 with observations.

[29]*Cassation criminelle*, 4 November 1971, *J.C.P.*,1972-II, 17, 256, note MAYER-JACK.

[30]Formerly called the *inculpé*, see *supra*, note 19.

aspects. Firstly, during the *instruction* the investigating judge is under an obligation to interrogate the accused at least once, in order to give him the opportunity to give explanations. Secondly, the accused does not take the oath, as this would infringe his right to act freely in his defence: he must be able to lie or alter his defence as he pleases during the proceedings. Thirdly, during his interrogation, the accused is assisted by counsel for the defence.

## 7.2. THE ASSESSMENT OF THE EVIDENCE

Before 1789, evidence was strictly regulated by statute: the weight of each bit of evidence was strictly determined in advance. Today, French law is governed by the principle that the evidence is free: what counts is the "intimate conviction" (*intime conviction*) of the trial judge, according to which he exercises a complete discretion in weighing the evidence presented to him. This rule is set out in art.353 CPP which sets out the formal warning to be read to the jurors by the president of the court in the *cour d'assises*:

> "The law does not ask judges for an explanation of the means by which they are convinced, it does not set out any particular rules by which they must assess the fullness and adequacy of the evidence; it stipulates that they must search their conscience in good faith and silently and thoughtfully ask themselves what impression the evidence given against the accused and defence's arguments have made upon them. The law asks them only one question which sums up all of their duties 'Are you personally convinced?" ("*Avez-vous une intime conviction?"*)

This principle is also applicable in proceedings before the *tribunal de police* (art.536 CCP) and the *tribunal correctionnel* (art.427 CCP ).

As a result of the *intime conviction* rule, the judge is not bound by any one piece of evidence. For example, he is not bound by a confession which "like any other item of evidence is left to his own independent evaluation" (art.428 CCP). It is possible to overturn the conviction of a defendant who has confessed[31].

However, the judge must give reasons for his decision. It is not sufficient for the judge to merely list the evidence relied upon without explaining the weight given to each piece. Judgments without *motivation* in this way may be overturned by the *Cour de Cassation*. Another important rule is that a judge may only rely on evidence which has been obtained in accordance with the law and without violating the rights of the defence (*droits de la défense*).

The *intime conviction*-principle is slightly infringed by the special weight which the legislator has given to certain formal statements (*procès-verbaux*). *Procès-verbaux* in principle merely convey information, which the judge may take note of if he so wishes (*procès-verbaux qui valent à titre de simple renseignement*). However, some procès-verbaux stand until the

---

[31]*Cassation criminelle*, 1 March 1929, S. 1930-I.73, note ROUX.

contrary is proved (*procès-verbaux faisant foi jusqu'à preuve contraire*). For example, those which formally record *contraventions* (art.537 al 2 CCP). A third category of *procès-verbaux* are those which must be believe up to the point at which fraud is established (*procès-verbaux qui valent jusqu'à inscription de faux*). For example, in customs matters, a statement drawn up by two customs officers is effective as proof until such time as it is proved that the officers are guilty of falsifying the document (art.336 *Code des douanes*)[32].

## 8. Special forms of procedure

### 8.1. PRIVATE PROSECUTION

In principle, the public prosecutor may prosecute any offence which has been brought to his attention. The victim's complaint has no other effect than to inform him of the existence of an offence, without, however, obliging him to prosecute.

Yet, in respect of certain offences, *i.e.* offences protecting values where the public interest is not really threatened, the proceedings can only start following a complaint by a victim. Examples are calumny and defamation (*injure et diffamation*), the invasion of privacy, poaching, failing to pay certain alimonies (*abandon de famille*). With respect to those offences, the withdrawal of the complaint (*désistement*) automatically terminates the prosecution (art.6 al 3 CCP).

### 8.2. SUMMARY PROCEDURES

As ordinary proceedings are very time-consuming and often pointless, summary proceedings have been laid down by statute, especially in respect of minor offences[33].

### 8.2.1. Proceedings by penal order (ordonnance pénale)

Proceedings by penal order have been created by a law of 3 January 1972. They consist of a judgment delivered by the *juge de police* without a hearing, with no reasons being given and without the presence of lawyer. Penal orders can be delivered in respect of all *contraventions* even the most serious ones and even in the case of repeated offending. There are only two exceptions: *contraventions* committed by a minor and those envisaged in the Code de

---

[32]*Cfr. supra*, Chapter 1, par.7.1.

[33]These summary proceedings must not be confused with the special procedures which are applicable to certain offences *in flagrante delicto*, that have already been cleared up by the police. Suspects in such proceedings can be immediately referred to the trial court (*comparution immediate*), where they are tried following the ordinary proceedings.

Travail. The sanctions that can be inflicted by penal order are fines only.

There are, however, limits which aim at guaranteeing both the suppression of crime and the respect of the rights of the defence. Firstly, the public prosecutor may chose to refer the case to a court for a public hearing, in the presence of the accused and his counsel. He may do so where the facts may present certain difficulties which can only be cleared up by a debate. Another reason for the public prosecutor to chose ordinary proceedings instead of proceedings by penal order is where he finds that a fine is not a sufficient punishment in the case under consideration.

Secondly the *juge de police*, may take the view that a more severe sentence should be imposed and can refuse to deal with a case by penal order which was referred to him by the public prosecutor's department in a less repressive frame of mind.

Thirdly, if a penal order has been issued against the accused, he may, within a month of notification of the order, apply for a review of the order (*opposition*). If he opposes the penal order, his case will be publicly heard by the *juge de police* in an ordinary proceeding.

In practice penal orders are frequently used and objections to such orders arise in fewer than 10% of the cases.

### 8.2.2. Fixed penalty procedure (amende forfaitaire)

For certain *contraventions* in the *Code de la route*, especially those in the first four classes (the least serious) a fixed penalty procedure exists. The officer reporting the offence makes a formal record of it and gives the offender a notice of the offence *(avis de contravention)*. The offender then has 30 days to pay the fine, but he may also dispute the facts of the case by making a request to the public prosecutor. The latter can either dismiss the case, or pursue the matter (by way of proceedings by penal order or direct summons). Accordingly, the accused has may submit his case to a magistrate, and even to a trial judge in the case of prosecution.

### 8.2.3. Transaction

French law does not recognise the anglo-saxon practice of plea bargaining. However, there are at least two situations quite similar to plea bargaining in France.

First of all, the law allows settlements (*transactions*) to be reached in relation to certain offences. For example, in tax matters, settlements may be proposed before legal proceedings are begun or, under the conditions fixed by art.L 249, before final judgment" (art.L 248 *Livre des procédures fiscales*). The competent administrative authority may propose to the suspect that he admits the facts and pays a sum of money, the amount of which is fixed by them, in exchange for which they will drop the case against him.

One fundamental difference between *transaction* and plea bargaining is that in the case of *transaction,* a court appearance is, or may be, eliminated, whereas this is not so with plea bargaining in the Anglo-Saxon sense.

Court appearance may also be excluded in the case of drug addicts who have accepted the public prosecutor's proposal to undergo treatment for drug addiction or to place themselves under medical supervision. If this person conforms to the therapeutic instructions of the public prosecutor, he will not be prosecuted (art.L628 -I *Code de santé publique*). Accordingly, the offender finds himself offered a choice: undergo the treatment and escape prosecution or refuse the cure and be subject to prosecution.

## 8.4. MINORS

Minors who are under eighteen years of age at the time of the offence are judged by specialist courts in accordance with rules drawn up by an *ordonnance* of 2 February 1945, the so called young offenders charter (*Charte de l'enfance délinquante*).

The preliminary judicial investigation (*instruction*), which is obligatory for minors prosecuted for *crimes*, *délits* or *contravention* of the 5th class, is normally carried out by the juvenile judge (*juge des enfants*): a judge appointed on the basis of his ability and interest in the problems of young offenders. However, in case of a *crime*, the investigation is conducted by a *juge d'instruction* who has special qualifications for dealing with minors.

The trial stage of the proceedings must comply with more complex rules. If the case concerns a simple *délit*, the juvenile judge can try the matter himself *in camera*, and will impose a reduced sentence due to mitigating circumstances. If the case involves a more complicated offence or an offence for which imprisonment appears to be the necessary punishment, the juvenile judge refers the matter to a juvenile court which comprises 3 members (a president who is the juvenile judge and two assessors who are laymen, chosen for their interest in young offenders). In the case of a *crime*, the *juge d'instruction* refers the case to the *chambre d'accusation* which can in turn either submit it to the juvenile court if the accused is under 16, or to the assize court for minors if he is between 16 and 18. This assize court is made up of a member of the court of appeal as president, two assessors who are normally taken from the juvenile judges within the court of appeal, and nine jurors.

## 8.5. THE MENTALLY ILL

French law has very few statutory provisions relating to the mentally ill. The practice is as follows. Once an offence committed by a seriously mentally ill person has been referred to the public prosecutor, the latter refrains from prosecuting the suspect. If the mental illness is slight, the public prosecutor will refer the case to a *juge d'instruction*, who will thereupon order a psychiatric examination. Depending on the results of the psychiatric examination, three options exist: (a) if the suspect seems to be apt to be subjected to

132

criminal sanctions, the *juge d'instruction* will refer him to a trial court, which will impose a lesser sentence due to mitigating circumstances; (b) if the suspect is not apt to be subjected to criminal sanctions, the investigating judge will discharge him; (c) if the suspect cannot be submitted to criminal sanctions and could prove a danger either to himself or someone else, the investigating judge submits the case to the *préfet* who can intern the detainee in a psychiatric institution.

### 8.6. TRIAL *IN ABSENTIA*

Unlike certain legal systems, French law does not preclude the judgment of a case in the absence of the defendant (judgment *par défaut* in the *tribunal de police or tribunal correctionel* and judgment *par contumace* in the case of *crimes*). The accused who fails to appear may not be represented by counsel[34], and, if the charge involves a *crime*, will be judged without a jury.

However, a judgment rendered in the absence of the defendant is subject to a special remedy, called *opposition*. In case of judgments rendered *in absentia* by the *tribunal correctionnel* or the *tribunal de police,* the accused may file an *opposition:* if the opposition is filed within the time limits, the original judgment will be considered to be non-existent, and the case will be heard again. However, the opposition will be without effect if the accused fails to appear at the new hearing, unless the court agrees to refer the case for a second time which is possible if a prison sentence has been passed.

A judgment rendered *in absentia* by the assize court in relation to a crime is even less secure: if the fugitive gives himself up or is arrested before the statute of limitation for the execution of the sentence expires, the decision is entirely revoked.

## 9. Remedies

### 9.1. THE INVALIDATION OF PROCEEDINGS: *LES NULLITES*

Since the OPJ and the courts may commit procedural errors, the question arises as to how these errors can be sanctioned. French law notably retains the penalty of *nullité, i.e.* of invalidating the act. However, this is a very complex matter.

The circumstances in which a procedural act can be set aside are quite limited. The general rule is that a party can only seek the invalidation of a procedural act if he has been prejudiced by the error in question: no invalidation without grievance (*pas de nullité sans grief*, art.802 CCP). However

---

[34]Except in the case where the accused, being prosecuted for an offence carrying a fine or a prison sentence of less than 2 years, asks to be judged in his absence (art 411 CPP).

*nullités d'ordre public*, *i.e.* procedural rules which concern fundamental rules such as the rules relating to judicial organisation and the competence of the courts, may be invoked even if the complainant has not suffered any prejudice[35].

The procedure for annulment is quite difficult and as such a disincentive for potential applicants. Until recently, only the public prosecutor and the *juge d'instruction* were allowed to raise *nullités* during the preliminary judicial investigation (the *instruction préparatoire*, supra, 6.1.2.), by submitting a plea for annulment to the *chambre d'accusation*. The laws of 4 January and 24 August 1993 have extended this remedy by allowing the private parties (the accused and the *partie civile*) to raise *nullités*. However, the private parties can only raise *nullités* within 20 days after the closure of the *instruction*. During the trial phase, *nullités* must be raised *in limine litis* on penalty of being rejected.

The effects of *a nullité* differ according to the nature of the procedural irregularity. If the irregularity concerns the judicial organisation, competence or the rights of the defence, the whole procedure ensuing from the irregurality is annulled. If it concerns search and seizure powers, only the irregular act of investigation is annulled. In other cases, the judge decides on the effects.

## 9.2. OTHER REMEDIES

A distinction exists between ordinary and extraordinary remedies.

### 9.2.1. Ordinary remedies

Ordinary remedies are the appeal, which refers the case to a superior jurisdiction, and the *opposition,* which submits the case to the court which took the original decision. The appellant or the *opposant* can rely on any legal or factual argument. One important principle is the exclusion of *reformatio in pejus*: judges, in rendering a second verdict, may not increase the sentence of a defendant who has merely availed himself of the appeal procedure. However this liberal rule only applies to appeals.

### 9.2.2. Cassation and révision

*Pourvoi en cassation* and *pourvoi en révision* refer cases to the *chambre criminelle* of the *Cour de Cassation*, but may only do so in a limited number of cases enumerated by the law.

*Pourvoi en cassation* is based on an error of law, notably procedural law. The *chambre criminelle* can, at its discretion, either accept the appeal,

---

[35] *Cassation criminelle*, 20 October 1986, *Bull Crim*, n°295.

thus overturning the original decision and consequently transferring the case to another appeal court, or reject the appeal which gives the original decision absolute authority.

In particular instances, a *pourvoi en révision* makes the *cour de cassation,* exceptionally, a judge of the facts. *Révision* is cassation with the purpose of revising a final judgment. If the court believes there has been a judicial error, it sends the accused back to a court of the same level as the one who rendered the first decision, but different to the one which rendered the decision which has been annulled. If the innocence of the convicted person is recognised, he has the right to compensation.

## 10. Other questions

### 10.1. STATUTES OF LIMITATION

The period during which an offence can be prosecuted is limited in time, depending on the seriousness of the offence. The limitation periods are set out in arts.7-9 of the Penal Code. They are 10 years for *crimes*, 3 years for *délits* and 1 year for *contraventions*.

The limitation period can be suspended, or interrupted. Interruption results in a renewal of the original time limit. It is not limited in time[36], with the result that the limitation period can be prolonged indefinitely. The prescriptive period can be interrupted by any act of prosecution (*acte de poursuite*) or of investigation (*acte d'instruction*).

## 11. Select bibliography

### *Books*

BRIERE DE L'ISLE, G. and COGNIART, P., *Procédure pénale*, Paris, Armand Colin, 1971.
HELIE, F., *Analyse et commentaire du Code de procédure pénale*, Paris, Libraries techniques, 1958-1959, 2 vols.
MERLE, R. and VITU, A., *Traité de droit criminel. Droit pénal général et procédure pénale*, Paris, Cujas, 1981-1984, 2 vols, 996p. and 1002p.
LARGUIER, J., *Droit pénal général et procédure pénale*, Paris, Dalloz, 1985, 222p.
LEVASSEUR, G., CHAVANNE, A. and MONTREUIL, J., *Droit pénal et procédure pénale*, Paris, Sirey, 1986, 292p.
PRADEL, J., *Droit pénal*, 8th ed., Cujas, 1992.
PRADEL, J. and VANIMARD, A., *Les grands arrêts du droit criminel*, 3rd.ed., Sirey, 1992.

---

[36]Cfr. Chapter 1 (Belgium), par.10 and Chapter 5 (Germany), par.10.

RASSAT, M.L., *Procédure pénale*, Paris, Presses universitaires de France, 1991.
SOYER, J.C., *Manuel de droit pénal et procédure pénale*, Paris, L.G.D.J., 1987, 386p.
STEFANI, G., LEVASSEUR, G. and BOULOC, B., *Droit pénal général et procédure pénale*, Paris, Précis Dalloz, 1987, 2 dln., 779p. and 1072p.

## *Periodicals*

Receuil de droit pénal
Revue internationale de police criminelle, Interpol
Revue internationale de droit pénal
Revue de science criminelle et de droit pénal comparé
Revue de la police nationale

# Chapter 5 - Germany

Prof. Hans-Heiner **KÜHNE**
Law Faculty
University of Trier

## 1. Sources

### 1.1. THE CODES ON CRIMINAL LAW, CRIMINAL PROCEDURE AND CIVIL PROCEDURE

Though Germany is a federation, the states (*Bundesländer*) have no competence in the field of criminal procedure. All Germany is ruled by federal laws in this field.

Central sources are the Code of Criminal Procedure (*StPO, Strafprozeßordnung*) and the Judicature Act (*GVG, Gerichtsverfassungsgesetz*). The latter sets out the prerequisites of the former, such as the jurisdiction of the different courts, the staffing of courts, choice and appointment of lay judges. Moreover, the Judicature Act (*GVG)* contains regulations which might have been expected to form part of the Code of Criminal Procedure (*StPO*), including provisions concerning the principle of public trial (§169 *et seq.*GVG) and those relating to the deliberation and voting of the court (§192 *et seq.*GVG).

The Code of Civil Procedure (ZPO, *Zivilprozeßordnung*) supplements the Code of Criminal Procedure in so far as the latter expressly refers to it. This is the case, for example, with respect of the notification of decisions (*Zustellung*, §34 StPO) and the taxation of costs (*Kostenfestsetzung* §464 b StPO). The Penal Code (*StGB, Strafgesetzbuch*) provides regulations with at least a strong relevance to criminal procedure. For example, §77-77b StGB deal with crimes that cannot be prosecuted without the complaint of the victim (*Antragsdelikte*).

All of these codes were created at the end of the 19th century. They all originate in scholarly works which aimed at the construction of a system of law applicable in any of the various German states. Both principles of the ancient Roman law and new ideas emerging from the Enlightment and the French revolution inspired these efforts. With *the Reichsgründung* in 1871, Parliament seized the opportunity and turned them into *Reichsgesetze* after very short committee and parliamentary discussions in the Seventies of that century.

These times are generally considered to be the most creative in the whole of German legal history. They helped to rid the German states from the strong remnants of a feudal system reaching back to medieval times. Thus, secret trials without defence counsel, conducted by judges who were not independent and who simultaneously occupied the position of prosecutor were abolished. In spite of numerous amendments and reforms, the essence of these codes subsists, and constitutes the basis of contemporary legal culture in Germany.

## 1.2. THE CONSTITUTION

The German Constitution (*Grundgesetz, GG*) has both a guiding and a correcting function with respect to criminal procedure. Both the general fundamental rights (arts.1-19 GG) and the so-called *judicial* fundamental rights (*justizielle Grundrechte*, arts. 101(1), 103, 104 GG) constitute fortresses that protect the individual against the power of the state. Criminal procedure must, both in theory and in practice, comply with the Constitution and its value-system. Criminal procedure in Germany has, therefore, been called "applied constitutional law".

## 1.3. THE EUROPEAN CONVENTION ON HUMAN RIGHTS

The European Convention on Human Rights, which became part of the federal law in 1953, is very similar to the German Constitution. Both individual rights of citizens and procedural guarantees are given, which leads to an overlapping between the two instruments[1].

Though the European Convention is looked upon as a set of norms that are hierarchically situated below the constitution, serious problems arise from the overlapping of both instruments. The following example may illustrate the problem: the Federal Court (BGH, *Bundesgerichtshof*) has rendered a decision in last instance which contains interpretations of procedural law in relation to the European Convention; in this decision the Court declares that if convicted, the non-German speaking accused has to pay for the interpreter's costs (art. 6(3)a of the European Convention). The person convicted complains to the Federal Constitutional Court (*BVerfG, Bundesverfassungsgericht*) arguing that his constitutional right to a fair trial (*Rechtsstaatsprinzip*, art 20 GG) has been violated, because he has been discriminated against in comparison with German speaking accused persons (*Verletzung des Gleichheitsgebots*, art. 3 GG). His claim is dismissed. The Court does not see any violation of constitutional guarantees even in the light of an interpretation paying special attention to the value system of the

---

[1]For details see KÜHNE, H.H., *Strafprozeßlehre, Eine systematische Darstellung für Prüfung und Praxis*, 4.ed.1993, p. 7-14.

European Convention[2]. Thereupon, the person concerned lodges an application with the European Commission of Human Rights, and the case is brought before the European Court of Human Rights. Contrary to the decision reached by the German Federal Constitutional Court, the European Court holds that art.6(3)a of the European Convention clearly gives the accused the right to the free services of an interpreter[3].

Despite the fact that the European Court does not formally interfere with the Federal Constitutional Court as far as the interpretation of the German Constitution is concerned, a conflict nevertheless arises in a material sense because the two courts render a decision with respect to the same factual situation on the basis of different legal instruments, the European Convention and the German Constitution.

The question therefore arises which of the two courts has the final authority in such cases. Behind this question lies the highly political issue of national judicial sovereignty and its constitutional implications. The German Constitution recognises the concept of immutability for the essence of the fundamental constitutional rights (*Grundrechte*). A dogmatic construction that has been defined as the essence of a fundamental right (*Grundrecht*) by the Federal Constitutional Court is no longer open to any changes. Even a qualified majority which enables parliament to change the constitution in general cannot touch this matter. Consequently the mere idea of a European Court going beyond these limits is abhorrent to German lawyers.

Yet in practice, the priority of the case-law of the European Court is accepted in Germany. This is done by virtue of a formal argumentation, in which the jurisdiction of the European Court is explained by international law obligations which do not concern constitutional law but exclusively the law of the European Convention on Human Rights.

## 1.4. VARIOUS STATUTES

Important principles defining the position of judges are laid down in the Constitution (art.92 *et seq*.GG) and, in more detail, in the *German Judges' Law* (DRiG, *Deutsches Richtergesetz*) which is a federal law applicable to judges in the federal courts and state courts.

The *Federal Advocates' Law* (BRAO, *Bundesrechtsanwaltsordnung*) transforms the canons of professional ethics and duties into binding rules of law. Here we find more information about defence counsel than we do in the Code of Criminal Procedure (StPO, *Strafprozeßordnung*).

---

[2]The Federal Constitutional Court (*Bundesverfassungsgericht, BVerfG*) uses the Convention as a stimulus for constitutional interpretations, see Federal Constitutional Court, 23 August 1965, *Entscheidungen des Bundesverfassungsgerichts*, 19, 342 (347); Federal Constitutional Court, 17 May 1983, *Entscheidungen des Bundesverfassungsgerichts*, 64, 135 (150).

[3]LUEDICKE, BELKACEM AND KOC v. Germany, European Court of Human Rights, 28 November 1978, *Publ. E.C.H.R.*, A, vol 29.

The Code of Criminal Procedure tells us who will have to bear the burden of costs. The *Court's Charges Law* (GKG, *Gerichtskostengesetz*) and the *Federal Advocate's Charges Law* (BRAGO, *Bundesrechtsanwalts-gebühren- ordnung*) give the basis for the calculation of these fees.

Witnesses and experts are indemnified according to the *Witness and Expert Compensation Law* (ZSEG, *Zeugen- und Sachverständigenentschä-digungs-gesetz*).

Persons who have been subjected to procedural coercive measures through no fault of their own are compensated pursuant to the *Compensation of Criminal Prosecution Law* (StrEG, *Strafrechtsentschädigungsgesetz*). This does not imply wrongful acts of criminal prosecution. These acts are indemnified by virtue of the general rules of civil law (see below 5).

Last but not least, the *Federal Central Register Law* (BZRG, *Bundes zentralregistergesetz*) sets out which sentences have to be registered for what time and which persons and institutions have access to such data.

## 2. Structure of the criminal justice system

### 2.1. INVESTIGATING AND PROSECUTING AUTHORITIES

#### 2.1.1. The police

The master of both the investigation and the launching of prosecutions is the public prosecutor. The police are merely auxiliaries of the public prosecutor (§152(2) GVG (*Polizei als Hilfsbeamte der Staatsanwaltschaft*). Special parts of the police forces are appointed to this function by state law. They must act on the instructions of the prosecutor, despite the fact that they remain at the same time within the organizational and hierarchical framework of the police. The police service is organized on the level of the state, as part of the Ministry of the Interior. As an auxiliary body for the prosecutor they take part in the duties of the Ministry of Justice. This is a source of quite a few problems.

At the state level, the police are organized in 3 units: the *Polizeipräsidium*, which is the unit of bigger towns, the *Polizeidirektion* and the *Polizeiinspektion* which are the units comprising villages and rural areas. The system of organization is strictly hierarchical going down from the Ministry to the last rural policeman. Within these police forces, there is an internal division of *Schutzpolizei* and *Kriminalpolizei*. The former have a general competence comprising petty crimes, they are the policemen on the beat. The *Kriminalpolizei* specialises in the investigation of crime.

At the federal level, there is the *Bundeskriminalamt* (Federal Police Agency) which has mainly a supporting function. The *Bundeskriminalamt* can only investigate a limited number of areas of federal concern, which are enumerated by statute (e.g. counterfeiting, terrorism, internationally organized crime).

Whereas, in theory, according to the law, the public prosecutor leads the investigations, the police, in practice, lead the investigations *de facto*. The prosecutor only intervenes in cases of special public or political interest. In such cases, he plays the role which the code has attributed to him, *i.e.*, that of the master of investigation, in cooperation with the police. Yet the lack of expertise in techniques of criminal investigation strongly impedes the prosecutor's ability really to lead investigations. The practical result is that the prosecutor acts mainly as a legal supervisor of the police.

## 2.1.2. The public prosecutor

The prosecutor's office is a part of the Ministry of Justice (*Justizministerium*). Within the *Länder*, the prosecutor's office is hierarchically organized from the "prosecutor general", who acts directly under the authority of the minister and has competence in the area of a high court, down to the district prosecutors who are locally attached to the district court and are subordinate to the prosecutor general.

At the federal level there is the federal prosecutor's office competent only for cases of subversive activities (*Staatsschutzdelikte*, §120, 142a GVG) and placed under the authority of the Federal Ministry of Justice.

The prosecutor's duties are to investigate crime, and in doing so, to look for both incriminating and exonerating circumstances (§ 160 II StPO). Empirical data demonstrate, however, that prosecutors usually do not obey this legal rule and predominantly look for incriminating evidence[4].

If sufficient evidence is available, the prosecutor is obliged to bring the charge before the court. Without this formal act the court is unable to proceed with the case. It is only with respect to petty crimes that the prosecutor may drop the case due to his limited discretionary power (*Opportunität*, §153 *et seq.*StPO).

The prosecutor must be present at the court proceedings. He acts as the representative of the state and has the responsibility of discharging the burden of proof.

## 2.2. THE JUDICIARY

Judges are independent by constitutional guarantee (art.97(1) GG) and have to be impartial. In cases where the accused has reasons to challenge the impartiality of a judge (even if these are purely subjective reasons) the judge can be disqualified by motion of the accused (§24 *et seq.*StPO).

It is the law, not the state which designates the competent judge: the competence of the judges in criminal procedure is defined by law. According to the principle of the "legal judge" (*gesetzlicher Richter*, art.101 GG), ad

---

[4]BLANKENBURG et al., *Die Staatsanwaltschaft im Prozeß strafrechtlicher Sozialkontrolle*, 1978, p. 257 *et seq.*

hoc tribunals are forbidden and no authority is able to match judges and cases.

In first instance courts (local court, *Amtsgericht* and district court, *Landgericht*), lay judges can be members of the court[5]. There are, however, no lay judges in the High Court (*Oberlandesgericht*) sitting in first instance.

Lay judges are in the same legal position as professional judges, which means that during the trial they have to decide on all matters, with the same vote as their professional counterparts. There is only one exception to this rule: lay judges have no right to inspect the files; their only source of information has to be the hearing, i.e. the trial.

The jurisdiction of the courts is ruled by the Judicature Act (*Gerichtsverfassungsgesetz*, GVG).

The *Amtsgericht* has first instance jurisdiction in cases where a penalty not exceeding 3 years is to be expected (§24(1) GVG). The Amtsgericht cannot exceed this limit (§24(2) GVG). Within the Amtsgericht, the seriousness of the case determines whether a single judge, a jury court or an enlarged jury is competent. The prosecutor determines according to these rules the competent court by bringing in the charge. The court before which the case is brought may correct the prosecutor's application by remitting the charge to another court.

First instance competence of the *Landgericht* exists with respect to crimes that do not fall under the jurisdiction of either the *Amtsgericht* or the *Oberlandesgericht*. §74 -74(c) GVG further enumerate the serious crimes that come within the jurisdiction of the *Landgericht*.

The only and exceptional first instance competence of the *Oberlandesgericht* exists in cases of terrorism and political crimes such as high treason and assaults against the highest representatives of the state (§120 GVG).

The presiding judge leads the trial. Defence counsel and prosecutor as natural opponents may only implement their procedural rights under the authority of the court. The court decides on the course of the proceedings and governs them.

## 3. Parties to the criminal proceedings

### 3.1. THE PROSECUTOR

The prosecutor leads the investigation and decides whether or not to bring the charges. During the trial, he bears the burden of proof, pleads at the end of the hearing and has the right of appeal both in favour and against the accused. For more details see *supra*, 2.1.2.

---

[5]There is a dispute whether lay judges ought to remain part of penal courts, see KÜHNE, H.H., "Laienrichter im Strafprozeß", *Zeitschrift für Rechtspolitik*, 1985, 237.

## 3.2. THE DEFENCE

At any stage of the proceedings, a suspect has the right to consult defence counsel of his choice (§137 StPO and art. 6(3)c European Convention on Human Rights). Any lawyer (*Rechtsanwalt*) who is admitted to this function by the Bar can act as defence counsel. Prerequisites for admission are two state examinations in law which can be taken after a minimum of 3 1/2 years of university studies and 2 1/2 years of practical training. There is no differentiation between lawyers practising at the bar and those who have an office practice and do not appear in court. University professors of law have the privilege of acting as defence counsel before any court without the requirement of admission by the chamber of lawyers.

If a suspect has no financial means to pay for his defence, he gets a voucher valid for any lawyer of his choice within the district to pay for legal advice. Only in serious charges, §140 StPO grants a free defence covering the costs of all proceedings if the suspect is indigent.

Defence counsel has far-reaching rights. He has unlimited access to the suspect in custody (§148 StPO). Correspondence between counsel and suspect is not subject to any control[6]. Defence counsel has the right of participation in any investigative activity that requires the presence of the suspect. He must be informed about investigative activities which are carried out by a judge (§167)[7]. During the hearing, the defence's presence cannot be restricted. In cases of serious charges and obligatory defence, the trial cannot be carried out without the defence (§140 StPO).

Defence counsel's position in trial proceedings is similar to that of the prosecutor though the defence bears no burden of proof whatsoever. The court has disciplinary power over all participants, including the prosecutor and the defence, as far as basic manners such as brawling and rampaging are concerned (§176 *et seq.*GVG (*sitzungspolizeiliche Gewalt*). In his procedural activities, defence counsel is under no authority of the court. Counsel cannot be dismissed by the court, except in extraordinary circumstances[8]. Breaches of his professional duties as laid down in the Federal Advocates Law (BRAO) can be sanctioned by the Chamber of Lawyers by means of disciplinary sanctions.

---

[6]There are exceptions in cases of terrorist charges (§148(2), 148a StPO and the Statute Banning certain Contacts (*Kontaktsperregesetz*) of 30 September 1977.

[7]An exception is laid down in §168(c)3 StPO which allows the judge to exclude the suspect in cases where there are reasons for believing that his presence will jeopardise the investigation. Yet the defence has a right of participation even in these cases.

[8]*E.g.*where there is a strong suspicion that the defence counsel has participated in the crime under investigation (§138(a) *et seq.* StPO).

### 3.3. THE VICTIM

Traditionally the victim had scarcely any procedural rights in German criminal procedure beyond the position of a mere witness. After a short and vigorous discussion in the early Eighties, the so-called *Victim's Rights Novel* (*Opferrechtsnovelle*) has entered into force (April 1987), which has drastically improved the victim's procedural situation. Henceforth, any victim has the right to be kept informed throughout the proceedings, which includes the right to consult the *dossier*. The latter, however, can only be exercised by his lawyer (§ 406(e) StPO). Consultation with and representation by a lawyer with rights of audience during the hearing are free of charge if the victim is indigent (§406(f) and (g) StPO). During the hearing of the victim as a witness, the public can be excluded in order to protect the victim's privacy (§171b and 173(2) GVG).

There are different forms in which a victim can formally participate in penal proceedings.

The victim may act *as a private prosecutor (Privatkläger*, §374 *et seq*.StPO), if the prosecutor does not exercise his right to public prosecution (using his right not to prosecute) or is unable to obtain sufficient evidence. In this role, the victim has the same legal position as the prosecutor, with the exception, however, that the victim has no authority to instruct the police. This makes private prosecution a procedural choice with hardly any practical relevance.

The victim of crimes enumerated in §395 StPO may act as a *"joint plaintiff" (Nebenkläger* §395 *et seq*.StPO), joining the public prosecution. Here the victim can support the prosecutor's case in his own right by pursuing his own interests.

*"Joint procedure" (Adhäsionsverfahren*), which enables the victim to bring a civil claim for the compensation of damages resulting from the crime within penal proceedings (§403 *et seq*.StPO), is in German forensic practice a merely theoretical concept. The judge may reject the application for a "joint procedure" without giving any reasons purely by stating that the application is not suitable (§405, 2 StPO). In practice, judges, as a rule, reject these applications[9]. This is extremely regrettable, because "joint procedure" could be very helpful for victims in saving the effort of going through a second ordeal of formal proceedings.

---

[9]See KÜHNE in SEPAROVIC (Ed.), *Victimology - International Action and Study of Victims*, Vol. II, Zagreb 1989, p. 261.

# 4. General principles concerning criminal procedure

## 4.1. GENERAL PRINCIPLES

### 4.1.1. The presumption of innocence

During the preliminary investigation it is up to the prosecutor, and during intermediate proceedings and the trial up to the court, to produce the necessary means of evidence. In other words, the burden of proof rests exclusively with the legal authorities.

### 4.1.2. The principle of "instruction"

The principle of "instruction" (*Instruktionsmaxime*), as opposed to the principle of negotiation (*Verhandlungsmaxime*), imposes upon all authorities involved in criminal proceedings the duty to search for the truth. Even courts are in no way bound by the evidence brought before them by the "parties". Any suspect is innocent until he is found guilty by a final judgment. This principle has been recognised in German criminal procedure from the beginning of modern procedural law in 1877, though it was never mentioned in the code itself. When the European Convention on Human Rights became part of German federal law in 1953, Art.6(2) explicitly enunciated this principle. For this reason, plea bargaining is not possible. Yet, in reality, something like informal plea bargaining in practice exists. In order to speed up proceedings, courts and prosecutors usually agree in advance on a reduced penalty, if the suspect or his defence promise to ease proceedings by a (partial) confession. The Federal Constitutional Court has admitted this practice[10], despite severe scholarly criticisms[11].

### 4.1.3. The principle of the right to be heard

No disadvantageous decision may be taken unless the person concerned was first given an opportunity to explain his point of view (*rechtliches Gehör*). Art.103 GG provides for a constitutional guarantee in this respect and many provisions in the Code of Criminal Procedure provide detailed implementations of this principle.

---

[10]Federal Constitutional Court, 27 January 1987, *Neue Zeitschrift für Strafrecht*, 1987, 419, acknowledging Federal Court, 21 September 1965, *Entscheidungen des Bundesgerichtshofs in Strafsachen*, 20, 268 and Federal Court, *Neue Zeitschrift für Strafrecht*, 82.

[11]SCHÜNEMANN, B., "Absprachen im Strafverfahren", *Deutscher Juristentag Gutachten* 1990.

### 4.1.4. The principle of acceleration

The principle of acceleration imposes a duty on all juridical authorities to avoid any unnecessary delay in criminal proceedings (*Beschleunigungsgebot, Konzentrationsmaxime*). Thus, there are no court holidays in criminal matters. However, acceleration may not impair the right of giving necessary time for preparation of the defence or a trial of the whole case. Art.6(1) of the European Convention on Human Rights provides the statutory basis. A more concrete and central provision is §229 StPO which limits the periods of interruption within trial proceedings.

### 4.2. PRINCIPLES GOVERNING THE OPENING OF CRIMINAL PROCEEDINGS

### 4.2.1. The "ex officio" principle

As a result of a long historical development, the state has acquired a monopoly of criminal prosecution and it has even assumed a duty to proceed *ex officio* (*Offizialprinzip*). This means that offences will be prosecuted irrespective of whether the victim desires so or not. Two exceptions to this rule must be mentioned: firstly, certain offences are only prosecuted on the basis of a complaint by the victim and secondly, certain offences of a political character may only be prosecuted on decision of the government or authorities concerned (§ 77-77e StGB).

### 4.2.2. The principles of legality and opportunity

The prosecutor is required by law to bring a charge whenever there are sufficient grounds to suspect a person of having committed an offence (*Legalitätsprinzip*). The opposite principle (*Opportunitätsprinzip*) which gives the prosecutor the discretionary power either to drop the charge (with or without informal sanctions) or to bring the case before the trial judge (Weisungen, Auflagen, §153 *et seq.*StPO), only applies to petty offences in Germany. This principle is prone to abuse though it helps to diminish the workload of prosecutors and courts.

### 4.2.3. The principle of accusation

The prosecutor's task is not only to conduct the pre-trial investigations, but moreover to bring the case before the court. Without the formal accusation of the prosecutor no court will be able to hear a case. The prosecutor's indictment will be decided upon by the court competent for the trial. The indictment permitted by the court defines the subject matter of the proceedings.

Until the procedural reform of 1974 pre-trial investigations were directed by a judge (*Untersuchungsrichter* §178-197 StPO (now abolished)). Ever since the creation of the first common Code of Criminal Procedure in

146

Germany in 1879, there has been a controversy with respect to the concept of the investigating judge[12]. A certain distrust in the neutrality of the prosecutor, at that time a fairly new position in the procedural system, made the legislator decide to install the investigating judge. By 1975, it had appeared that this distrust was unjustified. On the other hand, the position of the judge under the Basic Law (*Grundgesetz*) made it necessary to keep him out of any activity which was not of a purely judicial nature[13].

Accordingly, the legislator was not only able to abolish the preliminary judicial investigation conducted by the investigating judge in 1975, but could also praise this change as a step towards further acceleration of trials[14]. Furthermore there was no danger of restricting the rights of the accused: his rights during the investigation with respect to the prosecutor were the same as those which existed with respect to the investigating judge. In addition, the final decision on coercive measures (see *infra*, 5) remained with the judge as it did before.

### 4.3. PRINCIPLES GOVERNING THE TAKING OF EVIDENCE

#### 4.3.1. The principle of the free evaluation of the evidence

Breaking with the Germanic tradition, there are, in principle, no rules of evidence. The free evaluation of evidence laid down in §261 StPO is a logical consequence of the endeavour to look for substantive proofs. The decisive element is the conviction of the court (*richterliche Überzeugung*). In particular, the judge is in no way bound by a guilty plea. Of course this does not mean that all evidence is admissible (see *infra*, 7).

Yet there is one exception to the principle of free evaluation of evidence. According to §274 StPO, the official record of the trial can, as far as necessary formalities are concerned, only be refuted by proving the adulteration of the record.

#### 4.3.2. The principle of immediacy

The principle of immediacy *(Unmittelbarkeitsprinzip)* requires the taking of evidence live by the court. As a rule, no evidence which has been obtained elsewhere than during the trial can be used as a ground for conviction.

There are, however, exceptions to this principle. § 251-256 StPO give room for indirect evidence, for example in cases of inaccessibility of direct evidence.

---

[12]*See* LAMPE, "Ermittlungszuständigkeit von Richter und Staatsanwalt nach dem 1. StVRG", *Neue Juristische Wochenschrift*, 1975, 195.

[13]*Bundestagsdrucksache* 7/551, p. 39.

[14]*Ibid.*, p.38.

### 4.3.3. The principle "in dubio pro reo"

As a result of both the principle of instruction and the presumption of innocence (see *supra*), the accused can only be convicted if the court has found sufficient evidence for his guilt. If any reasonable doubt remains he must be acquitted. The court decides on whether or not doubts are reasonable.

#### 4.4. PRINCIPLES GOVERNING THE TRIAL

### 4.4.1. The principle of publicity

As a reaction against secret proceedings run by judges owing allegiance to non-democratic sovereigns, the publicity of trials was intended as a means of achieving public control over trials in the 19th century.

Today judges are independent and anybody may be appointed to the bench, provided that he has the required professional qualifications, flowing from two state examinations.

In recent times, the principle of the publicity of the trial has been criticized as a principle endangering the rights of the accused and other participants rather than a protection. It has been successfully argued that publicity may threaten the efficiency of both the presumption of innocence and the privacy of the accused and the witnesses. Cases of sexual assault, rape or violence within the family are good examples of this threat. For this reason, publicity can be restricted or even excluded in order to protect the rights of accused and witnesses (§170 *et seq*.GVG). The recording of the public trial, whether by means of photography, by film or by tape, is forbidden. (§169(2) and 176 GVG).

### 4.4.2. The principle of orality

This principle results from the fight against secret proceedings which existed in Germany until the end of the 19th century. Oral proceedings are a necessary prerequisite for publicity. Moreover, oral proceedings were meant to ease communication in court. Given the fact that even today about 90 % of all accused persons in Germany belong to the lower classes, which implies as a rule lower educational standards, resulting in insufficient knowledge to communicate on a written basis, oral proceedings are most probably helpful. This does not mean, however, that these persons have the proper oral communicating skills which are required in court. Since the sociolinguistic works of B. Bernstein we know about different language codes and competences, a problem which is of special significance in court proceedings[15].

## 5. Coercive Measures

Coercive measures (*Zwangsmaßnahmen*) are necessary to help the judiciary to secure evidence and to prevent the suspect being absent when his presence is required. As coercive measures interfere with individual rights, they must be based on statute and, in addition, comply with the principle of proportionality (*Verhältnismäßigkeitsprinzip*), even though this principle is not explicitly mentioned in the code.

Coercive measures, depending on their seriousness, may be ordered either by a judge, or by the prosecutor or the police. If the measure is taken by an authority other than a judge, the person can lodge a complaint (*Beschwerde*) against the measure which is brought before a judge.

Coercive measures can only be applied if a material suspicion exists. The code uses different levels of suspicion: *simple suspicion, sufficient suspicion and urgent suspicion*. These terms refer to an assessment of probability. They are meant to restrain state authority in criminal proceedings. Nevertheless, they are not very efficient since there are no criteria for distinguishing between the various levels of suspicion, which leads, in practice, to arbitrariness[16].

Coercive measures imposed on an innocent person are legal if a material suspicion exists in combination with the other legal prerequisites. Because of the vagueness of the term suspicion, cases in which a person can successfully argue that the measure was not justified for lack of suspicion are extremely rare. If the person is, in the end, found innocent, he will be compensated according to the Law for the Compensation of Criminal Prosecution (*Gesetz über die Entschädigung für Strafverfolgungsmaßnahmen, StrEG*). However, this legislation contains many reservations excluding former suspects from compensation if they actively or passively gave rise to the suspicion or if the trial has been suspended on discretion. Compensation rates are low: 20 DM are paid per day of confinement.

In cases of illegal use of coercive measures, compensation may be sought according to the general rules of civil law. The compensation claim is brought against the state (§839 Civil Code (BGB) and art. 34 GG).

---

[15]See KÜHNE, H.H., *Strafverfahrensrecht als Kommunikationsproblem*, 1978.

[16]See KÜHNE, H.H., "Die Definition des Verdachts als Voraussetzung strafprozessualer Zwangsmaßnahmen", *Neue Juristische Wochenschrift*, 1979, 617.

## 5.1. ARREST AND DETENTION ON REMAND

### 5.1.1. Arrest (Vorführung)

Persons who do not obey a summons to appear before a judicial authority (prosecutor or judge) can be ordered to be brought before such authority (*Vorführung*).

Persons who are found in the course of committing a crime or immediately after having committed a crime, may be arrested without warrant of a judge by anyone including private citizens (§127 StPO). They must, however, be brought promptly before a judge or another officer authorised by the law to exercise judicial power. While private citizens must proceed immediately to bring such an arrestee under the authority of a judicial officer or the police, the police must do so within a maximum period of 48 hours.

Arrest, in contrast to detention on remand (*Untersuchungshaft*), may be ordered not only by a judge but also by a prosecutor.

### 5.1.2. Detention on remand (Untersuchungshaft)

A person may only be detained on remand if the reasons mentioned in §112-112a StPO (*Haftgründe*) are given. These are:
- the suspect has escaped (*Flucht*)
- danger of absconding (*Fluchtgefahr*)
- danger of meddling with the evidence (*Verdunklungsgefahr*)
- danger of re-offending (*Wiederholungsgefahr*).

According to §112(3) StPO, in cases of extremely serious crimes, a person may be detained without any special ground for arrest. However, this provision has been restrictively interpreted by the Federal Constitutional Court (*Bundesverfassungsgericht*), which has held that, even in the case of §112(3) StPO, one of the legal *Haftgründe* must be given, albeit only in a minor intensity[17].

Only a judge is competent to order detention on remand. The prosecutor has a right to apply to a judge for detention on remand.

With the exception of §112a StPO (detention on remand based on the danger of re-offending), there is no absolute limitation of duration of detention on remand. A complicated system of optional and obligatory review of the decision is meant to reduce the duration of period of the arrest. Unfortunately, it has proved to be too complicated to live up to that expectation.

Release on bail or on a variety of other securing conditions is possible and very frequently applied (§116 StPO).

If the arrested person is not ultimately convicted at the end, he has the right to be compensated according to the Law for the Compensation of

---

[17]*Entscheidungen des Bundesverfassungsgerichts*, 19, 342 (350 *et seq.*).

Criminal Prosecution (*Gesetz über die Entschädigung für Strafverfolgungs-maßnahmen, StrEG*) which grants very low rates. In cases of illegal detention, higher compensation will be granted according to the general principles of civil law.

## 5.2. SEARCH AND SEIZURE

### 5.2.1. Seizure (Beschlagnahme)

Objects of proof, including proceeds of crime may be seized wherever they are found (*Beschlagnahme*). Seizure can be ordered by the prosecutor and, in case of urgency, even by a police officer. The foregoing, however, does not apply to the seizure of mail, which can only be ordered by a judge, except in case of urgency, where the prosecutor may order seizure of items of mail for a maximum of 3 days. Thereafter the order must be confirmed by a judge or it will loose effect automatically (§99 StPO). The prosecutor must transmit the mail which has been seized unopened in its original state to the judge (§97 StPO).

Objects containing information which are covered by legal privilege (e.g. the professional secrets of medical practitioners, priests or defence counsel) cannot be seized.

### 5.2.2. Search (Durchsuchung)

Suspects and their homes or offices or any other place where relevant objects or wanted persons are presumably to be found may be searched.

The prerequisites of search vary according to the procedural position of the person concerned. The suspect and his private or professional dwellings may be searched more easily than other persons and places. In any case, the search warrant must contain a statement of the alleged crime, a description of the objects to be found, and an explanation why these objects are expected to be found in the place to be searched. Objects that are relevant to a crime other than the one mentioned in the search warrant may be kept under the conditions of §108 StPO (*Zufallsfunde*).

The law provides that searches can only be made by virtue of a search warrant, issued by a judge (§105 StPO): exceptionally, and only in case of urgency, where there is no time to seek a warrant from the judge without endangering the effect of the search, the prosecutor, or even the police, may issue the warrant themselves. In practice, however, most searches are based on warrants issued by the prosecutor or the police. Consequently, the exception has become the rule: a search warrant issued by a judge has become in fact rather exceptional whereas the practice of police and prosecutor searching on their own has become the rule.

### 5.2.3. Special forms of search

As a reaction to actions by leftist terrorist movements in the Federal Repub-lic[18] two special forms of search have been introduced by the legislator.

In 1978, §111 StPO came into effect, which gives the judge, and in case of urgency the prosecutor and the police, the right to install *"checkpoints"* *(Kontrollstellen)* where any person passing by may be searched without a concrete suspicion. This applies only in cases of most serious crimes.

In 1987 the so-called *"dragnet investigation" (Schleppnetsfahndung)* was legalized in §163d StPO, giving the investigation authorities the power to scan general personal data obtained by police control, and to process this information according to given selection-criteria. In this process, persons under no suspicion may come into the files only because they share some characteristics with a suspect. Yet from the viewpoint of police work, this form of investigation is helpful in fighting organized criminality.

### 5.3. EXAMINATION OF BODY AND MIND

Irrespective of his consent, the suspect can be submitted to an examination of his body to verify relevant facts. Blood tests and medical examinations *(körperliche Eingriffe)* are permissible, if no detriment to health can be expected (§81a StPO). This measure should, in principle, be ordered by a judge, except in case of urgency, where the public prosecutor or even the po-lice may order it. With respect to blood tests, this is the general rule.

By order of a judge, the suspect can be submitted to a clinic for a mental examination (§81 StPO). However, the absolute time limit is 6 weeks. The suspect is under no obligation to cooperate with a mental examination. He is only obliged to remain in the hospital for the given time.

Other persons may be physically examined if they are potential witnesses, in order to look for traces of a criminal offence on their body. With the exception of blood tests, no medical invasion is admissible, how-ever, unless the person freely consents. A person can refuse to submit himself to any of these examinations under the same conditions as he is allowed to refuse to testify as a witness.

### 5.4. INTERFERENCE WITH THE RIGHT TO PRIVACY

*The taking of fingerprints and photographs* of the suspect is possible insofar as it seems necessary for the investigation or for police data systems (*für die Zwecke des Erkennungsdienstes*, §81b StPO). This question is determined by the police, but an appeal to a court can be lodged in order to control these

---

[18]Activities of the Baader-Meinhof-Group in the early Seventies and its successor the Red Army Fraction later on. This kind of criminality hitherto unknown in the Federal Republic caused somewhat hysterical reactions by both the legislator and the police forces.

orders.

*Telephone surveillance* may be ordered in some cases of very serious offences which are enumerated in §100a StPO. Both the suspect and persons who are suspected of cooperating with him can be put under telephone surveillance. The technique of such surveillance is restricted to going into the postal lines and recording the conversations. Bugging, which means placing a microphone elsewhere, is not permitted. Telephone surveillance requires a judicial warrant. If in case of urgency, the prosecutor has issued the warrant, it will expire automatically after three days unless a judge has confirmed it (§100b StPO).

Undercover agents, i.e. policemen who act under a false identity in order to investigate serious criminality by pretending to cooperate with criminals, may be used by order of the prosecutor's office (§110a-e StPO). Their are not obliged to disclose their real identity when they appear as a witness (§68 StPO).

## 6. The ordinary course of criminal proceedings

### 6.1. THE INVESTIGATION

Criminal proceedings start with the suspicion that a criminal offence has been committed. The prosecutor, in reality the police (see *supra*, 2.1.1.), opens the investigation. If there is sufficient evidence that a crime has been committed, the police transmit the file to the prosecutor. The prosecutor in charge may return the file to the police for further inquiries; he may also drop the case for lack of evidence or lack of violation of the criminal law; or he may decide to bring the charge before the court.

### 6.2. THE "INTERMEDIATE PROCEEDINGS" *(ZWISCHENVERFAHREN)*

If the prosecutor decides to prosecute the case, he brings the case before the court which would be competent for the trial proceedings. This court decides whether or not the "main" trial should be opened. This is the so-called *"intermediate proceeding"* (Zwischenverfahren §199 - 212b StPO), which is comparable to committal proceedings. The court is entitled to take more evidence before its decision, it may either refuse the opening of the trial or it may order the opening of the trial according to the prosecutor's indictment or with alterations.

The prosecutor has the right to appeal against a decision which is negative from his point of view. The suspect has no means of challenging the court's decision.

### 6.3. THE "MAIN" TRIAL *(HAUPTVERFAHREN)*

If the opening of the "main" trial (as opposed to the investigation and the intermediate proceedings) is ordered, the trial has to be prepared

*(Vorbereitung der Hauptverhandlung)* according to §213- 225a StPO by the court. At this stage of the proceedings, the accused, the defence counsel, witnesses and experts are summoned. If it is a first instance district court or high court trial, the names of professional and lay judges have to be given to the accused (§222 a StPO).

The main trial *(Hauptverhandlung)* is carried out as follows:
- summoning of the participants
- examination of witnesses and experts
- withdrawal of the witnesses; experts may be present during the trial
- interrogation of the accused as to his person by the presiding judge
- reading out the bill of indictment by the prosecutor
- instruction of the accused that he is free to remain silent
- interrogation of the accused as to the case (if he is willing to give evidence)
- taking of other evidence
- closing of the evidence taking
- pleas of prosecutor and defence counsel
- last word of the accused
- deliberation of the court (in camera)
- public announcement of the verdict and its reasons.

## 7. Evidence

### 7.1. PRESENTATION OF EVIDENCE

Although, according to the principle of instruction *(supra*, 4.1.2.), the court must look for the evidence, the prosecutor and, more often, defence counsel, have an interest in producing evidence themselves. In these cases a formal application for evidence *(Beweisantrag)* has to be filed which must indicate the prospective result of the evidence, the means of evidence, its location and, in cases of witnesses, the addresses. A properly submitted application for evidence can only be rejected on the grounds of the limited number of reasons given in § 244 StPO.

### 7.2. MEANS OF EVIDENCE

The accused has the right not to plead to the charge at any stage of trial and to remain silent. He may even tell lies without being held criminally responsible. The suspect must be informed about these rights (§136(1), 243(4) StPO).

*Witnesses (Zeugen)* are obliged to testify. To deliberately make a false statement in court (not to the police or the prosecutor) is punishable under §152 *et seq*.StGB. A witness is usually required to testify under oath. If a witness refuses to testify he is subject to coercive measures. Various reasons may, however, justify his refusal to testify. These include close relationship to the accused, risk of self-incrimination, and professional secrecy. Banking secrecy is not an accepted ground for refusing to testify. With the exception of professional secrecy, witnesses have to be informed of their right of refusal. After having been questioned by the court, the defence and the prosecution may examine the witness by asking the court to admit their questions. Even witnesses who are not victims of the alleged crime have a right to be assisted by counsel[19].

*Experts (Sachverständige)* have to give explanations on the evidence on the basis their special competence. They may not investigate on their own to provide new evidence. If so, they have to be questioned as witnesses. Experts must be impartial. The court is not bound by their findings but must give reasons if it does not follow it. In such cases a second expert is usually called.

*Investigation on the spot (Augenscheinsbeweis)* has to be understood in a broad sense as including all forms of sensual confrontation with objects related to the offence - looking at localities, persons, weapons or pictures taken thereof as well as listening to tape recordings.

*Documents* are mostly introduced by reading them aloud at the trial (*Urkundsbeweis*). If the particular appearance of the document itself is in question it will be an object of investigation on the spot (*Augenscheinsbeweis*).

### 7.3. INADMISSIBLE EVIDENCE

Though criminal investigations have as their very purpose the discovery of factual truth as far as an offence is concerned, it is important to mention that the truth cannot be discovered by whatever means or method. The rule of law (*Rechtsstaatsgebot*, art.20 GG) means that the state is subject to self-restraint when interfering with the individual rights of its citizens, even if such citizens are under criminal suspicion. Accordingly, there are forms of inadmissible evidence which are explicitly mentioned in the StPO and others which derive from constitutional interpretations.

The central rule so far is §136a StPO which bans all forms of so-called third degree interrogations, i.e. interrogations by means of, for example, torture, deception, exhaustion, threat or with the help of hypnosis. Any other method having a comparable impact on the freedom of the suspect's will are likewise prohibited. For example, interrogations supported by a polygraph - the so-called lie-detector - are not allowed.

All these forbidden forms of interrogation are banned even if carried out with the consent of the accused, which is of special relevance in the case of the polygraph.

Evidence obtained as a result of an interrogation in the sense of §136a StPO is inadmissible. The same is true for evidence obtained by illegally violating the constitutional guarantees of an individual.

---

[19]Constitutional Court, 8 October 1974, *Entscheidungen des Bundesverfassungsgerichts*, 38, 105.

Evidence acquired by an infringement of other procedural provisions-for example statements of an accused who has not been informed of his right to remain silent (§136(1) StPO) will not automatically be held to be inadmissible. The Federal Court has ruled that only where violations of procedural rights have a serious, decisive impact on the legal position of the accused, should inadmissibility be the consequence[20]. This case-law has been strongly criticized because there are no valid criteria to determine whether or not the infringement of a procedural rule has such an impact. Moreover it is difficult to understand why violations of the rules relating to the taking of evidence should not prevent judges from using this very evidence.

Another question is whether evidence which derives from illegally acquired knowledge is admissible, i.e. whether the original defect affects the subsequent results. May a judge use the accused's fingerprints from the weapon as proof, though the accused has notified the police about the hiding place of the weapon while being tortured? The Anglo-American "*fruit of the poisonous tree doctrine*", according to which all subsequent evidence is poisoned, and hence inadmissible, is disputed in German law of criminal procedure. Contrary to the views of the majority of scholars, the Federal Court generally rejects this doctrine. In exceptional cases, however, the possibility of exceptions in favour of the doctrine have been acknowledged by the court[21].

## 8. Special forms of procedure

### 8.1. PROSECUTORIAL DISCRETION/PLEA BARGAINING

### *8.1.1. Prosecutorial discretion*

The German prosecutor has a limited discretionary power (*Opportunität*) in the following cases: less serious offences (*geringe Schuld und fehlendes Verfolgungsinteresse*, §153, 153a StPO); political crimes, where prosecution would interfere with the state's interest (§153d StPO); or where the suspect has committed his crime in a situation of compulsion or under blackmail *(Opfer einer Nötigung oder Erpressung*, §154c StPO). Here the prosecutor is allowed to decide, sometimes with the approval of the competent judge, to drop the case. If the decision is based on §153a StPO, a resumption of the case is not possible, whereas all other forms of discretion do not impede the prosecutor's right to resume investigations at a later stage.

---

[20]Bundesgerichtshof, 14 May 1974, *Entscheidungen des Bundesgerichtshofs in Strafsachen*, 25, 325.

[21]Bundesgerichtshof, 18 April 1980, *Entscheidungen des Bundesgerichtshofs in Strafsachen*, 29, 244; Bundesgerichtshof, 24 August 1983, *Entscheidungen des Bundesgerichtshofs in Strafsachen*, 32, 68.

## 8.1.2. Plea bargaining

Under the principles of instruction and legality, there is no room for plea bargaining in the strict sense in German criminal procedure. Nevertheless, certain forms of plea bargaining exist which are even acknowledged by the Constitutional Court[22] (see *supra*, 4.1.2.). These so-called "informal agreements" (*informelle Absprachen*) have only recently come to the attention of legal discussion in Germany. It was found that, mostly in complicated cases with a lot of witnesses to be heard, defence counsel have developed a habit of discussing the case with the court and the prosecutor in advance. Counsel may, for example, promise a confession by his client on some points of the indictment, and in return the court will pronounce a sentence not exceeding a certain limit.

The problem with these arrangements is that they are reached *quasi* privately, outside the formal proceedings. Therefore, all procedural guarantees inherent in the formalized and public trial are running idle. That is why scholars seriously oppose these strategies[23], whereas courts accept them although they emphasize that such arrangements may neither unduly restrict the rights of the accused nor the finding of the truth[24].

## 8.2. PRIVATE PROSECUTION (*PRIVATKLAGE*) AND ACCESSORY PROSECUTION (*NEBENKLAGE*)

## 8.2.1. Private prosecution (Privatklage)

§374 StPO enumerates certain petty crimes which may be privately prosecuted if the prosecutor has decided not to prosecute because prosecution would not be in the public interest. The position of a private prosecutor can be held by the victim and by any other person in the case of offences which are prosecuted only upon request (*Antragsdelikte*). The private prosecutor exercises the function of the public prosecutor but without being endowed with his means of coercion and without the assistance of the police. Moreover the private prosecutor is burdened with the duty of paying an amount of money as a financial security for all persons being summoned. Consequently, private prosecution is not very attractive for people without the necessary financial means. In most cases, private prosecution ends with a settlement instead of a sentence.

---

[22]Bundesverfassungsgericht, 27 January 1987, *Neue Zeitschrift für Strafrecht*, 1987, 419.

[23]See SCHÜNEMANN, "Absprachen in Strafverfahren?", *Deutscher Juristentag Gutachten*, 1990.

[24]Bundesverfassungsgericht, 27 January 1978, *Neue Zeitschrift für Strafrecht*, 1987, 419; Bundesgerichtshof, 7 June 1989, NStZ 1989, 438; Bundesgerichtshof, 4 July 1990, *Neue Juristische Wochenschrift*, 1990, 3030.

## 8.2.2. Accessory prosecution (Nebenklage)

With the Victim Protection Law of 1987, the number of offences open to accessory prosecution has been multiplied. Accordingly, not only the petty offences that are subject to private prosecution (*supra*, 8.2.1.) but also such serious crimes as bodily assault, rape and robbery are open to accessory prosecution (§395 StPO). The victim of such offences may support the public prosecutor as joint plaintiff. He has the right of presence and application, he may plead and file an appeal.

An indigent joint plaintiff may apply for legal aid if the factual and legal problems are considerable.

Empirical analyses have shown that accessory prosecution is in most cases aimed at the enforcement of civil law claims[25].

### 8.3. SUMMARY PROCEEDINGS (*BESCHLEUNIGUNGSVERFAHREN UND STRAFBEFEHLS-VERFAHREN*)

Summary proceedings in the German Code of Criminal Procedure are known in two variations.

The first is the so-called accelerated trial (*beschleunigtes Verfahren*). In the case of minor offences which are dealt with at local court level, the prosecutor can initiate a main trial without a bill of indictment and without passing through the intermediate procedure (*Zwischenverfahren*), simply by moving for accelerated trial. If the court accepts, the trial will be carried out without undue delay (§212 - 212b StPO).

The other alternative of summary proceedings are the proceedings by penal order (*"Strafbefehlsverfahren"* (§407- 412 StPO)), which authorize the local court to decide solely on the prosecutor's application. The accused may object to the judgement which opens normal proceedings. The "Strafbefehlsverfahren" is helpful in coping with a great number of cases, mostly traffic offences, which can be dealt with quasi mechanically, as the facts and the legal rules to be applied are usually very similar.

### 8.4. JUVENILES

The Juvenile Court Law (*JGG, Jugendgerichtsgesetz*) provides for some procedural specialities for offenders between 14 and 21 years. These cases are brought before *juvenile courts*. Although juvenile courts are staffed according to the general provisions of the GVG, both the professional and the lay judges must comply with higher standards of knowledge and experience in educational affairs; the same is true for the prosecutor (§37 JGG). This legal requirement, as a rule, is usually not met in practice. Very often,

---

[25]KÜHNE, H.H. in SEPAROVICH (Ed.), *Victimology, International Action and Study of Victims*, Vol. II, Zagreb 1989 p. 261.

younger judges and prosecutors with no additional competence in other fields are appointed as judges and prosecutors in juvenile courts. If a woman happens to become a judge or a prosecutor, she will very likely be sent to a juvenile court just by the fact of her gender which, according to a well settled prejudice, guarantees her special skills in educational affairs.

With respect to juveniles, the principle of legality of prosecutions is not applicable: the prosecutor has the discretionary power to bring a formal charge against the juvenile or to refrain from doing so. This system is meant to avoid formal proceedings against juveniles (§45,47 JGG).

Detention on remand (*Untersuchungshaft*) is subjected to stricter rules than those applicable to adults. Juveniles, are, if possible, detained on remand in reformatories rather than in prisons (§72 JGG).

Judicial Aid for Juveniles (*Jugendgerichtshilfe*), a public welfare organisation giving social help to deviant juveniles, has the right to participate in any juvenile court proceedings. The main task of Judicial Aid is to explore the personal and social situation of the accused juvenile more thoroughly than the court would be able to do (§38 JGG). Thus the prognosis of the court when deciding on the sanction will be supported by additional information.

In order to prevent negative educational influences and labelling mechanisms by the juvenile's exposure to spectators, trials of juveniles are not public (§48 JGG).

Parents or other legal guardians of the juvenile may act as counsel, having the right to apply and to appeal (§67 JGG).

The juvenile may be partially excluded from the hearing, if the proceedings might be disadvantageous or detrimental to his education (§51 JGG).

Remedies are limited to one additional instance which, according to the juvenile's option may be general appeal (*Berufung*) or cassation (appeal on a point of law - *Revision*).

Finally, the court can decide to have the name and the case of the sentenced juvenile deleted from the official criminal records with the effect that legally, the juvenile is without a previous criminal record(§97 JGG).

## 8.5. THE MENTALLY ILL *(UNZURECHNUNGSFÄHIGE)*

If investigations show that the suspect is mentally ill *(unzurechnungsfähig)*, the court is restricted to committing the perpetrator to a psychiatric clinic or to a clinic for addicts (§71 StGB). There are no special procedural rules, the ordinary rules of criminal procedure are applicable.

## 8.6. TRIAL *IN ABSENTIA (ABWESENHEITSVERFAHREN)*

As a rule, a trial can only be held if the accused is present. Yet there are some exceptions to this rule.

The accused may, at his own request, be exempted from his duty to be present if the sentence will not exceed imprisonment of 6 months (§233

StPO). He has to be heard, however, by a judge to compensate for his absence (§233(2) StPO.

If a sentence of a fine of not more than 180 day's income (*Tagessätze*) is expected and the summoned accused has been informed that the trial can proceed without him should he not appear, *trial in absentia* is possible (§232 StPO). The sentence must remain within the given limits.

If the accused is unable to plead (*verhandlungsunfähig*) because of an intentional act of his own and if he has been heard once during the trial, the court may, if it considers it to be reasonable, proceed without him (§231a StPO). This provision was introduced into the code when in the Seventies leftist terrorists tried to obstruct trials by injuring themselves.

Another technique of obstructing trials was to terrorize the trial by shouting, laughing and making other noises. An accused who misbehaves can now be excluded without further interruption of the proceedings (§231 b StPO). The accused must, however, have had the chance to comment on the accusation.

## 9. Remedies

### 9.1. *BESCHWERDEN*

Intermediate decisions, i.e. decisions rendered before the judgment on the merits of the case, can be challenged by a complaint *(Beschwerde)* which is brought before a higher court (§304 *et seq*.StPO.)

### 9.2. APPEAL *(BERUFUNG)* AND CASSATION (*REVISION*)

The judgment on the merits rendered by a local court of first instance can be appealed against (*Berufung*). The decision of the appellate court can only be challenged on questions of law *(Revision)*. Whereas the appellate court, in appeal proceedings, repeats the whole proceedings, revision is restricted to the control of questions of law only.

No appeal is possible against a judgment in first instance rendered by the district court. This judgment can only be challenged by revision. This is indeed surprising, because serious cases which are tried at the district court cannot be controlled by a second fact finding instance. The reason for this situation can be found in an argument of the 19th century. At that time, local court judges were considered to be less competent than their colleagues in the district courts. Consequently, there was a need for more control with respect to the local courts. Today this argument is no longer valid in Germany. There is no difference in juridical competence or experience between local and district court judges. That is why the seriousness of the crime should govern access to remedies. For many years scholars and practitioners, have pleaded for a reform of remedies in this sense. Today's political perspectives, however, characterized by huge case loads and insufficient personnel point, rather, to a limitation of remedies in general.

## 9.3. CASSATION TO REVISE A FINAL JUDGMENT

A final sentence (*rechtskräftiges Urteil*) can be corrected only by a successful petition for retrial (*Antrag auf Wiederaufnahmeverfahren*, §359 *et seq.*StPO). Such a petition may be filed both in favour of a convicted and against an acquitted person.

A retrial in favour of *a convicted person* is possible if relevant new facts or evidence have been found which were not known to the court before. Other reasons, which are enumerated by the law are: the judgment was influenced by illegal means on the part of witnesses, experts or judges (e.g. perjury, bribery); the sentence was based on a civil court judgement which was finally quashed later on.

Against *the acquitted person* retrial is possible, if he has made a confession after final sentence.

In general, courts are extremely reluctant to respond positively to petitions for retrial.

## 9.4. CONSTITUTIONAL COMPLAINT AND APPLICATION TO THE EUROPEAN COMMISSION OF HUMAN RIGHTS

There are two more remedies though they do not belong to the canon of regular remedies of the criminal procedure.

The first is the *constitutional complaint (Verfassungsbeschwerde)*. Any citizen alleging to have been violated in his constitutional rights by state authority is allowed to address the Constitutional Court (*Bundesverfassungsgericht*) if the course of law is exhausted. That is why the constitutional complaint has developed into a so-called "superrevision", very much to the discontentment of the Constitutional Court. However, the Constitutional Court has taken several opportunities to correct last instance sentences of the Bundesgerichtshof on the occasion of constitutional complaints.

Even if the Constitutional Court has been of no help, there is still the possibility of *applying to the European Commission of Human Rights* in Strasbourg. As pointed out above (see above 1.4.) the European Convention on Human Rights has become part of German federal law, which entitles the Commission, and ultimately the European Court on Human Rights, to decide on the observance of the European Convention on Human Rights in Germany. In four cases Germany's interpretation of the European Convention on Human Rights has been corrected by the Court[26].

---

[26]LUEDICKE, BELKACEM AND KOC v. Germany, European Court of Human Rights, 28 November 1978, *Publ. E.C.H.R.*, A, vol 29; ECKLE v. Germany, European Court of Human Rights, 15 July 1982, *Publ.E.C.H.R.*, Series A, vol. 51; OZTURK v. Germany, European Court of Human Rights, 21 February 1984, *Publ. E.C.H.R.*, Series A, vol. 73.

## 10. Other questions

### 10.1. STATUTES OF LIMITATION

The period during which an offence can be prosecuted is limited in time, depending on the seriousness of the offence. The limitation periods are set out in Section 78 of the Penal Code. They vary between 30 years (for offences carrying life imprisonment), 20 years (for offences carrying a penalty of more than 10 years), 10 years (for offences carrying a penalty between 5 and 10 years), 5 years (for offences carrying a penalty between 1 and 5 years), and 3 years for all other offences.

The limitation period can be suspended, or interrupted. Interruption (*Unterbrechung*) results in a renewal of the original time limit. It is limited in time, *i.e.* it can only result in a prolongation to maximum twice the original time-limit. Whereas, under the old penal code, prolongation could result from any judicial act, it can, under the 1975 Code, only result from acts that are enumerated in the law.

## 11. Select bibliography

### Books

BLANKENBURG, E., SESSAR, K.and STEFFEN, W., *Die Staatsanwaltschaft im Prozeß strafrechtlicher Sozialkontrolle*, Berlin 1978
KLEINKNECHT, T., *Strafprozessordnung Gerichtsverfassungsgesetz Nebengesetze und Bestimmungen*, München, C.H. Beck, 1991, 40th ed, 1689p.
KÜHNE, H.H., *Strafprozeßlehre*, 4. Aufl. 1993
KÜHNE, H.H., *Strafverfahrensrecht als Kommunikationsproblem,* Heidelberg 1978
PETERS, K., *Strafprozess-Ein Lehrbuch*, Heidelberg, C.F. Müller Juristischer Verlag, 1985, 4e druk, 750p.
SEPAROVIC, P.(ed.), *Victimology, international action and study of victims,* Vol. II, Zagreb 1989
SCHÜNEMANN, B., "Absprachen im Strafverfahren", *Deutscher Juristentag*, Gutachten 1990

### Periodicals

Goltdammer's Archiv für Strafrecht
Monatsschrift für Kriminologie und Strafrechtsreform
Strafverteitiger
Zeitschrift für die gesammte Strafrechtswissenschaft
Zeitschrift für Strafvollzug und Straffälligenhilfe

# Chapter 6 - Greece

Associate Prof. Christos **MYLONOPOULOS**
Law Faculty
University of Athens

## 1.Sources

The main source of the Greek Law of Criminal Procedure is the *Code of Criminal Procedure* (CCP, Law Nr 1493 of August 17, 1950) which has been in force since 1 January 1951. This code has subsequently been amended and completed by several special statutes.

Another important source is the *Greek Constitution* of 1975, particularly the provisions relating to the protection of personal liberty (arts.5 §2-4 and 6), the prohibition of torture and any other humiliating treatment, and the compensation of persons who have been unlawfully detained or sentenced (art.7 §2 and 4). Other relevant constitutional provisions are the competence of the "natural judge" (*i.e.* the principle according to which only the law, and not the state or the parties, can designate the competent judge (art.8)), the protection of the right to privacy, the provisions concerning the criminal liability of the President of the Republic (art.49), of members of Parliament (art.61-62) and of the Government (art.86) and the provisions regarding the jurisdiction of criminal courts (art.96-97).

Another important source of rules of criminal procedure is the *European Convention on Human Rights* (ratified by legislative decree 53/1974), which is directly applicable and has priority over contrary domestic statutory provisions (art.28 of the Constitution). Accordingly, the procedural provisions of the Convention, including the prohibition of torture, the protection of personal liberty and security, the right to a fair trial, the presumption of innocence, the inviolability of privacy and correspondence (arts.3, 5, 6 and 8 of the ECHR) are part of Greek criminal procedure.

Finally, the *Military Criminal Code* (1941) and the *Statute on Judicial Organisation* and a great number of other statutes contain specific rules of criminal procedure.

## 2. Structure of the criminal justice system

### 2.1. INVESTIGATING AUTHORITIES

Depending on their seriousness, offences are investigated either by the police, under the direction of the public prosecutor, or by the investigating judge.

Investigation by the police is done by *investigating officers*, who are responsible for the so-called *"summary investigation"*, which, in practice, is the most common procedure (see *infra*, 6.1.).

The main or *"ordinary investigation"*, despite its name, is only applicable in a minority of cases, *i.e.* in case of a felony or grave misdemeanour. The ordinary investigation is carried out by the *investigating judge*, after the case has been submitted to him by the public prosecutor (see further *infra*, 6.1.).

## 2.2. PROSECUTING AUTHORITIES

In Greece, the State has, in principle, a monopoly over the prosecution of crime. This function is carried out by the public prosecutor, whose task is not only the prosecution of crimes, but, more generally, the enforcement of the law, the protection of the citizens and the application of rules concerning public order.

Although the public prosecutor is not a judge, he is a judicial officer *lato sensu*. Thus, he is not a party to the proceedings in the technical sense of the term, since he does not represent an interest contrary to that of other parties. On the contrary, he has duty of objectivity, *i.e* he is obliged to look for the objective truth, searching not only for evidence against, but also in favour of the accused (art.239 §2 CCP).

The function of the public prosecutor is characterised by two principles: (art.24 of the Statute of Judicial Organisation): the principle of hierarchical subordination, and the principle of indivisibility.

The *principle of hierarchical subordination* flows from the fact that the public prosecutor's office is hierarchically organised according to a pyramidal structure, in which subordinate officers of the public prosecutor are deemed to act on the orders of the latter. Accordingly, each member of the public prosecutor's office is under a duty to carry out orders and to follow instructions of his superiors. However, this does not prevent the individual member of the prosecutor's office from expressing his personal, dissenting, opinion during the trial.

The *principle of indivisibility* also flows from the hierarchical structure of the public prosecutor's office. It means that members of this office act in the name of the head of the pyramid, *i.e.* that each member of the public prosecutor's office is deemed to be a representative of the latter. Accordingly, acts performed by subordinates are always attributed to the public prosecutor.

Whereas the public prosecutor is also responsible for the investigation of offences (*supra*, 2.1.), his main duty is to prosecute, *i.e.* to bring the formal charge against the suspected offender. Depending on the case, he may order either a summary or an ordinary investigation (see *infra*, 6.1.) or, if the case is ready for trial, he may summon the accused directly before the trial judge. He may also, before bringing the charge, order a preliminary inquiry in order to determine whether a charge is appropriate.

The public prosecutor must summon all important witnesses, not only those for the prosecution, but also those for the defence (art.327 §1 CCP). If the evidence is not sufficient to prove the suspect's guilt, he is obliged to ask the court (or the judicial council) to acquit the accused (art.245 and 308 CPP). He may decide not to prosecute. However, once the accused has been formally charged, the prosecutor can no longer drop the charge. In such cases, he may submit the file to the judicial council with a request for the acquittal of the accused.

The public prosecutor is an essential participant in the proceedings. He must be heard before any judicial decision can be made whether of the trial court, the judicial council (*infra*, 2.3.2.), or even in case of an order of a judge or an investigating judge. Omission of this rule would entail the nullity of the judgment or order. The public prosecutor must always give the reasons for his submissions and his presence is required during the entire hearing. He has the right to appeal against decisions of both the trial courts and the judicial council.

Although, in principle, the public prosecutor is an independent judicial officer who acts upon his own initiative and freely decides whether or not to bring a formal charge (art.28 CCP), there are some exceptions to this rule. The Court of Appeal (gathered in plenary session) and the Minister of Justice can order the public prosecutor to bring a charge in a particular case (arts.29 and 30 CCP). In this hypothesis, the public prosecutor is obliged to bring the charge, even if he is personally opposed to doing so. However, nothing prevents him, when the case is brought before the trial judge, from requesting the acquittal of the accused.

## 2.3. THE JUDICIARY

### 2.3.1. Organisation of the judiciary

The judiciary in Greece consists of two different types of courts, which correspond to the two stages of the proceedings, the pre-trial stage and the trial stage (see *infra*, 6): during the pre-trial stage, the investigating judge and the judicial council are the competent judicial organs (*infra*, 2.3.2.), whereas, during the trial stage, judicial acts are performed by the trial courts mentioned in this paragraph.

### (i) trial courts

The organisation of the trial courts is based on the division of the crimes in the penal code, which is three-fold: felonies, misdemeanours and petty offences (art.18 Penal Code). A *felony* is any act punishable by death or by confinement in a penitentiary; a *misdemeanour* is any act punishable by imprisonment or by pecuniary sanction or by confinement in a reformative institution; a *petty offence* is any act punishable by jail or by a fine. The judiciary is organised according to this division.

*The mixed criminal court* is composed of professional and lay judges. There is a mixed criminal court in first instance and one appellate mixed criminal court. At first instance, it consists of the president of the misdemeanour court as the presiding judge, two professional assessors of the same court and four lay judges (art.8 §1 CCP). The mixed court of appeal is composed of the president of the Court of Appeal as a presiding judge, two judges of the same court and four laymen (art.81 CCP). It is competent with respect to felonies[1], except those which have been expressly submitted to the competence of the three-member court of appeal and the political offences (art.109 CCP). Though the mixed criminal court was initially competent to try the majority of felonies, most felonies have been submitted to the competence of the courts of appeal, because of the complex legal problems they present.

*The Court of Appeal* consists of professional judges only. A distinction must be made between the three-member court of appeal and the five-member court of appeal: the three-member court of appeal is composed of the president of the court and two judges of the same court; the five-member court is composed of the president and four professional judges (art.8 §1 CCP). The *three-member Court of Appeal* decides on appeals against the decisions of the three-member misdemeanour court (see below). Despite its name, it is also competent to render first instance decisions with respect to a number of felonies[2], and also with respect to misdemeanours committed by advocates, judges, bishops and prefects. The *five-member Court of Appeal* decides on appeals against the judgments of the above court (art.499 CCP). It is also competent with respect to acts of terrorism (Law 1916/90).

*The misdemeanour court* is composed either of three or of one professional judges. The *three-member misdemeanour court* has a residual competence, *i.e.* it is competent in respect of all misdemeanours, save those which are tried by the mixed criminal courts, the courts of appeal, the one-

---

[1]For example, it is competent to adjudicate intentional homicide (art.299 Penal Code), severe and deadly bodily harm (arts.310§3 and 311 Penal Code), infanticide (art.303 Penal Code), exposure to harm (art.306 Penal Code), rape (art.336 Penal Code), sexual abuse of mentally disabled (art.338 Penal Code), seduction of infants, (art.339 Penal Code), etc.

[2]See art.111 CCP. These include counterfeiting (art.207 Penal Code), forgery committed wit the author's intent to enrich himself or another (art.216 §§ 1 & 3 Penal Code), forgery of stamps (art.218 § 1 Penal Code), false certification or alteration of documents committed by an official with intent to enrich himself or another (art.242 § 3 Penal Code), felonies against property or against property interests (such as aggravated theft, aggravated embezzlement, extortion, fraud committed as a profession or habitually), breach of trust in office (art.256 Penal Code), embezzlement in office (art.258 Penal Code), piracy (art.215 § 11 of the Code of Public Maritime Law), felonies against the safety of air, rail or water transportation, intentional bankruptcy of Banks and Corporations and forest fires (Law 663/77), drug offences (Law 1722/89) and offences against the law on explosive substances (Law 495/76).

member misdemeanour court and the juvenile court (art.112 CCP). The *one-member misdemeanour court* hears the less serious misdemeanours, *i.e.* those which carry custodial sentences not exceeding one year or pecuniary sanctions only. The one-member court is also competent to hear appeals against judgments of the petty offences court (art.114 CCP).

The *petty offences court* is competent to try petty violations save those which are submitted to the competence of the three-member misdemeanour courts (committed by bishops, lawyers, judges, etc) and of the juvenile courts. It is composed of one professional judge.

### (ii) pre-trial courts

Whereas the courts mentioned in the foregoing paragraph are trial courts, which judge on the merits, the investigating judge and the judicial council decide questions that precede the trial on the merits.

The *investigating judge* is a judge in the court of first instance (the misdemeanour court) who is appointed for two years by presidential decree (art.26 of the Statute on Judicial Organisation). He conducts the preliminary judicial investigation, the so-called main or *"ordinary investigation"* which is ordered by the prosecutor in cases of felony or serious misdemeanour (*cfr. supra*). He also decides about coercive measures that are taken during the pre-trial stage.

The *judicial council* is a chamber of the misdemeanour court (first instance) or of the Court of Appeal (at appellate level). It is composed of three professional judges. The hearings of the judicial council are not public. The judges deliberate *in camera* and decide after having heard the prosecutor, who retires after submitting his case (art.306 CCP). The judicial council of second instance decides on appeals against decisions of the council of first instance. The decisions of both councils must be reasoned and in many cases they are subject to a plea of *cassation* before the Supreme Court.

A special competence of the judicial council of the Court of Appeal exists with respect to extradition (art.448 CCP).

### 2.3.2. The role of lay judges

Lay judges participate in the proceedings of the mixed court of appeal. Lay judges are selected by lot, from panels compiled every year by the judicial council. Only Greek citizens of both sexes who have not been deprived of their civil rights and who are domiciled at the seat of the court can qualify as jurors. There is also a requirement of age and education: for the mixed court of first instance, they must be more than 30 years old and have at least elementary education, whilst for the mixed court of appeal they must be at least 40 years old and have high school education. Clergymen, the President of the Republic, the Prime Minister, members of the Government, deputies, professors, prefects, judges and diplomats cannot be lay judges. An impediment for life exists with regard to persons who have been irrevocably convicted of an intentional offence and sentenced to imprisonment for more than three months (art.379-385 CCP).

The mixed court decides not only on the question of guilt but also on aggravating or extenuating circumstances, the sentence, etc. (art.404 CCP). Specific legal problems such as questions relating to competence, admissibility of the claim of the *partie civile*, preliminary questions, etc. are decided by the professional judges only. They also decide about the admissibility of the prosecution and are competent to declare that the charge must be dropped (art.405 CCP).

### 2.3.3. Independence and impartiality of judges and prosecutors

The independence and impartiality of the judicial authorities is recognised in Greek Law. It applies to both judges and prosecutors, who enjoy functional and personal independence, in the sense that they are not bound by any directive, order or intervention emanating from other authorities.

According to art.87 of the Constitution, they are subject to the Constitution and the Law only. They are not allowed to hold functions in the Government or to exercise any other profession.

Judges and prosecutors are appointed by presidential decree after a competition, according to a procedure provided for by statute (art.88 §1 of the Constitution). They are nominated for life, unless their appointment is terminated for the reasons provided for by the Constitution (art.88 §4), *i.e.* in case of a penal conviction, a grave breach of discipline, illness or mental or professional incapacity.

Disciplinary power over judicial authorities is exercised by judicial councils. However, the President, the Vice-Presidents and the Attorney General of the Supreme Court are appointed by the Government. This practice bears the risk of jeopardising the independence of the judiciary.

As far as *impartiality* is concerned, judges, prosecutors, investigating judges or law clerks have to be *excluded* in case of close relationship amongst themselves, according to art.14 CCP. The same applies when one of the aforementioned persons is the victim of the offence. The judicial authorities may also be *challenged* for the above reasons and on the basis of obvious doubts concerning their impartiality (art.15 CCP).

## 3. The parties to the criminal proceedings

### 3.1. THE PUBLIC PROSECUTOR: NOT A PARTY TO THE PROCEEDINGS

The prosecutor cannot be considered as a party to the proceedings. Rather than a person "opposing" the accused, he is a judicial authority, who has the duty to seek the objective truth.

## 3.2. THE ACCUSED

According to art.72 CCP, the accused is the person who is named in the public prosecutor's charge, the person mentioned in the denunciation, complaint, request or report concerning the offence, or the person to whom the offence is attributed at any stage of the investigation. The characterisation of a person as an accused person triggers a number of rights, which he would not have in the capacity of a witness. Accordingly, he cannot be compelled, nor is he entitled, to give evidence under oath, nor can he be charged with perjury. He has these rights until he is irrevocably acquitted or convicted (art.73 CCP).

The accused has the *right to counsel*: he is entitled to be represented by or to appear with two counsel in the pre-trial stage and with three counsel in the oral public-trial (art.96 CCP). The investigating judge or the court have the duty to appoint counsel if the accused so requests (art.100 §5 and 340 CCP). He can never be deprived of the right to communicate with his counsel (art.100 §4 CCP).

Furthermore, he has *the right to be present* with counsel at any act of investigation (art.97 CCP). He also has the right to have counsel present even during his interrogation (art.100 §1 CCP).

The accused *is entitled to put questions to witnesses and experts*, to make comments (art.99 CCP), submit applications and raise objections. He also has the right, after the examination of each witness, to comment on the reliability of the testimony, to make statements and give explanations with regard to the testimony (art.358 CCP).

In the pre-trial stage, the accused has the right to consult the file, to obtain copies of the documents in the file (art.101 CCP), and to give a written defence statement (art.273 §2 CCP). When he appears before the investigating judge or the court he has the right to be clearly informed of the charges and of his rights (art.103, 273 §2 CCP). Both in the pre-trial stage and during the trial, he has the right to remain silent (art.273 §2 and 366 §2 CCP).

When he is summoned by the investigating judge, he has the right to ask for a period of 48 hours to prepare his defence. This period may be extended after a new request (art.102 CCP).

He has the right to obtain the attendance and examination of defence witnesses but not in a number exceeding that of the witnesses summoned by the prosecutor and the *partie civile* (art.327 §2 and 5 CCP). He has nevertheless the right to obtain the attendance and examination of one witness in the case of misdemeanour and of two witnesses in case of a felony. The prosecutor is not obliged to summon a witness who is domiciled abroad (art.327 §2 CCP).

During the trial, the accused has the right to be heard (art.20 of the Greek Constitution) and to speak the last word, at the end of the trial. In presenting his defence, the accused may not be interrupted or hindered in referring to facts which contradict the charges against him. He also has the right to communicate with his counsel, but not in order to answer a question (art.366 CCP). The accused or his counsel are always entitled to have the last word (art.369 §3 CCP).

Although the accused must appear in person before the court, he has the right to be represented by counsel in case of petty offences or misdemeanours which carry only a pecuniary penalty or a custodial sentence not exceeding six months. The same applies in appeal proceedings, if the accused can show that he cannot attend the trial because of an insurmountable impediment. In this case he can be represented by his counsel, if the latter is duly empowered (art.501 §3 CCP).

### 3.3. THE *PARTIE CIVILE*

According to art.82 CCP, the victim of an offence has the right to bring a *civil action* before the criminal court by making a statement that he "constitutes himself" *partie civile* in the criminal proceedings. Any natural or legal person who has suffered direct damage as a result of the offence, may take part in the criminal proceedings as a *partie civile*. For example, the owner of the stolen objects, the person who suffered bodily harm, the insulted person, the corporation whose reputation has been undermined by the falsity of the defamatory statement, *etc.* may bring a civil action against the accused. As a rule, the partie civile has the same rights as the accused (art.108 CCP).

The *partie civile* may claim both material and moral damages, if he is entitled to such damages under civil law. Accordingly, relatives of a murder victim may claim moral damages, *i.e.* compensation for "pain and suffering" (art.63 CCP).

If, however, the prosecutor has decided not to prosecute the case, the victim can only bring a civil action, *i.e.* a claim for damages, he cannot launch a private prosecution.

The victim who wishes to become a party to the proceedings must formally declare that he "constitutes" himself as a *partie civile*, either during the pre-trial stage of the proceedings, or at the trial at first instance, before the taking of the evidence begins (art.63 CCP). If his constitution as a *partie civile* has no formal legal basis, the other parties may ask that he be dismissed (art.85 CCP).

If the victim is a minor, the civil action can only be brought by his legal representatives (art.82 §2 CCP). There are two cases in which the civil action may be brought by the public prosecutor: if the victim is mentally disabled, or in the case of offences against the State (art.70 CCP).

### 3.4. THE CIVILLY RESPONSIBLE PERSON

In Greek criminal procedure, the person who is vicariously responsible for an offence can be a party to the criminal proceedings as the *"civilly responsible person"*. The civilly responsible person is not personally charged with the offence, but can be held civilly liable for the damages caused by the offence, or, in some cases, for the pecuniary sanctions and expenses which the court imposes on the accused. For example, parents can be held civilly responsible for damages, caused by an offence committed by their children.

The civilly responsible person as a party to the proceedings has the rights of the *partie civile* (art.107 CCP) and may be summoned either by the victim or by the prosecutor (art.89 CCP). He also has the right to intervene in the criminal proceedings (art.91 CCP). His importance is however insignificant in practice.

# 4. General principles concerning criminal procedure

4.1. GENERAL PRINCIPLES

## 4.1.1. *The rule of the search for the material truth*

The judge, the investigating authorities and the prosecutor are under an obligation to search not only for evidence against the accused, but also for evidence in his favour. This principle is laid down in a series of provisions of the Code of Criminal Procedure, (see, for example arts.239 §2, 274 al b, 327 §1, 490 CCP).

## 4.1.2. *The right to be heard*

The right to be heard is recognised by the Greek Constitution (art.20 §1). Everyone is entitled to explain his point of view before a court, and the authorities involved in criminal proceedings must make sure that any suspect has the opportunity and facilities to exercise this right. Thus, the accused has the right to participate in the proceedings, to appoint a defence counsel, to be informed about the charge and to have adequate time and facilities to prepare his defence. Furthermore, he has the right to speak and to make comments and motions, to present evidence and to ask questions.

## 4.1.3. *The principle of motivation*

According to art.93 §2 of the Constitution and art.139 CCP, specific and full reasons must be given in every judgment. Failing to give such reasons may entail the nullity of the judgment. However, this principle does not apply to judgments rendered by the military courts, because no special statute has yet been promulgated, as required by the Constitution.

## 4.1.4. *The principle of acceleration*

In accordance with art.6(1) of the European Convention on Human Rights ("everyone is entitled to a fair and public hearing within a reasonable time"), every judicial authority involved in criminal proceedings must create the conditions necessary to allow the trial to take place as soon as possible, without, nevertheless, violating the accused's right to have adequate time and facilities for the preparation of his defence.

### 4.1.5. The principle of judicial care

Judicial authorities are under the obligation to remind the parties of their rights, in order to protect them from any unexpected development which might cause prejudice to them. For example, a court may postpone the hearing of a witness or of a party not duly summoned, if this might cause prejudice to the accused (art.174 §2b CCP).

### 4.1.6. The principle of equality

The fair-trial principle requires that the parties in the criminal proceedings, *i.e.* the victim and the accused, must be equally treated. This principle has been recognised in a number of provisions. For example, during the pre-trial stage of the proceedings, the victim has the same rights as the accused (arts.96-99, 107-108, 309 CCP), while during the trial, both parties have the right to make comments, motions or objections, to examine witnesses or experts and, after the taking of evidence is concluded, to speak.

However, the principle of equality, does not apply with regard to the public prosecutor, who is not a party to the proceedings (*supra*, 3.1.) and who, as a rule, is in a better position than the parties.

### 4.2. PRINCIPLES GOVERNING THE OPENING OF CRIMINAL PROCEEDINGS

### 4.2.1. The "ex officio" principle

Most offences are prosecuted *ex officio, i.e.* irrespective of the wishes of the victim. However, some offences of minor importance (e.g. defamation, insult, threat, disturbance of the home, *etc.*), can only be prosecuted after a complaint by the victim.

More generally, most procedural acts are performed *ex officio*, by the prosecutor and the court, whereas only exceptionally, procedural acts depend on the initiative of the parties, e.g. the act by which the victim "constitutes" himself as a party to the proceedings (*partie civile)*, the summoning of witnesses for the defence at the beginning of the trial, etc.

### 4.2.2. The principle of legality

In principle, the public prosecutor is obliged to prosecute each offence that has been reported to him (legality principle), provided that it is based on the law and that it is not manifestly ill-founded as to the facts. Decisions not to prosecute are communicated to the public prosecutor at the Court of Appeal. In addition, the public prosecutor has the discretionary power to suspend prosecution in case of a misdemeanour, if the expected sentence is insignificant compared with the sentence imposed or anticipated for another act (art.44 CCP). He may also refrain from prosecuting an alleged extortion, if the victim of the extortion was threatened with the revelation of an offence, and prosecution would risk revealing that offence.

Furthermore, the Minister of Justice may order the suspension of prosecution concerning a political offence, if prosecution bears the risk of endangering the international relations of the country (art.30 §1 CCP).

Finally, the public prosecutor may decline to prosecute in case of rape, if the victim states that publicity could cause her grave mental suffering (art.344 Penal Code).

### 4.2.3. The principle of accusation

The Greek Code of Criminal Procedure follows a mixed system based on the principle of accusation with elements of the inquisitorial model in the pretrial stage (*infra*, 6.1.), and elements of the adversarial system during the trial (*infra*, 6.3). As a rule, offences are prosecuted by the public prosecutor who represents the accusation during the entire proceeding. The accused has the right to be assisted by a counsel. Accordingly, the functions of accusation, defence and judgment are carried out by different persons.

The pre-trial stage is characterised by some features of the inquisitorial system, such as the principle of *ex officio* prosecution and investigation, the fact that proceedings in this stage are written and secret, and the fact that at this stage, the accused's participation to the proceedings is extremely limited.

During the trial, however, the characteristics of the adversarial system prevail, such as the principle of publicity, of orality, of opposition, of direct testimony and of concentration (see *infra*, 4.4.).

### 4.3. PRINCIPLES GOVERNING THE TAKING OF EVIDENCE

### 4.3.1. The presumption of innocence

The presumption of innocence laid down in art.6(2) of the European Convention on Human Rights ("everyone charged with a criminal offence shall be presumed innocent until proved guilty according to the law"), coincides with the principle of inviolability of human dignity (art.2 §1 of the Greek Constitution): an accused person is deemed innocent until he has been convicted by an irrevocable judgment. In connection with this principle, the maxim *in dubio pro reo* must be respected, according to which in criminal trials, doubt is to be resolved in favour of the accused.

### 4.3.2. The principle of the free assessment of the evidence

According to art.177 CCP, the court, in assessing the evidence, is not bound by formal rules. The judges must decide according to their *"intimate convic-*

*tion*", following the voice of their conscience, and led by an impartial assessment reached during the trial, concerning the truth of the facts, the reliability of witnesses and the value of the evidence.

This principle, however, does not mean that judges are free to convict a person without reason or to assess the facts arbitrarily. In case of doubt, they are obliged to apply the maxim *in dubio pro reo*. They must always give reasons for their judgments, and are, in doing so, bound by the rules of logic and of common experience.

An exception to the principle of the free assessment of the evidence is the exclusionary rule: judges may not base their conviction on unlawfully obtained evidence.

### 4.3.3. *The principle of direct testimony*

This principle is closely related to the principle of orality of the trial (see *infra*, 4.4.2.). The principle of direct testimony means that the trial judge may only form his conviction on the basis of evidence which has been produced in front of him, and which he has personally "perceived". It is, however, distinct from the principle of orality, because the latter is applicable to the whole trial, whereas the principle of direct testimony only applies to the taking of evidence.

The principle is laid down in several provisions, e.g. art.333 CCP (witnesses must be examined orally in the court and by the court), art.357 §4 CCP (written testimonies can only be read in court in exceptional circumstances), art.363 CCP (investigation *in loco* is carried out by the court) etc.

### 4.4. PRINCIPLES GOVERNING THE TRIAL

### 4.4.1. *The principle of publicity*

According to art.93 §2 and 3 of the Constitution and to art.329 §1 CCP, the trial must be held in public and the judgment must be publicly pronounced. However, the presiding judge has the right to exclude minors under the age of 17 from the courtroom, and in big trials, he may restrict the number of persons admitted to the courtroom.

Furthermore, art.93 §2 of the Constitution allows for an exception to the principle that the trial must be held in public in cases where publicity is deemed to cause prejudice to morals or to the private lives of the parties. Particularly, in case of rape, the public may be excluded if their presence might cause grievous suffering or defamation of the victim (art.330 CCP). Similarly, proceedings before juvenile courts are not held in public (law 3315/1955).

The so-called indirect publicity of trials via the press and mass media, which may lead to the exposure of the accused to TV- or radio- transmitted programmes, has been forbidden by law n°2145 of 1993.

### 4.4.2. *The principle of orality*

Whereas the pre-trial investigation takes place in secret and in writing, the trial is held orally, even if publicity is excluded. This rule enables the court to get information based on the direct contact with the evidence and to assess the personality of the accused. Thus, art.331 of the CCP provides that the trial must be held "live". The examination of a witness, as a rule, may not be replaced by reading the record of an earlier examination or by reading a written statement.

The *ratio legis* of the principle of orality is that the court may only rely on the evidence produced during the trial, *i.e.* on submissions which have been made orally before the judges and on documents which have been read out before the court. Any information in the *dossier* which was not read out during the trial may not to be taken into account. Violation of this rule may entail the nullity of the judgment.

### 4.4.3. *The principle of continuity*

According to the principle of continuity, the trial must be conducted without interruptions until the judgment is pronounced (art.339 §2 CCP). The presiding judge has the right to order interruption only in specific cases provided for by law, e.g. in the case of an insurmountable impediment, or when it is necessary to summon a witness. An ordinary trial may not be interrupted for more than five days. If, however, the trial lasts for more than one month, or in case of a felony, it may be interrupted for a period of 30 days (art.375 §2 CCP, as amended by art.1 Law 1952/91). This rule undermines the maxim of concentration and is the subject of repeated criticisms.

### 4.4.4. *The principle of unity (principle of continuous presence)*

The accused has the duty and right to attend the hearing (art.340 CCP). Moreover, it is obvious that the efficiency of the principle of orality relies upon the continuous presence of the same judges, so that they can have a personal perception of the evidence and of the personality of the accused. Thus, if a trial is expected to last for a long time, an additional judge may join the court, in order to replace a colleague in case of impediment (art.6 §5 of the Statute on Judicial Organisation).

## 5. Coercive measures

### 5.1. ARREST

As a rule, a person can only be arrested if two conditions are met: the offence must reach a certain threshold of seriousness, and there must be a duly motivated warrant of arrest or a decision of the judicial council (art.276 CCP, *cfr.* art.6 of the Constitution).

If, however, the offender is caught in the act of committing a felony or a misdemeanour, he may be arrested without warrant by the public prosecutor. In the same circumstances, every citizen has the right to arrest the offender, save where the offence can only be prosecuted on complaint (art.275 CCP). A suspect who does not voluntarily appear before the investigating officer, may be compulsorily brought before him, even in the case of non-arrestable offences (art.272 CCP).

### 5.2. DETENTION ON REMAND AND OTHER RESTRICTIVE MEASURES

Detention on remand or other restrictions of personal liberty such as bail, periodical appearance of the accused before police authorities or the investigating judge or restrictions (e.g. prohibition of travelling abroad, of visiting certain places or staying in certain places, or of meeting certain persons) can be ordered by virtue of art.272 *et seq.* CCP).

These measures may be ordered by the investigating judge with the consent of the prosecutor or by the judicial council (arts.283 §1, 276 §2b CCP) in case of felonies or serious misdemeanours, and only when serious indications of guilt exist. Moreover, they should be "absolutely necessary" in order to prevent the perpetration of further offences, or if there are reasons to believe that the accused will flee. They may also be ordered if the accused is considered to be particularly dangerous (art.282 CCP).

Detention on remand is limited in time: it cannot exceed 18 months with regard to felonies and 9 months with regard to misdemeanours (art.287 CCP).

Detention on remand may be suspended or replaced by another restrictive measure by the investigating judge or the judicial council. If the trial is postponed, the trial court can also order the suspension of detention on remand or its conversion into another restrictive measure.

### 5.3. SEARCH AND SEIZURE

According to art.9 of the Constitution a person's home may only be searched in the presence of a judicial authority. If this search is carried out during the night, further conditions are required (art.254 CCP). It is expressly provided that publicity and disturbance must be avoided.

### 5.4. EXAMINATION OF BODY AND MIND

An examination of a person's body can be ordered only if it is absolutely necessary, without, however, insulting him. The examination of a woman's body must be carried out by another woman in the presence of the investigating officer (art.957 CCP).

The mental health of the accused may be examined in the form of an *expertise* ordered by the investigating judge or by the court. The accused can be ordered to stay in a psychiatric hospital for a period not exceeding six months (art.200 CCP).

## 5.3. INTERFERENCE WITH THE RIGHT TO PRIVACY

It is an offence under Greek law to record telephonic communications and even any other oral communication in general (except when such communication takes place in public) (art.370A and 370D Penal Code). Evidence obtained by means of intercepting protected communications must, in principle, be declared inadmissible by the court (art.31 §2 Law 1941/91).

However, art.19 of the Constitution, which protects the secrecy of correspondence and communication, provides for the possibility of statutory exceptions. At present, legislative decree 792/1971 is still in force which permits the prosecutor or the investigating officers to violate the secrecy of correspondence and telecommunications, provided the investigating judge consents. The same rights exists, according to art.11 of Law 1910/90 with regard to acts of terrorism. It remains, however, controversial whether unlawfully obtained evidence is admissible if a ground of justification provided for by the penal code exists.

# 6. The ordinary course of criminal proceedings

## 6.1. THE PRE-TRIAL STAGE

According to art.43 and 46 CCP, the public prosecutor is obliged to prosecute the case as soon as it has been reported to him, whether by the police, or by a citizen, or by the victim-*partie civile*, or by an official report issued by another authority.

Depending on the circumstances of the case, he has three different options: he may order an investigation (either an "ordinary" investigation or a "summary" investigation, see below), he may summon the accused directly before the trial court, or he may proceed to a preliminary inquiry, in order to find out whether formulating a charge against the accused is appropriate.

The purpose of the *investigation* is to collect the evidence that is necessary to allow the prosecutor or the judicial council to decide whether there is a *prima facie* case against the accused (art.239 CCP).

An *ordinary investigation* is compulsory when the offence is a felony or a misdemeanour with regard to which detention on remand can be ordered. The ordinary investigation is a preliminary judicial investigation, carried out by the *investigating judge*. The investigating judge is obliged to examine the case and to carry out all investigations necessary for the discovery of the truth, e.g. the collection of information, the examination of witnesses, the hearing of the accused, investigations on the spot, ordering an expertise, etc. The investigating judge is restricted by the mandate of the public prosecutor, as described in the investigation request: whereas he may conduct his investigations freely, he may only investigate the offence mentioned in the investigation request. He may collect evidence with respect to the suspect and to all potential co-authors and accomplices, but not with respect to offences, even related offences, other than the one(s) mentioned in the request.

*Summary investigation* is ordered by the prosecutor in the case of minor misdemeanours, and is carried out by general or specialised investigating officers, such as petty offences judges, police officers, harbour police officers, etc. Summary investigations can also be done by the public prosecutor himself.

The case can be sent directly to *the trial court* in the case of petty offences or misdemeanours caught in the act. The same possibility exists if there has been no formal investigation, but only a preliminary inquiry.

6.2. THE TERMINATION OF THE INVESTIGATION AND THE COMMITTAL PROCEEDINGS

There is a difference according to whether the investigation was a summary or an ordinary investigation.

A *summary investigation* is terminated as follows: after the collection of the evidence is completed, the competent investigating officer transmits the file to the public prosecutor who may either send the case directly to the trial court or, if he believes that the evidence against the accused is not sufficient, request the accused's acquittal before the judicial council. He may also order an ordinary investigation if he finds that the summary investigation needs completion (art.245 CCP).

An *ordinary investigation* can only be concluded on the condition that the investigating judge has interrogated the accused, unless the latter has not appeared, after having been duly summoned (art.270 CCP). In principle, an ordinary investigation can only be formally concluded by the first instance judicial council which is, as a rule, the sole competent authority to terminate the ordinary investigation. If, however, the offence is a misdemeanour, the prosecutor may refer the case directly to the trial court. Likewise, if the investigation concerns a felony with regard to which sufficient evidence exists, the file may be referred directly to the second instance judicial council, which decides irrevocably (art.308 CCP).

The judicial council may either acquit the accused or order his committal to the trial court. It may also order that the investigation should be completed.

6.3. THE TRIAL

The "main procedure" or trial is divided into the preparatory proceedings and the public procedure before the trial court.

### 6.3.1. The preparatory stage

The *preparatory stage* consists of all judicial acts concerning the summoning of the accused: the prosecutor sends him either the decision of the judicial council accompanied by a simple citation, or a summons to appear directly in the trial court. In this case, the summons contains the charge, including a detailed description of the facts and the applicable articles of the Penal Code (art.321 CCP).

In both cases the trial court is bound by the committal order of the judicial council or the charge in the prosecutor's summons as far as the facts are concerned: the charge may not be changed, and the accused cannot be convicted on a different factual basis. For example, an accused charged with murder could not be convicted of larceny.

### 6.3.2. The hearing

The hearing begins with the call of the case. The presiding judge ascertains whether the accused, defence counsel and the summoned witnesses are present.

The presiding judge conducts the trial, examines the witnesses and the accused and takes the evidence. He authorises the assessors, the prosecutor and the parties and their counsel to put questions. The presiding judge may forbid questions and interrupt the prosecutor and the parties when they go beyond the case (art.333-335 CCP). It is possible to object to the rulings of the presiding judge regarding the conduct of the trial.

The Code of Criminal Procedure provides that the presiding judge must examine the accused concerning his personal circumstances (art.342 CCP) and inform him about his rights. Then the prosecutor briefly communicates the charges and the presiding judge asks the accused general information about the offence, reminding him that he will state his defence after the taking of evidence is concluded (art.343 CCP). Thereafter, he starts with the taking of the evidence. The *witnesses* are ordered to leave the court room. They are then summoned back individually to testify, without the presence of the other witnesses (art.350 CCP). After the examination of the witnesses, the reports of *experts* are read out and the experts themselves may be summoned in order to give clarifications on their reports. Written reports and other documents must be read aloud (art.364 CCP), according to the principle of orality (*supra*, 4.4.2.).

Witnesses and experts are examined not only by the presiding judge but also by the assessors, the prosecutor, the counsel of the *partie civile* and the counsel of the accused (art.357 CCP).

Thereafter the accused presents his defence. The presiding judge, the assessors and the prosecutor may ask questions.

Thereafter the civilly responsible person (see *supra*,3.2.2.) is examined (art.367 CCP).

When the taking of the evidence is concluded, the prosecutor and the parties have the right to speak. The accused is always entitled to have the last word.

Finally, the court deliberates *in camera* on the issue of the guilt and pronounces its judgment in public. If the accused is found guilty, the prosecutor and the accused intervene on the issue of the penalties, other measures that the court may order and of the claims of the *partie civile* (art.371 CCP). The sentence is pronounced in public. If there is a dissenting opinion, this must be contained in the written judgment (art.35 Law 184/75). In practice, it is very rare for the trial court to read out the grounds of the sentence when it is pronounced.

## 7. Evidence

See *supra*, 4.3.

## 8. Special forms of procedure

### 8.1. TRIAL *IN ABSENTIA*

The accused must appear in person before the court (art.340 CCP). If he is absent, the trial proceeds as if he were present, unless he has not been duly summoned. This applies not only with regard to misdemeanours (art.340 §3 CCP), but also in case of felonies (art.432 §2 as amended by statute 1941/91). If the offence, however, is a misdemeanour, an accused who has been sentenced *in absentia* has the right to ask for the annulment of the judgment on the grounds that he has not been legally summoned (art.430 CCP). In case of a felony he may be retried if he is arrested or appears voluntarily.

### 8.2. JUVENILE COURTS

Offences committed by children and adolescents, *i.e.* by persons aged 7-12 and 17 years respectively, are brought before *the Juvenile Court*. It is competent to try even offences which would be qualified felonies if committed by an adult. The *three-member Juvenile Court* decides on offences which are punishable by confinement in a Reformative Institution for at least five years. As far as other offences are concerned, the *one-member Juvenile Court* is competent (art.113 CCP).

### 8.3. OFFENCES COMMITTED BY THE PRESIDENT OR BY GOVERNMENT MEMBERS

*The Special Court* (art.86 of the Constitution) is competent try high treason and violation of the constitution committed by the President of the Republic. It can try offences committed by the Members of the Government according to art.1-5 of the legislative decree 802/1971.

8.4. PLEA BARGAINING AND TRANSACTION

Since most offences are prosecuted ex officio, *plea bargaining* is, in principle, not admitted. *Transaction* is permitted in a few cases only, *i.e.* with regard to tax-evasion and smuggling (art.103 of Law 1165/1918) etc.

8.5. SUMMARY PROCEEDINGS

*Summary proceedings* are used in cases of petty offences that are identified by a competent authority (art.414 CCP) and in cases of misdemeanours or petty offences when the accused has been caught in the act (art.409 *et seq.* and 417 *et seq.* CCP).

In summary proceedings, the accused is brought without delay before the competent prosecutor, who sends him directly to the trial court on the same day. The accused, however, has the right to request a delay of three days in order to prepare his defence. In this case the court decides on the continuation of the accused's detention (art.423 CCP).

# 9. Remedies

9.1. GENERAL PRINCIPLES

The main remedies are appeal and *cassation*. Their filing has the following effects:

*Extension*: in case of connexity or complicity, the effects of the remedy filed by one of the defendants are also extended to the defendants who have not filed it (art.469 CCP).

*Suspension*: if an appeal or cassation is filed, the decision or judgment against which it is filed cannot be executed, except in the case of detention on remand. However, when the accused has been convicted by the mixed criminal court or by the court of appeal, his appeal does not suspend the execution of the sentence unless the court, on his request, renders a specific decision in this respect (art.497 §6, 7 *et seq.*). The same applies with regard to *cassation* if imprisonment has been imposed (art.471 CCP).

*Devolution*: the filing of a remedy submits the case to a court which is hierarchically superior to the court against whose judgment the remedy is filed.

*Prohibition of the reformatio in peius*. The legal position of the accused cannot be worsened if he alone has lodged the appeal. If, however, the other parties have also appealed against the judgment, the appellate court may impose a higher or an additional penalty or a security measure (art.470 CCP).

*Time limit*: as a rule, appeals should be lodged within ten days after the pronunciation of the judgment or the communication of the decision of the judicial council. *Cassation* should be filed by the defendant within twenty days after the pronunciation of the decision.

## 9.2. APPEAL

In case of an *appeal*, the court re-examines the entire case in fact and law and passes a new judgment which replaces that of the judgment rendered by the court of first instance. The procedure to be applied is the same as before the former court.

Appeal may be filed by the defendant, the *partie civile* and the prosecutor. The defendant has the right to use this remedy if he has been sentenced by the three-member misdemeanour court to a custodial sentence exceeding three months or by the one member misdemeanour court to imprisonment for more than 30 days. In the case of a decision of the three-member court of appeal or of the mixed criminal court, the defendant has the right to appeal only if he has been sentenced to imprisonment for a period exceeding two years.

Decisions of the judicial council, however, are only open to appeal, as far as the accused is concerned, if he is committed for trial for an offence punished by imprisonment exceeding one year (art.478 CCP). in contrast, the *partie civile* may appeal against any decision of the judicial council in which it acquits the accused (art.480 CCP).

## 9.3. *CASSATION*

The accused and the prosecutor have the right to file a plea in *cassation* . This remedy can be used with regard to both a decision of the judicial council and a judgment of the trial court. The *partie civile* has the same right, but only to a limited extent. The Attorney-General of the Supreme Court has the right to ask for the annulment of any judgment.

The plea of nullity may be based only on certain reasons such as absolute or relative nullity of an act which has taken place in court, lack of reasons, violation of the provisions concerning publicity or the competence of the court, incorrect application or interpretation of a substantive criminal provision, violation of the *res judicata*-principle, violation of the provisions concerning jurisdiction, etc. Some of the aforementioned reasons are examined *ex officio* by the Supreme Court. If the plea is sustained, the court annuls the judgment and sends the case to the same court in order to have it re-tried by other judges. However, in the case of erroneous application of the law, the Supreme Court applies the provision correctly and it may, e.g. decide to acquit the accused (art.518 CCP).

## 9.4. *CASSATION* TO REVISE A FINAL JUDGMENT

Reopening a case is, strictly speaking, not a remedy but an extraordinary procedure which may take place after a judgment has become final, if new facts render the conviction obviously erroneous (art.525 *et seq.* CCP). For example, a case can be reopened if new and hitherto unknown evidence has been disclosed, if a person was convicted on the basis of false testimony, if the accused has already been acquitted by another court, etc. Applications aiming at the reopening of the case are very rarely sustained by the Supreme Court. Convicted persons tend to prefer the procedure of pardon (art.567 CCP) which may be granted by the President of the Republic after the opinion of the Council of Pardon.

## 10. Select bibliography

ANDROULAKIS, N., *Fundamental Concepts of the Penal Process*, fasc 1-4, Athens-Komotini (1972-1991)

BOUROPOULOS, A., *Commentary of the Code of Penal Procedure*, vols I-II, 2nd ed, Athens (1957)

DEDESS, C., *Penal Procedure*, 8th ed, Athens (1988)

GAFOS, I., *Penal Procedure*, fasc 1-3 (1966-1967)

KARRAS, A., *Lectures on Penal Procedural Law*, fasc 1-3, 3rd ed, Athens-Komotini (1990)

TSOUKALAS, K., *Penal Procedure*, vols I-II (1943-1947)

ZISSIADIS, I., *Penal Procedure*, vols I-III, 3rd ed, Thessaloniki-Athens (1976-1977)

# Chapter 7 - Ireland

Finbarr **McAULEY**
and
John **O'DOWD**
Law Faculty
University College Dublin

## 1. Sources

### 1.1. GENERAL REMARKS.

The common law is the residual source of Irish criminal procedure and the historical origin of basic constitutional rights such as trial by jury and freedom from arbitrary searches and arrests. Yet many of the original features of the common law would now be regarded as inconsistent with modern conceptions of procedural justice. For example, an accused could not be legally represented in cases of felony until 1837 nor testify in his own defence in any case until 1924. This situation was in practice ameliorated by the role of the jury, in particular, by its right to return a general verdict, and by the prerogative of pardon.

Although greatly modified by legislation since the Act of Union (1800), Irish common law remains a more significant source of criminal procedure than its English counterpart, the more so because the relevant legislation has often been ad hoc and piecemeal. The Constitution has also profoundly influenced the law of criminal procedure. Some common law rules have been held not to have survived the enactment of the Constitution, and many such rules, abrogated by statute before 1937, would probably have suffered the same fate.

### 1.2. THE CONSTITUTION.

The Constitution is the fundamental law of the State: any rule of common law, any statute in force in 1937 or any Act of the *Oireachtas* (the Irish Parliament) is devoid of legal effect to the extent that it has been held to be inconsistent with the Constitution. Many Articles of the Constitution have a bearing on the law of criminal procedure, viz., Art. 38 (trial of offences), Art. 34 (courts), Art. 40.3 (personal rights), Art. 40.1 (equality), Art. 30 (prosecution of offences). In interpreting the Constitution our courts have been greatly influenced by decisions of the United States Supreme Court and occasionally consider the law of other Member States and the provisions of international conventions.

## 1.3. LEGISLATION

There are many statutes dealing with criminal procedure. These vary greatly in date and mode of expression. One of the most striking features of our criminal law is the survival of a large body of Victorian, and, indeed, pre-Victorian statutes. For example, the Statute of Northampton (1328) (2 Edw. 3, c.3) remained part of our law until 1983!) A statute passed since 1937 must, where possible, be interpreted so as to be consistent with the Constitution.

Many important rules of criminal procedure are to be found in subordinate legislation. A statutory instrument dealing with court practice and procedure may not, however, substantially amend a statutory provision, nor may a statute delegate the power to make laws for the State, a power which the Constitution reserves for the *Oireachtas*.

Important statutes are: the Offences against the State Act of 1939 (hereinafter referred to as the "1939 Act"), the Criminal Procedure Act of 1967 (hereinafter referred to as the "1967 Act") and the Criminal Justice Act of 1984 (hereinafter referred to as the "1984 Act").

## 1.4. THE COMMON LAW

The common law is now mainly of relevance to the law of evidence rather than to the law of criminal procedure. Irish common law is derived from that of England, but many features once common to the law of the two countries, such as the distinction between felonies and misdemeanours, have been abrogated by statute in England; English authorities are, however, still frequently cited. The courts have considerable scope to develop the common law and on occasion do so along different lines to those taken in England, often favouring authorities from other common law countries.

## 1.5. THE EUROPEAN CONVENTION ON HUMAN RIGHTS

The Convention has not been incorporated into domestic law by an Act of the *Oireachtas*. Article 29.6 of the Constitution provides that international agreements shall be part of domestic law only where the *Oireachtas* so determines. Thus, our courts have refused to give any direct effect to the provisions of the Convention; but it is accepted that domestic legislation should, where possible, be construed so as not to involve the State in a breach of its obligations under the Convention.

## 1.6. LEGAL DOCTRINE AND LAW REFORM

Legal doctrine is enunciated by the courts and not by academic commentators; the main task of the latter is critically to evaluate the work of the judges. Oral argument in court is vital to the development of the law and judges respond most readily to arguments couched in terms familiar to the practising Bar. The citation of academic texts has, however, become more common. Academics thus influence judges through their writings and also often press for legislative reform of the law.

## 2. Structure of the criminal justice system

### 2.1. INVESTIGATING AUTHORITIES

#### 2.1.1. Garda Síochána

The *Garda* Síochána is the only police force in the State. All the powers exercisable at common law by a "constable" may be exercised by a *Garda* by virtue of his office. There are no specialised police forces, such as border or transport police. Other State agencies - such as officers of Customs and Excise - do, however, exercise important functions in preventing and detecting particular kinds of crime and have important and far-reaching powers of search, detention and interrogation.

Criminal proceedings normally follow a *Garda* investigation, often originating with a complaint from a victim of crime. There seems to be no general duty to report a crime to the *Gardaí* or to assist their inquiries. Nevertheless, concealment of the commission of a felony is an offence, as is a conspiracy to conceal the commission of any crime. The *Gardaí* may require a person in custody under the 1939 Act to give a full account of their movements and any information in their possession in relation to certain types of offences; the *Gardaí* have similar powers in relation to persons not in custody. It is an offence either to knowingly make a false report or gives false information to a *Garda* in connection with a criminal investigation.

All members of the *Garda Síochána* in the exercise of their duties are completely independent of the *Director of Public Prosecutions* (henceforth the "the D.P.P."), just as he is completely independent of them. The *Garda Síochána*'s function is to detect, record and investigate offences. *Gardaí* normally prosecute summary offences in the District Court, but in relation to indictable offences they investigate, gather evidence and attempt to identify and apprehend suspects. In most cases the *Gardaí* initially charge a person with an offence without reference to the Director of Public Prosecutions but they may inform the D.P.P. of their investigations and seek his "direction" as to whether or not to charge a suspect.

The *Gardaí* ultimately refer all indictable cases to the D.P.P. for a decision as to whether proceedings should be started or continued. He examines the evidence gathered by the *Gardaí* to assess if a prosecution should be brought and which charge(s) to prefer. Although the D.P.P. has no direct investigative function, he may require the *Gardaí* to seek further evidence which he considers necessary or desirable for a successful prosecution.

## 2.2. PROSECUTING AUTHORITIES

### 2.2.1. *Summary prosecutions*

In general, any person ("a common informer") may make a complaint to a District Judge in relation to a summary offence. This right may, however, be excluded by reason of the nature of the offence or by an express or implied statutory provision. Only the D.P.P., a *Garda* or a person specifically authorised by statute to prosecute may apply for a summons under the Courts (No.3) Act, 1986.

The D.P.P. may always initiate a summary prosecution - except where one has already been lawfully initiated. Moreover, a *Garda* may prosecute in the name of the D.P.P. without any specific authority to do so.

### 2.2.2. *Prosecution on indictment*

All crimes and offences prosecuted in any court, other than special court or a court of summary jurisdiction, must be prosecuted in the name of the People and at the suit of the Attorney General or of some other person authorised in accordance with law. Statute now effectively provides that the D.P.P. should be the sole prosecutor on indictment in ordinary criminal matters.

### 2.2.3. *The office of Director of Public Prosecutions*

The Director of Public Prosecutions (D.P.P.) is a civil servant appointed by the Government after an elaborate nomination process and who is free of party political or other influence. The D.P.P. is responsible for the selection of counsel and all other aspects of the conduct of a prosecution. The D.P.P. retains counsel in private practice on a case by case basis. Counsel engaged by the D.P.P. do not exclusively specialise in the prosecution of criminal cases; many have a civil practice and many regularly appear as defence counsel in criminal cases.

### 2.2.4. *Other prosecuting authorities*

Statutes provide for the prosecution of specified offences by persons other than the D.P.P. There is normally no need to obtain prior judicial authority before commencing a prosecution on indictment.

## 2.3. THE JUDICIARY

### 2.3.1. *General*

The District Court, the Circuit Court, the Central Criminal Court, the Court of Criminal Appeal, the Supreme Court and the Special Criminal Court all deal with criminal matters. Legally qualified judges preside in all criminal courts.

### (i) The District Court
The District Court has a local and limited jurisdiction. The main elements of its criminal jurisdiction are the summary trial of offences, the preliminary examination of indictable offences and the administration of the bail system.

### (ii) The Circuit Court
The Circuit Court is also a court of local and limited jurisdiction. The main elements of its criminal jurisdiction are the hearing of appeals from trials in the District Court and the trial of indictable offences with a jury.

### (iii) The Central Criminal Court
The Central Criminal Court is the name given to the High Court when it is exercising a criminal jurisdiction, the main aspect of which is to try offences on indictment with a jury. This jurisdiction, which is limited to certain grave offences, extends throughout the State. The Court sits in Dublin with a Dublin jury.

### (iv) The Special Criminal Court
The functions and composition of this Court are discussed below (8.2.2.).

### (v) The Court of Criminal Appeal
The functions and composition of this Court are discussed below (9.1.2.(i)).

### (vi) The Supreme Court
The Supreme Court is the court of final appeal and, subject to statutory exceptions, has appellate jurisdiction from all decisions of the High Court. It hears appeals from the Court of Criminal Appeal where that court confirms a conviction and it is certified that a question of law of exceptional public importance arises.

## 2.3.2. Competence

Apart from those tried in the District Court, offences are tried on indictment, either with a jury (the Circuit and Central Criminal Courts) or without one (the Special Criminal Court). The Constitution requires trial with a jury in all cases except those involving minor offences. Only minor offences may be tried summarily.

The main criterion for classifying an offence as minor is the severity of penalty, but some offences, such as murder, may be of such moral gravity that they can never be treated as minor. The general upper limits for the penalties appropriate to a minor offence seem to be six to nine months' imprisonment and a fine of several thousand pounds.

### 2.3.3. The nomination of judges

Only practising lawyers are appointed as judges; both barristers and solicitors may be appointed District Judges; but only barristers can be appointed to other judgeships. Judges are independent in the exercise of their functions. All Judges hear both civil and criminal matters and almost always sit alone - a single judge, for example, presides over all trials with a jury. In general, judges only sit en banc in the Court of Criminal Appeal and in the Supreme Court.

### 2.3.4. The role of lay judges

The jury remains of cardinal importance in our criminal process. Its composition and function are governed by the Constitution, by common law and by the Juries Act, 1976. The Constitution requires that a jury be a randomly selected cross-section of the adult community, in particular without distinction of sex. Since 1984, a jury may reach a verdict by a 10-2 or 10-1 majority.

The relationship of judge and jury is crucial to the criminal trial. Questions of fact are for the jury to decide and questions of law for the judge. Thus, the jury must be excluded from the trial while the judge determines the admissibility of evidence (the voir dire). Conversely, the judge is excluded from the jury's deliberations, which are strictly confidential. Moreover, a jury need not give reasons for its verdict.

## 3. Parties to criminal proceedings

### 3.1. THE PROSECUTOR

The prosecutor's duty is not to strive for a conviction at all costs but to lay before the court all the relevant facts known to him and to ensure that the court correctly applies the law, even if this favours the accused. He should inform the defence of any information favourable to the accused and furnish it on request. He should not seek the imposition of any particular penalty, but should impartially lay all matters relevant to sentence before the court.

### 3.2. THE ACCUSED

### 3.2.1. General

The accused has the benefit of the presumption of innocence, of a range of constitutional guarantees (see 3.2.2. infra), and of rules designed to prevent the introduction of unduly prejudicial evidence. Some of these protections, principally the right of silence, have been strongly criticised by the police and prosecutors in recent years.

### 3.2.2. Constitutional rights

Under the rubric of "due course of law," the Constitution guarantees an accused important rights in connection with the conduct of criminal proceedings. These include the right:
(a) to be heard in his own defence;
(b) to be legally represented;
(c) to a speedy trial;
(d) to notice of the charges against him;
(e) to an impartial adjudication;
(f) not to be placed in double jeopardy;
(g) to be tried and sentenced in public;
(h) not to be compelled to incriminate himself;
(i) to have evidence obtained as a result of a breach of his constitutional rights excluded;
(j) to have the case against him fairly prosecuted.
    Other rights - such as the right to confront witnesses - may be latent in the concept of "due course of law."

### 3.2.3. Fair hearing

The Constitution gives any person whose good name is seriously impugned in any proceedings the right to an effective defence, including the right to a copy of the evidence against him, to cross-examine his accusers, to give rebutting evidence and to be represented by counsel. An accused also has the right to present relevant evidence, and to an adequate opportunity to prepare a defence.
    The rule that an accused may not be tried *in absentia*, though fundamental, is not absolute, provided the essentials of justice are observed - as where he is disorderly or where he voluntarily absents herself. The court must have special concern for the rights of an absent defendant.

### 3.2.4. Defences

There is no burden on the accused to prove any affirmative case (except for the defence of insanity); he need only leave the jury in reasonable doubt as to whether the People have proved his guilt. He must, however, give or refer to evidence from which the jury could reasonably conclude that an asserted ground of defence might exist. Even if a jury rejects an accused's evidence it must still consider whether all the evidence proves his guilt beyond a reasonable doubt.

### 3.2.5. The accused's testimony

Until 1924 neither the accused nor his spouse could testify. The Criminal Justice (Evidence) Act, 1924 gave the accused the right either to testify or not and (subject to qualifications) to prevent him spouse from doing so. Safeguards for the accused were included, principally a prohibition on comment by the prosecution on his failure to testify. The prosecution cannot introduce evidence of the accused's prior convictions in order to impeach his character, unless certain conditions are satisfied.

### 3.2.6. Legal representation

A suspect or accused has a constitutional right to reasonable access to his legal advisers at all stages and to engage a lawyer to conduct his defence. An indigent person has no constitutional right to a lawyer at public expense in all cases, but fair procedures may often so require.

A person under interrogation has a constitutional right to consult a solicitor and to have unimpeded access to one, in order to enable him to make an informed decision whether or not to make a statement, thus helping to redress the inequality between a suspect and his interrogators. It seems a suspect can require questioning to be suspended until after he has consulted her solicitor. It has been held that the *Gardaí* are under no general duty to provide a lawyer for a person under interrogation or to inform him of his right to one. The latter holding has been doubted and the question appears to be an open one.

An accused who cannot afford his own lawyers can obtain legal aid in respect of each stage of a prosecution from his first remand onwards. The decision whether to grant legal aid is made by the appropriate court upon the accused's application. It must appear to the Court that the applicant's means are insufficient to enable him to obtain legal aid and that by reason of the gravity of the offence or of exceptional circumstances it is essential in the interests of justice that he should have legal aid.

### 3.3. THE VICTIM

Traditionally, the victim of a crime has had no standing in criminal proceedings. A victim has a right to make a complaint to a District Judge of the commission of an offence, but only in the case of summary offences may he prosecute to a final conclusion without the cooperation of the D.P.P. Nor can the victim prevent the entry of a *nolle prosequi*.

In general, a victim is not entitled to legal representation at a criminal trial arising out of his complaint. His main role is as a prosecution witness. However, in conjunction with the passing of the Criminal Law (Rape) Act 1990 the Minister for Justice announced that alleged victims of rape and serious sexual assaults would be given legal aid to retain lawyers to defend their interests in relation to the trial of their alleged attackers.

## 4. General principles concerning criminal procedure

4.1. GENERAL PRINCIPLES

### 4.1.1. Accusatorial criminal procedure

The Irish system is accusatorial: a person is accused of an offence, disputes the accusation and a court decides whether the accuser has adduced enough evidence to justify a conviction.

The Constitution guarantees that a person may be convicted only of offences whose elements have been specified with sufficient precision for him to make a proper defence. Equally, the presumption of innocence is not merely procedural or evidentiary, but gives an accused a constitutional right to be treated as innocent until proven guilty.

### 4.1.2. The burden of proof

The prosecution must prove beyond reasonable doubt that the accused is guilty of the charges against him. "Reasonable doubt" is not a technical concept, but should be contrasted with the proof on the balance of probabilities required in civil proceedings.

The presumption of innocence is an aspect of the "due course of law" guaranteed by Art. 38.1. of the Constitution. There are, however, statutes which, in different ways, place the burden of proof on an accused in certain specified circumstances.

### 4.1.3. Impartiality

An accused has a constitutional right to be tried by an impartial tribunal. This accords with the common law maxim *nemo iudex in causa sua*. Similar impartiality is required of judges and prosecutors.

### 4.1.4. Publicity

At common law the public were entitled to be admitted to any trial on indictment. The Constitution requires that justice be administered in public, save in such special and limited cases as may be provided for by law; the public may be excluded only where a public hearing would lead to a denial of justice.

### 4.1.5. Fair procedures

An accused is entitled to have the prosecution against him conducted fairly. A prosecutor may not discontinue a prosecution solely to avoid the consequences of an unfavourable judicial ruling; nor bring separate prosecutions or delay prosecution in order to harass the accused and subject him to successive rather than concurrent sentences. Evidence relevant to an accused's guilt or innocence must, so far as is necessary and practicable, be preserved until the end of his trial.

## 4.2. PRINCIPLES GOVERNING THE OPENING OF CRIMINAL PROCEEDINGS

### 4.2.1. Expedition

Statute generally requires that a prosecution for a summary offence must be initiated within six months of the cause of complaint. In relation to almost all indictable offences there is no time limit for the bringing of a prosecution.

An accused has a constitutional right to be tried, whether summarily or on indictment, without undue delay and may thereby be able to prevent his trial from proceeding. What is "undue" delay must be determined in the light of the circumstances of each case. The prosecution must show some cause for delay other than mere administrative inefficiency, but the court will take into account delay caused by the accused. It seems an accused must show that he has been prejudiced by the delay (for example, by losing the opportunity to present evidence in his defence). Delay is particularly serious where an accused is detained on remand and may result in release on bail.

The requirement of reasonable expedition applies primarily to prosecutions already initiated - delay between the date of the alleged offence and the charge will only bar proceedings where there has been an inexcusable failure to prosecute.

### 4.2.2. Prosecutorial discretion

The D.P.P. has sole responsibility for prosecuting criminal proceedings he institutes; the courts cannot compel him to initiate or to continue any prosecution. He is not obliged to, and does not normally, give reasons for a decision to prosecute or not to prosecute. However, it seems that the adoption by the D.P.P. of a policy not to prosecute a certain type of offence would be unlawful.

A prosecution may be discontinued by a *nolle prosequi* which the D.P.P. may enter for various reasons (inadequate evidence, a "bargain" with the accused to plead guilty to other charges etc.). A *nolle prosequi* is not a bar to fresh proceedings, but this common law principle is qualified by the Constitutional requirement of fairness.

The D.P.P. is generally exempt from judicial review in relation to discretionary decisions concerning prosecutions, unless it is shown that he acted mala fide or was influenced by an improper motive or policy. The courts recognise that the existence of probative evidence is not the only factor in prosecutorial decisions: matters such as the relative seriousness of the offence and the resources available to the *Gardaí*, may be considered.

## 4.3. PRINCIPLES GOVERNING THE PRE-TRIAL PHASE

### 4.3.1. Constitutional principles

All measures authorised by law to secure the due administration of justice - whether by preventing the flight of the accused, interference with evidence or the concealment of the proceeds of crime - must respect the constitutional presumption of innocence and the requirements of fair procedures, particularly where a restriction on personal liberty is concerned.

### 4.3.2. Disclosure and discovery

The accused's constitutional right to advance notice of the case against him is given legislative effect in relation to indictable offences by the Criminal Procedure Act, 1967. Under this Act he may insist on a preliminary examination by a District Judge to determine the sufficiency of the People's case. In all prosecutions on indictment the People must, before the trial, serve on the accused statements of the evidence which it is intended each prosecution witness will give together with any exhibits. The People may not introduce any evidence of which notice has not been given to the accused in this manner. The absence of more detailed discovery, however, limits an accused's opportunity to assess the process by which the People's case, presented in the Book of Evidence, has been assembled. A summary trial may, in exceptional cases, be enjoined pending disclosure of the prosecution case to the accused.

## 4.4. PRINCIPLES GOVERNING THE TRIAL

### 4.4.1. Scope of trial

Since our system is accusatorial the court must accept the limits which the parties impose on the issues and on the evidence. The court must convict an accused who pleads guilty, although such a plea may, in exceptional cases, be set aside on appeal. Similarly, the court can neither refuse to accept a *nolle prosequi* nor object to the prosecution's failure to make a case against an unindicted accomplice of the accused.

Equally, the right of the judge to question witnesses is limited and may not be employed so as to prejudice either side.

### 4.4.2. Oral evidence

At common law all evidence in a trial must be given by oral testimony on oath. Secondary evidence such as written or verbal admissions by the accused or exhibits must be proved by oral evidence. A trial on indictment proceeds by way of viva voce examination of witnesses conducted by counsel. Counsel decide what witnesses should be called and what legal submissions should be made to support the case being argued.

A judge's participation in the questioning of witnesses is kept to the barest minimum: a fortiori, the jury plays hardly any role in this. There is thus no systematic, disinterested interrogation of witnesses.

### 4.4.3. Unity of trial

A trial on indictment should as far as possible be continuous; an adjournment of more than a few days in the course of a trial may render a conviction unsafe. The unitary nature of a criminal trial is also emphasised by decisions which establish that, in principle, every issue relating to the accused's guilt or innocence must be determined at a single trial.

### 4.4.4. Judge and jury

The functions of a judge in a trial on indictment are:
a) to ensure that counsel observe proper procedure, particularly when examining witnesses; b) to rule on the admissibility of evidence before it can be presented to the jury; c) to make binding rulings as to the correct interpretation of the law; d) to deliver a speech to the jury indicating the correct interpretation of the law and giving a summary of the case made by each side and, e) in the event of a conviction, to pass sentence.

Even where an accused is tried without a jury, the judge must avoid all semblance of partiality, and in particular, of appearing to assist the prosecution; if he fails to do so, this is a grave defect in the trial. The judge's proper role is that of an impartial umpire intervening only to control a witness or to clarify an ambiguity. He may question witnesses, but must not thereby impede the presentation of either side's case. The judge may, very rarely, call a witness not called by either party.

The function of the jury is to consider the evidence given at the trial and to decide disputed issues of fact. The active participation of the jury in the conduct of a trial is minimal. The jury may put questions to witnesses and have a witness recalled to give further evidence after its retirement, but these rights are rarely exercised.

### 4.4.5. Nature of verdict

A jury can always return a special verdict, but invariably returns a general one of "guilty", "not guilty" or one of "guilty but insane". Such verdicts are not accompanied by any statement of findings of fact or of reasons; it is often impossible to determine the basis of a verdict, particularly of an acquittal which might often have been reached in several different and inconsistent ways.

## 5. Coercive Measures

A distinction must be drawn between measures intended to secure an accused's amenability to the process of criminal justice and those intended to facilitate the gathering of evidence.

### 5.1. ARREST

### 5.1.1. Purposes of arrest

A citizen may be deprived of his personal liberty only in accordance with law. The only lawful purposes of arrest are either to secure the appearance of the person in court or to detain him under s.30 of the 1939 Act. An actual deprivation of personal liberty for any other purpose (even to safeguard the life of the detainee) is unlawful; unless it is intended to protect the right to life of a victim in peril. Evidence obtained as a result of an unlawful arrest or of unlawful detention after a lawful arrest is prima facie inadmissible.

### 5.1.2. Identification of suspects

A person detained under the 1939 Act or the 1984 Act can be required to give his true name and address; failure to do so is a criminal offence. A senior *Garda* officer may authorise the taking of palm and fingerprints from, and the photographing of, suspects in custody under the 1939 Act and the 1984 Act.

A person can be arrested for the purpose of being identified by a witness only under the 1939 Act, s. 30 and a suspect may not be compelled to take part in an identification parade. There are detailed rules governing the proper conduct of such parades and where one has not been held the judge must draw the jury's attention to the serious nature of the omission; informal identifications must be treated with great caution.

### 5.1.3. Arrest without warrant at common law

Every adult is under a duty to attempt to arrest a person committing treason or felony in his presence and has power to arrest a person committing or about to commit a breach of the peace. Where anyone reasonably suspects that a felony has been committed he is entitled to arrest the suspect or to require a *Garda* to do so (although a *Garda* has some discretion to refuse to do so.) An arrest by a private individual is unlawful if it is proved that no felony was committed. By contrast, provided he reasonably suspects that a felony has been committed, a *Garda* is not legally liable for a wrongful arrest. There is no common law power to arrest on suspicion of a misdemeanour (save in a case of breach of the peace) nor on suspicion of a summary offence.

### 5.1.4. Arrest without warrant under statute

Many statutes authorise arrest without a warrant on suspicion of particular offences. Such statutes contain a wide variety of differently defined powers of arrest and vary in date from 1831 to the present day. The modern tendency is to confine powers of arrest to members of the *Gardaí* or other public officials. Statutes conferring powers of arrest are normally construed restrictively. Modern statutes normally require a reasonable suspicion that a particular offence is being, has been, or (more rarely) is about to be, committed. In the case of the 1939 Act, s.30 only a bare suspicion is required for a valid arrest, but such suspicion must be genuinely held.

### 5.1.5. Arrest under warrant

Arrest under warrant is rare since the necessity for an arrest is not normally anticipated. The District Court has power to issue a warrant for the arrest of a person within its jurisdiction suspected of an indictable or a summary offence. The purpose of a warrant is to secure the accused's attendance in court; the Judge may decline to issue a warrant if a summons appears adequate for this purpose.

### 5.1.6. Investigative arrest and detention

At common law the only purpose for which a person can be arrested is to ensure his attendance in court. An arrest (*i.e.* any actual restraint on personal liberty) or a prolongation of detention intended solely to make a person available for questioning is unlawful at common law.

As soon as the *Gardaí* suspect that a person willingly assisting them with their inquiries has committed an offence they must inform him that he is free to terminate the interview and leave the place where he is; if they do not do so they may be considered to have detained him unlawfully unless he is lawfully arrested. Where a person has been arrested he must be brought before a court and charged as soon as possible; thereafter the police may not question him. However, a person may be detained for the purpose of investigating crime under the 1939 Act, s.30 and the 1984 Act, s.4.

The 1939 Act authorises a *Garda* to arrest any person whom he suspects of having committed, being about to commit or being or having been concerned in the commission of a "scheduled offence". Such a person may be detained for up to 24 hours (usually, but not always, for interrogation) and for a further period of twenty-four hours if so authorised in writing by a senior police officer. Detention may not be lawfully prolonged beyond forty eight hours and it seems that a person may not be arrested under s. 30 more than once in relation to the same matter.

Under the 1984 Act, s.4 the member in charge of a *Garda* station may order the detention of a person whom he suspects of having committed an offence the sentence for which is greater than five years' imprisonment where such detention will assist the investigation of crime. A person must be brought to a *Garda* station as soon as practicable after their arrest; otherwise detention cannot lawfully be authorised under the section. The initial period of detention is six hours; a further six hours may be authorised in the same way as under the 1939 Act. Questioning may be suspended at the detainee's request to allow for sleep and refreshment. A person may only be held in detention for a maximum of twenty hours. The 1984 Act provides no new power of arrest: only those validly arrested at common law or under statute may be detained. The Act thus relieves the *Gardaí* only of the duty to bring an arrested person before a court as soon as possible.

## 5.2. SEARCH AND SEIZURE

### 5.2.1. Premises

The Constitution proclaims the dwelling of the citizen to be inviolable and guarantees it against forcible entry save in accordance with law. A *Garda* may only enter premises (without the owner's express or implied consent) in order to execute an arrest or search warrant or where otherwise authorised by law. Common law allows anyone to enter a dwelling to terminate an affray or avert serious injury and allows a *Garda* to enter to arrest a felon, to execute an arrest warrant or avert a breach of the peace or the commission of an offence. Many statutes confer powers of forcible entry without warrant - any such power must, however, be strictly construed. A statutory power of arrest without warrant is not, in the absence of express provision, to be construed as conferring a power to enter private property in order to carry out an arrest.

### 5.2.2. Search warrants

A warrant authorises its addressees to search specified premises and seize specified property. At common law a warrant may only be issued for a search for stolen goods. However, many statutes provide for the issue of search warrants for particular purposes. There is statutory authority for searches for stolen goods, firearms and drugs, but not for the body of a murder victim or for a murder weapon. Warrants are usually issued by a District Judge or by a Peace Commissioner, but senior *Garda* officers are occasionally authorised to do so.

### 5.2.3. Persons and vehicles

A person may only be searched without his consent where this is authorised by law. At common law an arrested person may be searched and dangerous weapons or items of evidence seized. Such a search may extend to things in his custody at the time of arrest or in the place where he is arrested; the lawful scope of such searches is unclear.

Some statutes authorise the stopping and searching of persons and vehicles outside the context of an arrest; or provide that persons found to be present in the course of a search of premises may themselves be searched. A person detained under the 1939 Act may be searched and anything in his possession may be seized and retained for testing. A person detained under the 1984 Act may be searched in a similar manner; but he may be strip searched only where the presence of drugs or explosives is reasonably suspected and only on the authority of a senior officer. A customs official or *Garda* may detain and search any person or vehicle where he suspects with reasonable cause that a controlled drug is present; this can include a strip search and "an intimate body search".

### 5.3. EXAMINATION OF BODY AND MIND

Without specific statutory authority bodily searches (including X-rays) and the taking of forensic samples without a person's consent are unlawful. Some statutes authorise the taking of samples of bodily substances for forensic testing. However, force may not be used to obtain such samples; rather, a refusal to provide them is a criminal offence.

Where a suspect is in custody under the 1939 Act or the 1984 Act or is in prison a *Garda* may take samples of bodily substances - such as blood, saliva or nails, a swab from any part of the body, a dental impression or a footprint or similar impression for forensic testing. A sample may only be taken on the authority of a senior police officer and, in relation to blood, pubic hair, urine, saliva, or a swab from a bodily orifice or genital region or a dental impression, only with the written consent of the person concerned. The person must be told that the results of any tests may be used as evidence, that his consent is required for the taking of a sample and must be informed of the possible consequences of refusal; where consent is refused without good cause a court may draw such inferences from that refusal as appear proper and may treat it as corroborating other evidence, but not as the sole evidence of guilt.

### 5.4. INTERFERENCE WITH THE RIGHT TO PRIVACY

Surveillance (*e.g.* openly following a suspect in public places) is, ipso facto, neither a deprivation of personal liberty, nor a violation of the constitutional right to privacy; but it may be so intense that it requires justification to be lawful. Surveillance involving trespass or the use of concealed listening devices or other prima facie unlawful acts requires specific lawful authority. The tapping of a citizen's telephone or the interception of his mail without legal authority is a breach of the constitutional right to privacy for which damages may be recovered.

## 6. The ordinary course of proceedings

6.1. INITIATION

### 6.1.1. Charge

Criminal proceedings are formally initiated by bringing a person before a District Judge and making an oral complaint against him. In summary proceedings, proceedings may also be initiated by the issue of a summons by the District Court Office.

Where a person is arrested without warrant a number of courses of action are open to the *Gardaí*. Where they are satisfied that the person is innocent or that there is insufficient evidence against him he must be released without being brought before a court. Where the *Gardaí* intend to initiate proceedings there is a detailed procedure for informing the accused of the intention to charge him and for the recording of particulars of the charge. The accused should be given a chance to reply to the charge; any such reply should be recorded as evidence. The *Garda* in charge of a station may, in most cases, admit an accused to bail on condition that he appear in the District Court.

A person "charged" in a *Garda* station and not admitted to station bail must be brought before the District Court within a reasonable time. In the District Court a *Garda* makes an oral complaint to the Judge alleging that the accused has committed the offence set out in the charge sheet. He may then be remanded in custody or on bail.

6.2. THE POSITION OF THE ACCUSED PENDING TRIAL

### 6.2.1. Remand

An accused's case is rarely disposed of on his first appearance in the District Court; the Court may therefore remand an accused from time to time (*i.e.* adjourn his case). A District Judge may, upon sending the accused for trial or remanding him, commit him to prison or other lawful custody, or - except where bail may be granted by the High Court only - release him on bail. An accused may be remanded in custody for no longer than eight days on his first appearance and subsequently for no longer than thirty days with the consent of both parties. With the consent of both parties he may be remanded for any period on bail. An accused on remand is entitled to be treated as an innocent person under a precautionary restraint; in particular, his right to consult with his legal advisers in privacy must be respected.

### 6.2.2. Bail

There is a right to bail, derived from the constitutional right to personal liberty, unless there are specific grounds on which bail may be denied. Bail is the release of an accused on specified conditions, one of which is invariably that he appear in court on his next remand date. Either the accused promises to forfeit a specific sum if he does not observe these conditions or else he is released into the custody of persons who promise to answer financially for his failure to do so. The amount of bail must not be so excessive as to be a denial thereof, but must balance the means of the accused and his sureties against the fundamental purpose of securing his appearance at trial.

There are no offences for which bail may never be granted; but where the charges are very grave, e.g. murder or treason, bail is most exceptional. The basic criterion for deciding whether a person should be given bail is whether he will try to evade justice if free to do so. The factors that may be considered in this regard include: the strength of evidence against the accused; the likely sentence which would be imposed on conviction and a reasonable probability of disposal of illegally acquired property or of intimidation of witnesses or jurors. Bail cannot be refused because it is likely that the accused will commit further crimes while on bail: this would be a form of preventive detention properly reserved for periods of national emergency only.

### 6.3. PRELIMINARY EXAMINATION

The right to a preliminary examination is statutory, not constitutional; the legislature could give the D.P.P. power to order return for trial in all cases. However, a preliminary examination by a judge is an exercise of the judicial power with which the D.P.P. cannot interfere and some requirements of the Act of 1967 - such as that of serving a Book of Evidence on the accused to permit adequate preparation of his defence - may be inherent in the concept of trial "in due course of law".

### 6.3.1. Book of evidence

Certain documents must be served on an accused even if he waives a preliminary examination: viz., a statement of charges, a copy of the information initiating the proceedings, a list of the People's witnesses (and statements of their evidence) and a list of exhibits. These documents are collectively known as the "Book of Evidence". Before trial, the D.P.P. may serve the accused with additional statements and/or a list of additional witnesses (and statements of their evidence) and/or a list of additional exhibits. Additional evidence may not normally be served during the trial and material evidence of which the accused has not been given notice may not be tendered by the People.

### 6.3.2. Procedure

Before an accused can be tried on indictment (except in the Special Criminal Court) a District Judge must normally conduct a preliminary examination, to decide whether the case against him is sufficient to put him on trial. The prosecutor must first serve the Book of Evidence. Both prosecutor and accused may give evidence (which is recorded in sworn depositions) or require witnesses to do so. However, given the limited scope of the inquiry and since the party who calls a witness may not cross-examine him this right is rarely exercised.

If the Judge is of opinion that there is a sufficient case to put the accused on trial for the offence charged he should send him forward for trial. If he is of opinion that a sufficient case has been made out in relation to some other indictable offence he should have him charged with that offence and send him forward for trial on it. Where he is of opinion that a summary offence only is disclosed, and the D.P.P. consents, he should cause him to be charged with that offence and deal with him accordingly. Otherwise, the accused should be discharged in respect of the offence under examination.

An accused often waives his right to preliminary examination, without prejudice to his right to plead not guilty. It is even more common for an accused to forego his right to call witnesses, and to confine himself to legal submissions on the sufficiency of the Book of Evidence.

### 6.3.4. Scope of inquiry

The nature of a preliminary examination has been summarised as follows:

> "The examination is preliminary in every sense; it is for the purpose of determining whether or not, on the face of the statements and/or depositions a case is made out; it does not attempt to measure the strength of the case; it does not purport to express a view as to whether or not there will be a conviction; it merely determines whether or not assuming the truth of all relevant detail that is given by way of statement or on deposition, the accused person could be convicted".

Thus, a return for trial does not involve any preliminary finding of guilt, nor does it oblige the D.P.P. to bring the accused to trial.

### 6.3.4. Return for trial

The return for trial is, in general, to the Circuit Criminal Court. In practice, only those cases excluded from the jurisdiction of the Circuit Court are returned to the Central Criminal Court. Where required by law, a valid preliminary examination and return for trial are necessary before the D.P.P. can prefer an indictment and before any court can have jurisdiction to try the accused.

6.4. PRE-TRIAL PROCEDURES

## 6.4.1. Indictment

The D.P.P. chooses the charges to be laid against the accused. Counsel for the D.P.P. prepares the indictment and must do so with great care; a defect in it cannot be cured by amendment, unless such amendment can be made without injustice.

An indictment may charge more than one offence; each offence being dealt with in a separate, numbered "count". Such offences, whether felonies or misdemeanours, need not be connected. Two or more persons may be charged in one indictment, where there is a connection between the offences charged. The inclusion of more than one accused and/or more than one offence in an indictment does not require that all the accused and/or offences be tried together.

Each count contains a statement of the offence charged, with enough particulars to give the accused reasonable information as to its nature. Generally speaking, no count should relate to more than one offence; thus a count should not refer to separate incidents each of which involves a distinct offence.

## 6.4.2. Separate trials

Either the People or the accused may wish to have particular offences and/or accuseds included in the same indictment tried separately. The D.P.P. may feel that a proliferation of counts confuses juries and that it is better to proceed on a few "specimen" charges, entering a *nolle prosequi* in respect of others; an accused may be unfairly prejudiced in the eyes of the jury because of the number of charges against him, undermining the presumption of innocence and his protection from evidence of bad character. It may also be desirable to remove from a jury the temptation improperly to treat evidence relating to one charge as corroborating that relating to others.

Similarly, several accused may be prejudiced by joint trial. A jury may improperly treat evidence which is admissible against one - *e.g.* a confession - as admissible against all. The court of trial again has power to order separate trials but only if an accused can show prejudice to his case.

6.5. THE TRIAL

## 6.5.1. Opening procedure

*(i) Arraignment*
The first procedure at a trial is arraignment, *i.e.* reading the indictment to the accused in open court and calling upon him to plead to each of the counts therein.

The decision whether to plead "guilty" or "not guilty" is one for the accused alone; counsel should provide professional advice only and must advise him not to plead guilty if he says he did not commit the offences charged. Unless he has been found unfit to plead the Court must accept a plea of guilty and convict him. An accused may change his plea to guilty at any time during his trial; such a plea aborts the trial of the counts to which it relates. A plea of guilty may be withdrawn at any time up to sentence. An accused may plead guilty to some or all counts and may plead guilty to an alternative offence where certain offences are charged, e.g. he may plead guilty to manslaughter to a count alleging murder.

Sentencing policy encourages guilty pleas by giving "discounts" of various kinds to those who plead guilty, such as shorter or non-custodial sentences. The ostensible justification for leniency is the remorse shown by the accused, but many see "administrative expediency" as the main motive for the policy.

### (ii) Jury selection
Jury service is regulated by the the Juries Act, 1976. In general, any citizen aged between 18 and 70 who is registered as a Dáil elector is liable for jury service.

A panel of jurors is selected from the Register of Electors, where necessary by some random or other non-discriminatory method. Random selection is required by the Constitution so that juries are, on average, "a fair cross-section of the community".

Both the People and defence may challenge any of the persons as they are selected, but before they are sworn. The Act of 1976 provides that the People and each accused may challenge no more than seven jurors without showing cause; any person subject to such a "peremptory" challenge cannot serve as a juror. The People and each accused may challenge any number of jurors for cause shown, *i.e.* by giving a reason why that person should not serve.

### 6.5.2. Trial

### (i) Opening speeches
Once a jury has been empanelled counsel for the People addresses it - summarising the nature of the case and the matters which the People intend to prove. This is known as opening the case to the jury. It should allow the jury to compare the intended proofs with the evidence given, but counsel should not mention evidence which he knows or suspects the defence intend to challenge as inadmissible. The defence makes no opening statement at the beginning of the trial. This reflects a reluctance to disclose a line of defence until the prosecution's evidence has commenced.

### (ii) Examination of witnesses
A witness is first examined by the party calling him ("examination in chief"); counsel for that party is limited in the type of questions he can ask. He may

not (except as to minor or undisputed matters) ask a "leading" question, *i.e.* one which suggests the answer desired or assumes the existence of disputed facts as to which the witness must testify - e.g. "Did you see the accused come out of the building alone?" rather than "Did you see anyone?".

The aim of these rules is to ensure that a witness's testimony is based on his own personal recollection and is expressed in his own words. The jury should hear the testimony of the witness with the least possible degree of modification or influence by counsel calling him. Neither counsel nor other persons should "coach" a witness, *i.e.* indicate that it would be desirable if the witness testified to particular facts or in a particular manner.

Even testimony which is purportedly based on personal recollection and expressed in the witness's own words may be seriously defective as evidence. Its probative value may be undermined by failure of memory, honest mistake, prejudice, bias, ill-will or downright concoction. The common belief is that the best method of determining whether a witness is lying or whether his evidence is otherwise unreliable is to expose him to cross-examination by counsel for the other party. In cross-examination counsel attempts to cause the witness to qualify or retract his testimony in chief or casts doubt upon his veracity or his capacity to give reliable evidence. Cross-examination also enables the defence to put its version of what happened to prosecution witnesses. This is particularly important in view of the fact that the defence makes no statement at the start of the trial indicating the nature of its case.

The party calling a witness may re-examine him in order to deal with matters arising out of the cross-examination, but only in relation to such matters and subject to the same restrictions as apply to examination in chief.

*(iii) Defence case*

The accused may choose not to give evidence, in which case he is limited to highlighting weaknesses in the prosecution case and to stressing the importance of the presumption of innocence.

The Act of 1924 prohibits any comment by the prosecution on the failure of the accused or of his spouse to testify. However, the judge may make such comment in his summing up. The judge must convey to the jury that they cannot infer guilt simply because the accused has failed to testify though they may properly regard such a failure as casting doubt on the veracity of a defence put forward.

An accused under cross-examination may be asked questions tending to incriminate him in relation to the offence charged. However, he may neither be asked nor required to answer any question tending to show that he has committed, been convicted of or charged with any offence other than that charged or that he is of bad character. This limitation does not apply where proof of the commission of or of conviction for such other offences is admissible to show that he is guilty of the offence charged, nor where he has attempted to show his good character or his defence impugns the character of the prosecution or of its witnesses or where he has given evidence against a co-accused.

### (iv) Closing argument
The right to make, and order of, closing speeches is now regulated by the 1984 Act. The People may make a closing speech unless the accused is not represented by counsel or a solicitor and does not call any witnesses, apart from witnesses as to character. The defence may make a closing speech in all cases. The closing speech for the People shall be made before that for the defence. In a closing speech counsel sums up the nature of his case and briefly indicates the evidence that has been given and the issues to be decided by the jury.

### 6.5.3. Verdict

The judge must sum up the case for the jury unless it is so simple that explanation of it would be otiose. His charge should be intelligible, concisely summing up the issues of fact and the evidence, and drawing attention to the points at which the cases presented by both sides conflict. The jury must be told to confine itself to the evidence, that the onus of proof is always on the People and that it cannot convict if there is a reasonable doubt about the accused's guilt. The judge must direct the jury as to the proper interpretation of the law, confining himself to those matters which are relevant to the issues which the jury has to decide. In particular, the elements of the offences charged, and the facts capable of affording a defence to them, should be clearly explained to the jury. The charge should present the law in a way that a lay person can easily understand and apply; each judge must choose his own form of words.

Until 1984 the verdict of a jury in a criminal case, whatever its nature, had to be unanimous. A verdict need not now be unanimous if at least eleven jurors participate and if at least ten of them agree with it. The judge cannot accept a verdict that is not unanimous unless he thinks that the jury has had a reasonable period of time for deliberation having regard to the nature and complexity of the case; and no such verdict shall be accepted unless the jury has deliberated for at least two hours.

A jury may bring in a general verdict ("guilty" or "not guilty") or a special verdict (in practice, that of "guilty but insane".) A general verdict states the jury's decision, without explanation; a special verdict recites the facts found by the jury, leaving the legal effect of those findings to be determined by the judge. Apart from "guilty but insane", which is only technically a special verdict, special verdicts are unknown in modern practice.

### 6.5.4. Sentence

The sentencing of offenders is the concern of the trial judge; the jury has no role therein. Statutes normally prescribe a maximum sentence for indictable offences, giving the trial judge wide discretion to take into account the circumstances of each case, including the personality and record of the offender. Where the sentence to be imposed is not fixed by law only the trial judge can determine what specific sentence should be imposed; statute cannot allow the prosecutor to interfere with this determination. Nor should the prosecution seek to have any particular sentence imposed.

The Criminal Justice Act, 1993, contains a number of imortant innovations with respect to sentencing. In cases of sexual offences or offences against the person, it is made mandatory for the court to take into account the effect of an offence before sentencing a convicted person. In particular, the court must hear evidence of the victim as to the effect of the offence, if the victim so desires. Criminal courts are given a general power to make compensation orders against convicted persons in respect of personal injury or loss resulting from their offences.

### 6.5.5. Closing procedures

*(i) Costs*
If an accused is acquitted, the court may, at its discretion, award him the costs of his defence. Where the accused is entitled to criminal legal aid there is generally no reason to award his costs.

*(ii) Leave to appeal*
If an accused wishes to appeal either conviction or sentence to the Court of Criminal Appeal, he must obtain leave to do so. He must apply in the first instance to the trial judge for a certificate that the case is fit for appeal; if such a certificate is refused, as is usually the case, he must appeal against that refusal to the Court of Criminal Appeal. A certificate must be sought at the close of the trial or within three days thereafter. The Court of Criminal Appeal may neither extend this time limit nor grant leave to appeal unless a certificate from the trial judge has been sought and refused.

## 7. Evidence

### 7.1. GENERAL

### 7.1.1. Role and rationale

The law of evidence is crucial to our system of criminal procedure. With minor exceptions, it applies equally to all criminal proceedings, from summary prosecutions in the District Court to trials in the Central Criminal

Court. The demands of jury trial have, however, particularly influenced many rules of evidence. Oral testimony, tested by cross-examination, has traditionally been accorded the highest probative value; stress is laid on the value of a witness's demeanour as an indication of his credibility.

### 7.1.2. Exclusionary character

The law of evidence mainly consists of rules preventing certain matters from being considered by courts in deciding issues of fact, even though such matters may be relevant.

## 7.2. WITNESSES

### 7.2.1. The oath

A witness must in general give evidence on oath - or, if he objects to taking an oath, on affirmation. However, in criminal proceedings, a child of tender years may give unsworn testimony, provided that he understands the obligation to tell the truth or is capable of giving an intelligible account of events.

### 7.2.2. Competence

An accused's spouse is generally competent to testify against him.

### 7.2.3. Compellability

In general, a person summoned as a witness must testify. An accused can choose whether or not he wishes to testify in his defence. An accused's spouse is compellable to give evidence for the defence and to testify for the prosecution where the offence charged is a sexual offence or an offence involving violence against the spouse, the child of the spouse or of the accused, or against any person under 17 years of age.

### 7.2.4. Privilege

Although a person may be compellable to give evidence he may be entitled to refuse to answer a particular question on the ground of privilege. Apart from the privilege against self-incrimination (see infra), the main head of privilege is that which relates to communications between lawyers and their clients. This privilege may be defeated, inter alia, if the lawyer participates in his client's criminal purpose. The categories of privilege are not closed; the acknowledgement of new heads of privilege reflects a balancing of competing public interests. Thus, although ministers of religion enjoy a privilege in civil proceedings, journalists do not in criminal cases.

### 7.2.5. Public interest immunity

A witness may claim to be immune from answering a question because it would be detrimental to the public interest to do so. The most significant instance of this in criminal proceedings is the right of police witnesses not to disclose the identity of persons providing information in confidence to them. However, such immunity is not absolute and it is for the court to balance the competing public interests. Communications between *Gardaí* are not privileged per se. There is a constitutional requirement that a claim for privilege should not generally be upheld if it would impede an accused's efforts to establish his innocence.

### 7.2.6. The privilege against self-incrimination

A witness is not bound to answer any question put to him in court, the answer to which would, in the judge's opinion, tend to expose him to any criminal charge, penalty or forfeiture. Some statutes, however, make it an offence for a person not to answer questions put to him by *Gardaí* in the course of an investigation, regardless of whether or not the answers might incriminate him. These statutes do not provide that such answers cannot be used in evidence against that person in subsequent criminal proceedings and courts have generally held that no such restriction can be implied. Indeed, some statutes explicitly provide that such compelled answers are admissible in proceedings against the persons giving them.

### 7.3. SPECIAL TYPES OF EVIDENCE

### 7.3.1. Hearsay

As a general rule, a witness's testimony as to a statement made by a person out of court is only admissible in relation to the issue of whether or not the statement was made or as "unwitting" evidence of the state of knowledge or intent of its maker. Such a reported statement may not be received as evidence of the truth of the matters which the statement expressly or implicitly asserts to be true. There are some exceptions to the rule. The most important are: admissions of guilt by an accused; a dying declaration by a homicide victim which identifies his killer; and statements which are part of the "*res gestae*".

### 7.3.2. Admissions by accused

*(i) Voluntariness*
No statement made by an accused is admissible in evidence unless the prosecution proves beyond reasonable doubt that it was "voluntary", a term which has in this context a technical meaning. A statement is not voluntary if

it was produced as a result of threats or inducements held out to the accused by a person in authority or as a result of oppression which overbore the accused's free will. Oppression is a relative concept and requires the Court to consider both the accused's character and the circumstances of the interrogation. Physical violence is one instance of oppression but practices such as sleep deprivation or unduly prolonged or persistent questioning may also be oppressive. The law is concerned primarily with the extraction of confessions by police use of improper means, not with an accused's mental condition as such.

*(ii) Judges rules*
There is an established set of judicial rules of practice governing the questioning of, and taking of statements from, suspects by the police. The Rules indicate how the inherent judicial discretion to exclude evidence should be exercised in specified situations. Thus the judiciary may continue to develop new rules of practice of the same nature. A statement obtained in violation of the Judges Rules may be admitted at the discretion of the trial judge.

*(iii) Corroboration*
A confession can be the sole, uncorroborated evidence upon which an accused is convicted and no warning to the jury about the reliability of confessions is required by law. In particular, it is not necessary to prove the existence of a corpus delicti by independent evidence.

### 7.3.3. Opinion evidence

As a general rule a witness may give evidence of facts only; his opinions are not evidence. He must testify as to facts he has observed and leave it to the court to interpret those facts. As an exception to this rule, a witness's opinions may be received as evidence in relation to an area in which he has a professional or technical expertise.

### 7.4. EXCLUSIONARY RULES

### 7.4.1. General

Relevance to the facts in issue is merely a necessary, not a sufficient, condition of admissibility.

### 7.4.2. Illegally obtained evidence

Every court has a discretion to exclude evidence obtained as the result of an illegal act if the public interest so requires. This discretion must be exercised judicially having regard to factors such as the seriousness of the illegality, whether or not it was intentional, whether it was excused by urgency and whether it indicates a policy of gathering evidence by illegal means. The purpose of excluding such evidence is primarily to deter police misconduct.

### 7.4.3. Unconstitutionally obtained evidence

The Constitution does not expressly require the exclusion of unconstitutionally obtained evidence: the doctrine is one developed by the Courts, primarily under the influence of U.S. case law. Evidence obtained as the result of "a deliberate and conscious violation" by the State or its agents of any of the accused's constitutional rights must be held to be inadmissible, unless there are "extraordinary excusing circumstances".

Where a person's right to personal liberty has been violated any statements he makes during such unlawful detention are, on that ground alone, inadmissible, being deemed to be the fruits of a violation of the Constitution. The voluntariness of the statement and the fairness of the means by which it was obtained are both irrelevant if the detention was unlawful.

Real evidence obtained through unlawful searches of dwellings violates the constitutional inviolability of the dwelling and would be a basis for the exclusion of evidence obtained by such means. A person's constitutional right to privacy in, for example, his telephonic and postal communications is well established and it seems that a violation of this right would of itself be a basis for the exclusion of any evidence thereby obtained. Thus, evidence obtained as a result of an unlawful search of premises other than the accused's dwelling might be inadmissible on *O' Brien* grounds, if his right to privacy had thereby been violated: an example might be an unlawful search of an accused's hotel room.

Evidence obtained as a result of an unlawful intrusion on the bodily integrity of an accused would presumably be excluded as the fruit of the violation of the right to bodily integrity.

### 7.4.4. Exclusion for unfairness

A trial judge has a residual discretion to exclude evidence which ought not to be admitted. However, this "discretion" must be exercised judicially on the basis of objective criteria and a decision to exclude evidence can be reviewed on appeal. A trial judge may exclude evidence obtained by unfair means.

> "[B]ecause our Constitution ... postulates the observance of basic or fundamental fairness of procedures, the judge presiding at a criminal trial should be astute to see that, although a statement may be technically voluntary, it should nevertheless be excluded, if by reason of the manner or of the circumstances in which it was obtained, it falls below the required standard of fairness. The reason for exclusion here is not so much the risk of an erroneous conviction as the recognition that the minimum essential standards must be observed in the administration of justice ...".

If the prejudicial effect of evidence outweighs its probative value the trial judge must exclude it from consideration. It is for the trial judge to balance probative force against prejudicial effect.

## 7.5. EVALUATION OF EVIDENCE

In criminal cases it is unconstitutional for a statute to require that a court should accept certain evidence as "conclusive" proof of some other fact. However, the weight which should be given to certain types of evidence is the subject of a number of rules of law and practice.

> "[A]ccumulated judicial experience eventually tends to crystallise into established rules of judicial practice, accepted rules of law and statutory provisions ... The category of circumstances and special types of case which call for special directions and warnings from the trial judge cannot be considered as closed".

The main effect of such rules is to require that the jury be warned of the danger of acting on particular kinds of evidence without independent corroboration. Thus a jury must be warned of the danger of convicting on the evidence of an accomplice.

# 8. Special forms of procedure

## 8.1. PLEA BARGAINING

An accused may offer to plead guilty to certain charges in an indictment in return for the entry of a *nolle prosequi* in respect of other, more serious, charges. Counsel for the D.P.P., if authorised by the Director, may accept such a proposal but cannot give the accused any assurances as to the sentence he may receive on the remaining charges, although judges usually give some "discount" for a guilty plea. It is improper for counsel for the D.P.P. to take the initiative in proposing such an accommodation. The accused must not be pressured into accepting a "plea bargain"; the trial judge should be highly circumspect about giving any advance indication of his attitude to the proper sentence in the event of a plea of guilty or of a conviction.

## 8.2. SPECIAL COURTS

### 8.2.1. Constitutional basis

Special courts may be established by law in cases where it may be determined in accordance with such law that the ordinary courts are inadequate to secure the effective administration of justice and the preservation of public peace and order. The constitution, powers and jurisdiction of such courts are to be determined by law. Such courts are exempt from the guarantee of jury trial; their members need not be judges nor enjoy full judicial security of tenure, trials before them need not be held in public and there need not be any right of appeal from their verdicts. Special courts are, however, subject to all other constitutional guarantees, notably that no person shall be tried on any criminal charge save in due course of law and that the State shall respect, and as far as practicable by its laws defend and vindicate, the personal rights of the citizen.

The Executive may not interfere with the independent functioning of a special court by dismissing or threatening its members. Other aspects of trial in due course of law - such as the exclusion of unconstitutionally obtained evidence and the right of an accused to make a proper defence, or to have his guilt determined beyond reasonable doubt - are fully applicable to proceedings in special courts. The High Court retains jurisdiction over proceedings in the special courts by way of judicial review and by way of an enquiry into the legality of an accused's detention.

### 8.2.2. Special criminal court

The 1939 Act provides for the establishment of a Special Criminal Court or Courts whenever the Government is satisfied that the conditions set out in Art. 38(1)1 are satisfied and makes a proclamation to that effect. Such a proclamation may be subsequently revoked by the Government or annulled by a resolution of the *Dáil Eireann* (the lower house of the Irish parliament).

The main jurisdiction of the Court relates to those offences which are - by order of the Government - "scheduled offences" for the purposes of the 1939 Act. This "schedule" currently includes arson, malicious damage, false imprisonment and a variety of offences under the 1939 Act. However, a person charged with a non-scheduled offence may be tried before the Special Criminal Court if the D.P.P. certifies that the ordinary courts are inadequate to secure the effective administration of justice and the preservation of public peace and order in relation to the trial of such person on that charge.

The Court's jurisdiction is not limited to "subversive" or "political" offences - it extends to any case where it is determined in accordance with law that the ordinary courts are inadequate within the terms of Art. 38(3)1. Thus, the Court could be used to deal with organised crime such as large scale drug-trafficking.

### 8.3. SUMMARY PROCEDURE

### 8.3.1. Summary disposal of indictable offences

#### (i) Consent to summary trial
Given the constitutional requirement of trial with a jury, only minor offences may be tried summarily. An indictable offence may or may not be a minor one, depending on the circumstances. There is, therefore, legislative provision for the District Court to try certain indictable offences summarily. The offences in question include assaults, offences under the Larceny Acts and

malicious damage. Other statutes make similar provisions in respect of other specific offences.

The conditions under which an indictable offence may be tried summarily are: (i) that the court is of opinion that the facts proved or alleged amount to a minor offence; (ii) that the accused, having been informed of his right to jury trial, does not object to summary trial and (iii) in certain cases only, that the D.P.P. (or exceptionally the Attorney General) consents to summary trial.

*(ii) Guilty plea*
Where an accused charged with an indictable offence (other than treason, murder, piracy, genocide and some other grave crimes) is before the District Court he may plead guilty. If the Judge accepts the plea as a properly informed one and the accused signs a written plea, he may be sent forward to the Circuit Court with that plea; alternatively, the Judge, if the D.P.P. does not object may deal with the offence summarily, but may in that case impose only such penalty as might be imposed on a summary trial of an indictable offence.

8.4. JUVENILE JUSTICE

There is no distinct system of juvenile justice as such. The general law of criminal procedure is adapted to deal with the case of a child or young person in three main ways.

First, a child under seven years has an absolute defence of doli incapax to any criminal charge, while there is a rebuttable presumption that a child between seven and fourteen years of age is doli incapax; persons aged fourteen and older are fully liable for their criminal acts. Secondly, when dealing summarily with an offence alleged to have been committed by a child or young person, the District Court - which holds special sittings as the Children's Court - may deal with the case with an appropriate degree of informality and may dispose as the best interests of the juvenile require. Thirdly, children and young persons are subject to a distinct regime of sanctions and penalties.

8.5. CONTEMPT OF COURT

The guarantee of jury trial does not generally impair the right of a court to try persons accused of contempt of court in a summary fashion and to punish them accordingly. The maintenance of the independence and authority of the courts requires that they be free to deal with such offences in a summary fashion. Any court can punish persons accused of contempt in facie curiae. The inferior courts - such as the District Court, the Circuit Court and the Special Criminal Court - must rely on the High Court to deal with other forms of contempt directed against them.

# 9. Remedies

## 9.1. APPEAL

### 9.1.1. Summary trial

Anyone convicted or bound over to keep the peace in the District Court may appeal against conviction or sentence to the Circuit Court. The Circuit Judge, sitting without a jury, conducts a complete re-hearing of the case. An accused cannot appeal against conviction only; the Court may always confirm the conviction and impose a harsher sentence (if it is one the District Court could impose). There is, however, provision for an appeal against sentence only. Conversely, the accused may require the prosecution to repeat their proofs and introduce new grounds of defence, not raised in the District Court. An appeal to the Circuit Court results in the release of the appellant pending the determination of the appeal.

The prosecution has no such right of appeal, but may appeal an acquittal by way of a case stated.

### 9.1.2. Trial on indictment

A conviction on indictment and/or sentence may be appealed in two ways: firstly, by the statutory mode of appeal to the Court of Criminal Appeal from decisions of the Circuit, Central Criminal and Special Criminal Courts, and secondly, by way of appeal from the Central Criminal Court to the Supreme Court, by virtue of Art. 34(4)3 of the Constitution.

### (i) Appeal to the Court of Criminal Appeal

The Court of Criminal Appeal consists of a Supreme Court and two High Court judges. The D.P.P. may appeal against an unduly lenient sentence imposed following a conviction on indictment. An acquittal cannot be appealed to the Court of Criminal Appeal. An accused may appeal against conviction or sentence or both; he has no right of appeal, but must first obtain leave to do so. If the trial judge refuses such leave the convicted person must seek it from the Court of Criminal Appeal. A person who pleaded guilty will be given leave to appeal against conviction in exceptional cases only.

The Court may affirm or reverse the conviction in whole or in part and may remit, reduce increase or otherwise vary the sentence. If the appeal is against conviction only the sentence may not be increased, but if the appeal is against sentence the Court may increase it if it thinks fit.

The Court may substitute a verdict of guilty of a lesser charge, e.g. a verdict of manslaughter in lieu of one of murder. If the Court quashes a conviction it may order the accused to be re-tried on some or all counts, whether or not fresh evidence has been heard. An accused may not be re-tried on different charges; nor where the People have omitted to adduce crucial evidence.

The Court's decision is final unless the Court itself or the D.P.P. certifies that the decision involves a point of law of exceptional public importance and that it is desirable in the public interest that an appeal should be taken to the Supreme Court. However, the quashing of a conviction cannot be appealed.

### (ii) Central Criminal Court to Supreme Court

Under Art. 34(4)3 the Supreme Court has jurisdiction to hear appeals from "all decisions of the High Court" with such exceptions as may be specified by law. A conviction by a jury in the Central Criminal Court can be appealed to the Supreme Court, even though it can also be appealed to the Court of Criminal Appeal; an accused must, however, choose which of these rights of appeal he wishes to pursue. An acquittal in the Central Criminal Court may be appealed to the Supreme Court.

### 9.2. HABEAS CORPUS UNDER ARTICLE 40(4)2 OF THE CONSTITUTION

Where a complaint is made to a High Court judge that a person is being unlawfully detained, the judge shall forthwith enquire into the complaint. The judge may order the person in whose custody such person is detained to produce his body before the Court on a named day and to certify in writing the grounds for the detention. Upon the detainee being produced before it and having given the person detaining him an opportunity to justify the detention, the High Court shall release the detainee unless satisfied that he is being detained in accordance with the law.

If the detention is not shown to be lawful the court has no discretion to refuse relief on the basis of the applicant's conduct or otherwise. Whilst a person released under Article 40(4)2 is not immune from re-arrest on the same or on a different charge, he should be allowed a meaningful period of time at liberty before a re-arrest is attempted.

### 9.3. JUDICIAL REVIEW

### 9.3.1. Supervisory jurisdiction of High Court

The High Court has a general supervisory jurisdiction over proceedings in all "inferior" courts - e.g. the District Court, the Circuit Court and the Special Criminal Court. The High Court not only reviews the legality of decisions of the inferior courts, but also prevents those courts from exceeding their powers and may require them to carry out their duties. The High Court's function is to ensure that lower courts and administrative bodies do not exceed or abuse the jurisdiction conferred on them by law; this function seems to be an essential aspect of its Constitutional jurisdiction.

## 9.4. CASE STATED

### 9.4.1. Appeal by case stated

Where a party is dissatisfied with a District Judge's determination of proceedings as being erroneous in point of law he may, within 14 days, apply to the Judge to state a case. The Case Stated sets out the facts and grounds of the determination and seeks the High Court's opinion on specific points of law arising from it. The Judge must state a case unless he is of opinion that the application is frivolous and a refusal to do so may be appealed to the High Court. Only points of law may be referred to the High Court; findings of fact are conclusive unless there was no evidence to support them. A mixed question of law and fact may be the subject of a case stated.

The High Court may reverse, affirm or vary the determination of the District Judge on the basis of its answer to the question of law posed; remit the matter to the District Court; or make whatever order it deems fit. It may not vary any penalty imposed. The case may not be remitted to the District Court for further evidence.

An acquittal in the District Court may be reviewed by way of case stated and set aside if it is found to have resulted from an error of law.

### 9.4.2. Consultative case stated

A District Judge shall, if requested by any person who has been heard before him, refer any question of law arising in the proceedings to the High Court - unless he considers the request to be frivolous; the Judge may also refer a question on his own initiative. The essential difference between this procedure and the traditional one is that a consultative case may be stated at any stage in the proceedings, which are then adjourned pending the High Court's answer - thus the Judge need not have heard all the evidence before stating a case of this type. A District Judge's decision whether or not to state a consultative case cannot be reviewed.

A Circuit Judge may - on the application of one of the parties - refer to the Supreme Court any question arising in a matter pending before him and may adjourn his judgment or order pending the determination of the Supreme Court. A Circuit Judge may not state a case relating to the constitutional validity of an Act of the *Oireachtas*, although it is proper to refer a question as to the validity of subordinate legislation.

A Circuit Judge may state a case at any point in the proceedings; for example, at the close of the prosecution case in an appeal from the District Court. However, where a person is being tried on indictment in the Circuit Court the Judge may not state a case after the jury has been sworn and before its verdict has been pronounced.

## 9.5. CONSTITUTIONAL CONTROL

Only the High Court (and on appeal the Supreme Court) has jurisdiction in relation to the validity of a law having regard to the provisions of the Constitution; no such question can be raised in any other court. For this purpose "law" means an Act of the *Oireachtas* passed since 1937. The District, the Circuit and the Special Criminal Courts and the Court of Criminal Appeal must treat an Act of the *Oireachtas* as valid and binding upon them. It may be, however, that these courts can determine other issues arising out of the interpretation of the Constitution - such as the constitutionality of a rule of common law or a pre-Constitution statute.

## 9.6. REFERENCE TO THE COURT OF JUSTICE OF THE EUROPEAN COMMUNITY

A court exercising criminal jurisdiction is clearly entitled to seek a preliminary ruling from the Court of Justice of the European Communities. However, it is unclear how the making of a such a reference can be accommodated within the framework of national criminal procedure. In a summary trial in the District or Circuit Court it is relatively straightforward for the judge to make a reference at whatever stage of the case seems convenient. However, the position in relation to trials on indictment is less clear. It is not generally desirable to fragment a trial on indictment by an adjournment of months if not years. Either the trial judge should make a reference after receiving the verdict or he should leave it to the appellate courts to make one.

## 9.7. TORT REMEDIES

The State may be sued for any tort, breach of constitutional rights or other wrong - "sovereign immunity" of the State from suit is inconsistent with the Constitution. The State is vicariously liable for the acts of its servants or agents - this liability may even extend to acts outside the scope of their employment. Thus, if a *Garda* is guilty of the tort of malicious prosecution or a prison officer unlawfully intercepts a prisoner's mail the State may be sued and damages recovered from it.

## 9.8. REVIEW OF MISCARRIAGES OF JUSTICE

There is no judicial procedure under which the propriety of a conviction may be investigated or reconsidered once an accused person has exhausted his rights of appeal; the matter is *res judicata* and cannot be re-opened by any court. Where there is serious concern about the reliability of a conviction only the Executive may take remedial action - by the exercise of its power of pardon or remission or by releasing an offender from custody. A judicial public inquiry may be established to investigate a case, but without power to affect the validity of a conviction.

The Committee on Miscarriages of Justice has recommended a new procedure for reviewing the reliability of doubtful convictions under which - in contrast with the existing system of criminal appeals - the facts of each case could be extensively investigated by a non-judicial agency.

## 10. Select bibliography

### Textbooks

The range of textbooks directly relating to Irish criminal procedure is severely limited. Irish practitioners still routinely refer to English works in this area. The following is a brief list of some of the most pertinent Irish texts:

RYAN & MAGEE, *The Irish Criminal Process*, Dublin & Cork, 1980
HOGAN & WALKER, *Political Violence and the Law*, Manchester, 1989
CASEY, *The Office of the Attorney General in Ireland* , Dublin, 1980
*The Garda Síochána Guide*, Dublin, 1991
KELLY, *The Irish Constitution*, 2nd ed., Dublin, 1984 & 1987
COLLINS & O'REILLY, *The State in Civil Proceedings in Ireland*, Dublin, 1989
FENNELL, *The Law of Evidence in Ireland*, Dublin, 1992
MCAULEY, F., *Insanity, Psychiatry and Criminal Responsibility*, Dublin, 1993.

### Case list

The following is a selection of a number of especially significant cases.
**General**
*Melling v. Ó Mathghamhna* [1962] I.R. 97
*The State (Quinn) v. Ryan* [1965] I.R. 70
*People (Attorney General) v. O' Callaghan* [1966] I.R. 501
*The State (Healy) v. Donoghue* [1976] I.R. 325
*King v. Attorney General* [1981] I.R. 233
*People (D.P.P.) v. Shaw* [1982] I.R. 1
*People (D.P.P.) v. T.* [1988] 3 Frewen 141
*Goodman International v. Hamilton* [1992] I.L.R.M. 145
**Minor Offences**
*Melling v. Ó Mathghamhna* (supra)
*Conroy v. Attorney General* [1965] I.R. 411
**Prosecution**
*The State (O'Connell) v. Fawsitt* [1986] I.R. 639
*The State (McCormack) v. Curran* [1987] I.L.R.M. 225
**Arrest**
*Dunne v. Clinton* [1930] I.R. 366
*People (D.P.P.) v. Quilligan* [1986] I.R. 495
**Bail**
*People (Attorney General) v. O' Callaghan* (supra)
*People (D.P.P.) v. Ryan* [1989] I.R. 399
**Preliminary Examination**
*Costello v. D.P.P.* [1984] I.R. 436
*O'Shea v. D.P.P.* [1988] I.R. 655
**Jury Trial**

*de Búrca v. Attorney General* [1976] I.R. 138
*People (D.P.P.) v. O'Shea* [1982] I.R. 384
**Sentence**
*Deaton v. Attorney General* [1963] I.R. 170
**Evidence**
*People (Attorney General) v. Casey (No.2)* [1963] I.R. 33
*People (Attorney General) v. O' Brien* [1965] I.R. 142
*Maher v. Attorney General* [1973] I.R. 140
*People (D.P.P.) v. Shaw* (supra)
*People (D.P.P.) v. Pringle* [1983] 2 Frewen 57
*D.P.P. (Hanley) v. Holly* [1984] I.L.R.M. 149
*People (D.P.P.) v. Hoey* [1987] I.R. 646
*People (D.P.P.) v. T.* (supra)
*People (D.P.P.) v. Healy* [1990] 2 I.R. 73
*People (D.P.P.) v. Kenny* [1990] 2 I.R. 110
**Offences Against the State Acts**
*People (D.P.P.) v. Quilligan* (supra)

## *Statutes*

The following is a selection of important statutes relating to criminal procedure.
Petty Sessions (Ireland) Act, 1851; Courts of Justice Acts, 1924 and 1928; Criminal Justice (Evidence) Act, 1924; Criminal Justice (Administration) Act, 1924; Offences Against the State Acts, 1939 to 1985; Criminal Justice Act, 1951; Criminal Procedure Act, 1967; Prosecution of Offences Act, 1974; Juries Act, 1976; Criminal Law Act, 1976; Criminal Law (Rape) Acts, 1981 and 1990; Criminal Justice Act, 1984; Courts (No.3) Act, 1986; Criminal Evidence Act, 1992; Criminal Justice Act, 1993.

# Chapter 8 - Italy

Prof. Piermaria **CORSO**
Law Faculty
University of Parma

## 1. Sources

### 1.1. THE CODE OF CRIMINAL PROCEDURE

The new Code of Criminal Procedure, which entered into force on 24 October 1989, is the first since the democratic republican regime was established in Italy in 1946, and the fourth since Italy was juridically and politically unified in 1861.

Between the first Code (1865) and the present, there were the 1913 Code of Criminal Procedure which bore a liberal imprint, and the 1930 Code of Criminal Procedure (*Codice Rocco*), which expressed the ideology of those times but which nevertheless outlived both the fascist regime and the first forty years of the present constitutional regime.

During this period, the Code was changed several times, altering its original inquisitorial nature. There were even attempts to introduce radical reforms. The most far-reaching of these proposals was the 1978 preliminary draft, which, at a time when the State was deeply troubled by problems of terrorism and political crimes, was considered to be biased by an over-emphasis of the rights of the accused. Once the "emergency season" (1974-1982) was over, the movement towards reform re-emerged. In 1987, the Italian Parliament passed a statute in which it set out the general guidelines to be incorporated in the new Code, and delegated the task of elaborating the text to the Executive. Its final draft, approved in 1988, was published in the *Official Gazette* on 24 October of that same year.

It is noteworthy that the Code of Criminal Procedure has already been, and continues to be, the subject of important modifications that are either suggested by practical requirements (see, *e.g.*, the delegated legislative decree no. 12 of January 14, 1991) or else are imposed by decisions of the Constitutional Court (*Corte Costituzionale*). Hence one may well conclude that, despite an imposing array of rules, the field of criminal procedure in Italy is in a transitional phase. Another important element is that proceedings pending when the new code entered into force, and which were started under the 1930 Code, are pursued under the old rules even though the laws on procedure have changed.

## 1.2. THE CONSTITUTION

There are many important rules relating to criminal procedure in the 1948 Italian Constitution, which is the primary formal source of the law and which cannot be modified by ordinary legislation. This factor led to numerous substantial modifications to the 1930 Code of Criminal Procedure, and had a decisive influence on the drafting of the 1988 Code. Moreover, rules of criminal procedure that are contrary to the Constitution, may be declared unconstitutional by the Constitutional Court.

It is impossible to give an exhaustive picture of all the provisions that have a direct bearing on procedure, and therefore the information given in the present contribution must remain general and fragmentary.

The most important principles are the following: equality before the law (art.3); the right to personal freedom, including the deadline beyond which detention on remand may not extend (art.13); inviolability of the home (art.14) and freedom and secrecy of communication (art.15); the right of access to a court to defend one's interests and the right to be assisted by counsel at every stage and degree of the proceedings (art.24); the right to have one's case heard by the "natural judge", *i.e.* the judge whose competence has been determined by law (art.25); the guarantee that extradition can only be granted on the basis of international agreements and never for political crimes (arts.10 and 26); the presumption of innocence (art.27); the autonomy and independence of the judges, *servi legum* (arts.101 and 104); the prohibition the State establishing extraordinary or special tribunals (art.102); the independence of the judiciary, which also applies to lay judges who participate in criminal proceedings (art.108); the legality principle with respect to prosecution, *i.e.* the rule that prosecution is obligatory (art.112); the guarantee that reasons should be given for all jurisdictional measures and that judicial decisions should be subject to appeal and to *cassation* before the Supreme Court *(Corte di Cassazione)* on legal issues (art.111).

The provisions on the organization of the Constitutional Court (arts.134-138) are also important, as are the following laws: No. 1 of February 9, 1948; No. 1 of March 11, 1953 and No. 2 of November 22, 1967; the rules on impeachment proceedings (No. 29 of January 25, 1962); No. 1 of January 16, 1989 and No. 219 of June 5, 1989 concerning the crimes of high treason and attempt on the Constitution (see arts.90 and 96 of the Constitution).

## 1.3. INTERNATIONAL LAW

Supra-national legislation, multilateral and bilateral agreements are also sources of Italian law. Italy is a party to both the European Convention on Human Rights (approved under law No. 848 on August 4, 1955) and the International Covenant on Civil and Political Rights of December 19, 1966 approved on October 25, 1977 (No. 881).

Another important source is the reciprocity principle which governs the fields of international co-operation and legal assistance.

## 1.4. OTHER STATUTES

In addition to the Code of Criminal Procedure, rules relevant to criminal procedure are to be found in the Law on the Organization of the Judiciary (*Ordinamento giudiziario*), in the Law on criminal procedure for juvenile offenders (*tribunale per i minorenni*), in the Law on Assize Courts (*corti d'assise*) of April 15, 1951 (No. 287), in the law on public legal aid for the indigent accused (*patrocinio a spese dello Stato*) of July, 31, 1990 (No. 217) and in the special legislation on organized crime (*mafia*) and on tax offences.

The *Military Code of Criminal Procedure* of 20 February 1941 (No. 303), is applied by the military judiciary to military crimes committed by persons belonging to the armed forces. Initially, military procedural law differed considerably from civilian law. Now the rights of the accused are equally protected in both civil and military proceedings with the difference tending to lie mainly in the judges composing the courts. The trend is towards turning military jurisdictions into to ordinary jurisdictions.

The *rules on drug offences* are contained in the Law of December 22, 1975 (No. 685) as amended June 26, 1990 (No. 162), which establishes an elaborate system of intervention by administrative and judicial authorities, the latter having final jurisdiction in the more serious cases and in those where the defendant refuses recovery therapy.

The *Penitentiary Regulations* of July 26, 1975 (No. 354), as amended October 10, 1986 (No. 663), govern the rights and duties of prisoners and of internees, providing judicial control during the enforcement of the custodial sentences, and also with respect to alternative measures such as parole, conditional discharge, early release, etc.

Lastly, judicial control is also available in the proceedings for enforcing preventive measures (*misure di prevenzione*) depending on what danger the accused presents for society (laws of December 27, 1956 (No. 1423); May 31, 1965 (No. 575); September 13, 1982 (No. 646) as amended).

## 1.5. CASE-LAW

Judicial precedents are not sources of the law of criminal procedure: in the Italian system, not even a decision by the Supreme Court (*Corte di Cassazione*) in plenary session (*sezioni unite*) is binding for the judge on the merits. Obviously, however, the authority of a Supreme Court judgment, and above all the fact that it is adequately grounded, may be sufficient to make different trends of interpretation of the law converge.

The Code of Criminal Procedure has been in force for too short a time to give rise to significant divergencies in case-law, but the Supreme Court has already clarified the meaning of some of the most widely applied procedural rules.

1.6. LEGAL DOCTRINE

Legal doctrine, being "professorial law", is not a source of the law *stricto sensu*. It, nevertheless, acts both as a thrust and a clarification of procedural problems. So far, neither the quality nor the quantity of the doctrine on the new code have developed to a meaningful extent, even though remarkable studies on the system as a whole and on specific subjects exist.

## 2. Structure of the criminal justice system

2.1. GENERAL PRINCIPLES

The 1988 Code of Criminal Procedure was drafted according to the guidelines laid down in the 1987 statute that gave the Executive the mandate to elaborate the Code (*supra*, 1.1.). These guidelines were: applying the constitutional principles; complying with the international rules concerning the rights of the individual in the criminal proceedings (particularly the European Convention on Human Rights and the International Covenant on Civil and Political Rights); introducing an adversarial trial system, taking into account that proceedings must be simplified to the maximum extent possible; adopting the principle of orality; making sure that the prosecution and the defence are equally treated at every stage of the proceedings.

This led to the abandoning of the inquisitorial system, which was characterised by secret, written pre-trial proceedings geared towards shaping the evidence at the pre-trial stage, with the result that the trial was only a mere verification of the evidence obtained during the pre-trial investigation.

In general terms, the reform brings the Italian criminal justice system into line with the adversarial system of common-law countries, albeit that important differences subsist: for example, prosecution remains mandatory (plea bargaining is not possible, see however the *patteggiamento*, *infra*, 8.3.), and the judge does not play a passive role, but has instead far-reaching powers of initiative with respect to the gathering of evidence, further amended as a result of some interpretative findings.

2.2. INVESTIGATING AUTHORITIES

The investigating authorities consist of the public prosecutor (*pubblico ministero*) and a specialized investigation body known as the judicial police (*polizia giudiziaria*).

The *judicial police* is generally the first authority to deal with an offence. They are obliged to collect information about offences, even on their own initiative, and to prevent offences from having further consequences. They must take the necessary steps to protect the evidence and gather any other element that may be useful for the enforcement of the criminal law.

The *public prosecutor* is a magistrate without judicial power, who is directly in charge of the investigation. Formally he is a public party, but his task is to act objectively, in the sole interest of preserving law and justice. He must collect the evidence, irrespective of whether it is evidence for the prosecution or for the accused (art.358). The public prosecutor may avail himself of the judicial police (art.109 of the Constitution), who must conduct any investigation ordered or entrusted to them, and follow the public prosecutor's guidelines.

Under the former criminal code, there was a third investigating authority, the investigating judge *(giudice istruttore)*, who had autonomous investigating powers, alongside those of the public prosecutor and the police. The new code has abolished the investigating judge, thus adopting the principle that investigative and judicial functions should be strictly separated. The successor to the investigating judge, the *judge for the preliminary investigations (giudice per le indagini preliminari* or G.I.P.) no longer has investigating powers of his own. However, he still plays an important role, because he may, to a varying degree, exercise control over the activities of the investigating authorities, and in doing so guarantee respect for the rights of the accused whenever measures must be taken that restrict personal freedom, or affect the right to privacy. Another important task of the *giudice per le indagini preliminari* is the *incidente probatorio*: when, during the preliminary investigations and thus before the trial, the need to give evidence arises, such evidence may be given to the judge for the preliminary investigations, during a special, adversarial, hearing called *incidente probatorio* (see further *infra*, 6.1.3.).

## 2.3. PROSECUTING AUTHORITIES

The public prosecutor is the *dominus* of the preliminary investigations. He decides whether or not to prosecute the offence (see further *infra*, 6.).

The organization of the board of public prosecutors consists of a public prosecutor's office at the level of the *pretore* and at the tribunal (*infra*, 2.4.1.), and of an attorney general's office at the level of the Court of Appeal and of the Supreme Court (*Corte di Cassazione*).

## 2.4. THE JUDICIARY

### 2.4.1. Competence

Judges in the first instance are the *pretore*, the tribunal, the Assize Court, the Minors' Court *(tribunale per i minorenni)* and the Military Court (*tribunale militare*). Their competence depends on the seriousness of the offence for the first three, and upon the age or the *status* of the accused for the last two.

The *judge for the preliminary investigations (giudice per le indagini preliminari* or G.I.P.) is likewise a judge in the first instance. He may judge crimes for which the *Pretore*, the *Tribunale* or the Assize Court are competent (art.596).

The *Pretore* is a single judge who is competent to try less serious crimes, *i.e.* offences carrying a sentence not exceeding four years' imprisonment. There are, however, noteworthy exceptions to this rule, such as receiving stolen goods, which carries a higher sentence.

The *Assize Court* (*Corte d'Assise*) is composed of two full-time judges (one as a president) plus six lay judges, and is competent to judge serious crimes (murder, manslaughter, slavery).

The *Tribunale* is composed of three full-time judges and is competent for all the crimes not assigned to the *pretore* or to the Assize Court. For example, it is competent for the more serious financial offences, slander by means of the press, robbery, kidnapping, corruption, extortion, and the more serious drug offences.

The *Minors' Court* is competent to judge any offence committed by persons who were under the age of eighteen years at the time the offence was committed. It is composed of four judges, two of whom are lay judges appointed because of their expertise in the fields of medicine, psychiatry and psychology.

The *Military Court*, composed of military judges and of persons who serve in the armed forces but are not judges, applies the military penal code, and is competent only in cases of military crimes committed by servicemen.

Wholly *extra ordinem* is the competence, in first and sole instance, of the *Constitutional Court* in plenary session (15 judges plus 16 lay judges chosen by lot), to judge the crimes of high treason, and attacks against the Constitution by the President of the Republic.

### 2.4.2. The role of lay judges

The Constitution (art.102) provides for the direct participation of the people in the administration of justice. The Law on the Organization of the Judiciary states who are to be the judges in criminal cases. Normally such competence is conferred to professional judges with legal training. However, ordinary citizens can also be appointed as judges on the basis of two criteria: a specific competence in a non-juridical field (courts for juvenile offenders, *infra*, 8.9.); court of surveillance on the execution (*tribunale di sorveglianza*, *infra*, 10.2.)), or else a generic competence determined, inter alia, by age and a minimum degree of education (assize courts).

According to the Italian law of criminal procedure, lay judges always sit together with professional judges. During the trial, they have the same functions as the professional judges, except for the fact that it is always a professional judge, not a lay judge who presides over the hearing (contrary to the Anglo-Saxon tradition, where the jury deliberates and reaches its verdict without the presence of the professional judges).

The 1988 Code has to a large extent reduced the competence of the Assize Court, following the general tendency to reduce the jury trial already apparent in the preceding period. The importance of the contribution of common sense to the administration of justice does not affect the fact that lay judges are less able to deal effectively with complicated cases because they lack legal training, which may lead to decisions of an emotional nature rather than decisions grounded on the findings during the trial.

### 2.4.3. The nomination of judges

Both magistrates and judges are appointed after an examination (art.106 of the Constitution) in accordance with the rules of the judicial system. Different criteria apply to honorary judges and to lay judges in general, who are instead appointed from previously established lists.

### 2.4.4. Independence and impartiality

Judges are subject only to the law (art.101 of the Constitution). This is intended to exclude conditioning by either the Government or Parliament: the independence and autonomy of the judiciary are ensured by the *Consiglio Superiore della Magistratura* and by special guarantees granted by law such as nomination for life.

Generally speaking, impartiality is ensured by a more clear-cut distinction between the functions of those who judge and of those who investigate. Some of the figures in the 1930 Code of Criminal Procedure, such as the investigating judge, who later also decided on the results of the investigations or on the merits, have been eliminated.

The new code lays down rules covering both situations of incompatibility between consecutive functions held by the same person (set *a priori* by the law) and situations in which the judge may be disqualified either on his own initiative (*astensione*) or upon request by the parties (*ricusazione*). For example, a judge must abstain from taking part in a decision on a case in which he has previously been involved in the capacity of an expert, counsel, public prosecutor or judge. The same rules apply where a close relative is a judge, or when a reasonable person would doubt his impartiality due to personal interest or other reasons.

## 3. Parties to criminal proceedings

### 3.1. THE PUBLIC PROSECUTOR

The strict separation between the role of the judge and that of the prosecution and investigation is meant to ensure equidistance from the parties and parity of the parties. The essence of the adversarial principle lies in the confrontation between the parties, each of them in pursuit of their own interest, and in their contribution to the evidence. The Italian criminal trial is now a *proceeding between the parties*, precisely in order to guarantee that the prosecution and defence can participate to the proceedings under equal conditions.

Hence the public prosecutor has become a party to the proceedings, since he has lost the substantial jurisdictional powers he enjoyed under the inquisitorial system in the 1930 Code of Criminal Procedure. He is, however, also a *public party* because his role is not necessarily to oppose the accused, but to perform his functions objectively.

It is not for the accused to select his prosecutor, but the public prosecutor may refuse to serve for reasons of propriety, which goes to show that the public party is expected to conduct independent and impartial investigations in the sole interest of serving law and justice. The magistrate who disqualifies himself is obviously replaced by a different one belonging to the same office.

### 3.2. THE DEFENCE

The right of defence is inalienable at any stage and degree of the proceedings: the Constitutional Court has specified that the second paragraph of art.24 of the Constitution guarantees both the right of access to a court to defend one's interests and the right to be assisted by a technical counsel. The Court also held that the accused may not waive his right to this technical defence. In holding so, the Court goes beyond art.6(3)c of the European Convention on Human Rights.

### *3.2.1. The accused (imputato/indagnato)*

The accused is the person mentioned in the *notitia criminis* (*i.e.* the official document in which the police reports the offence to the prosecutor, see *infra*, 6.1.1.), and in respect of whom the public prosecutor believes that the suspicion is well-founded.

In technical terms, the accused (*imputato*) is the person whom the public prosecutor, at the end of the preliminary investigation, requests to be committed for trial, to be tried summarily, to receive a penal order, to be allowed to ask for the enforcement of a penal sanction of up to two years with the prosecutor's agreement (*patteggiamento*) or to be tried immediately or directly (art.60, see further *infra*, 6 and 8).

However, the accused's rights and guarantees already exist during the preliminary investigation (*indagini preliminari*, see *infra*, 6.1.), with respect to both the public prosecutor and the judicial police. Even before the indictment (*imputazione*), which marks the passing from the preliminary proceeding (*procedimento*) to the trial proper (*processo*), the accused benefits from the presumption of innocence. He has the right to be heard and the right to remain silent (privilege against self-incrimination), which even includes the possibility to lie, except as regards his personal particulars and his prior criminal convictions.

There is no obligation on the part of the authorities to inform the accused that he is under investigation, but the public prosecutor has the duty to forewarn him of his intention to perform an act at which the defence counsel has the right to be present. This particular warning (*informazione di garanzia*) makes the person under investigation aware of the accusations against him, and includes a formal request to appoint counsel.

If the person under investigation is aware of the fact that a preliminary investigation is pending against him, he may spontaneously appear before the public prosecutor in order to make a statement. He may also be formally requested to appear, and even be brought *manu militari*, before the public prosecutor.

All of the above highlights the fact that the accused is an active subject of the proceedings as far as his rights are concerned (he must immediately be informed of such rights by the police), whereas he is a passive subject as regards the investigation.

The most invasive *servitutes justitiae* include submission to coercive measures such as deprivation of liberty or telephone-tapping. These are measures that the public prosecutor may request, but which can only be ordered by the judge for the preliminary investigations, due to the infringement on fundamental rights (see further *infra*, 5).

The accused cannot be required to speak under oath. Nor can devices such as a lie-detector, or methods such as narcoanalysis or psychotests be used on him, not even with his consent or at his own request. The reason for this is that they infringe the right to privacy, and that the results are not reliable (see further *infra*, 7).

The Code and the special statutes grant benefits to the accused who waives his right to remain silent and who cooperates in determining both his own and other people's responsibilities. In practice, ruses or pressure (such as the threat of a lengthy detention) may be applied in order to obtain statements.

### 3.2.2. Defence counsel

The presence of defence counsel is compulsory. The law does not allow the accused to defend himself in person. The compulsory presence of defence counsel next to the accused is justified by the fact that the right for the accused to defend himself in person may not be sufficient if he lacks the necessary juridical knowledge (*iura novit curia, reus nescit*) and when he is emotionally involved. Not even a lawyer may defend himself alone.   Anyone   who   is accused of an offence has the right to legal assistance, but not more than two counsel may be appointed. An indigent accused has the same right, but the State must bear the costs (Law No. 217 of July 31, 1990). This applies to the more serious crimes (*delitti*), but not to offences against tax laws (this provision does not seem to be in conformity with the presumption of innocence). The law also discriminates against low or middle-income tax payers who do not formally fall below the so-called poverty line.

An accused who does not appoint counsel of his own choice, or who has remained without one (e.g. because of a waiver) is assisted by counsel appointed by the judge or by the public prosecutor (*difensore di ufficio*, art.97), chosen from a list kept for this purpose. A court-appointed counsel is obliged to serve, but is paid by the accused. In practice, court-appointed counsel are not able to provide an efficient defence, and one is likely to see "undisputed disputes", or trials where counsel is only a passive bystander.

Counsel is the *alter ego* of the accused. The law forbids monitoring of conversations between counsel and his client. It also forbids intercepting the correspondence between them, and sets restrictions on searches and checks at counsels'office. Evidence that has been collected contrary to this rule may not be used. Pending detention on remand, the accused must be given the opportunity to consult his counsel privately, within sight but not within ear-shot of other people. However, if exceptional circumstances exist, the public prosecutor may request a restriction from the judge for the preliminary investigations, which prohibits contact between the accused and his counsel, for a period not exceeding seven days.

Counsel for the defence must do all he can in his client's interest. He may not, however, act against ethical principles or infringe the criminal law (e.g. by aiding and abetting) while at the same time not committing the crime of disloyal legal defence.

An important aspect of the right to technical defence is *the right to appoint a technical consultant* (an expert in a non-juridical field) *and a private investigator*. Like the defence counsel, these persons are subject to the duty of professional secrecy regarding the things they learn when carrying out their tasks.

### 3.3. THE VICTIM

### 3.3.1. General principles

The person who has been victim of an offence (*offeso dal reato*), or his close relatives if the victim has died as a consequence of the offence, can be an "active subject" in the criminal proceedings. Under the 1988 Code of Criminal Procedure, the victim's position in criminal proceedings may be twofold: he may either bring a private prosecution, or "constitute himself" as a *parte civile*.

Even in the presence of crimes that are prosecuted *ex officio*, the victim of an offence has the right to be informed of the beginning of the proceeding (*informazione di garanzia*) and of its progress. He has the right to counsel, the right to file briefs and motions, to present evidence, and to ask the public prosecutor that a special hearing with respect to the evidence, the so-called *incidente probatorio,* be held (see *infra*, 6.1.3.); he may lodge objections against the request for dismissal of the charge against the accused, may be summoned to the committal proceedings (preliminary hearing -*udienza preliminare*) and to the trial; he may ask the President to put questions to witnesses and request the public prosecutor to take legal remedies.

The victim may be represented in criminal proceedings by a body or an association representing his interests, but only with his consent.

### 3.3.2. Private prosecution

Certain offences can only be prosecuted upon complaint by the victim (*querela*).

Such a complaint authorises, but does not oblige, the public prosecutor to prosecute.

### 3.3.3. Civil claims: the parte civile and the civilly responsible person

The victim may also claim damages or restitution as a plaintiff in a civil action (*azione civile*), which is attached to the criminal prosecution. In such a case, the victim becomes a party to the trial (*parte civile*), but only in the pursuit of his civil interests. A claim for damages may also be filed by someone who, albeit not personally a victim of the crime, has suffered damage as a result of it. Such a claim may be filed against the accused and against the person vicariously responsible for the damages (*civilly responsible person*).

The civil claim may be filed during the committal proceedings (*udienza preliminare, infra*, 6.2.) and during the trial, but not during the preliminary investigations where the *thema decidendi* is only whether or not to prosecute.

An injured party who files a civil claim is a party to the criminal proceeding for all purposes: he has the right to counsel and to see the *dossier*; he may file briefs and motions with the judge, he has the right to be heard and to present evidence, to put questions to the witnesses, to be summoned to the trial, and to be heard in pleadings, and is entitled to take legal remedies.

If the party injured by the crime claims damages or restitution in a civil proceeding, the judgment reached in the criminal proceeding is not binding for the civil judge.

## 4. General principles concerning criminal procedure

### 4.1. PRELIMINARY OBSERVATIONS

The general principles which inspired the 1988 Code of Criminal Procedure have already been mentioned (*supra*, 2.1.). Among them are the 1948 Constitution and the international instruments on human rights.

### 4.1.1. The principle of maximum simplification

This is worth stressing because of its particular bearing on the structure of criminal proceedings as a result of recent choices in this respect. In the course of the proceedings, the principle of maximum simplification tends to eliminate all acts and activities that are not essential, this mainly in order to meet the requirement for speed and to ensure that there is the least possible time between the *tempus delicti commissi* and the decision. Justice delayed is justice denied.

The Constitution does not explicitly deal with this point, but art.6(1) of the European Convention on Human Rights states that every person has a right to a fair and public hearing within a reasonable time. So does the International Covenant on Civil and Political rights. Italy has been condemned several times by the European Court of Human Rights for violating this rule. In order to prevent further condemnation, the 1988 Code of Criminal Procedure has emphasized the need to simplify and speed up procedures.

Accordingly, the public prosecutor must finish the preliminary investigations within strict deadlines (6 months after the *notitia criminis*, *supra*, 3.2.1. and *infra*, 6.1.). This period can be extended by the judge for the preliminary investigations, but only if there are good reasons for doing so. For very serious crimes, preliminary inquiries may last 2 years. Particular diligence is required in cases where the accused is detained on remand: cases must be tried even in the periods of court recess (Law No. 742 of October 7, 1969 as amended on July 20, 1990, No. 193).

*Expertises* may be ordered during the preliminary investigations, when it is feared that ordering the expertise during the trial would protract the proceedings: the judge for the preliminary investigations may, by way of the special procedure which has now been created for such occasions (the *incidente probatorio*, see *infra*, 6.1.3.), order the *expertise*.

More generally, special procedures that speed up matters are encouraged, in order to avoid a trial which is lengthy and demanding (see *infra*, 8). Accordingly, the right to a speedy trial coincides with the legislator's choice for speedy procedures: see the *giudizio direttissimo* and *immediato* (*infra*, 8). However, such acceleration may not impair the accused's right to have adequate time for the preparation of his defence (*termine a difesa*).

### 4.1.2. The principle of due process of law

Proceedings must be conducted in accordance with the rules set forth in the Code of Criminal Procedure and in the special statutes. Compliance with the requirements of fairness and justice is both a guarantee of legality and a guarantee that the results of the investigation or of the judgment are correct: adequate judicial sanctions guarantee compliance with the norms, and thereby substantive due process.

There are four types of procedural deficiencies. If the irregularity merely consists of the violation of a formal rule which is not a condition for the validity of the procedural act, there is no sanction (art.124). However, the infringement of rules of major importance (concerning various rules relating to the judge, the public prosecutor, and the accused or his counsel), may entail a general nullity (*nullità di ordine generale*, art.178). This nullity may be ascertained also *ex officio* by the judge. Depending on the rule, general nullities can be ascertained either at any time during the proceeding (*nullità assolute*, art.179), or within fixed legal time-limits only (*nullità intermedie*, art.180). In other cases, which are determined by law, infringement of a procedural rule only entails nullity when one of the parties has raised the nullity. This must be done within legal time-limits (*nullità relative*, art.181).

## 4.1.3. The principle "iudici fit probatio"

The 1988 Code of Criminal Procedure has abolished the investigating judge and has deprived the public prosecutor of the judicial powers which he previously had *(supra*, 2.1.). As a consequence, the elements collected by the prosecutor during the preliminary investigations no longer have value as proper evidence, but only as a source of evidence. Under the old system, the results of the preliminary inquiry were gathered in the prosecution *dossier*, which was submitted to the trial judge before the trial. The trial was basically conducted on the basis of this *dossier* and the elements collected in the *dossier* by the public prosecutor constituted the evidence for the prosecution.

The new Code of Criminal Procedure has abolished this system, and requires all the evidence to be produced in court, in front of the trial judge, who must evaluate and assess it on the basis of the initiatives of the parties and of the confrontation between them *(iudici fit probatio)*. The legislator wished to avoid the situation in which preliminary investigations conditioned the trial and influenced the trial judge. However, recent legislative reforms and developments in case-law have greatly mitigated this rule, following the principle that evidence should not be dispersed (art.500).

Henceforth, the prosecution *dossier* can no longer be used in the trial proceedings, but only in the preliminary hearing *(udienza preliminare, infra,* 6.2.), where the decision whether or not to proceed with the case is made (art.326). The prosecution *dossier* is submitted to the judge at the committal proceedings. However, if the case is committed for trial, the prosecution *dossier* may not be transmitted to the trial judge.

There are two exceptions to the rule that all evidence must be produced during the trial and that the *prosecution dossier* may not be used in court.

The first is the *incidente probatorio*: this is a procedure which can be used if there is a risk that evidence available during the preliminary investigation may be dispersed by the time the case is referred to the trial court (see *infra*,6.1.3.). In such cases, the evidence may be produced before the judge for the preliminary investigations, in the same way as the evidence would be produced before the trial judge, with the exception, however, that the *incidente probatorio* takes place *in camera*. This derogation is limited in time, and may only be applied in the cases determined by law. In addition, the *incidente probatorio* can only take place on the request of the parties. This requirement is meant to exclude *ex officio* initiatives by the judge for the preliminary investigations, which would have created the risk of a return to the previous system where the investigating judge would conduct the investigation, which the 1988 Code of Criminal Procedure wanted to abolish.

The second exception lies in the possibility of using the prosecution *dossier* for settling the case by means of one of the special procedures such as the summary trial *(giudizio abbreviato)*, the *patteggiamento* and the penal order (see *infra*, 8). This can only be done with the consent of the accused. The accused's lack of interest in the trial is rewarded by procedural savings (reduced costs and time), by reduced sentences and other benefits (*infra*, ibid.).

### 4.2. PRINCIPLES GOVERNING THE OPENING OF THE CRIMINAL PROCEEDING

#### 4.2.1. The "ex officio" principle

Everyone has the right, but not the obligation, to report an offence to the police or to the public prosecutor. However, reporting is compulsory in case of serious crimes against the State.

Certain offences can only be prosecuted upon complaint of the victim (*querela*). Others can only be prosecuted with the authorization of Parliament (*autorizzazione a procedere*, e.g. art.68 of the Constitution), or on the request of the competent public authority (*richiesta di procedimento*).

Except for these cases, the public prosecutor has the duty to proceed *ex officio*, *i.e.* even without denunciation and even against the wishes of the victim. The State has pledged itself to protect the public against crime, and has acquired a monopoly over criminal prosecution *ne cives ad arma ruant,* and with an aim to forestall recourse to private justice. Criminal prosecution is a public duty, which excludes criminal prosecution by private parties. Accordingly the victim's complaint (*querela*) authorizes, but does not oblige, the public prosecutor to prosecute.

#### 4.2.2. The principle of the legality of prosecutions

The public prosecutor is under the obligation to prosecute (art.112 of the Constitution) whenever there are sufficient grounds to suspect a person of having committed an offence. The decision is taken after such preliminary investigations as he deems necessary. As a result of this, the Italian law of criminal procedure leaves no room for the "opportunity principle", which allows the public prosecutor to drop a charge at his discretion. Since, without amendment to the Constitution, no derogation can be made from the principle of legality, plea bargaining is not allowed. Agreements between the public prosecutor and the accused are permissible in a very circumscribed form (see *infra*, 8.3).

The application of the opportunity principle could be useful to reduce the work-load of judges and public prosecutors, but it bears the risk of opening the doors to abuse. In practice, however, the opportunity principle is a *de facto* development in the Italian judicial system because public prosecutors have no time to deal with all the crimes that are reported, and therefore choose to investigate only those that are socially more relevant (screening of the *notitiae criminis*). The other criminal cases are resolved by dismissal, expiry of the limitation period or periodical mercy measures (amnesty).

## 4.2.3. *The principle of secrecy*

The preliminary investigations conducted by the public prosecutor and by the police no longer engender evidence as was the case under the 1930 Code of Criminal Procedure, but are nevertheless covered by secrecy (art.329).

The person under investigation may not consult the register of the *notitiae criminis* and has no right to be informed of the beginning and the progress of the preliminary investigations (*indagini preliminari, infra*, 6.1.) against him. He only hears about these investigations when they are concluded.

Even in cases where the public prosecutor or the police have publicly disclosed that preliminary investigations are under way, the suspect and his counsel have no right to be present during acts of investigation (such as the questioning of potential witnesses), and have no right to be informed in advance of such acts (e.g. a search) (see further 6.1.2.).

The secrecy of the preliminary investigation lasts until the closing of the preliminary investigations, or even before if the public prosecutor deems it necessary. Secrecy also sets precise restrictions on the activity of the Press.

Since the preliminary investigations are henceforth "party investigations" which have no evidentiary value during the trial, it appears altogether acceptable that they take place without interferences by the defence. This brings the public prosecutor's investigations into line with the adversarial principle, according to which the plaintiff operates without the participation of the opposite party in collecting the material aimed at sustaining a possible indictment (*imputazione*). However, it may be argued that it is not a matter of indifference for the defence whether or not it plays a part in influencing the public prosecutor in his decision whether or not to prosecute.

### 4.3. PRINCIPLES GOVERNING THE TAKING OF EVIDENCE

The 1988 Code of Criminal Procedure devotes one of its eleven Books, Book III, to the subject of evidence. The first chapter enumerates a number of leading principles that are binding on the judge.

## 4.3.1. *The principle of the moral freedom of the individual*

Irrespective of the consent of the person concerned (be it the accused, the victim or a witness), methods or techniques that may have an influence on his "freedom of self-determination", or affect his capacity to remember and to evaluate the facts are forbidden (*libertà morale della persona nell'assunzione della prova*, art.188).

## 4.3.2. *The principle of the admissibility of evidence praeter legem*

The code enumerates the means of evidence (*mezzi di prova*, see *infra*, 3). This enumeration is, however, not exhaustive. The judge may rely on means of evidence even when they are not regulated by the law provided that they are useful and they do not adversely affect the moral freedom of the individual. In other words, the enumeration of the means of evidence in the Code is not a *numerus clausus*, and recently-acquired knowledge and science may be used as long as it is not contrary to the law (*prove non disciplinate dalla legge*, art.189).

### 4.3.3. The right to present evidence

The parties (public prosecutor and private parties) have the right to present evidence, which the judge must receive, with the exception of evidence forbidden by law, or obviously superfluous or irrelevant evidence.

In principle, *ex officio* evidence is only admissible in the cases provided by law. This idea is in line with the abolition of the investigating judge (art.507), but recent findings have upheld the contrary interpretation. The right to present evidence has been severely curtailed in respect of defendants, charged with organised crime (art.190bis).

### 4.3.4. The principle of the free evaluation of the evidence

Evidence must be produced in front of the judge by the parties- *iudici fit probatio* (*supra*, 4.3.1.)- even though he is in no way bound by it. In his decision, he must give reasons for both the results obtained and the criteria adopted in assessing the weight of evidence.

The judge may not rely on evidence that has been illegally acquired or evidence *contra legem* (such as evidence obtained by means of a lie detector or of narco-analysis), but he may be convinced on the basis of evidence obtained lawfully.

### 4.3.5. The principle of the burden of proof (onus probandi)

Art.27 para.2 of the Constitution and art.6(2) of the European Convention on Human Rights establish the rule that anyone charged with a criminal offence shall be presumed innocent until proved guilty by a final judgment.

This means that no one may be convicted as long as the public prosecutor has not proved his guilt beyond any reasonable doubt: *onus probandi incumbit ei qui dicit*. However, it is obviously in the interest of the accused to supply evidence in his favour (e.g. an alibi). If the accused wants to submit his own evidence, he must do so not later than seven days before the trial starts. He is not allowed to produce it during the trial, unless his evidence is new evidence.

### 4.3.6. The exclusionary rule

Evidence that has been illegally obtained may not be taken into account (*inutilizzabilità*, art.191). The question of the admissibility of the evidence may be raised by the parties, and *ex officio* by the judge.

## 4.4. PRINCIPLES GOVERNING THE TRIAL

The trial is the core of the criminal proceedings. During the trial, the adversarial model fully applies. The tasks of prosecuting and judging a case are now strictly separated.

The trial guarantees that both parties enjoy an equal opportunity to explain their point of view; it ensures that there is an impartial judge who is not aware of the elements gathered by the public prosecutor during the preliminary investigations; the case is referred to the trial judge only after having been committed for trial by the judge for the preliminary investigations after the committal proceedings (preliminary hearing- *udienza preliminare*).

Unlike under the former system, the *prosecution dossier* is no longer transmitted to the trial judge. The *dossier* submitted to the trial judge (*dossier of the trial*) only contains the following elements: the record of investigative acts of the public prosecutor and the police that cannot be repeated (*atti non ripetibili*, e.g. transcripts of telephonic conversations or investigations that cannot be repeated for instance, due to the health situation of the witness or the accused's failure to appear, his absence or his refusal to be examined), the record of evidence, received in the *incidente probatorio* (*infra*, 6.1.3.), the *corpus delicti*, the criminal record of the accused, the *notitia criminis*, and the documents concerning the civil claims.

### 4.4.1. The principle of immediacy (immediatezza)

According to the principle *iudici fit probatio* (*supra*, 4.1.3.), all evidence must be produced in front of the judge, and consequently, the elements collected during the preliminary investigations must be established in court, with the exception of the records of unrepeatable acts and the evidence received by the judge for the preliminary investigations during the *incidente probatorio*.

No statements made during the preliminary investigations may be read out in court; witnesses must be heard in person: hearsay (*de auditu*) testimony is forbidden as per the first-hand-knowledge rule.

The consequences of this principle are: that the trial judge is irreplaceable; that the judge who collected the evidence must be the one who decides on the merits of the case; that the trial must be held within a reasonable time in order to allow the clear recollections of the evidence and in order to bring the time when the evidence is collected close to the time when it is evaluated (principle of concentration of the trial).

### 4.4.2. The principle of orality

The principle of orality, according to which proceedings in court must be oral (contrary to the pre-trial investigations which are written), flows from the principle of direct testimony. Some documents, however, may be read aloud in court: the records of the unrepeatable actions performed during the preliminary investigations; the documents received on the parties' request or documents that are necessary to assess the accused's personality. Further significant exceptions to the principle of orality were introduced in 1992 (arts.190bis and 238).

Witnesses and experts may consult documents to aid their memories. However, anonymous documents cannot be retained as evidence (see further *infra*, 7).

### 4.4.3. The principle of publicity

Public attendance at criminal proceedings is a form of democratic control on the administration of justice. A trial *coram populo* guarantees that the activities of the parties, and particularly of the judge, are transparent.

Judgment must be pronounced publicly, but the press and the public may be excluded from all or part of the trial in the interest of morals, hygiene or the preservation of a public secret or of privacy. The judge may order that the examination of a minor, who was injured by the crime, be held *in camera*. However, the trial of an accused minor is never public.

Television is allowed in the courtroom either with the consent of the parties or when the judge believes that broadcasting part of the trial has a particular educational benefit. In this case, it is forbidden to film persons (parties, witnesses, experts) without their consent.

### 4.4.4. The principle "audiatur et altera pars".

The simultaneous presence at the trial of all the opposing parties lends substance to the principle *audiatur et altera pars* and its corollaries, such as the rules on refuting charges, on *ius vocatio* and on the need to take into account impediments for the appearance of the accused or his counsel. This principle is aimed at guaranteeing the equal standing of the parties during the trial and an equal opportunity to convince the judge: they have the right to have their evidence received in equal circumstances, and every decision of the judge is taken after hearing the parties (*sentite le parti*).

Most important, the parties have the right to cross-examine witnesses, experts, technical consultants and persons who have asked to be questioned or have agreed to be examined.

The judge decides on objections, ensures that no excessive or inadmissible questions are put (e.g. leading questions). He is passive, playing the role of an impartial audience, while the parties in fact conduct the trial. An exception in this respect is the examination of a minor , which is led by the president of the court, who has a power to collect absolutely necessary evidence *ex officio*.

## 5. Coercive measures

### 5.1. ARREST (*ARRESTO* AND *FERMO*)

The police may arrest a person caught while committing an arrestable offence, or immediately thereafter (*arresto in flagranza*) (arts.380 and 381). Private citizens may also arrest a person under certain conditions (art.383).

While private citizens are bound to proceed promptly to bring the arrestee under the authority of the judicial police, the police must do so within an average period of 24 hours (arts.380-383).

When there are serious reasons to believe that a person charged with a serious crime might abscond, the public prosecutor (and also the judicial police on their own initiative) may arrest him (*fermo degli indiziati di delitto*, art.384) even in cases other than those of flagrancy. Persons arrested or held must be brought within an average period of 48 hours before the judge for the preliminary investigations who, within the following 48 hours, must either confirm or withdraw the restrictive measure. This is done at a hearing (*udienza di convalida*), which is attended by the defence counsel.

### 5.2. DETENTION ON REMAND AND OTHER RESTRICTIVE MEASURES

The presumption of innocence does not exclude depriving a person of his liberty for the purposes of a criminal investigation, and does not exclude the use of other coercive measures. Coercive measures include: detention on remand, detention at health-care institutions, house arrest, restriction orders, compulsory residence orders, orders to report to the police at given intervals, prohibition to leave the country, etc.

### 5.2.1. Detention on remand (custodia cauttelare)

Detention on remand may only be ordered by a judge. As this is the most serious of all coercive measures, it can only be ordered when it is strictly necessary and where none of the other coercive measures is suitable (proportionality principle).

Detention on remand is deemed to be an exceptional measure. It can only be ordered if there is a danger that the accused will meddle with the evidence, if there are reasons to believe that he will abscond or when it is feared that he will commit serious crimes (art.274). The provision allowing detention on remand for reasons of "danger of reiteration" has been declared contrary to the presumption of innocence. Here the aim is the protection of the community and avoiding danger to any person in the community. However, art.275 was amended in respect of the more serious offences and in respect of organised crime: for these offences, detention on remand is mandatory, unless it can be established that there is no *periculum libertatis*.

Some persons may not be detained on remand: pregnant women, women who are breast-feeding, persons who are seriously ill, persons above the age of

70, and drug-addicts who are in therapy. Special rules apply to minors.

Detention on remand is limited in time. It may not exceed six years. After these, the accused must be released even if convicted following a judgment that is not yet final. This period may be extended by the judge for the preliminary investigations, but only if certain conditions are met.

Detention on remand ends when either the *fumus delicti* or the *periculum libertatis* end. It also comes to an end when a different coercive measure is applied, following a suspended sentence or a sentence shorter than the one already served, when the accused has not been questioned within 5 days and, lastly, the expiry of the terms for detention on remand.

Release may be conditioned by guarantees. Release on bail (*rilascio su cauzione*) is no longer permitted because of its potential for discrimination against the indigent accused.

### 5.2.2. House arrests (arresti domiciliari)

House arrest is a restriction of the right to personal liberty. A person subjected to this measure is in self-custody, but can be controlled at any time.

House arrests are restricted by the same time limits as detention on remand. The time spent under house arrest is deducted from the sentence that is eventually imposed.

### 5.2.3. Control of coercive measures

The judge for the preliminary investigations has the power to revoke and replace the coercive measures he has taken.

The law provides for the possibility of filing an application against his decisions with the *Tribunale della Libertà* in order to have coercive measures *de libertate* (such as a warrant) reconsidered, even on their merits (*riesame*). Cross-examination and recourse to the Supreme Court (*Corte di Cassazione)* are guaranteed.

The speediness of the proceedings is guaranteed by the short delays within which either a decision must be rendered by the *Tribunale della Libertà*, failing which the coercive measure must be terminated.

The measures restricting liberty which are not open to reconsideration (*riesame*) can be appealed against before the competent tribunal, or may be directly attacked - *per saltum* - before the Supreme Court in order to have the legality of the restriction determined.

### 5.2.4. The right to compensation

Detention on remand and house arrest are usually deducted from the sentence (art.657). When the accused has been acquitted by a final judgment, he is entitled to adequate compensation for having been unjustly detained on remand. The same right applies to a convicted person who has been unlawfully (*contra legem*) detained.

The extent of the compensation may not exceed one hundred million lire. Even though the right to compensation was laid down in art.5 of the European Convention on Human Rights in 1954, it was only implemented in the new code of 1988 (arts.314-315). The civil liability of judges in connection with measures concerning personal liberty was recognised in Law No. 117 of April 13, 1988.

### 5.3. INSPECTION, SEARCH AND SEIZURE

By stating that the domicile is inviolable, art.14 of the Constitution provides that inspections, searches or seizures are only permitted in the cases and forms provided for by the law. Inspection (*ispezione*) and search (*perquisizione*) are means of seeking evidence (*mezzi di ricerca della prova*, see *infra*, 7.1.): the former aims at finding traces of the crime, the latter at finding the *corpus delicti* or persons who are wanted.

*Ispezione* may be ordered with respect to the person of the interested party (*ispezione personale*), premises (*ispezione locale*) or objects (*ispezione reale*).

*Perquisizione* may concern people (*perquisizione personale*) or premises (*perquisizione locale*). Searches at banks and at the offices of defence counsel are of particular importance.

Another means of securing evidence is seizure (*sequestro*), which concerns the *corpus delicti* and the matters pertaining to the crime (*i.e.* objects which constitute the means and the product of the crime or its proceeds).

Search and seizure are closely related. Both are based on surprise, and it is therefore inconceivable that the interested party or his counsel should receive prior notice. Special rules exist with respect to the seizure of correspondence, seizure at banks, and also the relationship between seizure and professional, official and State secrets.

The seizure order may be challenged by filing a request for re-examination with the *Tribunale delle Libertà*, and the latter's ruling may be challenged on questions of law before the Supreme Court (*Corte di Cassazione)* (art.257).

### 5.4. EXAMINATION OF BODY AND MIND

As stated above, one type of inspection (*ispezione*) and of search (*perquisizione*) may concern the accused's or the victim's person, with the purpose of ascertaining whether the crime has left any traces.

This examination of the person must take place with due respect to the dignity of the person. The person subject to the examination is entitled to have the search carried out in the presence of a person he trusts. He may even require that it be carried out by a physician or by a person of the same sex.

Examination of the mind of the accused, of the victim or of a witness (mental examination) is done by means of an expert report (*perizia*) aimed at ascertaining criminal responsibility or the reliability of the statements made.

Insanity may be assessed either by the judge or on the basis of previous expert reports, or from the accused's behaviour.

Whereas psychiatric examination is admitted, neither psychological nor behavioural tests are allowed. Doctrine justifies this prohibition (which does not apply to juvenile offenders and to convicts serving a sentence) with the argument that the judge's good sense is sufficient, that such examinations are prejudicial to privacy, or that psychology does not obtain scientifically valid results.

### 5.5. INTERFERENCE WITH THE RIGHT TO PRIVACY

According to art.15 of the Constitution, freedom and privacy of correspondence and of any other form of communication are inalienable. They may be restricted only by judicial order, and subject to the guarantees offered by the law.

Intercepting a suspect's conversations and communications can be very useful to the investigations. Interceptions can be done by telephone tapping or by the use of miniature microphones and transmitters in order to monitor private conversations. This serious interference with the right to privacy can only be ordered for serious crimes specified by law, when there are serious reasons to believe that the accused is guilty and provided that there are no other means for collecting the evidence.

Interception is only permissible if carried out by virtue of a previous order of the judge for the preliminary investigations, given on the request of the public prosecutor. However, in exceptional circumstances, interceptions may be ordered by the public prosecutor, but he is under the obligation to report this immediately to the judge for the preliminary investigations who may confirm or reject it.

Prosecuting authorities are authorized by law to intercept postal communications from and to an accused, but the police may not open mail.

As interceptions are unrepeatable actions, the transcripts may be included in the *trial dossier* (*supra*, 4.4.1.).

Some interceptions are not permitted, e.g. intercepting communications from and to the counsel. Likewise, seizing and checking correspondence between the accused and his counsel are forbidden.

## 6. The ordinary course of the criminal proceedings

Very succinctly, and without mentioning the innumerable possible variations, criminal proceedings in Italy can be divided into the following successive stages: preliminary investigations by the judicial police and by the public prosecutor (possibly including an *incidente probatorio*); committal proceedings (preliminary hearing -*udienza preliminare*) with a possible indictment and, finally, the trial.

## 6.1. PRELIMINARY INVESTIGATIONS (*INDAGINI PRELIMINARI*)

### 6.1.1. *Police inquiry*

The purpose and scope of the police inquiry is to find out whether an offence has been committed, who is the suspect, where he may be found and what are the sources of evidence. Under the old code, the police often acted as a *de facto* investigating authority. In order to avoid this, the 1988 Code had set a time-limit for police investigations: within 48 hours, the judicial police had to inform the public prosecutor of their inquiry by transmitting the *notitia criminis*. The notitia criminis is immediately registered in the official record of the public prosecutor. Thereafter, the inquiry is continued on the instructions of the public prosecutor. Later amendments, however, have enlarged the independence of investigation officers.

### 6.1.2. *Preliminary investigations*

Preliminary investigations are carried out by the public prosecutor. Their purpose is to ascertain the facts and trace the evidence needed for a decision on whether or not to prosecute (art.326).

Like the inquiry, preliminary investigations are conducted in secret. Whereas defence counsel may not be present for important acts (such as the questioning of witnesses), he may, however, be present at others. For some of these investigative acts, he must be warned in advance (for example, inspections or confrontations), but not for others (for example search or seizure), which can be carried out without prior notice.

Preliminary investigations are limited in time: these should not, in principle, exceed a period of six months, starting from the registration of the name of the accused in the book of the *notitiae criminis*. According to arts.405-407, this period may be extended for up to two years for reasons of acknowledged need.

Preliminary investigations may be ended in different ways.

- The public prosecutor may the ask the judge for the preliminary investigations to have the prosecution dropped (*archiviazione*). *Archiviazione* may be requested in all the cases in which the public prosecutor finds that no offence was committed (*i.e.* when the *notitia criminis* was ill-founded) and in all those cases where he deems that the elements collected are not sufficient to obtain a conviction (art.125, provisions for the implementation of the Code of Criminal Procedure). *Nolle prosequi* produces dismissal without prejudice for the prosecution, *i.e.* it does not prevent the reopening of the case at a later stage. The case may be reopened when new evidence has emerged. This is decided by the judge for the preliminary investigations, on the request of the public prosecutor.

- The public prosecutor may ask the judge for the preliminary investigations to commit the accused for trial when he deems there is a probable cause against him, *i.e.* that the elements collected during his investigation are sufficient to obtain a conviction. The decision on whether or not to refer the case is taken in the committal proceedings (*udienza preliminare*, see *infra*,6.2.).

- The third way of concluding the preliminary investigations consists of a request for a special proceeding in which the public prosecutor formulates the indictment (*imputazione*) and submits the prosecution *dossier* either to the judge for the preliminary investigations (see *infra*, 8.2. and 8.3.) or to the trial judge (see 8.3 and 8.4. below).

### 6.1.3. The incidente probatorio

During the preliminary investigations, the public prosecutor (often on the request of the victim), and the person who is under investigation, have the right to ask the judge for the preliminary investigations to receive evidence in a special procedure called the *incidente probatorio*. This procedure is used when postponing the production of the evidence until the trial would either jeopardise the possibility of producing it, (for example, a witness or a co-accused is about to die or has been threatened), or would cause the trial to be suspended, which would be incompatible with the principle of concentration (art.392).

The request for this special hearing may be the subject of an objection by the person affected by it, but the decision rests with the judge for the preliminary investigations with whom the request is filed. Evidence received through such a procedure does not apply to persons other than those whose counsels took part in the *incidente probatorio*, and in particular does not apply to the civil party who does not consent.

### 6.2. COMMITTAL PROCEEDINGS (PRELIMINARY HEARING - *UDIENZA PRELIMINARE*)

The request for committal to trial put forth by the public prosecutor is followed by committal proceedings (*udienza preliminare*) before the judge for the preliminary investigations, unless the accused requests an immediate trial (*giudizio immediato*, see *infra*, 8.5.). The decision whether or not to commit a person for trial is taken by the judge. By conferring this decision to a judge, judicial control is guaranteed.

The *udienza preliminare* takes place *in camera*, but in the presence of the parties, *i.e.* the public prosecutor and the private parties (including the *parte civile*). A debate between the parties takes place, in which they develop their arguments on the basis of the documentation contained in the *prosecution dossier*.

The decision is taken on the basis of the documentation available (*rebus sic stantibus*), save for the limited power of the judge to acquire further information which he considers may be useful in reaching a decision (art.422). In this case it is the judge who leads the investigation.

*Committal* is ordered by a decree that must not be motivated (in order not to influence the trial judge): this decree states the charges, contains a summary indication of the evidence and sets a date for the trial. There are no remedies against the committal order. After the committal, the public prosecutor retains his right to conduct further investigations (art.430).

The judge for the preliminary investigations may also decide not to commit the accused and pronounce a *dismissal order (sentenza di non luogo a procedere*, art.425). The dismissal order is subject to appeal or cassation. Dismissing a case does not foreclose a reopening of the case should new evidence surface.

In theory committal proceedings are intended to be a "gate-keeper" aimed at restricting the work-load of trial judges and are supposed to act as "a sword and a shield" for the accused. In practice, however, dismissal orders are very rare because the judge's powers are limited. Consequently, committal proceedings often almost amount to a judicial backing of the public prosecutor's decision to prosecute.

## 6.3. THE TRIAL

### 6.3.1. Proceedings preliminary to the trial (atti preliminari al dibattimento)

Proceedings preliminary to the trial *(atti preliminari al dibattimento)* start with the closing of the preliminary investigations and end with the actions introducing the trial. There are at least three relevant moments:

Firstly, urgent acts of procedure *(atti urgenti)* can be performed, *i.e.* the collecting of evidence where necessary, when there is a risk of jeopardizing its authenticity or collection (when, for instance, a witness's life is in danger because of a serious illness). This may be done by the trial judge (or the president of the court if the court is composed of more than 1 judge) on a request by one of the parties.

Secondly, the parties must draft a list with the names of the witnesses, experts and technical counsel they wish to examine during the hearing, and indicate the circumstances which the examination must deal with. This list must be submitted to the court at least 7 days before the trial begins, in order to exclude surprise evidence, which is not admissible, save for evidence revealed after the submission of the list (art.468).

Thirdly, early dismissal can be requested if the public prosecutor and the accused do not object *(sentenza di non doversi procedere)*. This decision, caused for example by the crime's extinction under the statute of limitations, is not subject to appeal but can be challenged on questions of law before the Supreme Court *(Corte di Cassazione)* (art.469).

### 6.3.2. The trial

The trial must be held in public (see *supra*, 4.4.3.). The trial is recorded (in writing or by sound recording). At the trial, preliminary questions are dealt with first in order to ensure compliance with the parties' right to participation. Thus the judge verifies whether the parties have duly appeared, and examines whether reasons for non-appearance of the accused or his counsel are justified by a legal impediment.

If the accused is absent without justification (*contumacia*), the proceedings are continued without him, since he has the right not to participate to his trial. If, however, the accused does not appear due to a legal impediment, the trial is suspended or adjourned: the accusatorial system indeed requires that the accused be in a position to attend the trial if he so wishes. In order to avoid the guiltless absence of the accused, the 1988 Code requires the court to verify that the summons has been duly served, and allows for a new summons to be served if there are reasons to believe that the recipient was not aware of the original summons.

The trial judge is aware of the *thema decidendi*, *i.e.* of the indictment (*imputazione*) which is read through at the arraignment. He does not, however, know the results of the preliminary investigations, since the *prosecution dossier* is not transmitted to him (*supra*, 4.1.3.). The public prosecutor, and after him counsel of the private parties and of the accused develop their opening arguments (*esposizione introduttiva*), in which they indicate the facts to be proved and the evidence they ask to be received. This is the last moment at which documentary evidence may be filed. The judge decides on the admissibility of the evidence, and admits evidence both in favour of, and against the accused.

The trial begins with the setting out of the evidence in support of the case of the public prosecutor, and continues with the collecting of the evidence requested by the other parties: witnesses are the first ones to be heard, then the experts and technical consultants, and lastly comes the examination of the parties if they agree to it; the accused may issue spontaneous statements, or may ask to be examined.

The questions are asked by the parties. The president may add some questions, and may order *ex officio* that new, absolutely necessary evidence be collected. Then follow the readings of the documents that may be read aloud in court.

The charge may be modified during the trial (e.g. by contesting an aggravating circumstance), but in such a case the accused must be granted time to prepare his defence.

After evidence has been submitted, the public prosecutor and the counsels of the private parties set forth their closing arguments. After the pleadings, either the accused or his counsel have the right to make a final statement.

The court deliberates *in camera* (*camera di consiglio*). The judgment is pronounced in public. Full reasons may be read at the time of the judgment, or may be later put in writing by the judge. The timing is important for the purpose of impugning the judgment.

The verdict may be of acquittal, conviction or dismissal (*sentenza di non doversi procedere*, art.529), *e.g.* when no prosecution ought to have been brought, or when there has been an amnesty, or else when the limitation period has expired.

## 7. Evidence

### 7.1. GENERAL PRINCIPLES

Evidence is required to convince the judge of the existence of the facts allegedly committed by the accused, his liability to punishment, the measure of the sentence and civil responsibility deriving from the crime (art.187). The law itself is not subject to proof, except the law of a foreign country (relevant, for example, when applying the condition of double criminality with respect to extradition).

*Onus probandi incumbit ei qui dicit.* However, the public prosecutor is under the obligation to look for evidence both against and in favour of the accused. On the other hand, the accused may make a confession.

The *means for seeking evidence* (*mezzi di ricerca della prova*) are those procedures (inspection, search, seizure, wiretapping) which, in themselves, are not a source for convincing the judge, but are aimed at acquiring elements that have probative relevance (see *supra*, 5.).

On the contrary, the *means of evidence* (*mezzi di prova*) are those procedures which offer the judge elements that he can use directly for the purpose of the decision (testimony, examination of the parties, confrontations, recognizances, judicial experiments, expert opinions and documentary evidence).

### 7.2. THE HEARING OF WITNESSES

A witness is obliged to appear before the judge and to answer questions truthfully. Failure to appear, refusal to testify, being reticent and committing perjury are offences according to art.372 of the Penal Code. Witnesses may not be arrested during the hearing (art.476).

The accused may not be examined as a witness, and a witness may not be obliged to make self-incriminating statements (art.198). The victim may be questioned as a witness if he has any knowledge of facts that are relevant to the trial.

As a rule, witnesses are questioned by the parties themselves or by their counsel through direct examination, cross-examination and re-examination. The judge, or the presiding judge, may ask questions after the parties. He will allow only those questions that are related to the case at issue, and will not tolerate undue psychological pressure during cross-examination.

Witnesses are not obliged to testify when they have close family-ties with the accused (but if they do, the judge must previously inform them of their right to remain silent) or when professional or official secrets are concerned (here, instead, the judge is not obliged to previously inform the witness of his right). Privileged professional secrets are those of lawyers (client-attorney privilege), notaries public, physicians (physician-patient privilege), tax lawyers, clergymen (clergyman-penitent privilege) and public officials. Bank secrecy is no ground for a refusal to testify. Persons falling into one of those categories may choose whether or not to testify. In the latter case the judge may ascertain that the privilege applies, and may oblige the person to testify, in the cases when the law permits doing so. Journalists and the police are not allowed to testify unless they reveal the source of their information.

The existence of an official secret (*segreto di Stato*) bars testimony when it is confirmed by the Prime Minister.

## 7.3. THE EXAMINATION OF THE *PRIVATE PARTIES*

Examination of the private parties, not to be confused with the questioning (*interrogatorio*), is a possible means of evidence: it is only available on the interested party's request or with his consent. In particular, the examination gives an accused the opportunity to be heard, but he may also be questioned.

During the examination, the accused may choose not to answer questions, but this negative attitude may be held against him. His refusal to be examined, on the contrary, cannot have this effect since it is an expression of his right to remain silent.

## 7.4. CONFRONTATIONS AND "RICOGNIZIONI" OF PERSONS

Confrontations (*confronti*) are allowed only between persons already examined or questioned, when there are differences on relevant facts or circumstances (art.211).

*Ricognizione* of persons, objects, voices or sounds is aimed at obtaining a proof of identification. The legislator is aware of the fact that this is a delicate means of evidence, and has set strict rules for its application (arts.213-216). *Ricognizione* is in fact the same as the identification of persons and objects (*individuazione di persone e di cose*), performed by the public prosecutor during the preliminary investigations (art.361) with the difference, however, that the latter has no evidentiary value since it is a party action.

## 7.5. JUDICIAL EXPERIMENTS

Judicial experiments (*esperimenti giudiziali*) are aimed at ascertaining whether a fact could have occurred in a certain way. It consists of the reproduction, to the extent possible, of the situation in which the fact was committed. Here too, much attention is paid to the way judicial experiments are performed in order to guarantee the best possible result (arts.218-219).

## 7.6. EXPERT OPINIONS

Whenever there is a need for a contribution from a science outside the juridical field, the judge must appoint an expert who must be impartial, and, for this reason subject to the rules of abstention (*astensione*) and disqualification (*ricusazione*), which are decided upon by the judge.

An expert is obliged to accept the appointment. It is an offence for an expert to refuse the appointment. His services are remunerated.

The judge is not bound by the findings of the expert (*judex peritus peritorum*), but must give reasons if he does not follow them.

Experts must not be confused with technical consultants (*consulenti tecnici*) whom the public prosecutor and the parties may appoint even before the judge appoints an expert. Technical consultants are protected by professional secrecy.

## 7.7. DOCUMENTARY EVIDENCE

Documentary evidence are writings, or other documents, drawn up outside the courtroom. Such documents can only acquire "probative relevance" if they have been accepted as evidence by the judge, on the request of one of the parties. Obtaining documents emanating from the accused is always permitted, whereas documents concerning the *corpus delicti* must always be authorised.

# 8. Special forms of procedure

## 8.1. PRELIMINARY OBSERVATIONS

The adversarial system, introduced by the new Code of 1988 offers a maximum amount of procedural guarantees to the accused. It is, however, very costly and demanding in terms of time and personnel, as trials under the new code tend to last much longer than under the old code. If all cases were to proceed following ordinary proceedings, the judicial and prosecutorial authorities would be paralysed.

For this reason, the new code provides for the possibility of special forms of procedure, which are aimed at avoiding the ordinary proceedings (*supra*, 6.3.), and which aim at speeding up proceedings. It is hoped that 80% of all criminal proceedings will be dealt with according to these proceedings. Accordingly, the *procedimenti speciali*, despite their name, are in fact meant to be the way in which the great majority of criminal cases will be dealt with. They are regulated in a separate book of the new code.

Proceedings are shortened either by skipping committal proceedings (*udienza preliminare, supra*, 6.2.), by waiving the trial, or by waiving the preliminary investigations. The *udienza preliminare* is skipped in the case of a direct trial (*giudizio direttissimo,infra*, 8.4.) and in the case of an immediate trial (*giudizio immediato, infra*, 8.5.). The trial itself is waived in the case of a summary trial (*giudizio abbreviato, infra*, 8.2.) and in the case of punishment upon request by the parties (*patteggiamento, infra*, 8.3.). Preliminary investigations are waived when a penal order (*decreto penale, infra*, 8.6.) is imposed or when a settlement is reached (*oblazione, infra*, 8.7.).

The *procedimenti speciali* can only be used with the co-operation of the accused, who must waive his right to have his case dealt with under the general procedural rules (see *supra*, 6., the ordinary course of criminal proceedings). There are, however, several incentives intended to obtain the cooperation of the accused: depending on the procedure, the sentence may be reduced, he may avoid the publicity of the trial, the conviction will not be registered on his criminal record, etc.

### 8.2. SUMMARY TRIAL (*GIUDIZIO ABBREVIATO*)

Summary trial can be held on the request of the accused, provided the public prosecutor consents. It can be used for all offences, regardless of their seriousness, except for offences that carry a life sentence. In a summary trial, the case is judged not by the trial judge, but by the judge for the preliminary investigations. In derogation of the general rule that the trial should not be based on the prosecution *dossier*, the judge for the preliminary investigations in summary proceedings bases his decision on the prosecution *dossier*. Appeal against this decision is restricted, but cassation is always possible.

Despite the restrictions on his procedural rights, the advantages for the accused are considerable: if he is found guilty, the sentence will be reduced by one third, and the conviction will not be mentioned in his criminal record. Moreover, as the proceedings are held in camera before the judge for the preliminary investigations, he will avoid the publicity of a trial. Another advantage is that, unlike ordinary proceedings where the public prosecutor can modify the charge *in peius*, the charge cannot be changed in the case of a summary trial.

Summary trial involves an agreement on the form of procedure, not on the verdict (cfr *infra*, 8.3.). Consequently, the summary trial may end with an acquittal, if the elements collected by the public prosecutor are fragile. Seen in this perspective, summary proceedings are favourable to the accused because they prevent the case from being more deeply probed during the trial.

### 8.3. APPLYING PUNISHMENT UPON REQUEST BY THE PARTIES (*PATTEGGIAMENTO*)

The accused and the public prosecutor can ask the judge to apply a sentence which they agree upon amongst themselves. This procedure is called "applying the punishment upon request by the parties" *(applicazione della pena su richiesta delle parti, or "patteggiamento")*. The sentence imposed in such proceedings cannot exceed two years in prison (art.444).

The advantage for the State is that proceedings are shortened. The accused waives his right to contest the prosecution's charges, which is tantamount to *nolo contendere*, and his rights to file an appeal are restricted. The advantage for the accused is that, if he accepts the *pattegiamento*, the sentence will be reduced to two thirds. Moreover, no additional sanctions will be imposed on him, he will not have to pay for the costs of the proceedings. The sentence will have no administrative or civil effects.

The *patteggiamento* does not derogate from the principle of the legality of prosecutions (*supra*, 4.2.2.), according to which the public prosecutor is not entitled to drop the charge at his discretion. The agreement between the parties does not concern the decision whether or not to prosecute, but only affects the measure of the sentence. Despite the fact that the prosecutor must make a concession in return for the agreement of the accused, there is no risk that the sentence will be disproportionately mild or only symbolic because it is eventually rendered by a judge, who must assess the facts, verify the reduction of the sentence, and check on possible incongruities between the sentence agreed and the seriousness of the offence.

In theory, the judge may acquit the accused notwithstanding the agreement, but in practice, this seldom occurs. Usually, the verification by the judge of the factual basis of the *patteggiamento* is superficial or symbolic.

*Patteggiamento* is possible both during the preliminary investigations and during the trial. In exceptional cases, it is even possible in appeal proceedings.

In practice, *patteggiamento* has been accepted favourably by practitioners, but public opinion, and victims in particular, have reacted negatively.

### 8.4. DIRECT TRIAL (*GIUDIZIO DIRETTISSIMO*)

Direct trial is a proceeding in which the case is directly brought before the trial judge, without passing through committal proceedings (*udienza preliminare*) and, very often, even the preliminary investigations. The trial is conducted according to the ordinary procedural rules described above (*supra*, 6.3.).

Direct trial can be used either when the accused has been arrested while committing the offence (*arresto in flagranza*) or when he has made a confession (*confessione*) to the public prosecutor or to the judge. In other words, direct trial can only be used when there is a strong *prima facie case* against the accused.

In the case of *arresto in flagranza*, the case is brought before the trial judge within 48 hours, in the case of a confession, within 15 days from the entry of the *notitia criminis* in the appropriate register.

This simplified proceeding does not have any advantage for the accused. He is entitled to ask for either a summary trial (*supra*, 8.2.) or for a *patteggiamento* (*supra*, 8.3.).

### 8.5. IMMEDIATE TRIAL (*GIUDIZIO IMMEDIATO*)

When, after questioning the accused, the public prosecutor finds that there is no need for a preliminary investigation because there is enough evidence against him (*quando la prova appare evidente*, art.453), he may ask the judge for the preliminary investigations to refer the case to trial immediately. This may take place within 90 days, *i.e.* from the entry of the *notitia criminis* in the appropriate register (*supra*, 6.1.1).

The *giudizio immediato* may be requested, not only by the public prosecutor but also by the accused, e.g. in cases where the accused does not wish to disclose his case until the trial.

Legal doctrine has observed that immediate trial is very similar to direct trial (*supra*, 8.4.), and has commented upon the relative nature of the "obviousness" of the evidence.

### 8.6. PROCEEDING BY PENAL ORDER (*DECRETO PENALE*)

Penal orders are the most common form of summary criminal proceedings: the public prosecutor may ask the judge for the preliminary investigations to issue a penal order (*decreto penale*), which is in fact a conviction, issued in the absence of the accused and without a trial. This procedure may be used in the case of offences that are prosecuted *ex officio* and that carry fines only. The judge renders the decree without hearing the accused, and summarily explains the reasons for his decree.

The advantage of the penal order for the accused is that it allows the judge to reduce the sentence to half the minimum laid down by statute. Moreover, it can have neither civil nor administrative effects. These incentives are aimed at convincing the accused to accept the proposed solution. For the State, penal orders carry a considerable reduction in judicial workload.

The accused and his counsel may oppose the decree (*opposizione*) and ask for ordinary proceedings, for a *patteggiamento*, for summary or immediate trial, or, if possible, for a financial settlement. This *opposizione* must be filed within 15 days.

### 8.7. SETTLEMENT (*OBLAZIONE*)

When faced with petty offences that are punishable by fine only (*ammenda*) or by either fine or detention (*arresto o ammenda*), the accused is warned by either the public prosecutor or by penal order that if he pays a sum indicated in arts.162 and 162bis of the Penal Code, he will not be prosecuted.

If the accused pays, and complies with any formalities imposed on him, the judge issues a judgment by which the crime is extinguished.

### 8.8. PROCEEDING BEFORE THE *PRETORE*

The *pretore* is a single judge who, at first instance, is competent to try a large number of crimes (see *supra*, 2.3.1.). Proceedings before the pretore are significantly different from ordinary proceedings, to such an extent that the 1988 Code of Criminal Procedure devotes the whole of Book VIII to it.

Simplification has been obtained by eliminating committal proceedings (*udienza preliminare*) and by increasing the power which the judge for the preliminary investigations has in defining the proceeding beforehand.

The public prosecutor issues the summons without any jurisdictional filter, but the accused is given an incentive to agree to one of the special procedures if he wants to avoid trial.

The preliminary investigations are governed by the rules explained above (*supra*, 6.2.). There is, however, a tendency to reduce the *incidente probatorio* and to collect the evidence during the trial instead. At the end of the preliminary investigations, the public prosecutor has the following options: he may request the dismissal of the case, he may request a penal order; he may also summon the accused directly, with a notice concerning the possibility for the accused of asking for alternative procedures or of giving prior consent to a summary trial or to a *patteggiamento*. Once more the trial is conceived as an *extrema ratio* in a judicial system that pushes for early solutions.

One particularity of the proceedings before the pretore is the attempt to bring about a reconciliation between the accused and the victim in the case of offences that can be prosecuted on complaint only (*querela*). This *tentativo di conciliazione* (art.564) may be carried by the public prosecutor who summons both the complainant and the accused in order to obtain, circumstances permitting, the withdrawal of the complaint.

Proceedings before the pretore take place according to the rules of ordinary procedure (*supra*, 6.3.). However, if the parties agree, the transcript may be summed up, and questions to witnesses, experts and parties may be asked directly by the *pretore*.

In this procedure, the judge is not bound by the sentencing restrictions in the penal order opposed, and may even impose heavier penalties or detention, and deny a stay of sentence.

### 8.9. PROCEEDINGS AGAINST JUVENILE OFFENDERS

Proceedings against juvenile offenders are brought before a specialised court (minors'court and court of appeal for minors, see *supra*, 2.4.1.).

These proceedings differ fundamentally from those against adults. The general principle is to take into account the minor's personality and educational needs. Accordingly, a judicial police for minors exists, and it is permissible to assess a minor's personality, whereas it is forbidden to do so for an adult accused. Detention on remand can only be ordered in the most serious cases, and house arrests or placing the minor in a community are favoured. The *parte civile* proceedings are not open to a victim of an offence that is prosecuted before the minor's courts. Information supplied to the media is restricted. The trial is not public. The minor is examined by the president of the court. There is ample room for a suspended sentence, for a semi-custodial sentence, for a community-service order, for pardon and for a *nolle prosequi* "*per irrelevanza del fatto*".

## 9. Remedies

### 9.1. PRELIMINARY OBSERVATIONS

The Constitution guarantees two degrees of jurisdiction: the first one on the merits, the second on questions of law before the Supreme Court (*Corte di Cassazione*). The legislator has gone beyond the constitutional minimum rules by providing, in most cases, for three degrees of jurisdiction, the first two (first instance and appeal) on the merits, the third (*cassation*) on legal issues only.

## 9.2. APPEAL

Appeal is an ordinary remedy against judgments rendered at first instance. The accused may appeal all decisions that condemn or acquit him (provided he has an interest in filing the appeal) or that dismiss his case.

There are, however, some restrictions on the right of appeal. Appeal is generally excluded when the sentence is a fine (*ammenda*) and in cases where the accused has been acquitted or his case dismissed when he was charged with offences punishable by either a fine or alternative penalties (art.593).

There are also restrictions on appealing against judgments rendered in summary trials and in cases of *patteggiamento*. Appeal is excluded when the accused is acquitted before trial (art.469).

When one of the parties files an appeal within the time-limit, the non-appealing party may file a late appeal (*appello incidentale*) within 15 days. This procedure may possibly be unconstitutional, since a delayed appeal by the public prosecutor is contrary to his duty to prosecute within the legal time-limit.

Appeal proceedings are public. The court of appeal re-examines the whole case in fact and law within the limits of the reasons for the appeal (*tantum devolutum, quantum appellatum*), but it also has powers of *ex officio* re-examination (art.597(5)). In the appellate proceedings, further investigations are possible when the judge feels that he cannot decide *rebus sic stantibus* (*allo stato degli atti*). Otherwise, proceedings are limited to the report by the judge, the pleadings and the decision under appeal.

To restrict the work-load of the courts of appeal, decisions *in camera* are provided for on the request of the parties following an agreement concerning the reasons for the appeal and concerning the sentence (art.599).

*Reformatio in peius* (*i.e.* altering the judgment appealed against to the disadvantage of the accused) is forbidden in cases where only the accused, and not the other parties, have filed the appeal. If, however the appeal was filed by the public prosecutor (or the civil party in the case of art.577), the previous decision may be altered *in peius*.

## 9.3. *CASSAZIONE*

Resorting to the Supreme Court *(Corte di Cassazione)* is an ordinary (and last instance) remedy against judgments rendered at second instance and against judgments which are not subject to appeal. The Supreme Court may even decide on the legality of judgments at first instance *per saltum*.

Cassation can only be filed on questions of law (both substantive and procedural law, failure or inconsistency in the reasons, given for the decisions, abuse of discretion, failure to receive a decisive item of evidence: art.606). The Supreme Court is also competent in cases of restriction of personal liberty, conflicts of jurisdiction, competence and remittal of proceedings for "serious local situations", and in general has the duty to watch over the uniform application of substantive and procedural criminal law.

The Supreme Court either admits the application for review and quashes the original decision with or without remittal, or declares that the application is inadmissible or is rejected. When the original decision is quashed, the case is referred again to the judge of first or second instance. The latter will be bound by the principle of law affirmed by the Supreme Court.

As a rule, decisions of the Supreme Court are taken by a chamber composed of 5 judges, but when it is necessary to prevent or settle diverging interpretations, the court decides in combined chambers (composed of 9 judges).

### 9.4. *OPPOSIZIONE*

The term *opposizione* refers to different procedures. Strictly speaking, opposition is a complaint brought before the authority which rendered the decision (or failed to do so) against which the complaint is directed. For example, an *opposizione* can be made against a penal order by an accused who wants to have his case dealt with according to ordinary procedure.

At times, *opposizione* is a request filed with a judge asking him to reject a request of the public prosecutor (e.g. the victim of the offence can oppose the public prosecutor's request for the *archiviazione* of the case, art.410) or to prevent a particular act of one of the parties (e.g. the contemporaneous objection rule, *opposizione nel corso dell'esame dei testimoni*, art.504).

In other cases *opposizione* may consist of a complaint brought before a judge other than the one who has performed the action: for example, a judgment by the judge for the preliminary investigations may be opposed before the minors' court (art. 32, Presidential Decree No. 448 of September 22, 1988).

### 9.5. *CASSATION* TO REVISE A FINAL JUDGMENT (*REVISIONE*)

In the cases provided for by law, the case against a person who has been convicted by a final judgment can be reopened and retried, even if the convicted person has died. Retrial is not possible where the accused was acquitted. Being an "extraordinary remedy", an application for retrial may be filed at any time.

The application may be filed by the public prosecutor, by the condemned person, or a close relative of his. The grounds for retrial are: that the judgment in question and another judgment in the same case are contradictory; that the judgment was influenced by unlawfully obtained evidence; that new evidence has surfaced which was unknown to the judge at the time of the trial; that the civil or administrative preliminary ruling on which the conviction was based was quashed.

The application for retrial is brought before the court of appeal which may either reject it or receive it, repeal the sentence and acquit. An application for cassation may be lodged with the Supreme Court against the decision of the court of appeal.

### 9.6. COMPENSATION FOR JUDICIAL ERRORS

In the same manner as the right to compensation is recognised if a person has been the victim of unlawful detention (see *supra*, 5.2.4.), the accused who has been wrongfully convicted is entitled to compensation.

The amount of the compensation, which may take the form of a lump sum or a life annuity, is decided *in camera* by the court of appeal even after the convicted (now acquitted) person is deceased. A cassation can be lodged against this decision before the Supreme Court.

### 9.7. INDIVIDUAL APPLICATION TO THE EUROPEAN COMMISSION OF HUMAN RIGHTS

Since 1973, Italy has recognized the right of individual application to the European Commission of Human Rights together with the jurisdiction of the European Court of Human Rights (Arts. 25 and 46 of the European Convention on Human Rights) if an individual claims that his rights under the European Convention on Human Rights were violated.

By doing so, Italy has undertaken to comply with the decisions of an international, impartial body and where applicable to take part in a procedure in which the individual and the State hold a substantially equal position. The 1988 Code of Criminal Procedure has not changed this individual right. The right to individual application can only be used provided that all local remedies have been exhausted (art.26 European Convention on Human Rights).

## 10. Other questions

### 10.1. EXECUTION OF JUDGMENTS

A judgment becomes final after all ordinary remedies have been exhausted. An acquitted or convicted person may not be tried for the same offence after the judgment has become final - not even if relevant new facts or evidence become available (e.g., if an acquitted person later makes a confession), according to the principle of *ne bis in idem.*

The final judgment is not binding in civil and administrative proceedings against a person who was not a party in the criminal proceeding (e.g. when the victim has not formally taken part in the proceedings by becoming a *parte civile*).

The public prosecutor is responsible for the execution of custodial sentences (*sentenze di condanna*). He issues an order of execution (*ordine di esecuzione*) taking into account any time spent in detention on remand.

Questions arising from the execution of a sentence can be submitted to the judge who has ordered the execution (e.g. amnesty or *abolitio criminis*). Proceedings on questions relating to the execution of the sentence are held *in camera* and with a debate. The judge has investigating powers. He decides by means of an order that may be challenged before the Supreme Court.

In accordance with art.27 of the Constitution, which states that penalties must aim at the rehabilitation of the condemned, the 1988 Code and the 1975 Penitentiary Regulations provide that the courts are competent for checking every measure concerning the treatment of the condemned in such areas as rehabilitation, delaying execution, entrusting to an appropriate institution in the case of the condemned becoming mentally ill, safety measures, cancelling of a debt, replacing serving in jail by work, the parole system, etc. Debate and remedies are guaranteed. Proceedings before the court of surveillance on the execution of penalties (*tribunale di sorveglianza*) are held *in camera*.

10.2. JURISDICTIONAL RELATIONS WITH FOREIGN AUTHORITIES

The general principle is that international conventions and international law prevail over the provisions of the 1988 Code. For example, the granting of immunity, which is normally excluded, is permitted under art.728.

Extradition to a foreign country is excluded for political crimes and when there are reasons to believe that the fundamental rights of the requested person will not be respected. The decision on the admissibility of the extradition request is taken by the court of appeal.

The Code also deals with such subjects as letters rogatory, the transfer of proceedings and the execution of penal judgments to and from Italy.

## 11. Select bibliography

*Books*

CHIAVARIO, M., *La riforma del processo penale*, Torino, 1988
CONSO, G. and GREVI, V., *Profili del nuovo codice di procedura penale*, Padova, 1991
CORDERO, F., *Procedura penale*, Torino, 1993
CRISTIANI A., *Manuale del nuovo processo penale*, Torino, 1989
DALIA, A. and FERRAIOLI, M., *Corso di diritto processuale penale*, Padova, 1992
NAPPI A., *Guida al nuovo codice di procedura penale*, Milano, 1989
PISANI, M., MOLARI, A., PERCHINUNNO, V. and CORSO, P., *Appunti di procedura penale*, Bologna, 1992
RUGGIERO G., *Codice di procedura penale*, Bari, 1990
SIRACUSANO, D., DALIA, A., GALATI, A., TRANCHINA, G. and ZAPPALA, E., *Manuale di diritto processuale penale*, Milano, 2 vols., 1990-1991.

*Periodicals*

Archivio penale
La Giustizia penale
L'Indice penale

La Questione criminale
Rivista di diritto processuale
Rivista italiana di diritto e procedura penale
Rivista penale

# Chapter 9 - Luxembourg

Alphonse **SPIELMANN**
Procureur général d'Etat adjoint
Judge in the European Court of Human Rights
and
Dean **SPIELMANN**
LL.M (Cantab.)
Advocate at the Bar of Luxembourg
Assistant at the Law Faculty of the University of Louvain (U.C.L.)

## 1. Sources

### 1.1. INTRODUCTION

Luxembourg still applies the Napoleonic *Code d'Instruction Criminelle* (1808), although it has been thoroughly modified in recent years. As a result, there is a great resemblance with Belgium, where that Code is still in force. The resemblance with the Belgian system is even greater due to the fact that the Luxembourg penal code of 1879 is almost identical to the Belgian Penal Code of 1867, which in turn strongly draws from its predecessor, the French Penal Code of 1810. Therefore, this chapter will mainly focus on the differences between the Luxembourg system and the Belgian system, which is described in the first chapter of this book.

### 1.2. THE CONSTITUTION

The most important rules of criminal procedure are laid down in the Constitution of the Grand Duchy of Luxembourg of 17 October 1868, as modified in 1919, 1948, 1956 and 1972. It provides, for example, that trials should be held in public, save where publicity would jeopardise public order or public morality (art.88). Judgments should be motivated, *i.e.* judges should give the reasons for their judgments, both in law and in fact (art.89), thus allowing the parties to asses the chances of an appeal. According to the same article 89, judgments should be pronounced in public. The *ratio legis* for this provision is that judgments should be submitted to the control of public opinion.

    Article 87 provides for the organisation of a *Cour Supérieure de Justice*. This provision required the introduction of remedies (*voies de recours*), which allow appeals against judgments rendered by lower courts to be brought before higher courts, thus offering guarantees against potentially partial decisions or judicial errors.

## 1.3. INTERNATIONAL TREATIES

The Supreme Court decided, as early as 1950, that, in case of a conflict between an international treaty and a national statute, the former should prevail[1]. This decision was taken outside any constitutional or legal framework. Accordingly, the priority granted to international treaties is an achievement of the courts only[2].

This principle, particularly with respect to the European Convention on Human Rights, has obviously had repercussions on the Code of Criminal Procedure.

## 1.4. THE CODE OF CRIMINAL PROCEDURE

The Code of Criminal Procedure is, as in Belgium, still the old Napoleonic Code. However, the Luxembourg legislator has combined the talents of an intelligent imitator with those of a relatively prudent reformer[3]. Gradually, Luxembourg has shown its intellectual independence and has emancipated itself from its larger neighbours: whereas, in the 19th Century, Parliament, in accordance with the general spirit of conformism of the time, mainly followed the example of legislative changes in the neighbouring states, the 20th Century legislator has adopted a more progressive position and has, especially in the field of criminal procedure, introduced changes which were in advance of their time. As a result, the present *Code d'instruction criminelle* of Luxembourg could serve as an example for other countries.

Accordingly, unlike in Belgium, where the Napoleonic Code has remained virtually intact, Luxembourg has considerably adapted it in the course of time. For example, the Statute of 19 November 1929[4] introduced adversarial elements in the preliminary judicial investigation (*instruction*), thus softening the harsh features of the inquisitorial proceedings in the pretrial stage.

Many important changes were introduced in the course of the Eighties. In 1981, a Statute was passed which lays down the rules concerning the reopening of a case (*révision*) and which allows for the compensation of

---

[1]Cass. 8 June 1950, *Pasicrisie luxembourgeoise*, XV, 41. See PESCATORE,P., "Observations sub arrêt de la Cour Supérieure de Justice du Grand-Duché de Luxembourg du 7 mars 1953 (appel corr.) et du 14 juillet 1954 (cass.) dans l'affaire Pagani c.M.P. et Chambre des Métiers (part.civ.)", *Journal des Tribunaux*, 1954, 696; PESCATORE, P.," La préeminence des traités sur la loi interne selon la jurisprudence luxembourgeoise", *Journal des Tribunaux*, 1953, 645.

[2]SPIELMANN, A., WEITZEL, A. et SPIELMANN, D., *La Convention européenne des droits de l'homme et le droit luxembourgeois*, Bruxelles, Nemesis, 1991, 100-105.

[3]SPIELMANN, A., "D'un certain conformisme à un libre examen certain", in *Mémorial -Publications mosellanes (150 ans d'indépendance)*, Luxembourg, 1990, 93-104.

[4]*Loi sur l'instruction contradictoire, Mémorial*, A, 1929, 997.

victims of miscarriages of justice[5]. In the same year, a statute was passed allowing for the compensation of persons unjustly detained on remand (*détention préventive inopérante*[6]). In 1982, the Code was amended so as to allow the recording of telephonic conversations[7] (see *infra*, 5.3.) and in 1987, the court of assizes (*cour d'assises*) was abolished[8]. Finally, the Statute of 16 june 1989 substantially modernised the provisions on pre-trial investigations[9].

Most of these statutes have been incorporated into the Code, unlike in Belgium, where they were enacted in special statutes outside the Code.

## 2. Structure of the criminal justice system

### 2.1. INVESTIGATING AUTHORITIES

According to art.9 CCP *et seq.*, criminal investigations (*actes de police judiciaire*) are conducted by the "judicial police", *i.e.* persons invested with the capacity of judicial police officer (*officier de police judiciaire*), judicial police agent (*agent de police judiciaire*) or judicial civil servant (*fonctionnaires et agents chargés de certaines fonctions de police judiciaire*)[10]. These persons act under the direction of the *procureur d'Etat* (art.9), and are supervised by the *procureur général*; they are subject to the control of the judicial council of the court of appeal (art.9-1) (*chambre du conseil de la cour d'appel, infra,* 2.1.3.).

It is the task of the police to "find" (*constater*) offences, to collect the evidence and to trace the authors, as long as no formal inquiry (*instruction*) has been opened. When an inquiry has been opened, the police act on the instructions of the courts of investigation, *i.e.* the investigating judge and the judicial council (art.9-2).

Save in case of an offence *in flagrante delicto*, the investigating judge can only proceed to investigations after he has been seized of the case by either the public prosecutor or by the *partie civile*[11].

---

[5]*Loi concernant la révision des procès criminels et correctionnels et les indemnités à accorder aux victimes d'erreurs judiciaires, Mémorial*, A, 1981, 755.

[6]Statute of 30 December 1981, *Mémorial*, A, 1981, 1874.

[7]*Mémorial*, A, 1982, 2022, modified by the Statute of 7 July 1989, *Mémorial*, A, 1989, 1060.

[8]Statute of 17 June 1987, *Mémorial*, A, 744

[9]*Mémorial*, A, 1989, 774.

[10]Cfr. *supra*, Chapter 1, par.2.1.

[11]Cfr. *supra*, Chapter 1, par.2.1.3.

## 2.2. PROSECUTING AUTHORITIES

The "public action" (*action publique*)[12] can only be set in motion by the magistrates and the civil servants who have been invested with this competence by law, or by the victim, again in the cases provided for by law (art.1 CPP).

The powers of the *ministère public* are somewhat restricted in this respect for, although he may start the "public action", he does not further decide about it, as he has no powers to conclude transactions, engage in plea bargainings, abandon prosecutions, *etc.* (see, however, *infra*, 8.1., on prosecutorial discretion). Likewise, the *ministère public* does not have the monopoly of prosecutions, as both the *partie civile* and certain administrative authorities may bring offences before the courts.

## 2.3. COURTS

### *2.3.1. Composition*

As in Belgium, a distinction exists between courts that are competent at the pre-trial stage, and trial courts that are competent to judge on the merits[13].

Courts that are competent at the *pre-trial stage* are the investigating judge (*juge d'instruction*, one single judge), the judicial council of the court of first instance (*chambre du conseil,* three judges), and the judicial council of the court of appeal (three judges). Their functions are more or less the same as those held by their corresponding numbers in Belgium[14].

Courts that are competent at the *trial stage* are: the police court (*tribunal du juge de paix*, sitting as a *juge de police*, a single judge), the *correctional chambers* of the *tribunal d'arrondissement* (3 judges), and the *criminal chambers* of the *tribunal d'arrondissement* (3 judges). These courts correspond to the tripartite subdivision of offences in the Penal Code (*contraventions, délits, crimes*). *Contraventions* are judged by the police courts, *délits* by the chambre correctionnelle and *crimes* by the chambre criminelle.

The correctional chamber of the *tribunal d'arrondissement* is competent to hear appeals against judgments of the police judge. The correctional chamber of the Court of Appeal can hear appeals against judgments of the correctional chamber of the *tribunal d'arrondissement*. Judgments of the criminal chamber of the *tribunal d'arrondissement* can be appealed against before the criminal chamber of the court of appeal, which is composed of 5 judges.

---

[12]See *supra*, Chapter 1, par. 4.2.1.

[13]See *supra*, Chapter 1, par.2.3.

[14]There is a difference in terminology as far as the judicial council of the court of appeal is concerned, which in Belgium is called *chambre des mises en accusation* (court of indictment), *supra*, Chapter 1, 2.3..

## 2.3.2. The role of lay judges

On 7 May 1775, French revolutionary troops occupied the city of Luxembourg. On 9 december 1808, the *Code d'instruction criminelle* was promulgated. This code, which abolished the jury of accusation (*jury d'accusation*), retained the trial jury. Nevertheless, the jury in those times was only short-lived in Luxembourg: in 1814, it was abolished again by the Dutch sovereign prince William of Nassau, in a decree of 6 November 1814. However, it was re-introduced in 1831, after the Belgian decree of 19 July 1831 repealed the decree of 1814 and declared that the provisions of the Napoleonic Code of Criminal procedure would be in force again.

This situation lasted until 1987, when the *cour d'assises* was abolished in Luxembourg. There were many arguments in support of this change. Firstly, there was no possibility of appeal against judgments of the *cour d'assises*, which was considered contrary to the 7th Additional Protocol to the European Convention on Human Rights, where the principle of a double level jurisdiction has been laid down explicitly[15]. Another argument was that the jury did not give reasons for its decisions.

The Statute of 17 June 1987[16] has abolished the jury and attributed the competence to judge *crimes* to the criminal chamber of the *tribunal d'arrondissement*. Appeals against judgments of this court can now be lodged with the criminal chamber of the court of appeal. Furthermore, the same statute has modified the rules of competence and procedure in respect of the investigation and the judgment of *crimes*[17].

## 2.3.3. Nomination of the judges

Judges of the peace and judges in the tribunals (*tribunaux d'arrondissement*) are directly nominated by the Grand Duke. Judges in the court (*conseillers*) and presidents and vice-presidents in the tribunals are nominated by the Grand Duke, following advice of the *Cour Supérieure de Justice* (art.90 of the Constitution). Judges in the *Cour Supérieure de Justice* and judges in the Supreme Court (*Cour de Cassation*) are also nominated by the Grand Duke, following the advice mentioned above, as are the president of the Cour Supérieure de Justice, the presiding judges in the chambers of the Court of appeal, and the president, first vice-president and vice-president of the

---

[15]See SPIELMANN, D., "Le droit au double degré de juridiction en matière pénale dans le système européen de protection des droits de l'homme", *Bulletin du Cercle François Laurent*, IV, 1991, 1-44.

[16]Mémorial, A, 1987, 743.

[17]See further SPIELMANN, A., "De l'abolition du jury à la suppression de la cour d'assises", *Revue de droit pénal et de criminologie*, 1987, 719-733.

*tribunal d'arrondissement* (art.43 Statute on the Organisation of the Judiciary[18]).

The procedure by which the advice is taken is conducted as follows: for each vacant chair, the *Cour Supérieure de Justice*, gathering in plenary session, proposes three candidates. In addition, the procureur général d'Etat gives his advice. Only persons whose names have been proposed in this way can be appointed by the Grand Duke, which excludes arbitrary nominations.

Judges are nominated for life. They cannot be removed or suspended without a judgment. A judge can only be transferred to another court as the result of a new nomination, and only with his consent. However, in case of infirmity or of misbehaviour, judges can be suspended, revoked or transferred, according to the conditions laid down by statute (art.91 of the Constitution).

### 2.3.4. Impartiality

According to art.209 CPP, a person who has been a first instance judge in a particular case, may not thereafter hear the same case as an appellate judge.

In addition, the statute of 16 June 1989 has laid down a number of incompatibilities between different judicial functions. According to the newly introduced art.64-1 of the Statute of 7 March 1980 concerning the judicial organisation, the following functions are incompatible, if they are consecutively held by the same person in the same case:
- investigating judge and trial judge
- judge in the judicial council (*chambre du conseil*), involved in the committal proceedings or the proceedings concerning the release of an accused detained on remand, and trial judge
- public prosecutor and trial judge (if the magistrate in his capacity of public prosecutor has been involved in the case, by taking *conclusions* (or ordering such conclusions to be taken)), or by making *réquisitions*).

## 3. Parties to criminal proceedings

### 3.1. THE PROSECUTOR

The function of public prosecutor is held by the *ministère public*, who decides about the "public action[19]", launches the prosecution, is responsible for the good order of the proceedings and is competent to lodge appeals. The functions of the *ministère public* are discharged by:
- at the police court: a *substitut* of the *parquet* of the tribunal of first instance, or by a judicial officer (*attaché de la justice*)

---

[18]Statute of 14 March 1980, *Mémorial*, A, 1980, 143.
[19]*Supra*, Chapter 1, 4.2.1.

- at the tribunal of first instance (both in respect of the trial courts and the *investigation* courts (investigation judge, judicial council)): by the *procureur de l'Etat* or one of his substitutes
- at the level of the appellate instance (crimes and délits): the *procureur général d'Etat* or one of his advocates general.

As in Belgium, the ministère public is hierarchically organised, indivisible, but yet independent and "non-recusable" (*i.e.* cannot be disqualified)[20].

## 3.2. THE DEFENCE

The rights of the defence, which were underdeveloped in the -imported- Napoleonic Code of 1808, have been considerably strengthened in recent times.

The first substantial step was taken already in 1929, when the statute on the contradictory *instruction* (*i.e.* the preliminary judicial investigation conducted by the investigating judge) was introduced[21]. During the Eighties, a considerable number of changes were made, which contributed to reinforcing the legal position of the accused (and also of the *partie civile* and even of third parties) during the pre-trial investigation. The Statute of 16 June 1989[22] has replaced the old provisions in the Napoleonic Code with a totally new Book II, in which the "public action" and the *instruction* are regulated.

In general, the accused is in a much more advantageous position than he was under the Napoleonic code. The contrast with Belgium, where the Code still applies in its original form, is very sharp.

### 3.2.1. The accused[23]

Persons, including potential suspects, who are subjected to an identity check by the police have a number of clearly enforceable rights, set out in art.45 (see further *infra*, 5.1.1.).

Persons who are subjected to interrogation, either by the police (in case of an arrest in *flagrante delicto*, art.39(7)) or by the investigating judge (art.81(8)), have the right to be assisted by counsel during their interrogation,

---

[20]See *supra*, Chapter 1, par.2.2.

[21]*Mémorial*, A, 1929, 997.

[22]*Mémorial*, A, 1989, 774.

[23]Like in Belgium there are different terms to designate the person who is the subject of a criminal investigation, depending on the stage in which the proceedings are. Each of these terms correspond to different procedural rights. For example, there is a difference between suspects in the police station (*les personnes contre lesquelles il existe des indices graves et concordantes de nature à motiver leur inculpation*, cfr. art.38 CPP), persons who are the subject of a formal investigation (*instruction*), called "*inculpé*", and persons who are committed for trial, called "*prévenu*". As there are no equivalent terms in English to reflect these *nuances*, the term "accused" will be used throughout this contribution. *Cfr.supra*, Chapter 1, 3.2.1..

unless they have waived this right (see further, *infra*, 5.1.2.).

When interrogated by the investigating judge, the accused must be informed about the charges against him, before the interrogation starts (art.81(1)). In addition to counsel, the *ministère public* and the *partie civile* may be present at the hearing (art.81(8)). However, no party is entitled to speak during the interrogation without the authorization of the investigating judge.

After the first interrogation, the accused and the *partie civile* have access to the investigation *dossier*, each time a new interrogation is to take place or each time an investigation at which the parties may be present is to take place. The parties may request that parts of the *dossier* must be communicated to them. The communication of reports drafted by expert witnesses may never be refused (art.85).

Unlike in Belgium, where the pre-trial investigations are completely secret, which implies that neither the accused nor the *partie civile* may be present during investigative acts, their presence is allowed in certain cases in Luxembourg. For example, both the accused and the *partie civile* have the right to be present during an investigation on the spot (*transport sur les lieux*), and must even (except in case of urgency) be notified in advance that such investigations are going to take place (art.63). Likewise, when an *expertise* has been ordered by the investigating judge, the accused has the right to have the expertise attended by an expert of his own choice (art.87(3)).

In addition, the parties may request specific investigative acts from the investigating judge during the preliminary judicial investigation (*instruction*). Here too, the contrast with Belgium is again striking, because no such possibility has been provided for in Belgian law. For example, whereas witnesses, as in Belgium, are heard *in camera*, outside the presence of the accused and the *partie civile* (art.70), both parties may address a reasoned request to the investigating judge in which they ask him to hear additional witnesses (art.69(3)). Likewise, as far as *expertises* are concerned, the parties may ask the investigating judge to order specific expertises (art.88). Last but not least, the parties, including the accused and the *partie civile*, may appeal against *ordonnances* of the investigating judge (art.133).

A special remedy has been introduced in respect of seizures (*saisies*): if objects have been seized, the accused, the *partie civile* and any other interested party, may adress a request for the restitution of such objects from a court of law (art.68).

Another radical novelty in Luxembourg is that all parties, including the accused (*inculpé*), who claim that certain investigative acts performed during the pre-trial investigation are void, may now bring a request for nullification before the judicial council (*chambre du conseil*). This request may be directed against the investigation as a whole (*instruction*[24]), or against certain specific investigative acts (art.126 CPP).

### 3.2.2. *The defence counsel*

According to art.81(1) CPP, the investigating judge is under an obligation to inform the person of his right to chose an advocate, even an advocate registered in another E.E.C. member state (subject to the condition that this choice does not hinder the proceedings). If the person concerned does not appoint an advocate of his choice, an advocate *ex officio* may be designated, with his consent.

### 3.3. THE VICTIM

The Luxembourg CPP has adopted the *partie civile* system of the Code of 1808. The general principles are the same as those explained in the Belgian chapter. However, the procedural rights of the *partie civile* during the pre-trial stage of the proceedings are much better protected than in Belgium. For example, he has access to the investigation *dossier* prior to each interrogation of the accused (art.85), he may be present at certain investigations (*e.g.* the interrogation of the accused (art.81(8)), and investigations *in loco* (art.63)), he may ask the investigating judge to hear particular witnesses (art.69(3)), *etc.* In addition, he may appeal against *ordonnances* of the investigating judge (art.133) and he has the right to file a request for the nullity of the investigation or of certain particular investigative acts (art.126). Accordingly, he is, as from the pre-trial stage of the proceedings, a full party with all procedural rights that are given to the other parties.

## 4. General principles concerning criminal procedure

In general, the principles concerning criminal procedure of the Napoleonic code, such as they have been described in the Belgian chapter, are applicable in Luxembourg, with, however, one fundamental difference: the rights of the accused and of the *partie civile*, and even those of third parties, are much better protected in the pre-trial stage, as a result of the modifications set out in the preceding paragraphs.

Accordingly, as far as the *general principles* are concerned, the Luxembourg criminal proceedings are, as in Belgium, characterised by two stages (a pre-trial stage and a trial stage)[25], and the principles of the search for the material truth[26] and of the right to a fair trial[27] are likewise applicable.

---

[24]See *supra*, Chapter 1, par.6.1.3.
[25]See *supra*, Chapter 1, par.4.1.1.
[26]See *supra*, Chapter 1, par.4.1.2.
[27]See *supra*, Chapter 1, par.4.1.3.

As far as the *principles governing the opening of criminal proceedings are concerned*, the *ex officio* principle and the principle of "opportunity" are applicable, along the lines explained in the Belgian Chapter[28].

The *principles governing the taking of the evidence* are likewise comparable to the Belgian system[29], as are the *principles governing the trial, i.e.* the principles of publicity, orality and contradiction[30].

## 5. Coercive measures

### 5.1. ARREST AND DETENTION ON REMAND

### 5.1.1. Identity checks (vérifications d'identité)

According to art.45 of the CPP, "judicial" police officers and agents (*officiers et agents de police judiciaire*) are entitled to stop, at any moment, persons suspected of:
- having committed an offence or having attempted to do so
- preparing the commission of an offence (*crime* or *délit*)
- being able to give useful information to the authorities relating to an investigation concerning an offence (*crime* or *délit*)
- being subject to an investigation ordered by judicial or administrative authorities.

A person thus stopped must be identified immediately. The person in question must be informed of his right to inform his family or any person of his choice and to notify the public prosecutor. To this end, a telephone must be put at his disposal.

The identification check may only last for the time that is strictly necessary, and may in no case exceed 4 hours. The *procureur d'Etat* can, at any moment, stop the temporary detention *(rétention)* carried out for the purpose of an identity check.

Fingerprints and photographs may only be made if it is absolutely necessary to identify the person in question (art.45(5)), and must be authorised by the *procureur d'Etat* or the investigating judge.

If the person concerned is not the subject of any judicial investigation or enforcement measure, the records (*procès verbaux*) and any other document relating to the identification must be destroyed within 6 months.

---

[28]See *supra*, Chapter 1, par.4.2.
[29]See *supra*, Chapter 1, par.4.3.
[30]See *supra*, Chapter 1, par.4.4.

## 5.1.2. Arrest

In the case of offences *in flagrante delicto*, the police may arrest any suspects, who are defined as persons against whom there are serious suspicions (*les personnes contre lesquelles il existe des indices graves et concordantes de nature à motiver leur inculpation*)), for a period of time not exceeding 24 hours (art.39(1)). Arrestees have the right to inform any person of their choice (art.39(3)), and are entitled to be assisted by counsel during their interrogation by the police, who must previously inform them of this right (art.39(7)).

## 5.1.3. Restriction order (interdiction de communiquer)

According to art.84, the investigating judge may, immediately after interrogating the accused, issue a restriction order (*interdiction de communiquer*), for a period which may not exceed 10 days, which may be prolonged once. This restriction order, however, does not extend to the accused's defence counsel. The accused, his counsel, his spouse and any person having a legal interest in the lifting of the communication ban may request the judicial council to revoke it.

## 5.1.4. Detention on remand

Detention on remand may only be ordered by a judge, by virtue of a warrant called *mandat de dépôt*. A *mandat de dépôt* can only be delivered if the following conditions are met: (a) the offence must be an *arrestable offence*, *i.e.* an offence carrying a sentence of 2 years in prison or more; (b) there must be serious reasons to believe that the suspect has committed the offence and (c) one of the following reasons for the detention must be present: there must be reasons to believe that the suspect will abscond (which is presumed if he is suspected of a *crime*), that he will meddle with the evidence or that, if left free, he will commit new offences.

Prior to issuing a *mandat de dépôt*, the investigating judge must interrogate the accused. The *mandat de dépôt* must be duly motivated.

If the accused has not been committed for trial within a month after the warrant has been delivered, he will be released, unless the judicial council decides unanimously that he should be further detained (art.94-3). This decision has to be renewed each month, as long as the accused has not been committed for trial by the judicial council.

On the request of the accused, the judicial council may order his conditional release, subject to the condition that he appears at all proceedings where his presence is required, and submits himself to the execution of the judgment (art.113). This conditional release may be subject to bail (art.114).

### 5.1.5. *"Immediate arrest upon conviction": no longer possible*

Until the Statute of 7 July 1989, it was possible for trial courts to order the immediate arrest of a convicted person, pending the point at which his conviction became final. This immediate arrest was meant to bridge the period between the day of judgment and the day when the judgment becomes final, in the sense that no further remedy (appeal, *opposition*, *cassation*) would lie against the judgment any longer. Judgments are not enforceable as long as they are not final. For example, when the accused appeals his conviction, the judgment does not become final, and enforcement is suspended until the appellate court has rendered its judgment. Accordingly, "immediate arrest" was in reality a form of detention on remand, as the authority on which it was based was not the judgment, but a temporary authority, which allowed detention on remand pending the final judgment.

Whereas this form of detention still exists in Belgium[31], it has now been abolished in Luxembourg. The criticisms against it were based on the idea that, whereas, in former times, immediate arrest was justified because it was relatively easy for a condemned person to find shelter abroad, such justification no longer exists in a period in which multiple international conventions in the field of cooperation in criminal matters, particularly extradition, are available. Moreover, it was considered to be unjust for condemned persons to have to undergo their custodial sentences before having had the occasion to lodge an appeal or to apply for a pardon, and without having had the opportunity of contacting the magistrate, responsible for the execution of sentences[32].

### 5.2. SEARCH AND SEIZURE (*PERQUISITIONS AND SAISIES*)

The rules on searches (*perquisitions*) and seizures (*saisies*) are set out in arts.65-67 CPP. Searches may never be used to "find" an offence that has not yet been reported to the authorities (or discovered *in flagrante delicto*), only to collect evidence with respect to an offence that has already been discovered. The old case-law in which this principle was enounced is still valid today[33].

Searches can be ordered by the investigating judge, after notifying the public prosecutor, in all places where objects may be found that might be useful for the discovery of the truth. Exceptionally, searches can be performed without a warrant, *i.e.* in case of an offence caught in the act (*in flagrante delicto*), and when the occupant of the house consents to the search.

---

[31]See *supra*, Chapter 1, 5.1.3.

[32]*Documents parlementaires*, session 1988-89, n°3121, 4, p.2-3.

[33]Court of indictiment of the Court of appeal, 5 June 1912, *Pasicrisie luxembourgeoise*, VIII, 547.

Except in the case of an offence discovered *in flagrante delicto*, searches cannot be commenced before 6.30 in the morning, or after 8.00 at night, even with a warrant of the investigating judge.

The accused, the *partie civile*, or any other person who claims to have an interest in the objects seized, may claim their restitution from a court of law. As was already mentioned above, this provision departs from the old Napoleonic Code, and from the Belgian system, where the code is still in force: in Belgium, there is no possibility of claiming the restitution of objects that have been seized, except for the very unsatisfactory complaint with the *juge des référés*.

### 5.3. INTERFERENCE WITH THE RIGHT TO PRIVACY

Telephone tapping and control of correspondence is regulated in arts.88-1 CCP[34]. The following principles apply: surveillance of telephonic conversations and of any other form of communication may be ordered, in exceptional circumstances, by the investigating judge, in a specially motivated warrant and subject to the following conditions: (a) the offence which is the subject of the investigation must carry a penalty of at least 2 years in prison or more; (b) particular facts must cast suspicion upon the person to be put under surveillance, either as a perpetrator, or as an accomplice, or or as a person who receives or transmits information that is addressed to or originate from the accused and (c) ordinary means of investigation are not sufficient because of the nature of the facts and the special circumstances of the case.

Measures of surveillance must be lifted as soon as they are no longer necessary. They will cease automatically one month from the day on which the surveillance warrant was issued. This delay can be prolonged, on each occasion by a month, but may in no case exceed one year. Prolongation is decided by the investigating judge, in a motivated order which must be approved by the president of the judicial council of the court of appeal, within two days after its delivery and after hearing the *procureur d'Etat*.

The investigating judge cannot issue surveillance orders prior to the first interrogation of the accused. Some persons can never be put under surveillance, *i.e.* persons who are protected by an obligation of professional secrecy, laid down in art.458 of the Penal code, unless such persons are themselves suspected of an offence.

A person who has been put under surveillance must be informed of the fact that his correspondence or telephone has been under surveillance, not later than 12 months after the surveillance has ceased[35].

If the surveillance measures have had no concrete result, the copies and

---

[34] *supra*, note 7.

[35] See further SPIELMANN, A., WEITZEL, A. et SPIELMANN, D., *La Convention européenne des droits de l'homme et le droit luxembourgeois*, Bruxelles, Nemesis, 1991, 163-231.

transcripts and any other information added to the *dossier* will be destroyed by the investigating judge not later than 12 months after the termination of the surveillance was ordered. If the investigating judge finds that these copies and transcripts or supplementary information may serve the ongoing investigation, he may order that they be maintained in the dossier, by virtue of a special order. The *procureur d'Etat* and the person concerned may oppose this order (art.88-2, second par.).

If, as a consequence of the surveillance measures, the case against the person concerned has been dismissed, or if he has been acquitted or convicted by a final judgment, the copies, transcripts and supplementary information must be destroyed by the public prosecutor not later than a month after the final judgment.

## 6. The ordinary course of criminal proceedings

In comparison with the changes that were introduced in respect of pre-trial proceedings, the modifications of the Napoleonic CPP have been less drastic as far as trial proceedings are concerned. Proceedings before the trial courts in Luxembourg are, in general terms, conducted according to the rules set out in paragraph 6.2.2. of the Belgian Chapter (except, of course, for what has been said concerning the assize court, which has been abolished in Luxembourg).

There is a striking difference in respect of the committal proceedings (*règlement de la procedure*) before the judicial council (*chambre du conseil*), which are written in Luxembourg, whereas they are conducted in camera, but in the presence of the accused and the *partie civile* in Belgium[36]. If, however, the committal order of the judicial council is appealed against before the judicial council of the court of appeal, there is a hearing in the presence of the parties.

The article on the proceedings before the police court is identical to the one applicable in Belgium (art.153). As far as the proceedings before the tribunal of first instance (both in respect of *délits* and *crimes*) is concerned, there are some small differences, particularly in respect of the role of interpreters during the trial (art.190-1).

## 7. Evidence

The rules of evidence in Luxembourg are largely the same as in Belgium. The article in the Napoleonic Code on the subject, art.153, has remained unchanged in both countries. Hence, what has been said in this respect in the Belgian Chapter is applicable, *mutatis mutandis*, in Luxembourg[37]. Accor-

---

[36]See *supra*, Chapter 1, par.6.1.4.
[37]See *supra*, Chapter 1, par.7.

dingly, *procès-verbaux* may be used as evidence, and confessions, the testimony of witnesses, *etc.* have the same evidentiary weight as in Belgium.

There is, however, a fundamental difference due to the fact that pre-trial investigations in Luxembourg are in part adversarial, as the *accused and the partie civile* have, unlike in Belgium, the right to be present during the performance of most investigative acts. Accordingly, whereas *procès verbaux* in Belgium usually record evidence that has been collected in secret, the evidence recorded in the *procès verbaux* in Luxembourg has often been obtained in a more adversarial manner.

## 8. Special forms of procedure

### 8.1. PROSECUTORIAL DISCRETION (*CLASSEMENT SANS SUITE*)

As in Belgium, the public prosecutor has the right, but is not under an obligation to prosecute. The criteria regulating a decision whether or not to prosecute are not laid down in statute, but are drawn from a decision of the French *Cour de Cassation* of 1826, in which the practice was acknowledged in the following terms:

> "The legislator has not wished to oblige the public prosecutor to prosecute *ex officio*, without the intervention of the *partie civile*, after each and any denunciation, even the lightest and the most insignificant one, or after complaints which do not directly interest public order, and which often have no other purpose than to satisfy individual passion or hatred, vanity or self-esteem, or to procure, at the expenses of the State, and without any social utility, the reparation of some light losses suffered by private persons".

Accordingly, the public prosecutor is not obliged to prosecute whenever a crime has been reported to him: he has a discretionary power not to prosecute. Very often, he will decide not to do so, even in the presence of an offence, if prosecution is not necessary to protect the public interest.

Prosecutorial discretion can be based on various circumstances. For example, the public prosecutor may decide not to prosecute behaviour which, despite the fact that it is still punishable by law, does not meet with social disapproval, *e.g.* in abortion cases, or, before its decriminalisation, adultery.

It is, in this respect, noteworthy to remember the 6th Conference of the Ministers of Justice, held in The Hague, 1970, in which the principle of subsidiarity, proclaimed in the Declaration of Human Rights of 1789 was reaffirmed, according to which the law should only establish penalties that are strictly and obviously necessary (*la loi ne doit établir que des peines strictement et évidemment nécessaires*). In addition, the youth of the accused, or the lack of objective seriousness of the offence, may influence the public prosecutor's decision not to prosecute. It is obvious that such *"décisions de classement"* must be objectively reasoned[38].

## 8.2. PROCEEDINGS BY PENAL ORDER (*ORDONNANCES PENALES*)

The rules governing penal orders are set out in arts.216-1 till 216-10 CPP. The system works as follows: *if*, in case of a relatively minor offence, *i.e.* an offence carrying a sentence not exceeding five years, the public prosecutor does not wish to request a sentence other than a fine, he may address a written request to the trial judge, in which he asks the judge to impose a fine. The proceeding is conducted in writing, without a hearing or a debate. If the accused is found guilty, the judge imposes a fine by penal order (*ordonnance penale*), which is communicated to the accused. If the accused does not agree with the sentence thus imposed, he may oppose it, in which case the normal proceedings will be followed. In fact, the penal order is assimilated to *trial in absentia*, against which the accused may file an *opposition* (art.216-8 a)). He may also decide to appeal against the penal order (art.216-8 c)).

In case of road traffic offences, judges may not only impose fines, but also issue a penal order by which the convicted person's driving licence is suspended, but only for a period not exceeding 3 months (art.216-1 c)).

A penal order is not possible in the following cases: if there is a *partie civile*, if a formal investigation has been opened (*i.e.* a preliminary judicial investigation, conducted by the investigating judge), if the accused has no known domicile or residence, if compensation the damages caused by the offence has not been made or if the accused has not returned the goods.

## 8.3. *TRANSACTIONS*

There is no possibility of *plea bargaining* in Luxembourg, nor of *transactions*, as they are known in Belgium. Instead, the legislator has opted for the above-described penal orders, which are applicable to the same offences and under practically the same conditions as *transactions* in Belgium[39]. Transactions in Luxembourg are only known in the limited fields of tax offences and violations of the customs and excise legislation.

## 8.4. PRIVATE PROSECUTION

The rules on private prosecution are, *mutatis mutandis*, the same as those described in the Belgian Chapter[40].

---

[38]See SPIELMANN, A., "Criminalité et comportement déviant", *Bull. du Statec*, n°3/1973, p.84; SPIELMANN, A., "Le principe de l'opportunité et l'exécution des peines", *Revue de droit pénal et de criminologie*, 1974-75, 316-324.

[39]See *supra*, Chapter 1, par.8.2.

[40]See *supra*, Chapter 1, par.8.4.

## 8.5. TRIAL *IN ABSENTIA*

Here too, the rules are largely the same as in Belgium, as the relevant provisions in the Napoleonic Code have remained virtually unchanged in both countries[41].

# 9. Remedies

### 9.1. ORDINARY REMEDIES

Ordinary remedies are: *opposition* against *in absentiae* judgments and *appeal* against judgments, rendered in first instance. The rules explained in Chapter 1 relating to *opposition* and appeal are applicable, *mutatis mutandis*, to Luxembourg[42].

### 9.2. EXTRAORDINARY REMEDIES

Extraordinary remedies are *cassation* and retrial. Again, the rules on cassation and retrial basically correspond to what has been explained on these points in the Belgian Chapter[43].

However, as far as *cassation to revise a final judgment* is concerned, an important modification of art.443 CPP was brought about in 1981[44]. Firstly, rules have been laid down to allow for the compensation of victims of miscarriages of justice. Secondly, in addition to the classical grounds which may justify a retrial[45], a new ground for an application for retrial has been laid down: an application may be made if it follows from a decision of the Committee of Ministers of the Council of Europe, or of a judgment of the European Court of Human Rights in application of the European Convention on Human Rights, that a criminal conviction and sentence have been pronounced in violation of the Convention (art.443(5)).

# 10. Other questions

### 10.1. STATUTES OF LIMITATION

As in Belgium, all offences, regardless of their seriousness, prescribe after a certain amount of time has elapsed. The same difference exists between the prescription of the right to prosecute (art.637, 638, 640 CPP )and the prescription of the right to execute a sentence (art.635, 636, 639 CPP). Also,

---

[41]See *supra*, Chapter 1, par.8.7.
[42]See *supra*, Chapter 1, par.9.1. and 9.2.
[43]See *supra*, Chapter 1, par.9.3. and 9.4.
[44]Statute of 30 april 1981, *Mémorial*, A, 1981, 755.
[45]See *supra*, Chapter 1, par.9.4.

the length of the delays vary in accordance with the seriousness of the crime[46].

There is, however, a fundamental difference with the Belgian system, as far as the prescription of the right to prosecute is concerned: Luxembourg does not recognise the limitation that is applicable in Belgium, according to which prescription can only be interrupted during its first period, with the result that many offences in Belgium prescribe before they can be tried[47]. In Luxembourg, interruptions always result in a renewal of the prescriptive period, which can be renewed without limit. The only the limit is the "reasonable time" of art.6 of the European Convention on Human Rights, according to which prosecutions should not last longer than is necessary, in view of the particular circumstances of each case[48].

## 11. Select bibliography

THIRY, R., *Précis d'instruction criminelle en droit Luxembourgeois*, Luxembourg, Editions de Bourcy, 1971, 411p.

SPIELMANN, A., "De l'abolition du jury à la supression de la cour d'assises", *Revue de droit pénal et de criminologie*, 1987, 719-733.

SPIELMANN, A., "D'un certain conformisme à un libre examen certain", in *Mémorial -Publications mosellanes* (150 ans d'indépendance), Luxembourg, 1990, 93-104.

SPIELMANN, A., WEITZEL, A. and SPIELMANN, D., *La Convention européenne des droits de l'homme et le droit luxembourgeois*, Bruxelles, Nemesis, 1991, 605p.

SPIELMANN, D., "Le droit au double degré de juridiction en matière pénale dans le système européen de protection des droits de l'homme", *Bulletin du Cercle François Laurent*, 1991, IV, 1-41.

SPIELMANN, D., "L'exigence du délai raisonnable des articles 5,3 et 6,1 de la Convention européenne des droits de l'homme", *Revue trimestrielle des droits de l'homme*, 1991, 75-79.

---

[46]See *supra*, Chapter 1, par.10.1.

[47]Ibid.

[48]See SPIELMANN, D., "L'exigence du délai raisonnable des articles 5,3 et 6,1 de la Convention européenne des droits de l'homme", *Revue trimestrielle des droits de l'homme*, 1991, 75-79.

# Chapter 10 - The Netherlands

Prof. A.H.J. **SWART**
Faculty of Law
University of Utrecht

## 1. Sources

### 1.1. GENERAL OBSERVATIONS

### *1.1.1. Historical background*

The Kingdom of the Netherlands is divided into three parts: the Netherlands (that part of the kingdom situated in Europe), the Dutch Antilles and Aruba (islands in the Caribbean). According to article 3 of the Charter of the Kingdom of the Netherlands (*Statuut voor het Koninkrijk der Nederlanden*), powers of legislation on criminal matters and criminal procedure are entrusted to the separate parts of the Kingdom. The law of criminal procedure of the Dutch Antilles and Aruba will remain outside the scope of this article.

Two historical events played a fundamental part in shaping Dutch criminal law and criminal procedure. The first is the French Revolution, later followed by Napoleon's annexation of the Netherlands. The second is the establishment of a unified Dutch state, replacing the old Republic of the United Provinces in 1814.

In the days of the Republic, all criminal law and criminal procedure was a matter of local concern, and a great diversity of local customs prevailed regionally in both fields. The French Revolution was to change all this. It is especially important that the Netherlands was part of the French Empire between 1810 and 1813. During those years, the French *Code Pénal,* the *Code d'Instruction Criminelle* and the French system of judicial organisation were introduced in the Netherlands. After the end of French domination, this legislation remained in force for some time, the Code Pénal even until 1886.

The establishment of the Kingdom of the Netherlands in 1814 also meant a break with the past. The Netherlands was no longer a coalition of highly autonomous provinces. Since 1814, the Constitution has proclaimed uniformity of legislation and justice in the whole country and it prescribes that codes of criminal law and criminal procedure be introduced. Article 1 of the current Code of criminal procedure (*Wetboek van Strafvordering*) still declares that the creation of rules of criminal procedure belongs to the sole competence of the central legislator. Municipalities and provinces, for example, have no such powers.

As we have seen, it took some time before the French laws were replaced by legislation of Dutch origin. The Act on the organisation of the judiciary (*Wet op de rechterlijke organisatie*) and the first Dutch Code of criminal procedure (*Wetboek van Strafvordering*) date from 1838. They still reflect a great deal of French influence. Indeed, the Code of criminal procedure of 1838 is not much more than a translation of the French code upon which it was modelled. However, there are three differences which still prevail today. There is no jury in Dutch law; injured parties cannot institute proceedings against the suspected perpetrator of a criminal offence; and, finally, the position of the investigating judge or judge of instruction (*rechter-commissaris*) is somewhat different from that of the French *juge d'instruction*.

In 1926 the new Code of criminal procedure was introduced; it is still in force. The most important innovations brought about by this Code concern the pre-trial stage, which lost much of its secret nature, while the suspect's rights were greatly reinforced.

History shows that Dutch criminal procedure and the organisation of the judiciary were strongly influenced by French law. However, at the same time, we can trace the development of an emphatically national system of law, influenced by specific circumstances in the Netherlands and adapted to Dutch culture.

### 1.1.2. The influence of the European Convention on Human Rights

In referring to criminal law, we usually mean that part of the law that has been defined as criminal law within the national legal system. It is important to realise that the European Court of Human Rights considers article 6 of the European Convention for the Protection of Human Rights applicable to all procedures involving the application of sanctions which either deprive a person of his liberty or which are of a punitive and deterrent nature, irrespective of whether such procedures are considered criminal procedures under national law[1].

In the Netherlands, such pseudo-criminal law plays an important role in some fields, especially with respect to military offences of a disciplinary nature, tax and traffic offences. Disciplinary proceedings in the military field have recently been changed following the Act on the revision of military disciplinary proceedings of 1989 (*Rijkswet tot herziening van het militaire tuchtrecht*) and brought more into line with the European Convention. The Act on the administrative sanctioning of traffic regulations of 1989 (*Wet inzake de administratieve handhaving van verkeersvoorschriften*) provides non-criminal sanctions for road traffic offences, while a special act pertains to parking

---

[1]See, for example, ENGEL v. The Netherlands, European Court of Human Rights, 8 June 1976, *Publ. E.C.H.R.*, Series A, vol. 22 and ÖZTÜRK v. Germany, European Court of Human Rights, 21 February 1984, *Publ. E.C.H.R.*, Series A, vol. 73.

offences. With regard to fines for tax offences, case-law has developed guarantees in accordance with article 6 of the Convention since 1985[2].

## 1.2. THE CONSTITUTIONAL LEVEL

### 1.2.1. The Constitution

In the revised version of 1983, two chapters in the Dutch Constitution are especially significant for criminal procedure. Chapter 1 of the Constitution concerns fundamental rights. Essentially, its provisions correspond more or less to the comparable provisions of the European Convention for the Protection of Human Rights and the International Covenant on Civil and Political Rights. In some cases, the Constitution is more far-reaching than the conventions. For example, according to article 12, entry into a person's home against that person's will, requires prior identification and information as to the aim of such entry. Other important provisions, partly of a constitutional nature, are to be found in chapter 6, which deals with the administration of justice. Article 113, for example, forbids deprivation of liberty by any other authority than a court, while article 114 explicitly forbids capital punishment.

The provisions of the Constitution are directed exclusively towards the legislator. According to article 120, Dutch courts are forbidden to pass judgment on the question of whether the law is in accordance with the Constitution.

### 1.2.2. The European Convention on Human Rights and other human rights instruments

The most important human rights treaties to which the Netherlands is a party are the European Convention for the Protection of Human Rights and Fundamental Freedoms and the International Covenant on Civil and Political Rights. With respect to both treaties, the Netherlands has accepted the right of individual petition and, in the case of the European Convention, also the jurisdiction of the European Court.

Important decisions by the European Court on applications against the Netherlands include the Engel-case on military disciplinary law[3], the case of De Jong and others on military criminal procedure[4]; the X and Y-case on the impossibility for mentally handicapped victims of an offence to file complaints[5];

---

[2]The first decision is Supreme Court (*Hoge Raad*), 19 June 1985, *Nederlandse Jurisprudentie*, 1986, 104.

[3]See *supra*, note 1.

[4]DE JONG, BALJET & VAN DEN BRINK v. The Netherlands, European Court of Human Rights, 22 May 1984, *Publ. E.C.H.R.,* Series A, vol 77.

[5]X and Y v. the Netherlands, European Court of Human Rights, 26 March 1985, *Publ. E.C.H.R.*, Series A, vol 91.

the Kostovski-case on the use of statements by anonymous persons as evidence in a criminal trial[6] and the cases of Abdoella and Bunkate on trial within a reasonable time[7]. The Court ruled against the Netherlands in all these cases.

This by no means exhausts the importance of Strasbourg case-law. Decisions by the European Court against other European countries are regularly of great significance for Dutch criminal procedure, especially those on detention on remand (Brogan)[8], the impartiality of the tribunal (De Cubber[9] and Hauschildt[10]), the hearing of witnesses (Unterpertinger[11]), telephone-tapping (Kruslin and Huvig[12]) and extradition (Soering[13]).

A typical feature of Dutch constitutional law is that, while the courts may not examine laws in the light of the Constitution, they may test a law against a convention. According to article 94 of the Constitution, directly applicable provisions of conventions take precedence over provisions of national law. In the Netherlands, most of the provisions of the European Convention and the International Covenant on Civil and Political Rights are regarded as self executing. Consequently, the European Convention especially is as important in Dutch case-law as a constitution is in some other European countries. On average, each year the Dutch Supreme Court (*Hoge Raad*) renders some forty to fifty decisions in which the European Convention is involved, although the substance of these judgments is not always as important as their number would suggest. The Supreme Court's approach is very cautious indeed. It has rarely accepted a broad interpretation of the Convention unless forced to do so by the case-law of the European Court or the European Commission on Human Rights.

---

[6]KOSTOVSKI v. the Netherlands, European Court of Human Rights, 20 November 1989, *Publ. E.C.H.R.*, Series A, vol. 166.

[7]ABDOELLA v. the Netherlands, European Court of Human Rights, 25 November 1992, *Publ. E.C.H.R.*, Series A, vol.248-A and BUNKATE v. the Netherlands, European Court of Human Rights, 26 May 1993, *Publ. E.C.H.R.*, Series A, vol.248-B.

[8]BROGAN e.a. v. United Kingdom, European Court of Human Rights, 29 November 1988, Publ. E.C.H.R., Series A, vol. 145.

[9]DE CUBBER v. Belgium, European Court of Human Rights, 26 October 1984, *Publ. E.C.H.R.*, Series A, vol. 86.

[10]HAUSCHILDT v. Denmark, European Court of Human Rights, 24 May 1989, *Publ.E.C.H.R.*, Series A, vol. 154.

[11]UNTERPERTINGER v. Austria, European Court of Human Rights, 24 November 1986, *Publ. E.C.H.R.*, Series A, vol. 110.

[12]KRUSLIN v. France and HUVIG v. France, European Court of Human Rights, 24 April 1990, *Publ. E.C.H.R.*, Series A, vol. 176.

[13]SOERING v. United Kingdom, European Court of Human Rights, 7 July 1989, *Publ. E.C.H.R.*, Series A, vol.161.

1.3. STATUTES ON CRIMINAL PROCEDURE

### 1.3.1. The organisation of the judiciary

The Act on the organisation of the judiciary of 1838 (*Wet op de rechterlijke organisatie*) is of basic importance. It also governs the position and the work of the Public Prosecution Service (*Openbaar Ministerie*).

Separate rules concerning the trial of war criminals are to be found in the Act on War Crimes (*Wet oorlogsstrafrecht*), while economic offences are dealt with in the Economic Offences Act of 1950 (*Wet op de economische delicten*).

The administration of justice in military matters and the corresponding judicial organisation were separate until the end of 1990. As from January 1st 1991, however, they have been incorporated into the ordinary justice system by means of the Act on new rules concerning military justice of 1990 (*Wet houdende nieuwe regels inzake de militaire strafrechtspraak*). Criminal offences perpetrated by members of the armed forces are now dealt with by ordinary criminal courts. However, there is still a separate ruling on the administration of military disciplinary law, which was totally revised in 1990.

### 1.3.2. The Code of criminal procedure

Of overriding importance is the Code of criminal procedure of 1926 (*Wetboek van Strafvordering*). The Code has been amended many times since its introduction. Currently, there are plans for drastic amendments to the provisions governing the investigation of criminal offences, especially the preliminary judicial investigation under the supervision of an investigating judge.

As a result of the incorporation of military justice into the ordinary justice system, military criminal procedure is no longer separate. Some additional rules were added to the Code in the Act on new rules concerning military justice.

### 1.3.3. Special statutes

Despite its overriding importance, the Code of criminal procedure is not the only Act to contain rules of criminal procedure. Coercive measures pertaining to the investigation of criminal offences are to be found in many special statutes which provide investigating authorities with special powers, for example with regard to search and seizure. Almost invariably, these powers are more far-reaching than those provided by the Code of criminal procedure. Moreover, these special acts often provide powers of control and supervision with regard to compliance by citizens with those acts and therefore allow for coercion without there necessarily being a reasonable suspicion that an offence has been committed. This is usually linked to an obligation on the part of the citizen to co-operate.

The most important of these statutes are the Opium Act of 1928

(*Opiumwet*), the Traffic Act of 1935 (*Wegenverkeerswet*), the Economic Offences Act of 1950 (*Wet op de economische delicten*) and the Act on weapons and ammunition of 1986 (*Wet wapens en munitie*).

### 1.3.4. The Police Act and the Police Registration Act

In the Netherlands, the organisation of the police is based on the Police Act of 1957. Although this Act does not explicitly provide the police with the power to infringe upon individual rights in connection with the exercise of police authority, the Supreme Court deduces such powers from the Act itself. For example, the police may shadow persons of whom it is suspected that they will commit a criminal offence in the near future [14]. This means that more and more, the Act has come to provide a basis for preventive and pro-active police action.

A second important act worth mentioning is the Police Registration Act of 1990 (*Wet politieregisters*). This Act governs the collection and use of data in (computerised) data-files.

### 1.3.5. Pseudo-legislation

Criminal procedure is not only governed by statutes. In practice it is also influenced by a phenomenon known in the Netherlands as pseudo-legislation.
The Code of criminal procedure provides the Public Prosecution Service and the police with powers in a great many areas. The use of that authority is often the subject of instructions or memoranda with which individual prosecutors or police officers must comply. Many of these guidelines (*richtlijnen*) are made by the heads of the prosecution service, the procurators general (*procureurs-generaal*) (see *infra*, 2.2). The guidelines are concerned with three fields in particular: the penalties to be demanded by the public prosecutors at criminal trials; the question of which offences are to be prosecuted and which offences are to be dealt with out of court; and the use of certain techniques or tactics of investigation (such as the deployment of undercover agents). Most guidelines have been officially published. Recently, the Supreme Court recognised these guidelines as laws within the meaning of article 99 of the Act on the organisation of the judiciary[15]. Consequently, a citizen can now invoke a guideline in court. It is, for example, a valid defence that, according to the guideline, the accused should never have been prosecuted, or that undercover agents should not have been used in his case.

However, pseudo-legislation still differs from real legislation in that the Public Prosecution Service and the police are not absolutely bound to guidelines. It is possible to deviate from them for reasons of overriding importance.

---

[14]Hoge Raad, 14 October 1986, *Nederlandse Jurisprudentie*, 1987, 564.
[15]Hoge Raad, 19 June 1990, *Nederlandse Jurisprudentie*, 1991, 119.

## 1.4. CASE-LAW AND LEGAL DOCTRINE

### 1.4.1. Case-law

In Dutch criminal procedure, case-law plays an extremely important part. Each year, the Supreme Court renders hundreds of decisions in cases involving criminal procedure. Many feel that the Supreme Court is overburdened, and at present the question of whether a leave to appeal system should be introduced in the Netherlands is being debated.

The Supreme Court is a court of cassation, modelled on French lines. According to article 99 of the Act on the organisation of the judiciary, the Supreme Court can overturn a decision on two grounds: because of failure to observe formal procedure and because of incorrect interpretation of the law. The word "law" here does not only mean written law, but also unwritten principles of law and treaties.

The Supreme Court's most important task is still to determine the meaning of legal provisions and to decide whether lower courts have complied with them. There has, however, been a development which could be called the emancipation from written law. In increasingly ignoring the letter of the law, the Supreme Court has become an important creator of new criminal procedure. A few examples may serve as an illustration of this development. The Supreme Court examines decisions by lower courts not only in the light of legal provisions but also of unwritten principles of due process (*beginselen van behoorlijke procesorde*). The main principles are: the principle of equality of treatment (*gelijkheidsbeginsel*), a prohibition of abuse of power (*machtsafwending, détournement de pouvoir*), the principle that legitimate expectations must be fulfilled (*vertrouwensbeginsel*), and the principle of proportionality (*proportionaliteitsbeginsel*). Another example is the rule that illegally obtained evidence be excluded as proof, a rule that does not derive from the Code of criminal procedure but from case-law. The same applies to the rule that the public prosecutor may lose his right to prosecute if a serious violation of fundamental principles of due process has occurred, for example because the accused was not brought to trial without undue delay. The fact that the court, the public prosecutor, or the police officer has acted in accordance with the Code of criminal procedure does not, therefore, necessarily imply that those actions do not constitute a violation of law.

All this could create the impression that the Supreme Court has reinforced the rights of the defence alone. But that would be wrong. Less strict adherence to the letter of the law can also mean that actions which contravene written provisions are not always deemed contrary to law. The most important example is case-law relating to the use of statements by anonymous witnesses. This is forbidden by the Code of criminal procedure, but the Supreme Court has created a wide margin within which it has become possible (see *infra*, 7.2.).

## 1.4.2. Legal doctrine

At present, academic attention in the Netherlands remains focused on criminal procedure, on which a great deal has been written during the past decades - more indeed than on substantive criminal law. Criminal procedure is also changing at an ever faster rate under the influence of new developments (drug related crime, economic crime, new investigation tactics, etc.).

# 2. Structure of the criminal justice system

The investigation and prosecution of criminal offences requires an organisation able to undertake such tasks. In the Netherlands, four institutions are involved: the police (*politie*), the Public Prosecution Service (*Openbaar Ministerie*), the judiciary (*rechterlijke macht*) and the probation service (*reclassering*).

### 2.1. THE POLICE

Few subjects are so complicated as the organisation of the Dutch police force (*politie*). The larger municipalities in the Netherlands have their own municipal police force (*gemeentepolitie*). Smaller towns are served by a national police force (*rijkspolitie*) for which the Minister of Justice is responsible. Thirdly there is the royal constabulary (*Koninklijke Marechaussee*) who performs the duties of military police and border control and also regularly assists the municipal and national police force. The Minister of Defence is responsible for the Marechaussee. Recently, a Bill has been introduced providing for a total revision of the organisational structure. The police force will be divided into twenty-five regional forces on a territorial basis.

According to the Police Act of 1957, the tasks of the police are twofold: to maintain public order and to investigate criminal offences. The final responsibility for the first task belongs to the Burgomasters of the municipalities and the Interior Minister, for the second to the public prosecutors and the Minister of Justice. The distinction between the different tasks performed by the police in the Netherlands is not, therefore, reflected in any organisational division into different forces. According to the Code of criminal procedure, the public prosecutor directs the investigation of criminal offences. In practice, the prosecutor is rarely able to actually direct the police.

To make things even more complicated, there are, besides the regular police force which is organised on a territorial basis, special investigation services charged with the investigation of special categories of criminal offences. The three most important are the Fiscal Inquiry and Investigation Service (*Fiscale Inlichtingen- en Opsporingsdienst*, FIOD) under the authority of the Minister of Finance, the Economic Investigation Service (*Economische Controle Dienst*, ECD) under the authority of the Minister of Economic Affairs and the General Inspection Service (*Algemene Inspectiedienst*, AID) under the authority of the Minister of Agriculture and Fishing.

## 2.2. THE PUBLIC PROSECUTOR

The Act on the organisation of the judiciary refers to the judiciary in the broadest sense, comprising both the Public Prosecution Service and the judiciary. The former's function is to prosecute criminal offences, the latter must adjudicate them.

The Public Prosecution Service (*openbaar ministerie*) has a threefold task: to direct the investigation of criminal offences, to prosecute the perpetrators of criminal offences and to execute the decisions rendered by the courts. At the sub-district and district courts, the Prosecution Service is represented by public prosecutors (*officieren van justitie*), at the appellate courts and at the Supreme Court by procurators general (*procureurs-generaal*) and advocates general (*advocaten-generaal*).

The Public Prosecution Service is an hierarchical organisation, at the head of which stands, according to the law, the Minister of Justice. The relationship between the Minister of Justice and the Prosecution Service is a sensitive issue. The Public Prosecution Service is keen on emphasizing its independence and own responsibility. The procurator general and advocate general at the Supreme Court stand outside this hierarchy, because one of their tasks is the prosecution of criminal offences perpetrated by those in public office. That also explains why they, like judges, are appointed for life.

The procurators general at the appeal courts occupy a special position within the public Prosecution Service. In practice, they direct the Service in consultation with the Minister of Justice by means of the guidelines which they make (see 1.3.5.).

In Dutch criminal procedure, the Public Prosecution Service is the only body empowered to bring a prosecution for a criminal offence. On the other hand, the Prosecution Service is never obliged to prosecute. The Netherlands is one of the countries that has adopted the "opportunity principle" (*opportuniteitsbeginsel*). The monopoly on prosecution in combination with the opportunity principle make the Public Prosecution Service one of the central institutions in the Dutch criminal justice system.

## 2.3. THE JUDICIARY

### 2.3.1. Competence

The Criminal Code distinguishes between crimes (*misdrijven*) and misdemeanours (*overtredingen*). The competence of the different courts is linked to this distinction.

*Overtredingen* are first brought before a sub-district court (*kantongerecht*) of which there are sixty one. *Misdrijven* are first tried by one of the nineteen district courts (*rechtbank*) which are composed of three judges, although simple cases may be brought before a single member of the district court (see also *infra*, 8.1.). Appeals against decisions by the sub-district court are heard by the district court. Appeals against decisions by the district court are heard by one of the five courts of appeal (*gerechtshof*). The Supreme Court (*Hoge Raad*) stands at the head of the judicial organisation.

The courts try cases. But they are also involved in various ways in pre-trial investigations. A so called preliminary judicial investigation may be carried out by an investigating judge (*rechter-commissaris*, see 6.1.2.). This judge may also decide on detention on remand (*bewaring*, see 5.2.1.). Special tasks have also been entrusted to the judicial council (raadkamer), a panel consisting of three judges. Like the investigating judge, the judicial council may have to decide about detention on remand (*gevangenneming*, see 5.2.1.) and on a number of coercive measures (see 3.2. and 5.3.). It also deals with complaints against summonses.

### 2.3.2. The role of lay judges

For a few years during the Napoleonic era, juries did exist in the Netherlands. They were quickly abolished in 1813, never to reappear.

In the Netherlands, the judicial function is a matter for professional judges. The only real exception is to be found in the Act on new rules concerning military justice (*supra*, 1.3.1.). If a criminal offence, perpetrated by a member of the armed forces, is tried by a district court, that court must include a member of the armed forces. Substitute judges could perhaps also be considered an exception: it is not unusual for persons who are not professional judges but who do possess both knowledge and experience of the criminal justice system (for instance defence lawyers or lecturers in criminal law), to be appointed as judges and to participate more or less regularly in the administration of criminal justice. In this way they relieve the courts of some of the workload and allow the professionals to profit from their specific expertise.

### 2.3.3. The appointment of judges

According to article 118 of the Constitution, judges are appointed for life by the Crown. Members of the Supreme Court are appointed from a list of nominees drawn up by the Second Chamber of parliament.

### 2.3.4. Independence and impartiality

The Act on the organisation of the judiciary contains a number of provisions meant to guarantee the judge's independence. The most important are those concerning dismissal. Judges can only be dismissed by the Supreme Court on the grounds that they are manifestly unsuitable. It is also important that the position of judge is considered incompatible with a number of other public positions. However, there is no legal barrier to a judge's also being a member of a representative body such as parliament or a municipal council. In practice such combinations are rare.

As far as the impartiality of the judge in specific cases is concerned, arts.

512-524 of the Code of criminal procedure contain an extensive ruling intended to guarantee such impartiality. If facts or circumstances occur that would endanger the impartiality of the judge in a particular case, the judge may abstain from participation in the case, or be challenged by one of the parties.

According to the European Court of Human Rights in the cases of De Cubber and Hauschildt (*supra*, 1.2.2.), the participation of a trial judge hearing a case in which he has previously been involved during the pre-trial stage, could constitute a violation of article 6 of the European Convention. Article 268 of the Code of criminal procedure is based on the same notion, by laying down the rule that the judge who was in charge of the preliminary judicial investigation into a certain case, shall not take part in the trial itself. Elsewhere, however, the Code makes an exception for the juvenile judge. Meanwhile, case-law from Strasbourg has persuaded the Supreme Court that this provision should not be applied[16]. On the other hand, the Supreme Court does not consider situations in which the trial judge judging an offender was previously involved in decisions relating to the detention on remand of the same person, to be incompatible with article 6 of the European Convention[17]. The Dutch Code of criminal procedure does not forbid this; indeed, article 67a assumes that the judges who decided on detention on remand will, preferably, be the judges who decide the case itself.

## 2.4. THE RECLASSERING

The fourth institution to play an important part in the Dutch criminal justice system, is the *reclassering*. There is, to my knowledge, no equivalent of this service in the English speaking world although there may be some resemblances with the probation service in, for example, Great Britain. However, translating reclassering into "probation service" would be misleading.

The *reclassering* comprises a number of private organisations which have combined to form the Dutch Federation of Probation Institutions (*Nederlandse Federatie van Reclasseringsinstellingen*) which is subsidized by the Ministry of Justice.

The *reclassering* provides information to the courts on the accused's personal and social circumstances. Such information is either requested by the court, or provided by *reclassering* on its own initiative or at the request of the accused. A report by the *reclassering* is provided in a majority of cases in which there is a chance that a prison sentence will be imposed. The accused is not obliged to co-operate.

The *reclassering* also provides aid and support to accused persons and those sentenced, a task that is sometimes at odds with that of reporting to the court on the accused. In all, the *reclassering* most resembles a social service whose field of work is the criminal justice system as a whole.

---

[16]Hoge Raad, 13 November 1990, *Nederlandse Jurisprudentie*, 1991, 219.
[17] Hoge Raad, 27 November 1990, *Nederlandse Jurisprudentie*, 1991, 220

## 3. Parties to criminal proceedings

### 3.1. THE PUBLIC PROSECUTOR: NOT A PARTY TO THE PROCEEDINGS

Strictly speaking, there are no parties in Dutch criminal procedure. As far as the public prosecutors are concerned, the term is inappropriate, for they represent the public interest which will benefit most from the correct and just application of law. This means that the prosecutor must not attempt to secure the conviction of the accused at all costs, but must approach the case impartially.

### 3.2. THE DEFENCE

In the Netherlands, the term defence refers to both the accused (*verdachte*) and his counsel (*raadsman/vrouw*). There is only one word in Dutch criminal procedure for the person suspected of or on trial for committing a criminal offence: regardless of the stage the trial has reached, that person is known as the *"verdachte"*. The word, however, means two different things: during the preliminary investigation, the *"verdachte"* is the suspect, against whom there is probable cause. During the preliminary judicial investigation and the trial, indeed, as soon as a member of the judiciary has become involved in the proceedings, the *"verdachte"* is the accused against whom the prosecution is directed.

### *3.2.1. The accused*

Dutch criminal procedure occurs in two stages: the pre-trial investigation and the trial stage before a court. This distinction is of fundamental importance because in each stage there are essential differences in the position of the accused.

The *trial stage* is accusatorial, with the accused a party to the case. He has a number of rights, such as the right to be present, the right to examine witnesses, the right to be assisted by counsel, etc. These rights imply that, during the trial, the accused is in principle on an equal footing with the prosecutor.

During the *pre-trial stage*, the position of the accused is very different. Although the Code of criminal procedure of 1926 reinforced the rights of the suspect considerably and greatly reduced the secret nature of the preliminary investigation, nevertheless at this stage he is not only the subject of rights but also, or perhaps more so, the object of investigation. We see this, for instance, in the fact that he must, if necessary, undergo all sorts of investigatory measures such as arrest, searching, fingerprinting, etc. This gives the pre-trial stage a more inquisitorial character. It does, however, make a difference whether one is dealing with an investigation directed by the prosecutor, or a preliminary judicial investigation directed by a judge. See further *infra*, 6.1.1. and 6.1.2.

### 3.2.2. Defence counsel

Defence counsel is there to assist the accused. That is why, as a matter of principle, counsel may not act for the accused during the trial if the latter is not present. See *infra*, 8.2.

According to article 38 of the Code of criminal procedure, every accused has the right to be assisted by one or more lawyers of his own choice. This applies to every criminal case. Articles 40 *et seq.* deal with the allocation of counsel. If counsel is allocated, the accused is not free to choose his own lawyer, although preferences are often taken into account.

If the accused is remanded in custody, a defence counsel must be allocated by law, even if the accused has not requested that he be allocated a lawyer. The accused does have the right to replace allocated counsel by a lawyer of his own choice. If the accused has not been deprived of his liberty and is unable to pay for counsel, he may request the allocation of a lawyer. In that case it must be reasonably clear that the accused is in need of legal assistance.

According to Dutch law, counsel can never act against the will of the accused. If the accused refuses to accept counsel, the lawyer cannot act for him. During criminal proceedings, counsel has all the rights to which an accused is entitled. Article 50 of the Code affords counsel the right of unrestricted and unsupervised access to the accused who has been remanded in custody, both in person and by means of correspondence. However, some restrictions are allowed during the pre-trial stage. The most important ground for imposing such restrictions is that serious suspicion has arisen that contacts between accused and counsel are being used in an attempt to hinder the investigation. Such restrictions may be imposed by the public prosecutor or by the judge of instruction, although both must lay their decisions before the court as soon as possible.

Counsel has the right to be present whenever the accused is questioned. However, it has been established in case-law that this right does not apply to police interrogations. According to the Supreme Court, this restriction does not constitute a violation of article 6 of the European Convention[18].

Counsel must always act in the interest of the accused and in that interest only. At the same time, lawyers are bound by the ethics of their profession. This professional code of behaviour is a matter of disciplinary law, exercised by the Bar Association in the Netherlands (*Nederlandse Orde van Advocaten*) on the basis of the 1952 Lawyers Act (*Advocatenwet*).

### 3.3. THE VICTIM

The victim does not occupy a very prominent position in Dutch criminal procedure and is more or less without rights. During the past years there have been some attempts to improve the victim's position, for example by

---

[18]Hoge Raad, 22 November 1983, *Nederlandse Jurisprudentie,* 1984, 805.

systematically informing him of the progress being made in the case or by establishing a special fund for reimbursement of victims unable to seek satisfaction from the perpetrators. A more dubious practice that has arisen during the past decade is that of allowing victims to testify anonymously in order to protect them from possible threats by the accused. See *infra*, 7.2.

### 3.3.1. Private prosecution

In Dutch law, the victim cannot act as party to a criminal case in his own right. Only the public prosecutor has the authority to prosecute for a criminal offence. However, the Code of criminal procedure does allow interested parties to complain against decisions by the prosecution service not to prosecute. The complaint is heard by the Court of Appeal, which will then hear the victim. If the Court is of the opinion that the accused should be prosecuted, it will order the public prosecutor to bring a prosecution. In practice, this complaints procedure is not used very often.

### 3.3.2. Civil claims

The victim of a criminal offence can always seek compensation from the perpetrator quite simply, by joining the criminal case as a civil party (*civiele partij*). Due to a recent change in legislation, there is no longer a limit to the amount of damages that may be claimed by the victim.

The victim rarely appears in criminal cases, especially not if the accused has confessed. The explanation for this phenomenon is that statements by witnesses made during the preliminary investigation, can be used as evidence in court. See *infra*, 6.2. and 7.2.

## 4. General principles concerning criminal procedure

Dutch criminal procedure is governed by a number of principles, i.e. basic determinants of the structure of procedural law. Sometimes these principles are mutually reinforcing, sometimes they coexist in an uneasy relationship. Moreover, it is here that the influence of the European Convention is probably the greatest, as it provides its own norms of due process in criminal matters.

4.1 GENERAL PRINCIPLES OF PROCEDURE

### 4.1.1. The "principle of instruction"

As in most European countries, in the Netherlands the principle applies that the judge must attempt to arrive at the material truth in an independent manner. In determining what the facts of the matter are, he is not bound to accept the versions of either the prosecutor or the defence. There is, therefore, no such thing as plea-bargaining in court. (However, for agreements between prosecution and defence, see *infra*, 4.2.2.).

## 4.1.2. The right to be heard

According to article 35 of the Code of criminal procedure, the accused must be heard on every decision that the court could take in his case. This provision pertains not only to the trial proper, but also to the (preliminary) investigation. However, there are exceptions to the general rule with regard to decisions by the investigating judge during the preliminary judicial investigation. These exceptions concern the application of a number of coercive measures such as search and seizure and telephone taps.

## 4.1.3. The principle of acceleration

A number of provisions in the Code of criminal procedure give the court or the prosecution a fixed period of time within which certain action must be taken, or urge action with the least possible delay. The Code does not contain a general provision giving the accused the right to trial within a reasonable time. Article 6 of the European Convention on Human Rights does. No other aspect of article 6 has given rise to so many decisions by the Supreme Court during the past years. The problems that arise in the Netherlands in complying with this provision are especially evident in appeal cases, both to the appeal courts and to the Supreme Court. It is not unusual for one, or even more than two years to go by before a case is dealt with in appeal. Recently, the European Court of Human Rights condemned the Netherlands on two counts for having violated the European Convention on Human rights (see the Abdoella and Bunkate-cases, *supra*, 1.2.2.). The reason for these long delays is a lack of manpower and resources within the Dutch criminal justice system.

In 1980 the Supreme Court decided that prosecution should be inadmissible in cases of undue delay[19]. The primary result of this decision was that the lower courts became extremely reluctant to conclude that the right to a speedy trial had indeed been violated. They preferred a different approach, namely that, while there was no undue delay, the length of the trial nevertheless provided grounds for mitigating punishment. The Supreme Court later ruled that such mitigation can be considered a suitable sanction in cases of lesser violations of the right to a speedy trial[20].

---

[19]Hoge Raad, 23 September 1980, *Nederlandse Jurisprudentie*, 1980, 116.
[20]Hoge Raad, 7 april 1987, *Nederlandse Jurisprudentie*, 1987, 587.

## 4.2. PRINCIPLES GOVERNING THE OPENING OF CRIMINAL PROCEEDINGS

### 4.2.1. The "ex officio" principle

The power to prosecute is the exclusive prerogative of the Public Prosecution Service. There are, however, a number of legal restrictions. Some criminal offences cannot be prosecuted unless the victim of the offence has filed a complaint. In some cases the law requires that other authorities be consulted about, or even agree with, the decision to prosecute or not. This is the case, for example, with regard to offences concerning juveniles, or tax offences.

The Public Prosecution Service not only possesses a monopoly on prosecution, the law also allows it freedom in the way in which that monopoly is used. In other words, Dutch legislation on criminal procedure is based on the "principle of opportunity" (*opportuniteitsbeginsel*). It does, however, contain several corrective mechanisms with regard to the use to which that principle is put. For example, a decision not to prosecute can be revised by order of the Minister of Justice. More important than this somewhat theoretical possibility is the complaints procedure that allows the victim of a criminal offence to request that the decision not to prosecute be overturned by the Court of Appeal (see also *supra*, 3.3.1.).

On the other hand, the accused may file a complaint with the District Court against a decision to prosecute. The Court will dismiss the case against the accused if it is highly unlikely that he will be convicted.

### 4.2.2. The principles of "legality" and "opportunity"

As we have seen, Dutch legislation is based on the principle of opportunity. This principle plays a very important part in the day to day practice of the criminal justice system. If one wishes to understand that system, one must understand the use to which the principle of opportunity is put.

According to article 167 of the Code of criminal procedure, the public prosecutor may decide not to proceed with prosecution "for reasons of public interest". A public prosecutor will use this power if he does not expect prosecution to succeed, for example because there is not enough proof. This is called a *technical waiver*. However, a practice has developed in the Netherlands in which prosecutions that would certainly have succeeded are nevertheless waived. Such cases are referred to as *policy waivers*.

Policy waivers are extremely important in the Dutch criminal justice system. Each year, between 15 and 20 % of all crimes are dealt with in this way by the prosecution service; the percentage is much greater where misdemeanours (*overtredingen*) are concerned. This policy is based on two very different considerations: one is idealistic, the other pragmatic. The first is that criminal law should always be the ultimate solution (*ultimum remedium*). This implies that prosecution should only take place if the public interest so requires (a line of reasoning that turns article 167 upside down). The public prosecutor must always ask himself whether a different, non-criminal solution is preferable. The second consideration is purely pragmatic. Waiving large numbers of criminal cases helps prevent the courts from becoming overburdened, at least not more so than they already are. Considering the significance of waivers in criminal cases, it is understandable that the procurators general at the courts of appeal have devised guidelines in order to promote a uniform policy of waiver (see *supra*, 1.3.5.).

The public prosecutor can waive prosecution in an unconditional manner, but he can also waive prosecution provided that the accused accepts a number of conditions. The accused is not obliged to accept the conditions. A similar means of dealing with criminal offences is that of transaction (*transactie*), provisions on which are to be found in the Criminal Code. The nearest equivalent in anglo-saxon law is compounding, although transaction is used much more widely (for example for ordinary crimes) in Dutch criminal law.

By accepting a proposal by the Prosecution Service for transaction, the accused can avoid criminal proceedings. The *quid pro quo* usually involves the payment of a sum of money, the reimbursement of the victim, the relinquishing of stolen goods, or some such "sanction". Transaction is always possible in the case of misdemeanours. Since an amendment of law in 1983, it is also possible in the case of crimes that carry a penalty of no more than six years'imprisonment. In practice, conditional waivers and transactions also occur frequently; and here too the procurators general have drawn up guidelines. Such conditions, however, are often a matter of negotiation between the Prosecution Service and the defence, a practice that closely resembles plea bargaining.

The majority of criminal offences known to the authorities in the Netherlands are dealt with by means of waiver, conditional waiver or transaction. Nevertheless, in practice the need was felt for yet another way of disposing of cases, especially where traffic offences are concerned. The *Act on the administrative sanctioning of traffic regulations* of 1989 provides for administrative sanctions for traffic offences. Procedurally this system of sanctions differs from conditional waivers and transactions with which the accused can refuse to comply (in which case the public prosecutor will go ahead with the prosecution). The 1989 Act reverses this system, requiring the person who disagrees with the sanction to appeal to the court himself.

### 4.2.3. The principles of "accusation" and "inquisition"

As we have seen, Dutch criminal procedure is a mixture of accusatorial and inquisitorial elements, with inquisitorial aspects predominant during the phase of investigation, and accusatorial aspects dominating the trial proper. The trial however does have some inquisitorial characteristics, the most important of which is that the judge is not only responsible for the orderly course of events, but also directs an investigation into the true facts. This is apparent, for example, in the fact that it is the judge who examines the accused, the witnesses and other persons first, after which the public prosecutor and the defence are able to ask further questions. This is a consequence of the "principle of instruction" (see *supra*, 4.1.1.). The public prosecutor is always present during a trial.

### 4.3. PRINCIPLES GOVERNING THE TAKING OF EVIDENCE

#### 4.3.1. *The principle of the free evaluation of the evidence*

Dutch law on evidence is based on a number of principles. On the one hand, the Code contains several important rules with regard to the questions of which data may be used as evidence and how much evidence is necessary for a conviction. Statements by one suspect cannot, for example, be used against another in the same case, while the law prohibits convictions based on the accused's own statement alone or solely on a statement by a single witness. However, many of these rules have gradually been eroded in case-law. The case against a fellow suspect is often dealt with separately, so that statements by the one suspect can be used against the other. In case-law there is a tendency towards a free system of evidence.

On the other hand, a court is never obliged to convict. Whatever the evidence in a criminal case, the court may not convict unless it is convinced beyond reasonable doubt that the accused is indeed guilty.

#### 4.3.2. *The presumption of innocence*

The Code is based on the presumption of innocence, although it is never formulated as such. However, article 302 does forbid the court from demonstrating any feeling with regard to the accused's innocence or guilt. The accused has the right to remain silent, and the fact that he exercises that right may not be taken into account as evidence of guilt[21]. On the other hand, it is deemed admissible in case-law that an accused person's statement of denial be used as evidence, if that statement is so lacking in credibility and evidently untruthful as to be aimed purely at disguising the truth[22].

A different problem, pertaining more to the field of substantive criminal law, concerns provisions in which certain facts are regarded as the truth unless the accused can provide prima facie proof to the contrary. Such provisions are often to be found outside the Criminal Code. In such cases, Dutch courts adhere to the decision by the European Court of Human Rights in the Salabiaku-case[23]. They will, therefore, examine whether presumptions of fact or of law

---

[21]Hoge Raad, 8 November 1988, *Nederlandse Jurisprudentie,* 1988, 657.

[22]Hoge Raad, 17 January 1978, *Nederlandse Jurisprudentie,* 1978, 341.

[23]SALABIAKU v. France, European Court of Human Rights, 7 October 1988, *Publ. E.C.H.R.*, Series A, vol. 141.

are confined within reasonable limits which take into account the importance of what is at stake, and whether the rights of the defence are maintained[24].

### 4.3.3. The principle of "nemo tenetur"

Closely linked to the presumption of innocence is the principle that no one can be obliged to provide evidence against himself. This principle is laid down in Dutch criminal procedure in two different ways.

In the first place, the principle implies that persons under suspicion may not be coerced into giving a statement. Article 29 of the Code of criminal procedure centres around this right to remain silent. It adds that an accused person must be reminded of that right before each examination. The significance of remaining silent in the context of the evidence was discussed above.

At the same time, the Code is based on the idea that an accused person must suffer certain violations of his rights passively, such as search and seizure, but is not required to co-operate actively. He is not, for instance, obliged to give up an object, to open the door of his house, or to undress. Meanwhile, the Code also contains a number of exceptions to the rule that an accused person "need not co-operate in his own conviction". Such exceptions are even more frequently found in special statutes pertaining to special categories of crimes. For example, the Traffic Act obliges a person suspected of driving under the influence to co-operate with a breathalyser test. One could say that the second aspect of the principle of *nemo tenetur* has come under increasing pressure. According to the Supreme Court, human rights conventions do not embody any general principle regarding the right not to co-operate in one's own conviction[25].

### 4.4. PRINCIPLES GOVERNING THE TRIAL

### 4.4.1. The principle of immediacy

In the Code of criminal procedure, the trial is of course governed by the principle that the court may only use material that has been discussed in court as evidence (for example, art.297 Code of criminal procedure). This guarantees that evidence is not kept secret from the defence and that counsel can express an opinion on its value.

The Code also embodies the principle of immediacy (*onmiddelijkheidsbeginsel*) or of direct testimony, obliging witnesses to appear at the trial, for example, and declaring statements made in court only to be valid evidence. A limited exception to this rule concerns witnesses who will probably

---

[24]Hoge Raad, 11 October 1989, *Nederlandse Jurisprudentie*, 1990, 812, and 11 October 1989, *Nederlandse Jurisprudentie*, 1990, 813.

[25]Hoge Raad, 15 February 1977, *Nederlandse Jurisprudentie*, 1977, 557, and 20 November 1990, *Nederlandse Jurisprudentie*, 1991, 303.

be unable to appear in court, for instance for reasons of poor health. If necessary, such witnesses can be heard during the preliminary judicial investigation by the investigating judge. Counsel has the right to be present at such hearings.

However, the rule that statements by witnesses do not constitute valid testimony unless made in court has almost entirely been eroded in case-law. Soon after the introduction of the Code of criminal procedure in 1926, the Supreme Court accepted hearsay testimony as evidence[26]. This case-law is still of fundamental significance for criminal procedure in the Netherlands

In the first place, it has been one of the main reasons why the focus of investigation into the truth of the matter gradually shifted from the trial proper to the investigative stage, that has become the phase most crucial to the evidence. This means that the trial proper is very often restricted to discussing the value of data in files compiled long beforehand. Witnesses are not called to testify unless special circumstances make their actual presence during the trial desirable. Ordinary criminal cases are cases where no witnesses are present in person.

Because all relevant data have usually already been collected during the investigative phase, the trial itself does not normally take very long, especially not if the accused has confessed. Even a murder case in the Netherlands need not take more than a couple of hours if the accused has made a confession.

The main problem with this development is that it encroaches on the rights of the defense. Counsel has the right to examine witnesses during the trial, but not at the investigative stage (bar the exception mentioned above). This means that one of the most important rights of the defence has been seriously undermined, to an extent that only became apparent in the Eighties in a number of decisions by the Supreme Court on anonymous witnesses (see *infra*, 7.2.).

Since 1986, the right to examine witnesses laid down in article 6 of the European Convention has figured in many decisions by the European Court of Human Rights (for example the above-mentioned Kostovski-case, *supra*, 1.2.2.). These are highly significant for Dutch criminal procedure and have been the focus of a great deal of attention in the Netherlands. They have forced Dutch courts to change their course, giving the defence more opportunities to question witnesses for the prosecution. However, the exact meaning of the European Court's case-law is a matter of considerable controversy among Dutch lawyers.

### 4.4.2. The principle of orality

The Code of criminal procedure requires that the trial be oral. However, in appeals to the Supreme Court written proceedings are the rule, because the Supreme Court does not give any judgment on the facts of the case, but only on legal matters.

---

[26]Hoge Raad, 20 December 1926, *Nederlandse Jurisprudentie,* 1927, 85.

### 4.4.3. The principle of publicity

In accordance with article 6 of the European Convention, article 121 of the Constitution requires criminal trials to be held in public. The verdict must also be given in public. Some exceptions to the principle of publicity are allowed. They correspond to those detailed in article 6 of the European Convention.

## 5. Coercive measures

#### 5.1. PRELIMINARY REMARKS

Coercive measures (*dwangmiddelen*), either against the accused or against other persons, can be applied under many different circumstances in Dutch criminal procedure. Such measures may also serve different ends. In the first place, coercive measures are important in order to ensure effective investigation of the case, more especially during the trial. It is to that end that evidence can be seized or the accused be deprived of his liberty. Secondly, coercive measures are important because they may anticipate judicial decisions, thereby ensuring that such decisions can be executed at a later date. This may also be the reason for seizure or for depriving the accused of his liberty. Finally, sometimes coercive measures can be applied in order to prevent the commission of further criminal offences.

As coercive measures always imply a violation of a person's rights, they must be based upon formal law. Although it is not unusual for the Supreme Court to arrive at a broad interpretation of a legal provision concerning coercive measures, it will nevertheless not accept entirely new forms of investigation involving coercion without an explicit legal basis[27].

The legality of coercive measures does not solely depend on whether the power to apply them is granted by law. Their use must also be in accordance with principles of due process developed in case-law (see *supra*, 1.4.1.). The principle of proportionality is of the utmost importance in this respect.

The Code of criminal procedure contains detailed rules on coercive measures. The further such a measure intrudes upon a person's rights, the more the use thereof is restricted by conditions and guarantees. The most far-reaching measures of coercion (e.g. lengthy deprivation of liberty, telephone-tapping) can only be applied by order of, or with a warrant from, a court. The Code of criminal procedure is not the only statute to allow for the application of coercive measures. Many special statutes also contain provisions on coercion (see *supra*, 1.3.3.) with fewer conditions and guarantees than the Code. This can give rise to difficult questions regarding the relationship between the Code of criminal procedure and special legislation.

Coercive measures represent a violation of individual rights. The Supreme

---

[27] Cfr. Hoge Raad, 26 June 1962, *Nederlandse Jurisprudentie*, 462, 470 (blood sample), and 2 July 1990, *Nederlandse Jurisprudentie*, 1990, 751 (DNA sample).

Court therefore assumes that, with the exception of the deprivation of liberty, there is no coercion involved if a person co-operates voluntarily in an investigation, for example by allowing the police to enter his home or by agreeing to an examination of his car. The police have, therefore, a special interest in voluntary co-operation by the accused or by third parties, for this will negate any restrictions pertaining to the use of force. Courts are inclined to assume that citizens have co-operated voluntarily with an investigation unless they have made some clear indication to the contrary.

5.2. ARREST AND DETENTION ON REMAND

### 5.2.1. Types of deprivation of liberty in criminal proceedings

The following does no more than outline the most important ways of depriving a person of his liberty.

a. A person suspected of having committed a criminal offence may be stopped by a police officer and requested to provide personal data. This amounts more to a restriction than to a deprivation of liberty.

b. If a person is discovered *in flagrante delicto*, any citizen has the power to arrest him and bring him before a public prosecutor or so-called assistant public prosecutor (a high ranking police officer). In other cases, arrest may be ordered by a public prosecutor or assistant public prosecutor, but only if a criminal offence for which the law allows for detention on remand is concerned (see e).

c. Persons suspected of a criminal offence who have been arrested may be held for questioning for a maximum of six hours, not including the period between midnight and nine a.m. Such suspects may therefore be held for a maximum of fifteen hours, depending on the time of arrest.

d. Both the public prosecutor and the assistant public prosecutor can order that a suspect be held in police custody for a further period of two days (*inverzekeringstelling*), if necessary in the interests of the investigation. This is only possible if the law allows for detention on remand with regard to the offence. The public prosecutor can extend the original period of two days for a maximum of two days.

e. The Code of criminal procedure provides for three different forms of detention on remand by order of the judge. Persons may be held on remand (*voorlopige hechtenis*) if they are suspected of an offence that carries a penalty of at least four years' imprisonment or of a number of other specifically mentioned crimes. A suspect with no fixed abode, or one who refuses to reveal his address, can be held on remand for any crime. As we have seen, these criteria also pertain to arrest and police custody. The first type of detention on remand is known as *"bewaring"*. It can be ordered by the investigating judge for a maximum of ten days.

f. The second type is called *"gevangenhouding"* (literally: keeping in custody). It follows directly after *bewaring* by order of the judicial council (*raadkamer*). If the trial has not yet commenced, this form of remand may not last longer than thirty days; this period may be extended repeatedly for thirty days at a time by the judicial council.

g. The last type of detention on remand is called *"gevangenneming"*, which literally means taking into custody. It can be ordered by the court during trial with regard to a person who is not in custody. This form of remand may also be ordered by the court with a view to an extradition-request to another state.

As can be seen from this brief outline, it takes a relatively long time before a judge becomes involved in the deprivation of liberty in connection with a suspected criminal offence. Together, arrest and police custody can last for a maximum of four days and fifteen hours. The Dutch public prosecutor cannot be considered an "officer authorised by law to exercise judicial power" as meant by article 5, par. 3 of the European Convention on Human Rights.

For a long time, doubts were expressed as to whether Dutch law always meets the requirement that the detainee shall be brought promptly before a judge or other officer authorised by law to exercise judicial power. The decision of the European Court of Human Rights of 29 November 1988 in the Brogan-case (*supra*,1.2.2.), put an end to such doubts. Dutch criminal procedure does indeed infringe the European Convention on this point. A bill has now been presented to Parliament, amending the rules on arrest and police custody. In future, the investigating judge will decide on detention after a period of three days.

## 5.2.2. The prerequisites of detention on remand

In accordance with Dutch law, detention on remand is taken here to mean detention ordered by a judge. A general requirement is the existence of serious suspicions with regard to the accused, i.e. considerably more serious than a reasonable suspicion that he may have committed a criminal offence. The Code of criminal procedure also requires at least one of the following three conditions: (a) a risk that the accused might flee and avoid trial or the execution of sentence; (b) a danger that the accused might commit another offence which carries a penalty of at least six years imprisonment or which would seriously endanger the state or persons or property; (c) a risk that the accused might prevent or obstruct the investigation into his case were he not detained.

Detention on remand may also be imposed if the offence concerned has seriously shocked the community. These are cases in which society would be unable to understand why such offenders could remain at large, and this criterion applies solely to offences which carry a penalty of life imprisonment or at least twelve years.

In deciding about detention on remand, the judge must take the sentence into account that is likely to be imposed if the offender is convicted of the offence at a later date. Remand should only be imposed if the expected sentence involves the unconditional deprivation of liberty and if that sentence is not likely to be shorter than the proposed detention on remand would be. According to Dutch law, the court must always deduct time spent in detention on remand from a prison sentence.

### 5.2.3. The duration of detention on remand

As far as the duration of detention on remand is concerned, we must distinguish between remand before the trial proper has commenced and remand after that time. During the preliminary investigation, remand is limited in time; first to a period of ten days and then several periods of thirty days. After the trial proper has commenced, remand can last until thirty days after the court's decision in the case, although the accused can be released by order of the court in the meantime. Should the accused appeal against his sentence, this could result in detention on remand being extended.

The rules on the duration of detention on remand during the preliminary investigation were introduced into the Code of criminal procedure in 1974, and are complicated. The aim was to speed up criminal proceedings and so reduce the length of time spent in remand custody. Essentially the rules require that the accused must be released if the period of detention consisting of *"gevangenhouding"* has already been extended for two periods of thirty days, unless the trial proper has commenced within that period. This forces the public prosecutor, as it were, to hurry up with the preliminary investigation in order to be able to summon the accused in time.

In complicated cases the preliminary investigation is not usually finished before the summons goes out. However, the law allows the public prosecutor to request that the trial be suspended immediately with a view to finishing and closing the preliminary investigation. The court is free to grant or refuse the request. In these cases the normal rule is that detention on remand may last until thirty days after the court has reached a decision in the case.

### 5.2.4. Conditional release

Persons who are detained on remand may be conditionally released by the court. The accused is free to accept the conditions or not, one of which could be the payment of bail.

Conditional release from remand occurs quite frequently in the Netherlands, although persons who are conditionally released are rarely required to put up bail; most of them do not have sufficient funds anyway so that conditional release on bail would favour well-to-do defendants above poor defendants.

### 5.2.5. The control of legality

According to the Code, the suspect cannot appeal against a decision to detain him for questioning or against the first form of remand (*bewaring*, see *supra*). He can however appeal to the Appeal Court against decisions with regard to the second two forms of detention on remand and decisions to extend such detention, although he may only appeal once.

Because there is no appeal to a criminal court against deprivations of liberty ordered by the public prosecutor or the assistant public prosecutor, in practice the control of legality is often a matter for the civil courts in summary proceedings based on the Civil Code. The Supreme Court does not accept that a civil court could decide on the legality of decisions by the investigating judge. A Bill is currently before Parliament which allows for an appeal to the investigating judge against deprivations of liberty by order of the public prosecutor or assistant prosecutor.

Although this is not a legal remedy in the strict sense, it should also be noted that the accused can always file a request with the court competent to judge his case, that he be released from remand. This request is granted if circumstances have rendered the continuation of detention on remand undesirable.

## 5.2.6. The right to compensation

The Code of criminal procedure provides for financial compensation to the accused after the trial for time spent in arrest and detention on remand. Such compensation may be awarded if the case ends without the imposition of a punishment or measure, or if the sentence involves a punishment or a measure for an offence for which the Code does not allow detention on remand. However, the court is not obliged to grant full compensation, or, indeed, to grant compensation at all.

If it is a matter of illegal deprivation of liberty, there is always the possibility of a civil claim against the State. The concept of illegality is rather broad. According to case-law, any deprivation of liberty that appears to be in conformity with the law but which, nevertheless, in retrospect, is found to have been without good reason, may give rise to an obligation for the State to pay damages[28].

### 5.3. SEARCH AND SEIZURE

Objects can be seized if they may contribute to clarifying the case, or if there is a chance that they will be confiscated or withdrawn from circulation by a court at a later date.

The Code contains detailed rules on the question of who is authorised to seize goods in what situations. Seizure can often only be effected if a person's home has been entered against his will. It is important to note that a complete search of a dwelling place with an eye to seizure is normally only allowed by order of the investigating judge or court in chambers. If speed is required, others are authorised to order such a search.

Documents containing privileged data, i.e. data that are specially protected by the rules on professional secrecy relating to lawyers, doctors or other professionals sworn to secrecy, may not be seized. If documents are concerned

---

[28]Hoge Raad, 26 January 1990, *Nederlandse Jurisprudentie*, 1990, 794.

that could have some bearing on a lawyer's professional secrecy, the investigating judge and the local chairman of the Bar Association will usually decide together with defence counsel whether that is indeed the case.

## 5.4. EXAMINATION OF BODY AND MIND

The Code of criminal procedure distinguishes between examination of a person's clothes and examination of a person's body. Examination of the body means examination of the body's surface, but does include the so-called natural bodily recesses (mouth, anus, vagina). The Code does not allow substances to be introduced into the body or fluids to be extracted from it. In other words, the examination may not violate a person's physical integrity. Such violations are only allowed if based on a specific legal ruling (see also *supra*, 5.1.). For example, the Traffic Act allows a blood sample to be taken for analysis of the blood's alcohol content. At present, the necessity of a legal ruling with regard to DNA-samples is under debate.

The investigating judge may order that the accused be placed in a psychiatric institution in order to examine his mental faculties. Such an order may only be given if the accused has been detained on remand.

## 5.5. INTERFERENCE WITH THE RIGHT TO PRIVACY

Letters, telegrams and other documents handled by the postal services, may be seized by order of the investigating judge. In some cases, others may be authorised to give the order.

Since 1971, the Code of criminal procedure also provides for the tapping of telephones; messages conveyed by means of walkie-talkies and telefax are not included. The law restricts telephone-tapping to the investigation of offences for which detention on remand is possible. Conversations may be tapped if it is suspected that the accused is taking part. Tapping is not allowed in order to obtain information about offences that may be committed in the future. However, such information may be used if it was obtained by means of a tap with a view to the investigation of offences that have already been committed. Information obtained during the investigation into a certain offence, may be used as evidence of other criminal offences, even if detention on remand is not allowed for those offences.

Telephone-tapping may only be conducted after prior authorization by the investigating judge. There are no rules on the duration of a telephone-tap. After the tap has been concluded, the investigating judge must have all material destroyed that has no further bearing on the investigation in hand. The Code does not contain watertight rules on informing the person whose conversation was tapped after the tap has been concluded.

There is some controversy about the legal ruling on wire-tapping. Some find it too broad, and some too restricted. The debate has recently been rekindled by the decisions by the European Court of 24 April 1990 in the cases of Kruslin and Huvig against France (*supra*, 1.2.2.).

## 6. The ordinary course of criminal proceedings

Dutch criminal proceedings are divided into two parts: the pre-trial investigation and the trial proper before a court. The pre-trial investigation is also divided into two parts: a preliminary investigation conducted by the police under the direction of the public prosecutor, followed, if necessary, by a preliminary judicial investigation under the direction of an investigating judge.

### 6.1. THE PRE-TRIAL STAGE

### 6.1.1. The preliminary investigation (opsporingsonderzoek)

Every criminal case begins with an investigation into events by the police under the direction of the public prosecutor, either because an offence has been reported to the police, because a victim has filed a complaint, or because the police themselves have discovered something that has given rise to a reasonable suspicion that an offence has been committed.

A "reasonable suspicion" is the minimum requirement for the use of coercive measures. A "reasonable suspicion" is a suspicion that is based on facts and circumstances.

The preliminary investigation need not be restricted to preliminaries with regard to the suspected offence; indeed it is sometimes lengthy and extensive.

### 6.1.2. Preliminary judicial investigation (gerechtelijk vooronderzoek)

If the necessity arises as a result of the preliminary investigation, the public prosecutor can request the investigating judge to open a preliminary judicial investigation. The public prosecutor usually makes that request because certain coercive measures have become necessary. The most important of these are a search of a home, a telephone tap, the questioning of unwilling witnesses or an examination of the suspect's mental faculties. Although there are some exceptions, such drastic measures are normally only possible by order of the investigating judge. This is one of the reasons why a judge is involved in the preliminary investigation in Dutch criminal procedure. The second reason is that a preliminary investigation requires a certain degree of objectivity. Not only should incriminating evidence against the suspect be collected, but circumstances in his favour must also be examined. Such objectivity is better guaranteed by a judge than by the public prosecutor or the police.

The investigating judge directs the preliminary judicial investigation. He questions persons and decides on the application of coercive measures. The preliminary judicial investigation is aimed primarily at clarifying the case to such an extent that the public prosecutor can duly decide on whether or not to take the prosecution further. A second aim is to collect any information that may help the trial judge to reach a correct decision.

From the point of view of the defence, the main difference between the preliminary investigation directed by the prosecutor and the preliminary judicial investigation is that the latter affords the defence considerably more rights. For example, defence counsel has the right to be present when the suspect and witnesses are questioned, and a more extensive right of access to the documents of the case. Meanwhile, it is often possible to restrict these rights if the interests of the case so require.

Although not so obvious at first sight, it is assumed that the preliminary investigation by the police and under the direction of the public prosecutor may simply continue parallel to the preliminary judicial investigation. In some cases this can result in erosion of the rights of the defence during the preliminary judicial investigation.

During the past years, there has been considerable controversy about the preliminary judicial investigation, and some people have proposed doing away with it. One of the most important objections to the preliminary judicial investigation in its present form, is that the investigating judge is not really able to direct the investigation or bring it to a satisfactory conclusion, especially in complicated cases, because he has too much work and too little specialised knowledge of investigatory techniques. The government has installed a committee to study existing problems. In 1990, the committee produced a report, advocating a number of reforms. A bill has now been introduced, adopting most of these proposals.

### 6.1.3. The "criminal financial investigation"

In 1993, a new form of pretrial investigation has been introduced in the Code. It is called the "criminal financial investigation" (*strafrechtelijk financieel vooronderzoek*) and is concerned with the proceeds of crime. Its purpose is to establish what illegal gain suspects may have made in order to provide the courts with the evidence that may enable them to confiscate the proceeds of crime. The investigation is not carried out by the investigating judge, whose role is limited to allowing the investigation and to deciding on the application of a number of coercive measures. It is the public prosecutor who is in charge of the investigation. The investigation itself is secret in nature. Compared to the preliminary judicial investigation, the rights of the defence are more limited.

### 6.1.4. The indictment

At the end of the preliminary investigation, the public prosecutor must decide whether to bring the case to trial, to drop it or to bring it to some other conclusion. The freedom enjoyed by the prosecution in making this choice, and the available alternatives have been outlined above (*supra*, 4.2.1.).

If the prosecutor decides to bring the case to trial, he will summon the accused. In normal criminal cases, the Code of criminal procedure requires a period of at least ten days between the day on which the summons is served and the day on which the trial begins. This period may be shorter if less serious offences are involved. The Code also allows certain cases in which the accused was arrested *in flagrante delicto* to be tried on the same day. These procedures, however, are not frequently followed.

The accused may file a complaint against the summons. The case is then not heard before a trial court, but judged by a special court in chambers (*raadkamer*), which decides on whether the prosecution has any chance of succeeding and which will release the accused from prosecution if it is highly unlikely that the trial judge will reach a verdict of guilty.

The summons contains the charge(s) against the accused (*telastelegging*). The charge, usually formulated in formal and even archaic legal style, forms the basis of the trial. The court is strictly bound by the charge and the trial may not be conducted beyond the boundaries imposed by the facts detailed in the charge. Likewise, the court may not convict the accused for any other offence than that with which he has been charged. The public prosecutor may only alter the charge under certain restricted circumstances.

There is a rather curious exception to the foregoing that betrays a highly pragmatic attitude. The public prosecutor often decides not to charge the accused with all of the offences of which he is suspected, for example a long series of thefts, and issues a summons for one or two. At the same time, the prosecutor may add information on the other offences to the case-file which is available to the court during the trial. In this way, the prosecutor can induce the court to take into account the offences with which the accused has not been charged when pronouncing sentence for the offences contained in the charge. The Supreme Court has accepted this practice, albeit on certain conditions. The most important of these is that the accused has not denied having committed the offences. In its sentence, the court will then pronounce that it has taken the offences outside of the charge into account. In this way, the public prosecutor is prevented from ever issuing a summons for the same offences[29]. This practice relieves all those concerned in a criminal case of a great deal of bother and paperwork (and the accused from the threat of further prosecution).

## 6.2. THE TRIAL

The trial commences when the president of the court asks the accused his name and address. He will then inform the accused of his right to remain silent, after which the public prosecutor will read the charge (or a summary of it).

The trial is conducted under the direction of the president of the court. Normally, he will question the witnesses first, then any experts, and then the accused. After the chairman has concluded his examinations, the other judges, the public prosecutor and the defence have an opportunity to ask questions. The chairman will announce which documents are to be found in the file and he will read them aloud if so requested. If necessary, such documents can be discussed separately.

After the investigation has finished, the public prosecutor speaks, and then

---

[29]Hoge Raad, 13 February 1979, *Nederlandse Jurisprudentie,* 1979, 243.

the defence. The prosecutor gives his opinion on the case and then demands a sentence if he considers the accused guilty. The defence thereupon gives its opinion on the case. After the debate between the prosecution and the defence, the accused has the final word.

The court gives its verdict within fourteen days of concluding its trial sessions; in less serious cases, the verdict is often given immediately after the trial. A written verdict is often not available until much later. Together with the verdict, the court will inform the accused of any legal remedies available to him.

In Dutch criminal procedure, it is not possible to divide a criminal case into two separate phases, one in which the matter of the accused's guilt is decided, and one in which adequate punishment is discussed. However, a difference exists in respect of the confiscation of proceeds of crime. Here, the public prosecutor has to start a separate procedure the sole purpose of which is to allow the court to reach its decision with respect to the confiscation (see *supra*, 6.1.3., the criminal financial investigation).

## 7. Evidence

According to article 338 of the Code of criminal procedure, the court may only consider the case proven on the basis of legal evidence. Article 339 details what is considered legal evidence: the court's own observations, statements by the accused, statements by a witness, statements by an expert and written evidence. The article goes on to say that no proof is required of facts or circumstances that belong to the realm of common knowledge. The provision further implies that the same applies to rules of law. The court is deemed to be familiar with the law.

### 7.1. QUESTIONING THE ACCUSED

The accused has the right to be present in court and to be heard. The judge may order him to be present and, if necessary, to be brought to court, in the interests of the case. The accused has the right to remain silent, and he must be informed of that right. Failure to inform the accused will result in the trial being void, unless the accused was assisted by counsel. If the accused was not informed of his right to remain silent before being questioned during the investigative phase, any statements he may have made may not be used as evidence. (See for the significance of the accused's attitude *supra*, 4.4.2. and 3 above).

The accused's statement can only be used as evidence in his own case and not in the case against a fellow suspect. As we have seen, this rule is now devoid of meaning because such cases can be heard separately if necessary, so that the accused in the one case may then appear as a witness in the other.

Statements made during the preliminary investigation can also be used as evidence, even if the accused denies being guilty or refuses to speak during the trial.

The Code prohibits conviction on the sole basis of a confession.

## 7.2. THE HEARING OF WITNESSES

According to Dutch law, witnesses are bound to appear in person, to testify and to speak the truth. Before testifying they are required to either swear or promise to speak the truth. Failure to comply with any of these requirements constitutes a criminal offence.

Some categories of witnesses have the right to refuse to appear as a witness: persons who would incriminate themselves or a close relative by testifying; close relatives of the accused; and persons whose function in society requires that they be able to help others without there being any fear of their passing on information obtained in the course of such activities. This applies mainly to professions such as doctors, lawyers and the clergy, and persons in their service or employment. The courts are very reluctant to acknowledge the right to refuse to testify for other professions. It was refused, for instance, in the case of accountants, tax-advisers, journalists and police officers. However, a separate provision in the law does allow the court to prevent certain specific questions from being asked of witnesses in so far as such questions are detrimental to the interests of the police investigation[30].

The witness is questioned by the court, after which the public prosecutor and the defence have the opportunity to ask questions. There is no such thing as cross-examination in the Netherlands.

As we have seen, the Supreme Court has accepted that statements made by witnesses not present in court during the trial may be used as evidence (*supra*, 4.4.1). In this connection, the following should be borne in mind with regard to anonymous witnesses: an anonymous witness is a person whose identity and other personal data are not known to the trial judge or to the defence. Witnesses are promised anonymity if, during the preliminary investigation, they refuse to testify for fear of threats by the accused or by third persons. Protecting the interests of police investigation work is also sometimes considered sufficient reason for allowing a witness to remain anonymous. Such witnesses are heard by a police officer, or by an investigating judge. The verbatim report of this hearing will then omit all data that could make identification of the witness by third parties possible. The accused and/or his counsel are not, of course, present during the hearing. The investigating judge often offers counsel the opportunity of submitting written questions.

It is obvious that this practice severely affects the rights of the defence. Although the Code of criminal procedure does not allow anonymous witnesses,

---

[30]Hoge Raad, 27 March 1981, *Nederlandse Jurisprudentie*, 1981, 382.

the Supreme Court does not consider this practice unacceptable[31]. Its logical conclusion was reached in a case in which the Supreme Court accepted conviction on the basis of anonymous testimony only[32].

The decision by the European Court of Human Rights of 20 November 1989, in the case of Kostovski against the Netherlands (*supra*, 1.2.2.), has forced Dutch courts to change direction. Testimony by an anonymous witness who was heard by a police officer only, seems to have been outlawed by the Court as evidence, while an accused cannot be convicted solely on the basis of anonymous testimony. However, differences of opinion on the scope of the Kostovski decision have arisen. According to the Supreme Court, the decision does not prohibit the use of anonymous testimony in general. In a number of recent cases, the Supreme Court has readily accepted the use of anonymous testimony in several situations[33]. At the beginning of 1992, a bill was introduced to alter legislation.

Convictions may not be based on the testimony of a single witness only.

## 7.3. EXPERTS

As a result of technical and social developments, experts have come to play an increasingly important part in criminal cases. Experts are often appointed by the court, either during the trial or, more often, by the investigating judge during the preliminary judicial investigation. This is not, however, necessary. The nature of police investigations is also often that of a technical analysis.

The Code of criminal procedure gives the accused a somewhat restricted right to be present during an expert examination. There is also a restricted right to appoint a second expert, although the Supreme Court does not accept any general right to a second opinion. On the other hand, partly due to article 6 of the European Convention, parliament and courts definitely seem more prepared to recognise the interests of the defence in seeking a second opinion[34].

The court is not bound to accept the expert's opinion.

## 7.4. OBJECTIVE PROOF

### 7.4.1. The court's own observations

Whatever the court has itself observed may be used as evidence. The court's own observations as a means of proof refer, for example, to photographs that

---

[31]Hoge Raad, 5 February 1980, *Nederlandse Jurisprudentie,* 1980, 319, and 4 May 1981, *Nederlandse Jurisprudentie*, 1982, 268.

[32]Hoge Raad 25 September 1984, *Nederlandse Jurisprudentie,* 1985, 426.

[33]See inter alia Hoge Raad, 2 July 1990, *Nederlandse Jurisprudentie*, 1990, 692, and 2 October 1990, *Nederlandse Jurisprudentie*, 1991, 130.

[34]See *inter alia* Hoge Raad, 6 March 1990, *Nederlandse Jurisprudentie*, 1990, 467 (breathalyzer-test).

have been seen by the court, or to tapes to which it has listened. The photograph and the tape do not constitute proof themselves, rather that which the court has determined by means thereof. The court's own observations are not restricted to whatever occurs in the courtroom, but may include, for example, observations in the presence of the public prosecutor and the defence, at the place where the crime was committed (investigations on the spot).

### 7.4.2. Documents

Finally, the Code refers to documents as a means of proof. The word document refers to a written document and does not include, for example, photographs or drawings, which may be used as evidence through the court's own observations.

Reports by police officers occupy a special place among the documents. A report by an officer with powers of investigation in criminal cases may in itself be enough to convict, but only, of course, if that report and the trial have convinced the court of the accused's guilt.

### 7.5. INADMISSIBLE EVIDENCE

There is no provision in the Code of criminal procedure concerning evidence that has been obtained illegally. For a long time, it was assumed that the way in which evidence was obtained did not affect its value as a means of proof. In 1962, in a case concerning the taking of a blood sample against the accused's will and without a basis in law, the Supreme Court ruled that the results of the blood test carried out on that sample could not be admitted as evidence of driving under the influence[35]. For a long time this was the only decision on this subject.

Since the end of the Seventies, however, there have been many more, so that we can now refer to an established rule. Meanwhile, it has become clear that important restrictions to this principle have been accepted in case-law, the most far-reaching requiring that the legal rule, violation of which resulted in evidence being obtained, must serve to protect the interests of the accused himself. Violation of the rights of third parties does not affect the admissibility of the evidence. Illegally obtained evidence may also be used if it could have been obtained in another manner anyway. The third restriction is that violation of a legal rule serving to protect the interests of the accused, must have resulted in actual harm to the accused's interests. Finally, there is no objection against using evidence that has been illegally obtained by private persons and then put at the disposal of the authorities[36].

---

[35]Hoge Raad, 26 June 1962, *Nederlandse Jurisprudentie*, 1962, 470.

[36]Hoge Raad, 22 January 1990, *Nederlandse Jurisprudentie*, 1991, 401 and Hoge Raad, 16 October 1990, *Nederlandse Jurisprudentie*, 1991, 175.

## 8. Special forms of procedure

### 8.1. SIMPLIFIED PROCEDURES

The Code of criminal procedure is based on the general rule that criminal cases are tried by a court of three judges (district court). However, less serious offences may be tried by single judge. Crimes that come under the jurisdiction of the district court may be brought before a single member of that court if they are simple, from the point of view of proof, and if the penalty will not exceed six months' imprisonment. Single judges who are also members of the district court may also hear military cases, economic offences and juvenile cases under the same conditions.

Misdemeanours that come under the jurisdiction of the sub-district court, are always tried by a single judge.

Trials before a single judge are governed by special procedural rules. As a whole, the procedure is somewhat simpler.

### 8.2. TRIAL *IN ABSENTIA*

Dutch criminal procedure does not forbid a criminal trial in the absence of the accused; indeed, in practice this is a relatively frequent occurrence. The accused may be absent because he is not willing or able to appear, although he has been informed of the date of the trial. His absence may also be due to the fact that he never received the summons. In this connection, it is important to note that the provisions on serving a summons do not require that it be handed to the accused personally. For that reason, it can happen that a criminal case is heard while the accused neither knows nor could have known about it. This state of affairs can be problematic in the light of article 6, par. 1 of the European Convention on Human Rights, for this provision guarantees the right to be present in person when one's case is heard[37].

The accused who is prevented from appearing at his trial, may ask the court to postpone the hearing of his case. The court is not obliged to grant this request, unless it considers the reasons for postponement to be of an urgent nature and postponement itself compatible with the interests of due enforcement of the law. The protection of those interests may, therefore, result in the hearing of a criminal case in the absence of the accused, even though he has been unable to appear through no fault of his own.

It has always been assumed in case-law that counsel cannot act for the accused if the latter is not present. Someone who is absent cannot be assisted. However, there is an exception to this rule in case-law, namely if the accused,

---

[37]Cfr COLOZZA v. Italy, European Court of Human Rights, 12 February 1985, *Publ. E.C.H.R.*, Series A, vol. 89.

in the opinion of the court, has given an urgent reason for his absence, while postponement would be incompatible with due enforcement of the law[38].

For appeals against convictions in the absence of the accused, see *infra*, 9.2.

### 8.3. PROCEEDINGS AGAINST CHILDREN AND JUVENILES

A different set of rules pertains to the prosecution and trial of persons who have not yet reached the age of eighteen on the date when prosecution commences, the reason being that ordinary criminal procedure is considered unsuitable for the trial of juveniles. In juvenile criminal procedure, the emphasis is very much on the education and protection of underage persons. One result of this approach, however, has been that the juvenile accused often has fewer rights than the adult.

Perhaps the most remarkable characteristic of juvenile criminal procedure is the central position occupied by the juvenile judge, to whom, above all others, the interests of the juvenile offender are entrusted. Hardly a decision of any importance can be taken during the preliminary investigation, without the juvenile judge somehow being involved. The lengths to which this may go are well illustrated by the fact that the juvenile judge acts both as investigating judge during the preliminary judicial investigation, and as trial judge. This combination, quite different from the normal procedure that is applicable to adults, is now, however, considered as being contrary to article 6 of the European Convention on Human Rights (see *supra*, 2.3.3.).

Gradually, new ideas on juvenile criminal procedure are gaining ground. The idea that the interests of the juveniles themselves justify different rules of procedure, even if this means fewer procedural rights, is no longer accepted. In 1989, a bill was presented to parliament in which a revision of the criminal procedure pertaining to juveniles is proposed: this bill stems from the notion that, if juveniles are recognised as full legal subjects, the differences between adult and juvenile procedure must be kept as small as possible.

### 8.4. OTHER PROCEDURES

Other deviations from normal procedure exist with regard to some categories of offences and accused persons, for example defendants who are suspected of being seriously mentally disturbed, and corporations.

## 9. Remedies

The Code of criminal procedure provides all sorts of remedies against all sorts of decisions. Here we shall discuss only remedies against the most important decision in criminal procedure: the court's decision on the charge after the trial,

---

[38]Hoge Raad, 16 February 1988, *Nederlandse Jurisprudentie,* 1988, 794.

the final decision as it is called in Dutch (*einduitspraak*).

The system in the Code of criminal procedure is based on a distinction between ordinary and extraordinary remedies. *Ordinary remedies* must be pursued within a fixed time limit. As long as the limit has not been exceeded, or as long as there has been no decision on the remedy, no *res iudicata* exists. Leaving aside a limited exception with regard to decisions *in absentia*, this means that sentences by the court against which a legal remedy is still possible or has been pursued, cannot be executed.

*Extraordinary remedies* have no fixed time limit and can only be pursued after a decision has become *res iudicata*. The execution of judicial decisions is not suspended because an extraordinary remedy has been pursued.

Ordinary remedies are: appeal (*hoger beroep*), opposition (*verzet*) and revision (*cassatieberoep*). Extraordinary remedies are appeal to the Supreme Court in the interests of the law (*cassatie in het belang van de wet*) and judicial review (*herziening*).

### 9.1. APPEAL (*HOGER BEROEP*)

Appeal to an appellate court (*hoger beroep*) is the ordinary remedy that both the accused and the public prosecutor may use against almost all final decisions by a criminal court. Appeals against decisions by a sub-district court must be lodged with the district court, and against decisions by a district court with a court of appeal. The courts of appeal deal with appeal cases only.

Appeal involves a complete retrial by another, higher, judicial authority. The results obtained during the first trial may, however, be used in appeal.

If the accused was acquitted at the first trial he may not be convicted in appeal unless the court's decision is unanimous. If the appeal has been lodged by the accused only, a more severe penalty cannot be imposed unless the court's decision is unanimous.

### 9.2. OPPOSITION (*VERZET*)

Another legal remedy available to the accused against decisions given in his absence only, is known as "*verzet*" (literally: opposition). The result is a complete retrial by the court that rendered the original decision.

This remedy is subject to many restrictions. Originally it could be pursued against all decisions *in absentia*, both by the first trial court and by the appeal court, a system that could result in one case being heard four times, and which was amended in 1935. Since then, this remedy cannot be pursued against decisions in appeal, and it is available against decisions by the first trial court only if the law does not allow an appeal to an appellate court. As the latter is very rare, this form of appeal is fairly unimportant in Dutch criminal procedure.

### 9.3. CASSATION (*CASSATIEBEROEP*)

The public prosecutor and the accused may appeal to the Supreme Court

314

*(cassatieberoep)* against decisions that have been rendered upon appeal. But this remedy is not available against all decisions; the Code of criminal procedure forbids appeal to the Supreme Court if the accused has been acquitted.

An appeal to the Supreme Court is limited to matters of legal significance; the Supreme Court does not give judgment on the facts of the case, but on the questions of whether the previous court has followed the correct procedure and whether it has interpreted the law correctly. It follows from this that the Supreme Court has two tasks: to supervise compliance with criminal procedure, and to promote uniform judicial decision-making (see also *supra*, 1.4.1.).

The Supreme Court may dismiss the appeal or declare it well-founded, usually then either referring the case back to the court that gave the decision, or referring it to another court. Sometimes, however, the Supreme Court decides the case itself.

### 9.4. CASSATION IN THE INTERESTS OF THE LAW (*CASSATIE IN BELANG DER WET*)

This form of appeal to the Supreme Court is an extraordinary remedy that is only available to the procurator general at the Supreme Court. It is aimed at promoting uniformity of judicial decision-making. The procurator general will sometimes lodge an appeal in the interests of the law if different decisions have been given by lower courts on one and the same important legal issue, while a definite answer within the near future is considered desirable. It is rare for this remedy to be pursued in the Netherlands.

If a decision is overturned by the Supreme Court as a result of an appeal in the interests of the law, this cannot affect the ex-accused.

### 9.5. *CASSATION* TO REVISE A FINAL JUDGMENT (*HERZIENING*)

Cassation for the purposes of retrial (*herziening*) is an extraordinary remedy in the interests of the accused against miscarriages of justice. It is available to the ex-accused only, not to the public prosecutor and it cannot adversely affect the ex-accused.

A request for *herziening* may be made if contradictory verdicts have been reached, or if new facts have emerged that cast serious doubt on the validity of a conviction. The remedy is not available against decisions by a court that has interpreted the law incorrectly, nor can it be based on changes in legislation or case-law.

A request for *herziening* is decided by the Supreme Court. If it finds the request well-founded, the case is referred to a court of appeal for a retrial.

### 9.6. INDIVIDUAL APPLICATION TO THE EUROPEAN COMMISSION AND THE HUMAN RIGHTS COMMITTEE

The Netherlands has recognised the right of individual application under the European Convention on Human Rights, together with the jurisdiction of the

European Court. The Netherlands is also a party to the Optional Protocol to the International Covenant on Civil and Political Rights.

## 10. Other questions

### 10.1. STATUTES OF LIMITATION

The period during which an offence can be prosecuted is limited in time, depending on the seriousness of the offence. The limitation periods are set out in art.70 of the CCP. They vary according to the seriousness of the offence. Offences carrying life imprisonment prescribe after 18 years. Offences carrying a custodial sentence of more than 3 years prescribe after 12 years. Offences carrying a custodial sentence not exceeding 3 years prescribe after 6 years. Petty offences (*overtredingen*) prescribe after 2 years.

The limitation period can be suspended, or interrupted. Interruption results in a renewal of the original time limit. It is not limited in time[39], with the result that the limitation period can be prolonged indefinitely. The period in which prosecutions can be brought is, however, limited by the "reasonable time" of art.6 of the European Convention of Human rights.

## 11. Select bibliography

### Books

CORSTENS, G.J.M., *Het Nederlandse Strafprocesrecht*, Arnhem, 1993.
HENDRIKS, L.E.M. a.o., *Hoofdstukken Strafprocesrecht*, Alphen aan den Rijn, 1990.
KNIGGE, G. a.o., *Leerstukken van Strafprocesrecht*, Groningen, 1991.
MELAI, A.L. a.o. (ed.), *Het Wetboek van Strafvordering*, Arnhem, 1982, 7 vols. (the most important commentary on the Code of criminal procedure)
MINKENHOF, A., *De Nederlandse Strafvordering*, 5th print, by J.M. REIJNTJES a.o., Arnhem, 1990.
VAN BEMMELEN, J.M. and VAN VEEN, Th.W., *Strafprocesrecht*, 11th print, by D.H. DE JONG and G.KNIGGE, Alphen aan den Rijn, 1993.

### Periodicals

Delikt en delinkwent
Nederlands Tijdschrift voor Criminologie
Penitentiaire Informatie
Proces

---

[39]Cfr. Chapter 1 (Belgium), par.10 and Chapter 5 (Germany), par.10.

# Chapter 11 - Portugal[1]

Prof. Jorge **DE FIGUEIREDO DIAS**
and
Maria Joao **ANTUNES**
Assistant
Faculty of Law
University of Coimbra

## 1. Sources

The most important source of the current law of criminal procedure is the 1987 *Code of Criminal Procedure* (henceforth referred to as CCP), which entered into force on January 1st, 1988. Its predecessor, the 1929 Code of Criminal Procedure, is still temporarily in force as the 1987 CCP only applies to proceedings initiated after it first entered into force.

Besides this principal source, other legislation exists, regulating certain chapters or problems of criminal procedure. Decree 387 - A/87 (the jury system in criminal procedure), Decree 78/87, 387 -E/87 and 17/91 (proceedings in respect of transgressions and contraventions) and Decree 38/87 (the fundamental law of judicial courts) are examples of such secondary sources.

Matters of criminal procedure are also regulated by instruments which, in general, refer to other legal disciplines. This is the case, for example, with the European Convention of Human Rights, the Constitution of the Portuguese Republic, the Organization for the Protection of Minors, the Code of Military Justice and the Code of Labour Procedure.

In this context, reference should also be made to legal doctrine and case-law: legal doctrine constitutes the most relevant legal source after statute law, to the extent that it too, in its task of constructing the principles of juridical procedure in criminal cases, searches just and adequate solutions for concrete problems of community life ; case-law is also important because the courts can attain and develop a series of juridical principles, by resolving analogous problems in a consistent manner during a certain period of time.

## 2. Structure of the criminal justice system

The administration of criminal justice is fundamentally carried out through the activities of two distinct entities, the public prosecutor and the judge, who

---

[1]English translation by Cheryl Marie Webster

share between them the functions of investigating, indicting and judging offences.

## 2.1. THE PUBLIC PROSECUTOR

In this *accusatorial system* of criminal procedure, it is the responsibility of the public prosecutor to investigate the existence of a crime, to find its perpetrators and to discover and collate the necessary evidence with a view to reaching a decision concerning indictment (art.262 CCP). In this role, the public prosecutor is assisted by the organs of the criminal police which act under his direct guidance and whose functions are dependent upon him (arts. 263 and 56 CCP). This, however, does not prevent the criminal police from performing procedural acts within their own competence (for example, urgent and necessary acts intended to secure evidence - arts. 55, 249 et seq.CCP).

The public prosecutor in Portugal is a magistrate who benefits from individual status and autonomy in relation to the government (art.221 of the Constitution of the Portuguese Republic). It is his duty, in criminal procedure, to collaborate with the courts in the discovery of the truth and in doing justice, obeying criteria of strict objectivity in all his interventions in procedure (art.53 CCP).

## 2.2. THE JUDICIARY

Once the indictment has been moved by the public prosecutor, it is the responsibility of the judge or the court to try the offence. The exercise of the judicial function in Portugal, carried out by professional judges, is characterised by the independence and impartiality of the judiciary (art.206 of the Constitution of the Portuguese Republic and art.6 of the European Convention on Human Rights) : *independence*, in the sense of independence vis-à-vis the executive and legislative State powers, any lobbies, the judicial administration, and the other courts of justice; *impartiality*, in the sense that the law creates an atmosphere of pure objectivity, namely through the form of impeachments and suspicions of the judge (art.39 *et seq*.CCP)[2].

There are three types of courts in Portugal : the jury court, the "collective" court and the single court. The competence of each court is determined by the type of crime or its seriousness.

---

[2]For a more detailed analysis of these two aspects of Portuguese law of criminal procedure, see FIGUEIREDO DIAS and Maria Joao ANTUNES, "La notion européenne de tribunal indépendant e impartial. Une approche à partir du droit portugais de procédure pénale", *Révue de Science Criminelle et de Droit Pénal Comparé*, 1990, p.733 *et seq*.

## 2.2.1. The jury court

The jury court is composed of the judges of the "collective court" (see 2.2.2.) and of four lay judges, the jurors. Cases are brought before this court by the public prosecutor, the victim (*assistente*, see *infra*, 3.3.) or the accused. It is competent to try the following crimes: crimes against peace or against humanity, crimes against the security of the State, and crimes carrying a penalty of more than eight years' imprisonment (art.13 CCP).

## 2.2.2. The "collective" court

This court is composed of three professional judges. It tries those cases which are not judged by either the jury court or the single court. It has jurisdiction with respect to premeditated crimes or crimes with aggravating circumstances involving the death of a person, and with respect to crimes carrying a penalty of more than three years' imprisonment (art.14 CCP).

## 2.2.3. The single court

The single court is composed of one professional judge. It has jurisdiction over all crimes that do not belong to the jurisdiction of the jury court or the "collective court", including crimes against public authorities, cheques without sufficient funds or crimes carrying a penalty not exceeding three years' imprisonment. The single court is also competent with respect to crimes which in principle are tried by the "collective court", but which, in the given case, according to the indictment of the public prosecutor, should not be punished with more than three years' imprisonment (art.16 CCP). There is a tendency in Portugal towards enlarging the sphere of competence of the single court. In the future, its jurisdiction will be extended to crimes carrying a penalty of up to 5 years' imprisonment.

# 3. Parties to criminal proceedings

### 3.1. THE PUBLIC PROSECUTOR: NOT A PARTY TO THE PROCEEDINGS

As the intervention of the public prosecutor is motivated by the intention to discover the truth, to do justice and operate upon strictly objective criteria, it is clearly not possible for Portuguese criminal procedure to be classified as a procedure of parties[3] which would make the public prosecutor the party responsible for representing the interests reflected in the indictment.

---

[3]For a discussion of *procedure of parties*, see FIGUEIREDO DIAS, *Direito Processual Penal*, Coimbra Editora, 1984, p.242 *et seq.* By the same author, see also "Sobre os sujeitos processuais no novo Código de Processo Penal" in AAVV *O Novo Códi go de Processo Penal*, Almedina, Coimbra, 1988, p.30 *et seq.*

This principle, however, does not prevent Portuguese criminal procedure from being structured largely on an accusatorial basis as is, moreover, imposed by art.32, clause 5 of the Constitution of the Portuguese Republic[4]. The accusatorial structure of criminal procedure not only results from the division of procedural functions between the court of justice and the public prosecutor, but is also due to the status of *active subjects* which is given to certain participants in the procedure : the court of justice, the public prosecutor, the accused, the defense counsel and the *assistente* (*infra*, 3.3.) all benefit from autonomous rights to influence the actual course of the proceedings as a whole, in view of a final decision. In contrast, organs of the criminal police, witnesses, experts *etc.* perform individual acts whose procedural content is limited to their own sphere of competence. As such, these participants in the proceedings are thus prevented from being considered active subjects[5].

### 3.2. THE DEFENCE

According to art.60 CCP, the accused in the proceedings "is assured the exercise of rights and duties in the procedure, despite the fact that he may also be subject to both coercive measures and patrimonial guarantees and investigative measures". In this way, the accused may be guaranteed an all the more consistent and real position of *active subject* not of a mere object, as is the case in proceedings of an inquisitorial nature or even, in many cases, of a mitigated inquisitorial nature.

This status of active subject is reflected in the provisions relating to the *right of the defence* (art.32, clause 1 of the Constitution of the Portuguese Republic and art.61 CCP), granting him, at the same time, the fundamental presumption of innocence until such time as he is definitively convicted (art.32, clause 2 of the Constitution of the Portuguese Republic)[6].

The *presumption of innocence* has a direct impact on the legal position of the accused in two respects: the use of coercive measures and the use of the accused himself as a source of evidence.

As to the first aspect, this presumption implies that the accused may only be subjected to those measures that are socially acceptable given the possibility that they may be applied to an innocent person. Accordingly, the CCP establishes the principles of necessity, adequacy, proportionality, subsidiarity, and precariousness. In addition, the presumption of innocence leads

---

[4]For more information concerning this article, see FIGUEIREDO DIAS, "La protection des droits de l'homme dans la procedure penale portugaise", in *Boletim do Ministério de Justiça*, Lisboa, 1980, p.9 *et seq.*

[5]For a detailed analysis, see FIGUEIREDO DIAS, *Sobre os sujeitos processuais no novo Código de Processo Penal*, p.6 *et seq.*

[6]For more information concerning article 32 of the Constitution of the Portuguese Republic, see FIGUEIREDO DIAS, *op. cit.*, footnote 3, p. 15 *et seq.* and p.21 *et seq.*

to the limitation on the using of the accused as a source of evidence, out of respect for his free will. This respect implies, apart from the prohibition against the use of certain types of evidence (evidence obtained by torture, coercion or attacks on the physical or moral welfare of persons in general, art.126 CCP), the recognition of the right to be silent. Accordingly, the accused has the right, at any stage in the proceedings, not to answer questions about facts attributed to him or about the content of declarations made about those facts (art.61, clause 1 CCP).

The nature of active subject is also shared by the *defence counsel* who does not merely represent the interests of his client but also plays a part in the administration of justice, acting exclusively in favour of the accused. As such, he can be nominated to be present at certain acts without or even against the wishes of the accused (art.64 CCP), as he can also represent him to all intents and purposes when the hearing or some of its elements occur in his absence (arts. 334, clause 3 and 332, clause 5 CCP).

### 3.3. THE VICTIM ("*ASSISTENTE*")

Along with the court of justice, the public prosecutor, the accused and the defense counsel, Portuguese criminal procedure also recognizes the victim as an active subject as such. He is referred to as the "*assistant*" (*assistente*). The figure of the *assistente* is very characteristic of Portuguese law of criminal procedure and has a long tradition within it. The *assistente* is, in principle, the person particularly affected by the offence but who is nevertheless allowed to participate in proceedings not only as an injured party according to civil law (and thus as a *partie civile*) but as "a collaborator (*assistente*) with the public prosecutor to whose participation in proceedings the *assistente* is subordinated" (art.69 clause 1 CCP). Accordingly, the *assistente* participates in the actual criminal proceeding as a real party to the proceedings, even in relation to public crimes. In doing so, he represents the juridical interests infringed by the offence. In other words, the *assistente* has the role of "representative of the interests to which the law wished to give special protection in its definition of a criminal offence" (art.68, clause 1, paragraph a CCP). As such, the *assistente* benefits from autonomous rights in procedure. He may, for instance, move an indictment, independent of the indictment of the public prosecutor. The *assistente* may also appeal any decision which affects him, even where the public prosecutor does not opt to lodge such an appeal.

# 4. General principles concerning criminal procedure[7]

## 4.1. PRINCIPLES GOVERNING THE OPENING OF CRIMINAL PROCEEDINGS

Under Portuguese law, the prosecution of crimes is based on the principles of *"ex officio"* prosecution and the principles of legality and indictment.

### 4.1.1. The "ex officio" principle

In accordance with the law, it is the responsibility of a state organ, the public prosecutor, to initiate investigations concerning the commission of an offence (art.48 CCP) and to decide whether or not to submit it to a judge in order to obtain a judgment (art.276 CCP). The *"ex officio"* principle, which is based on the idea that the prosecution of crime is a matter of public interest, is, however, subject to certain limitations and exceptions. The limitations result from the existence of semi-public crimes, in which the legal title of the public prosecutor to bring proceedings needs to be supported by the charges brought by the victim or by others (arts. 49 CCP and 111 of the Penal Code). The exceptions result from the existence of private crimes, *i.e.* offences that can only be prosecuted on charges brought by the victim and thus on private indictment. It is, however, important to note that these limitations and exceptions are very few, especially in the latter case.

The justification for the existence of semi-public and private crimes is as follows: (a) as society does not consider certain crimes as serious offences, the public prosecutor only becomes involved where the victim requests his intervention; (b) the existence of a criminal prosecution against the wishes of the victim or without his authorization may, in certain cases, be detrimental to him. This situation is applicable to crimes which violate the privacy of the victim. An obvious example would be in the case of rape.

### 4.1.2. The legality principle

The public prosecutor is under a *duty to investigate* all offences which come to his attention (art.262, clause 2 CCP), also under a *duty to present an indictment* whenever sufficient information has been gathered to establish the commission of a crime and to identify a perpetrator (art.283 CCP). From this derives the *principle of immutability*, according to which the indictment cannot be withdrawn once a court of law has been called to rule upon it. This rule, however, does not apply to semi-public offences and private crimes, as the persons entitled to press charges and to bring a private prosecution can withdraw them until the passing of sentence in the first instance (arts.51 and

---

[7]For a more in depth analysis of the general principles of criminal procedure, see FIGUEIREDO DIAS, *Direito Processual Penal*, note 2, p. 113 *et seq*.

114 CCP). This withdrawal is, however, dependent on the consent of the accused (art.51, clause 3 CCP), as he may have an interest in his innocence being recognized by the court of justice.

The *principle of legality* however, is not absolute. For example, an exception exists in respect of petty crimes. This difference in procedural treatment is justified by the fact that such crimes differ from serious crimes (criminological background, the degree of threat to society, the public concern they provoke, etc.). For these offences, the public prosecutor has the possibility of shelving proceedings in the case of dismissal or immunity to punishment (art.280 CCP). He may also suspend proceedings provisionally by means of imposing injunctions and rules of conduct upon the accused (art.281 CCP). These concessions signify that, in Portuguese law, the *principle of opportunity* exists.

However, as these innovatory provisions enable the public prosecutor to drop the charges on the basis of criminal policy considerations underlying substantive criminal law, they represent, in fact, the adoption of a new and richer principle of legality which is founded on those very considerations. That same program is characterized by the subsidiary and fragmented character of the criminal intervention and the subsequent attribution to the punishment of the function of re-affirming the validity of the violated norm and wherever possible, rehabilitating the offender[8].

### 4.1.3. The principle of indictment

The *principle of indictment* is likewise recognised in Portugal. In addition to what has already been mentioned with respect to this principle, it is important to note that it also means that the trial court does not have the function of making preliminary investigations or presenting the indictment. The court investigates and judges within the limits set by the indictment, which is motivated, *i.e.* provided with grounds, and presented by a distinct organ, the public prosecutor. However, the definition and establishment of the object of proceedings, which is to say the contents of the indictment by which the court is bound, may also be brought about by another element of procedure : the request to open a preliminary judicial investigation, called *instruction* (arts. 303, 358 and 359 CCP, see *infra*, 6.2.)[9].

---

[8]For more information on articles 280 and 281, see COSTA ANDRADE, "Consenso e Oportunidade (reflexoes a propósito da suspensao provisória e do processo sumaríssimo)", in AAVV *O Novo Código de Processo Penal*, Almedina, Coimbra, 1988, p.319 *et seq.*

[9]See *infra* 6. The ordinary course of criminal proceedings.

## 4.2. PRINCIPLES GOVERNING THE TAKING OF EVIDENCE

In relation to evidence, three principles should be mentioned: the principle of instruction, the principle of the free evaluation of the evidence and the principle *in dubio pro reo*.

### 4.2.1. The principle of instruction

The structuring of Portuguese criminal procedure according to an accusatorial model is especially related to the *principle of instruction* (art.340 CCP). According to this principle, courts have the power and duty to clarify and investigate ex officio the facts presented to them for judgment. As such, the courts establish the necessary basis for their decisions, independent of the contributions of the prosecution and the defence. This principle illustrates the more general and inalienable nature of the purpose and of the content of criminal proceedings, *i.e.* its aim of establishing the whole truth. Hence, it assumes a markedly subsidiary nature[10].

### 4.2.2. The principle of the free evaluation of the evidence

According to this principle, the judge is free in evaluating the evidence that is put before him. It is recognized in art.127 CCP and defined as the "evaluation of evidence according to the rules of experience and the free judgment of the competent body".

### 4.2.3. The principle "in dubio pro reo"

It flows from the principle of instruction that none of the relevant facts can be considered proven, despite any evidence produced, if they are subject to reasonable doubt on the part of the court. In reality, though it is an intrinsic part of this principle that the court is obliged to collate the evidence necessary for its decision, it is understood that their absence cannot, in any way, be unfavourable to the position of the accused. Hence, a *non liquet* on the question of evidence must always weigh in favour of the accused. In this sense, the principle *in dubio pro reo* is affirmed, constitutionally supported in the principle that the accused shall be presumed innocent until such time as he is definitively convicted (art.32, clause 2 of the Constitution of the Portuguese Republic).

---

[10]For a more detailed analysis of the structuring of penal procedure on an accusatorial model integrated into the principle of instruction, *see* FIGUEIREDO DIAS, *Direito Processual Penal*, mimeographed edition, Faculdade de Direito de Coimbra, 1988-9, p.54 *et seq.*

4.3. PRINCIPLES GOVERNING THE TRIAL

Among the principles relating to the trial stage of the criminal proceedings in Portugal (see further 6.3.), the principles of contradiction, publicity, continuity, orality of proceedings and direct testimony should be mentioned.

### 4.3.1. The principle of contradiction

Whilst the judge, in accordance with the principle of instruction, is ultimately responsible for assuring a basis on which to make his decision, he should not, however, fulfil his functions alone but should hear both the prosecution and the defence. This requirement, obliging the judge to pay special attention to not only the arguments of the prosecution but also those of the defence, and to accept initiatives from the active subjects in the proceedings, represents the *principle of contradiction*, laid down in art.32, clause 5 of the Constitution of the Portuguese Republic. Arts. 321 and 327 CCP also refer directly to this article.

### 4.3.2. The public character of the trial

Under the terms of art.209 of the Constitution of the Portuguese Republic, trial hearings are *public*, except when the court of justice decides otherwise in order to safeguard the dignity of persons and of public morality or to guarantee its proper functioning. This constitutional principle is enshrined in art.321 CCP. In addition, according to art.86 of the same instrument, publicity implies the presence of the general public at this act of procedure, as well as the reporting and reproduction of the act by the media.

### 4.3.3. The continuity of the trial

The hearing is also governed by the *principle of continuity* which is recognized in art.328 CCP. Accordingly, the hearing must be held without interruption or adjournment, until the case is fully heard. This principle is, moreover, closely related to another principle, that of oral proceedings and direct testimony, which results from a series of guidelines found in the CCP (arts. 343, 345, 346, 360 and 363 CCP).

## 5. Coercive measures

Coercive measures are those acts that interfere with a person's liberty or privacy. Within this group, the following distinction can be made: measures of coercion on the one hand, and means of obtaining evidence on the other[11].

### 5.1. MEASURES OF COERCION AGAINST THE ACCUSED

Measures of coercion are only applicable to the accused. They are always applied by virtue of an order of a judge (art.194 CCP). Their purpose is one of prevention. As a consequence, such measures may be used in cases of abscondment or danger of abscondment; in cases of danger of interference with the course of the preliminary investigation or the "instruction" proceedings (see *infra*, 6.2.2.), *i.e.* danger in relation to the acquisition, conservation or reliability of evidence; and finally, in cases of danger of disturbance of public order or peace or of the continuing of the criminal activity, this being based on the nature and circumstances of the crime or on the personality of the accused (arts 191 and 204 CCP).

With this end in view, the following are the coercive measures which may be applied:

1) stipulation of identity and place of residence (art.196 CCP)

2) payment of bail (art.197 CCP)

3) obligation to present oneself at certain times (art.198 CCP)

4) suspension of exercising one's profession or one's rights (art.199 CCP)

5) prohibition on visiting given places, on leaving a designated area or on contacting certain persons (art.200 CCP)

6) obligation to remain at place of residence (art.201 CCP)

7) detention on remand (art.202 CCP) which has a subsidiary nature because it represents the most severe measure of coercion (arts. 193 and 202 CCP).

Arrest of persons found in the course of committing a crime or otherwise differs from detention on remand. Arrest *in flagrante delicto* or otherwise, is a simple deprivation of liberty, which may not exceed 48 hours' duration (arts. 141 and 254 CCP). Its objectives are: (1) to submit the arrestee to summary procedure; (2) to present him to the judge for the initial judicial interrogation or to apply for a coercive measure; (3) to ensure the immediate presence of the detained before the judge in a procedural act.

---

[11]For more information with respect to these coercive measures, see CASTRO SOUSA, "Os meios de coacçao no novo Código de Processo Penal", *Estudos em Homenagem ao Prof. Doutor Eduardo Correia*, 1989, p.471 *et seq.*

## 5.2. COERCIVE METHODS OF OBTAINING EVIDENCE

In relation to methods of obtaining evidence, the CCP allows for the examination of persons, places and objects (art.171 *et seq.* CCP); search and examination (art.174 *et seq.* CCP); seizure (art.178 *et seq.* CCP); and telephone-tapping (art.187 *et seq.* CCP). With respect to this second type of coercive measures, an attempt has been made to find a practical balance between the purpose of discovering the whole truth and efficiently administering justice on the one hand and the protection of citizens' fundamental rights on the other.

# 6. The ordinary course of criminal proceedings

## 6.1. THE INQUIRY

### 6.1.1. *The opening of the inquiry*

Proceedings begin with the *reporting of the crime*, either directly by the public prosecutor, by the police or by a complaint made by a public body or a private individual. It is the public prosecutor's task to receive such reports (art.241 CCP). Upon receiving the reports the public prosecutor opens an *inquiry* (art.262 CCP). The public prosecutor directs the inquiry, and in doing so, is assisted by the police (art.263 CCP).

The fact that the public prosecutor is the *dominus* of this phase of procedure does not, however, exclude the possibility of a judge's intervention, namely an investigating judge (*juiz de instruçao*). This involvement is, on the contrary, justified to the extent that only a judge can order acts which affect rights, freedoms and guarantees protected by the Constitution. Accordingly, parliament has either removed the exercise of certain acts from the jurisdiction of the public prosecutor (art.268 CCP) (for example, the interrogation of a person who has been arrested, searches and seizures in lawyers' offices, doctor's surgeries, or banking establishments) or has conferred certain measures to the exclusive jurisdiction of the investigating judge (art.269 CCP) (for example the search of dwellings, the seizure of correspondence and the listening to or recording of conversations or telephone calls).

### 6.1.2. *The closure of the inquiry*

The closure of the inquiry is brought about by a decision to present the indictment or to shelve the case (art.276 CCP), depending on whether the public prosecutor has gathered enough evidence to establish the commission of a crime and to identify a potential suspect. In terms of art.284 CCP, the *assistente* can also move an indictment based on the facts set out in the public prosecutor's indictment, on part of them or on other facts which do not substantially alter them[12].

## 6.2. THE INSTRUCTION

The decision whether or not to present the indictment can then be confirmed by a phase referred to as preliminary judicial investigation or *"instruction"*. According to the Constitution, these proceedings come within the jurisdiction of a judge, the investigating judge (*juiz de instruçao*, art.32, clause 4 of the Constitution of the Portuguese Republic). *Instruction* only occurs at the request of the *accused,* in relation to facts on the basis of which the public prosecutor or the *assistente* have moved the indictment, or at the request of the *assistente,* in relation to facts on the basis of which the public prosecutor has not moved the indictment (art.287 CCP). These possibilities confirm the status of active subject conferred upon these participants by Portuguese law of criminal procedure.

The optional nature of the *instruction* (art.286, clause 2 CCP) is explained by the fact that these proceedings have been provided in order to control the activities of the public prosecutor. As such, the *instruction* is meant as a *judicial corroboration* of the public prosecutor's decision either to file an indictment or to drop the case. In other words, the *instruction* aims at confirming, by means of a judicial ruling, the decision whether or not to bring the case to trial (art.286, clause 1 CCP). This phase in the proceedings consists, essentially, of the investigative acts carried out by the judge, assisted by the organs of the criminal police whose functions are dependent on him (art.209, clause 2 CCP). The "instructional debate" is obligatory, oral and intrinsically contradictory (arts. 297 and 298 CCP).

The *instruction* is closed by a decision whether or not to proceed to trial, depending on whether the *dominus* of this optional phase of procedure considers that the case should be submitted to judgment or not (art.308 CCP). However, the investigating judge may not decide to proceed to trial on the basis of facts which represent a substantial alteration of the indictment or to the request to start the *instruction*. Should the judge exceed this limitation, the *instruction* is void. For example, a modification of the facts with the effect of accusing the defendant of a different crime or of increasing the maximum penalty (arts 303, clause 1 f and 309, clause 1 CCP) would have

---

[12]For more information concerning the inquiry, see Anabela RODRIGUES, "O Inquérito no novo Código" in AAVV *O Novo Código de Processo Penal*, Almedina, Coimbra, 1988, p.61 *et seq.* and Germano M. DA SILVA, *Do Processo Penal Preliminar*, Lisboa, 1990.

the immediate effect of invalidating any decision of *instruction*[13]. Whilst these provisions confirm, on the one hand, that the object of procedure is delimited and defined by the request to open an *instruction*, they show, on the other hand, that *instruction* is not an autonomous supplement to the investigation, but merely a form of controlling the public prosecutor's activities.

### 6.2.1. Hierarchical intervention

There is yet another mechanism which exists in order to control the public prosecutor's decision at the end of an inquiry: the *hierarchical intervention* (art.278 CCP). If the public prosecutor has decided not to prosecute and if there is no request for an *instruction*, the hierarchical superior of the public prosecutor may determine whether the indictment is to be drawn up or whether investigations are to continue.

### 6.3. THE TRIAL

The next stage in the proceedings is the trial stage, or *judgment stage*. This stage is reached either after the inquiry or after the *instruction*: after the inquiry, if the latter is closed by an indictment and the instruction proceedings are not requested; after the *instruction*, if the instruction has been concluded with a decision to proceed to trial.

In relation to the trial stage, special mention should be made of the option given to the court of reopening the hearing to allow for the presentation of additional evidence in order to determine the type and severity of sanction to be applied (arts. 369, 370 and 371 CCP). Even though the 1987 CCP has not followed the "two stages model", in which the trial is divided in two stages, judgment and sentence, it has opted for the separation of the verdict into two distinct parts, thus obliging the court to decide on the question of guilt (art.368 CCP) and, in the event of a guilty verdict, to render another, separate, decision on the question of the sanction. These hearings allow the court to chose the appropriate sanction from the large variety of alternatives to imprisonment which exist in Portugal[14].

---

[13]For an in depth discussion of the object of proceedings, see Eduardo CORREIA, *Unidade e Pluralidade de Infracçoes*, Coimbra, 1948, reprinted by Almedina, 1983 and Mário TENREIRO, "Consideraçoes sobre o objecto do processo penal", *Revista da Ordem dos Advogados*, 47, 1987, p.997 *et seq.*

[14]For a detailed account of these alternatives, see Anabela RODRIGUES, "Critério de escolha das penas de substituiçao no Código Penal Português", *Estudos em Homenagem ao Prof. Doutor Eduardo Correia*, 1989, p. 21 *et seq.*

# 7. Evidence

### 7.1. GENERAL PRINCIPLES

Having as a backcloth both the principle of the free evaluation of the evidence (art.127 CCP) and the principle of the legality of evidence (article 126 CCP), defined as the admission of forms of evidence not forbidden by law, the 1987 CCP expressly admits as forms of evidence the following types:

1) evidence given by witnesses
2) the declarations of the accused, of the *assistente* and of the civil parties
3) evidence by means of confrontation of witnesses
4) evidence by means of recognition
5) the reconstruction of the fact in question
6) evidence given by experts
7) documentary evidence

Special mention should be made of evidence given by witnesses, the declarations of the accused, evidence given by experts and documentary evidence, particularly as, in some cases, a restriction is made in the system and rule of free evaluation of evidence.

### 7.2. THE EXAMINATION OF WITNESSES

Despite the fact that the Code of Criminal Procedure adheres to the principle of the free evaluation of the evidence, it has opted for a *system of witness-interrogation* similar to the Anglo-American system of cross-examination. According to this procedure, the witness is questioned by the party who called him to the stand, and afterwards is subject to counter-interrogation. If, during the course of this counter-interrogation, issues are raised which were not raised in the direct interrogation, the party who called the witness to the stand may question him again upon these issues, which may then be followed by another counter-interrogation of the same scope (art.348, clause 4 CCP). The judges and the jurors may, at any time, put to the witness those questions which they consider necessary for the clarification of the deposition and the correct determination of the case (art.348, clause 5 CCP). This possibility reveals once again the subsidiary nature of the principle of instruction and also demonstrates the objective of discovering the whole truth that presides over Portuguese criminal procedure.

The rules relating to the *privilege against self-incrimination* should also be singled out. According to this privilege, a witness is not obliged to answer questions when he alleges that his replies will be self-incriminating (art.132, clause 2 CCP). *Hearsay testimony*, referred to as indirect deposition, is also banned (art.129 CCP).

## 7.3. THE INTERROGATION OF THE ACCUSED

In matters relating to the declarations made by the accused, it is necessary to distinguish between declarations which relate to his personal identification and criminal record and those relating to the fact imputed to him. The explanation for this is as follows: in relation to declarations concerning his personal identification and his criminal record, and contrary to what occurs in respect of declarations concerning facts imputed to him, the accused is under a duty to answer questions and to answer them truthfully, under penalty of being criminally liable (art.342 CCP).

As to questions put to the accused with respect to facts imputed to him, Portuguese law of criminal procedure recognizes three possible solutions: (1) the accused says nothing. There is no possibility of using his silence against him. This flows from the *right to silence* (art.61, clause 1, C, art.343, clause 1 and art.345, clause 1 CCP); (2) the accused answers but does not tell the truth. In this case, he does not commit an offence; (3) the accused confesses (art.344 CCP).

It is noteworthy that the rules with respect to *confessions* in the 1987 *Code of Criminal Procedure* are completely different from those laid down in the 1929 Code. It is also noteworthy that this divergence brings the current Portuguese law of criminal procedure closer to the Anglo-American system. However, it is only a slight approximation as is shown by art.344 CCP, in which a distinction is made between petty offences (offences carrying a penalty of up to three years' imprisonment) and serious offences.

With respect to *petty offences*, a complete and unreserved confession has several implications: (1) the removal of the necessity to prove the allegations, which are consequently considered proven; (2) the immediate passage to final statements and, if the accused is not be acquitted for other reasons, to the decision determining the appropriate sentence; (3) the reduction of court costs by half. However, the court may decide not to take the confession into account, if it suspects that the confession was not made entirely freely, or if there are doubts as to the truth of the confession. This flows from the principle of the free evaluation of the evidence (see *supra*, 4.2.2.), and from the more general principle, underlying Portuguese criminal procedure, that the purpose of the trial is to discover the truth. In such cases, a confession will not have the results noted above.

With respect to *serious offences*, the courts always decide freely whether and to what extent evidence should be presented in relation to the facts which have been confessed by the accused.

## 7.4. EXPERT EVIDENCE

Expert evidence constitutes an exception to the principle of the free evaluation of the evidence (art.163, clause 1 CCP): judges are to some extent bound by the *expertise*. The underlying idea is that technical, scientific or artistic judgment, by its very nature, may only be questioned by equally technical, scientific or artistic criticism. If the judge considers that he has the necessary expertise to make such a criticism, he may diverge from an expert opinion, but in doing so, he must provide grounds for this divergence (art.163, clause 2 CCP). However, the judge is not bound by the assessment of the facts in the expert's opinion: here, the principle of the free evaluation of the facts is fully upheld, and the judge may disregard the expert's opinion at his discretion.

### 7.5. DOCUMENTARY EVIDENCE

Finally, *documentary evidence* should also be mentioned, and, in particular, the value of authentic or authenticated documents. In such documents, the material facts included are considered proven as long as the authenticity of the document or the truth of its contents are not fundamentally questioned (art.169 CCP).

## 8. Special forms of procedure

The individualized treatment of petty crimes in criminal procedure is very markedly visible in special proceedings. One could even say that the element distinguishing normal and special proceedings (summary (*processo sumário*) and extra-summary (*processo sumaríssimo*)), lies in the type of crime which they involve[15].

### 8.1. SUMMARY PROCEEDINGS

Summary proceedings can be used when the accused has been arrested while committing an offence (*in flagrante delicto)*, in cases where the offence does *not* carry a penalty of *more than three years imprisonment*. The accused must be brought before the trial judge within 48 hours of his arrest, or exceptionally, within a maximum time of five days (art.381 CCP).

The most characteristic element of this special procedure is, in effect, the rapidity which it makes possible. As the detention *in flagrante delicto* is carried out by a judicial authority or the police, the inquiry becomes unnecessary, as does the optional stage of instruction, as is expressly recognized in art.286, clause 2 CCP. This does not, however, exclude the possibility of the public prosecutor shelving proceedings, under the terms of art.280 CCP, or of temporarily suspending them according to art.281 CCP (art.384 CCP).

---

[15]For a detailed presentation of these criteria, see FIGUEIREDO DIAS and Anabela RODRIGUES, "La phase décisoire du jugement dans la procédure penale portugaise", *Revue Internationale de Droit Pénal*, 1986, p.534 *et seq*.

## 8.2. EXTRA-SUMMARY PROCEEDINGS

The extra-summary proceedings (art.392 CCP), to which it is also possible to apply arts. 280 and 281 CCP, affect those cases which are considered to be petty crimes. As such, extra-summary proceedings only take place in the case of: (1) offences carrying a penalty of either imprisonment not exceeding 6 months, or a fine, or both; (2) offences whose prosecution does not depend on private indictment; (3) offences for which the public prosecutor, in the concrete circumstances of the case, would request only a fine or a security measure not involving the deprivation of liberty.

Once these conditions are met, the public prosecutor requests the court that the punishment he proposes be applied in extra-summary proceedings. This means that no *instruction* is possible (art.286 CCP) and that there is an understanding between the court and the accused to the effect that the accused accepts the sentence proposed by the public prosecutor (art.396 CCP). Where this is the case, the judicial and criminal conflict is immediately resolved without subjecting the accused to a formal trial, and thus avoiding the stigmatizing effects that this "degrading ceremony" (Garfinkel) may involve. When this is not the case, proceedings return to normal procedure (art.396 CCP)[16].

# 9. Remedies

## 9.1. ORDINARY REMEDIES

Although the 1987 Code of Criminal Procedure upholds the general principle that, as a rule, decisions should be subject to appeal (art.399 CCP), it nevertheless expresses the idea that an appeal should always be exceptional[17]. Accordingly, a person who wishes to lodge an appeal must give reasons for his appeal and specify its basis in written "conclusions" (art.412 CCP). Any appeal may be summarily rejected (art.420 CCP). In addition, appeal is only available if a relevant interest exists. For example, the decision by which the *instruction* is closed (*supra*, 6.6.2.), cannot be appealed against when the case is committed for trial on the basis of the same facts as those on which the public prosecutor's indictment was based (art.310 CCP). As the public prosecutor and the investigating judge have both given the same assessment of the case, and because the final decision on the merits lies with the trial judge anyway, there is no relevant interest for the accused to appeal the decision by which the "instruction" is closed. Conversely, there

---

[16]For a more detailed discussion of extra-summary proceedings, see COSTA ANDRADE, *op. cit.*, p.356 *et seq.*

[17]For more information concerning the system of remedies of the 1987 CCP, see CUNHA RODRIGUES, "Recursos" in AAVV *O Novo Código de Processo Penal*, Almedina, Coimbra 1981, p.381 *et seq.*

would be a relevant interest where it was decided not to proceed to trial or if there was a difference between the decisions of the public prosecutor and the investigating judge

In courts of appeal, the stages through which all ordinary appeals pass are alike. The appeal may be based on any question relating to the decision under review, except where the scope of the appeal is restricted by statute (art.410 clause 1). However, where statute has restricted the scope of the appeal to questions of law only, the appeal court may nevertheless consider questions of fact in certain exceptional circumstances. The error appealed against must flow from the text of the appealed decision, or from the rules of common sense. An appeal may be based on the following grounds: (1) insufficient factual evidence to support the conviction; (2) a fundamental inconsistency in the grounds on which the decision is based; (3) an obvious error in the assessment of the evidence (art.410, clause 2 CCP).

This appeal, which is not restricted to the traditional "question of law", is referred to in legal doctrine as the *appeal of amplified review*[18]. The appeal in Portuguese law corresponds not to twin levels of appeal but to a single-level. As such, there exists a division of competence between the intermediate court (*tribunal da Relaçao*) and the Supreme Court of Justice. The first deals with appeals lodged against decisions of the single court and the second with those lodged against decisions of the collective court or the jury court (arts. 427 and 432 CCP).

In principle, the Supreme Court only reviews questions of law (CCP art.433). However, the possibility of an amplified review remains (art.410, clause 2). The intermediate court, on the contrary, considers both questions of law and of fact. An appeal concerning points of fact is only possible insofar as those facts flow from declarations made in hearings before the single court and documented in minutes. However, the public prosecutor, the defence lawyer or the lawyer of the *assistente* may wave the possibility of an appeal with respect to factual matters not requesting such documentation. In those cases, the review powers of the intermediate court are identical to those of the Supreme Court (art.428 CCP).

Regardless of whether the appeal is brought before the intermediate court or the Supreme Court of Justice, both courts are bound by the *principle of the prohibition of reformatio in pejus*. As such, when an appeal against the final decision is lodged exclusively by the accused, by the public prosecutor, in the exclusive interest of the accused, or by the accused and the public prosecutor, again in the exclusive interest of the accused, the higher court of justice may not aggravate the type or severity of sanctions resulting from the decision under review (art.409 CCP).

---

[18]For a more detailed description, see FIGUEIREDO DIAS "Para uma reforma global do processo penal português. Da sua necessidade e de algumas orientaçoes fundamentais" in AAVV, *Para uma Nova Justiça Penal*, Almedina, Coimbra, 1983, p.240.

9.2. EXTRAORDINARY REMEDIES

With respect to extraordinary appeals, the CCP recognizes the following possibilities:

*9.2.1. Appeal in the interests of a consistent application of the law*

If different courts have given opposite decisions under the same legislation, and no ordinary appeal is possible, the Supreme Court decides about the conflict. This decision is rendered in plenary session. The interpretation of the Supreme court is binding upon the lower courts (art.437 CCP).

*9.2.2. Appeal to revise a final judgment)*

This form of appeal is admissible in the following circumstances:
1) when another definitive verdict considers evidence used in the determination of the decision as false
2) when another verdict has definitively proven a crime committed by a judge or juror, related to the exercise of his functions in procedure
3) when facts which served as the basis for guilty verdicts are contradictory with those definitively proven in another verdict, and thus creating grave doubts as to the justice of the guilty verdict
4) when new facts or evidence are discovered which in themselves or in combination with those which were evaluated in proceedings, arouse grave doubts as to the justice of the guilty verdict (art.449 CCP).

## 10. Other questions

10.1. MENTAL ILLNESS

The fact that the accused suffers from mental illness does not significantly change criminal procedure. It does not, for instance, imply the suspension of proceedings to protect his right of defence. In Portuguese law, incapacity to take part in proceedings resulting from mental illness is remedied through obligatory representation by defence counsel (arts. 64 and 334 CCP).

The solution of Portuguese law is especially justified in cases where the mental illness of the accused begs the question of whether he is criminally responsible. Art.20 of the Penal Code requires that the question of his/her non-imputability be linked to the actual fact alleged. As such, criminal procedure should create the necessary mechanisms to permit the question to be put and decided during the proceedings of the facts themselves, as would occur with any other question relative to guilt. Thus, the proceedings run their course regardless of his/her mental illness. The question of non-imputability is only resolved at the point of sentencing, in the part relative to the question of guilt (art.368 CCP). Afterwards, if the court of justice concludes he is not imputable, it decides, during the part of sentencing relative to the determination of sanctions (art.369 CCP), whether or not to apply a security measure.

## 10.2. TRIAL *IN ABSENTIA*

Unlike the 1929 Code of Criminal Procedure, the 1987 Code does not treat the question of the absence of the accused in the context of special proceedings (proceedings in the absence of the defendant) which would lead to the judgment of an absent accused.

The present law of criminal procedure is inclined towards not judging absent defendants. In affirming the rule of the obligatory presence of the accused at the trial hearing (art.332, clause 1 CCP), the CCP deals with the absence of the accused through a *declaration of contumacy* (art.335 *et seq.* CCP). Hence, if it is not possible to notify the accused of the order which specifies the day of the trial hearing or to detain or remand him in custody in order to assure his/her presence, the accused is informed by public notices that he should present himself for judgment within 30 days, under penalty of being declared contumacious.

The declaration of contumacy implies for the accused that contracts of a patrimonial nature occurring after the declaration may be annulled. In addition, when it is shown to be necessary in order to discourage contumacy, the court of justice may prevent the accused from obtaining certain documents, certificates or records from the public authorities. Finally, it may also confiscate all or part of the assets of the absent accused.

## 10.3. COMPENSATION

Art.71 CCP recognizes the *principle of adhesion*, according to which a request for civil damages resulting from a crime being moved in the respective criminal proceedings. It may only be moved separately, before the civil courts, in certain cases allowed for by the law.

This compensation preserves its nature of a true civil lawsuit given that compensation of loss and damage resulting from a crime is governed by civil law (art.128 CCP). This status has led the law of criminal procedural to adopt the principle of request (art.74 CCP), which is typical for civil law. In the previous CCP, the reparation of losses and damage decided in criminal proceedings was of a specifically criminal nature and was a criminal consequence of a guilty verdict. Thus, it was automatically awarded by the courts without the necessity of request.

## 10.4. CONSENSUS SOLUTIONS

Using the terminology of several contemporary experts in procedure[19], the new Code of Criminal Procedure has conceived criminal procedure as a system of coordinates defined by a horizontal and a vertical axis (Preamble CCP, II, 6). The first of these coincides with the distinction between serious and petty crimes[20]. The second delimits and distinguishes what can be referred to as "areas of consensus" and "areas of conflict" in criminal procedure[21].

The 1987 Code shows many examples of consensus solutions. They are consistent with both the accused's and the victim's (the *assistente*) position as "active subjects" in the proceedings, with autonomous rights to influence the course of the legal proceedings (see *supra*, 3). Examples of consensus solutions are: *the provisional suspension of the proceedings*, which depends on the agreement of both the accused and the "assistente" (art.281, clause 1, a CCP) and *extra-summary proceedings*, which presuppose that the accused accepts the sanctions proposed by the public prosecutor. A final example of consensus solutions is that of the *complete and unreserved confession* to the facts charged to the accused, having, as a consequence, their being considered proven (art.344, clause 2, a CCP).

## 10.5. STATUTES OF LIMITATION

Matters of prescription in criminal law are dealt with in the Penal Code (arts. 117 et seq.). The time beyond which a crime is no longer enforceable is established by reference ot the abstract seriousness of the crime. For example, the term of 15 years - the longest term applicable in Portuguese law - would correspond to a crime whose maximum available punishment exceeds 10 years.

Criminal law prescription may be suspended in certain circumstances, only resuming the day that the reason for suspension ceases to exist. Prescription may also be interrupted, in which case the original term does not resume but, on the contrary, a new term is begun.

---

[19]See Jurgen WOLTER, "Strafverfahrensrecht und Strafprozeßreform", *Goltdammers Archiv für Strafrecht*, 1985, p.49 *et seq.*

[20]See supra 4.1. Principles governing the opening of proceedings, 7. Evidence and 8. Special proceedings.

[21]For an approach to the question of consensus in criminal procedure, see COSTA ANDRADE, with bibliography, op. cit., p.325 *et seq.*

## 11. Select bibliography

BARREIROS, A., *Manual de Processo Penal*, Universidade Lusiada, 1989.

CENTRO DE ESTUDOS JUDICIÁRIOS, *Jornadas de Direito Processual Penal. O Novo Código de Processo Penal*, Almedina, 1988.

COSTA ANDRADE, M., *Sobre as Proibições de Prova em Processo Penal*, Coimbra Editora, 1992.

COSTA PIMENTA, J., *Código de Processo Penal anotado*, Rei dos Livros, 1991.

FIGUEIREDO DIAS, J., *Direito Processual Penal*, Coimbra Editora, 1974.

FIGUEIREDO DIAS, J., *Direito Processual Penal*, Faculdade de Direito da Universidade de Coimbra, 1988-1989.

ISASCA, F., *Alteração Substancial dos Factos e sua Relevância no Processo Penal Português*, Almedina, 1992.

MAIA GONÇALVES, M., *Código de Processo Penal Anotado*, Almedina, 1992.

MARQUES DA SILVA, G., *Do Processo Penal Preliminar, Lisboa, 1990.*

# Chapter 12 - Scotland[1]

Prof. Christopher **GANE**
Director, Centre for Legal Studies
University of Sussex

## 1. Sources

### 1.1. HISTORICAL BACKGROUND

In 1603 James VI of Scotland became King of England and the two coun-tries, which had been enemies for centuries, became one kingdom. For over a hundred years following this "Union of the Crowns" Scotland and England retained their separate legislatures and distinct legal systems. In 1707 the Parliaments of Scotland and England dissolved themselves to create the new parliament of Great Britain. However, the Act of Union between Scotland and England expressly preserved the separate legal systems of the two countries, with the result that today, while forming part of a single state, with a common head of state, government and legislature, Scotland and Eng-land have separate legal systems[2]. These two systems, while inevitably influenced by the Acts of the Parliament of the United Kingdom, continue to reflect their different historical development. Nowhere is this more marked than in respect of their systems of Criminal Law and Criminal Justice. While other areas of Scots law have been significantly influenced by English ideas, Scottish criminal law and procedure remain largely untouched by English theory or method. There are several reasons for this. One of the most important is that while the House of Lords was quickly accepted after 1707 as the final court of appeal for both England and Scotland in civil matters, it was held in *Mackintosh v Lord Advocate*[3] that there could be no appeal from the Scottish courts to the House of Lords in criminal matters. The Scottish courts have, therefore, retained the "last word" in the interpretation and development of Scots criminal law. They do not even consider themselves bound to follow English interpretations of United Kingdom legislation common to both jurisdictions[4].

---

[1]I would like to thank Christine Gane BA, LLB and Sheriff C. N. Stoddart LLB, LLM, PhD for their helpful comments on earlier drafts of this article.

[2]Act of Union 1706-1707, Articles XVIII and XIX.

[3](1876) 3 R (HL) 34.

[4]See, for examples, *Ritchie v Pirie* 1972 JC 7; *Keane v Gallacher* 1980 JC 77.

## 1.2. GENERAL OBSERVATIONS

Scots law is an uncodified system. There is nothing in the realms of private law or public law which corresponds to the general, systematic and authoritative codes adopted in many other European jurisdictions. Nor are there any legal norms of "constitutional" status in the Scottish legal system. All branches of Scots law are based on ordinary legislation (Acts of Parliament or subordinate measures), the common (judge-made) law, legal writings of "institutional" status or a mixture of these elements.

The relative importance of these three sources varies. Some areas of the law are virtually untouched by legislation, and depend heavily on the common law and institutional writings. This is the case for many areas of substantive criminal law where, apart from modern "regulatory" offences, and in particular matters relating to road traffic, public health and welfare, statute has made little impact on the substantive criminal law of Scotland.

The situation is rather different in the case of criminal procedure. Since the nineteenth century, Scottish criminal procedure has been substantially based on legislation. However, this is subject to some important qualifications. Much of the law regarding powers of arrest, search and seizure and the questioning of suspects is derived from the common law. The bulk of the law of evidence in criminal cases is non-statutory, and while the sentencing powers of the courts are contained within a broad legislative framework, the discretion left to the courts is such that sentencing "tariffs" and guide-lines can fairly be described as judge-made.

## 1.3. LEGISLATION

Modern solemn criminal procedure[5] dates from the Criminal Procedure (Scotland) Act 1887 and the Criminal Appeal (Scotland) Act 1926. Modern summary procedure[6] dates from the Summary Jurisdiction (Scotland) Act 1908. Legislation governing criminal procedure was consolidated in 1975, and the basic statute is now the Criminal Procedure (Scotland) Act 1975[7]. Several Acts of Parliament have amended the 1975 Act, and care must be taken to read its provisions in the light of subsequent legislation, in particular the Criminal Justice (Scotland) Act 1980[8] and the Prisoners and Criminal Proceedings (Scotland) Act 1993.

Some important aspects of criminal procedure are not dealt with in the

---

[5]That is, procedure which is commenced by *indictment* and in which trial takes place before a judge and jury in the High Court of Justiciary or the Sheriff Court.

[6]That is, procedure which is initiated by *complaint* and in which trial takes place, without a jury, before a judge in the Sheriff Court or before a justice or justices in the District Court.

[7]Unless otherwise indicated, this Act is referred to throughout as 'the 1975 Act'.

[8]Unless otherwise indicated, this Act is referred to throughout as 'the 1980 Act'

1975 Act. The special procedures for dealing with juvenile offenders are to be found in Part III of the Social Work (Scotland) Act 1968. Access to bail in criminal proceedings is governed by the Bail etc. (Scotland) Act 1980. Important police powers of detention are contained in sections 1 and 2 of the Criminal Justice (Scotland) Act 1980. Sections 51 to 55 of the Criminal Justice (Scotland) Act 1987 contain special provisions for the investigation of serious or complex fraud.

### 1.4. CASE-LAW

In developing the common law, and in the process of statutory interpretation, the Scottish criminal courts observe a system of precedent. Decisions of the High Court of Justiciary on points of law, when sitting as an appellate court or a court of review, are binding on all lower courts. Although the matter has not been conclusively settled, it appears that the High Court also considers itself to be bound by such decisions[9]. It is possible, however, for a larger bench of judges to over-rule a previous decision of the High Court, so that a decision of three judges may later be over-ruled by a bench of five.

Decisions of single High Court judges on points of law are binding on all lower courts unless and until over-turned on appeal[10]. Such decisions are not, however, binding on other single judges[11] of the High Court, or on a bench of the High Court. Decisions of lower courts are not binding.

### 1.5. LEGAL WRITINGS

A distinction should be made here between the so-called "institutional writers", whose works have a particular legal authority, and ordinary legal writings which do not.

#### 1.5.1. Institutional writings

The concept of the "institutional writer" as a source of legal norms is of relatively recent origin. The modern understanding of the place of institutional writings is that in the absence of any statutory rule or judicial precedent, the views of certain writers may be accepted by a court as determining the law. This is not a status which is accorded to living writers, and in the field of criminal law and procedure it has not been accorded to the work of any author writing after the middle of the nineteenth century.

In relation to criminal law and procedure only one work is universally recognised as having "institutional" status and that is Baron David Hume's

---

[9]See, T.B. SMITH, *A Short Commentary on the Law of Scotland*, pp.38-39; *Sugden v H.M.Advocate* 1934 JC 103; 1934 SLT 465.

[10]*Jessop v Stevenson* 1988 SCCR 655.

[11]*H.M.Advocate v Higgins* 1914 JC 1.

*Commentaries on the Law of Scotland Respecting Crimes*[12]. But even this work is much less influential in relation to criminal procedure than it formerly was. The principal reason for this is that the rules of procedure have been so substantially changed by statute since the time of Hume that apart from some matters of principle his views have been largely superseded. (It remains, however, a very influential work in relation to substantive criminal law.)

### 1.5.2. Other legal writings

Apart from the so-called "institutional" writers, legal writings have no particular status, and are not formally recognised as a source of law. The weight that a court is prepared to give to the views of a writer will depend in part on the reputation of the individual, and in part on whether his or her views accord with the general attitude of the court towards the issue under discussion.

### 1.6. THE EUROPEAN CONVENTION ON HUMAN RIGHTS AND THE INTERNATIONAL COVENANT ON CIVIL AND POLITICAL RIGHTS

### 1.6.1. The European Convention on Human Rights

The United Kingdom is, of course, a party to the European Convention on Human Rights. Parliament has taken no steps to enact the Convention into United Kingdom law, and since the United Kingdom law adopts a dualist approach to the incorporation of international treaties, the Convention cannot be invoked before the Scottish courts as conferring enforceable rights at the domestic level.

The English courts take the view that the terms of the Convention may be relied upon as an aid to the interpretation of legislation. Where there is uncertainty or ambiguity in the language of a statute, regard may be had to the Convention so that the court may adopt the interpretation of the legislation which conforms to the principles of the Convention. This approach is based on the theory that when enacting legislation Parliament is presumed not to act against the international treaty obligations of the United Kingdom. It is, however, only a presumption, and in the face of clear statutory language the terms of the Convention have no role to play even if the legislation in

---

[12]This work was based on two earlier works by HUME, namely, *Commentaries on the Law of Scotland respecting the Description and Punishment of Crimes* (1797) and *Commentaries on the Law of Scotland respecting Trial for Crimes* (1800). The standard reference edition is the 4th ed. by B.R. BELL, 2 vols., Edinburgh 1844 (Herafter, 'Hume').

question violates the terms of the Convention[13].

Even this secondary reliance on the Convention is not permitted in the Scottish courts. In *Surjit Kaur v Lord Advocate*[14] it was held that the Convention, not being part of the domestic law of Scotland, could not be invoked, even as an aid to the construction of a United Kingdom statute. Indeed, it was suggested in *Montes and Others v H.M. Advocate*[15] that it was not even competent for the court to consider, within the context of a criminal appeal, decisions of the European Court of Human Rights on the interpretation of the Convention.

Nevertheless, the United Kingdom does recognise the right of individual application under article 25 of the Convention and the compulsory jurisdiction of the European Court of Human Rights, and the decisions of the Court have undoubtedly been influential in correcting defects in certain aspects of the domestic law of the United Kingdom.

### 1.6.2. *The International Covenant on Civil and Political Rights*

Although the United Kingdom had signed and ratified the International Covenant on Civil and Political Rights, it is not a party to the first Optional Protocol to that convention. The right of individual application to the United Nations Human Rights Committee is not, therefore, recognised by the United Kingdom. It is for this reason that the Covenant has had much less of an impact on the law of the United Kingdom than has the European Convention on Human Rights.

## 2. Structure of the criminal justice system

### 2.1. INVESTIGATING AUTHORITIES

Responsibility for the investigation of crime rests, at least in theory, with the local public prosecutor, the procurator fiscal. In practice, much of the day-to-day responsibility for the investigation of crime is delegated to the police who conduct the investigation under the general supervision of the procurator fiscal. Section 17(2) of the Police (Scotland) Act 1967 provides that in

---

[13]*Salomon v Commissioners of Customs and Excise* [1967] 2 *Q.B.* 11; *Malone v Metropolitan Police Commissioner* [1979] 2 *WLR* 700; *R vSecretary of State for the Home Department, ex parte Brind* [1990] 1 *All ER* 469, 141 *NLJ* 199 (1991).

[14]1981 SLT 322. For a discussion of this case See, *inter alia*, C.H.W.GANE, 'The European Convention on Human Rights - A Scottish View"[1982] *Liverpool Law Review* 169; W.FINNIE, "The European Convention on Human Rights: Domestic Status" (1980) 25 *Journal of the Law Society of Scotland*, 434. The decision in *Surjit Kaur* was confirmed by the decision of the Inner House of Court of Session in *Moore v Secretary of State for Scotland* 1985 SLT 38. See also, P.L. BEAUMONT *et al.*, "Treaties in the Courts" 1986 *SLT* (News) 61.

[15]1990 SCCR 645.

relation to the investigation of offences the chief constable of a police force shall comply with such lawful instructions as he may receive from the appropriate prosecutor.

The responsibilities of the police are limited to investigation. It is for the prosecutor and not the police to decide whether or not the results of the investigation justify a prosecution, and the police must put the result of their investigations fairly before the prosecutor so that he has a proper basis on which to decide whether or not to prosecute[16]. In practice prosecutors rely heavily on the reports submitted by the police, and in the vast majority of cases the prosecutor's decision is based entirely on these reports without further or additional investigation.

## 2.2. PROSECUTING AUTHORITIES

In common with most western legal systems, Scots law regards the prosecution of crime as primarily a public function, to be performed in the public interest by an official appointed for that purpose. The public prosecutor does not have an exclusive title to prosecute and in certain circumstances it is possible for a private citizen to initiate a prosecution. But for most practical purposes, responsibility for the prosecution of crime rests with a public official.

In Scotland, that official is the Lord Advocate who is the chief Law Officer of the Crown in Scotland. The Lord Advocate is appointed by the Prime Minister and if he (or she) is not already a member of the House of Commons, a peerage will be granted to enable him or her to sit in the House of Lords.

In the discharge of his functions as public prosecutor, the Lord Advocate is assisted by the second Law Officer, the Solicitor-General for Scotland, and a permanent staff of civil servants in the Crown Office in Edinburgh headed by the Crown Agent.

All prosecutions on indictment, whether in the High Court or the sheriff court, are conducted in the name of the Lord Advocate[17]. While the Lord Advocate may appear personally to prosecute, and occasionally does so in cases of particular difficulty or public importance, it is customary today for him to be represented. In the High Court this task is performed by Crown counsel appointed from members of the Scottish bar by the Lord Advocate and known as advocates-depute. Prosecutions on indictment in the sheriff court are conducted on behalf of the Lord Advocate by the procurator fiscal of the court.

Summary prosecutions are conducted in the sheriff courts and the district courts by the procurator fiscal of the appropriate court. In such cases

---

[16]*Smith v H.M.Advocate* 1952 JC 66.
[17]1975 Act, section 41.

the procurator fiscal does not prosecute in the name of the Lord Advocate but in a personal capacity as fiscal of the court. However, he remains responsible to the Lord Advocate and acts under his general supervision and guidance.

## 2.3. COURTS OF CRIMINAL JURISDICTION

Apart from courts of special jurisdiction (such as courts martial) three courts exercise criminal jurisdiction in Scotland - the High Court of Justiciary (commonly referred to as the High Court), the sheriff court and the district court. The High Court has both an original and an appellate jurisdiction. The sheriff and district courts sit only as courts of first instance.

### 2.3.1. Territorial jurisdiction

The jurisdiction of all three courts is subject to the principle of territoriality. Subject to certain exceptions[18], no court has jurisdiction to deal with a matter occurring beyond its territorial limits[19]. At the same time the criminal jurisdiction of the Scottish courts will normally extend to any person who commits an offence within those limits[20].

Only the High Court has general territorial jurisdiction. This extends to the whole of Scotland and the territorial waters around Scotland. The jurisdiction of the sheriff and district courts is more limited.

For the purposes of sheriff court jurisdiction, Scotland is divided into six sheriffdoms[21]. These six sheriffdoms are further divided into sheriff court districts. In general, a sheriff cannot try an offence committed outside his sheriffdom, but he does have jurisdiction in all the districts of the sheriffdom for which he is appointed[22].

The jurisdiction of the district court is based on the "commission area", i.e., a district or island area within the meaning of the Local Government (Scotland) Act 1973 and the authority of that court is limited, again subject to certain exceptions, to the relevant commission area.

---

[18]At common law the crime of piracy may be tried by the Scottish courts irrespective of where the offence was committed, or of the nationalityof the offenders or the ship: *Cameron and Others v H.M.Advocate* 1971 *SLT* 333. Similarly, under section 134 of the Criminal Justice Act 1988 the Scottish courts have jurisdiction to try persons for the crime of torture even if committed outside the United Kingdom. Section 6 of the 1975 Act confers jurisdiction on the Scottish courts to try any British subject who, in a country outside the United Kingdom, commits what would in Scotland be the crime of murder or culpable homicide.

[19]*H.M.Advocate v Hall* (1881) 4 Couper 438.

[20]*Lewis v Blair* (1858) 3 Irvine 16. For exceptions to this rule see the Visiting Forces Act 1952.

[21]Grampian Highland and Islands; Tayside Central and Fife; Lothian and Borders; Glasgow and Strathkelvin; North Strathclyde; South StrathclydeDumfries and Galloway: Sheriff Courts (Scotland) Act 1971, section 2 and Sheriffdoms Reorganisation Order 1974.

[22]1975 Act, ss. 3(4) and 288(5).

## 2.3.2. Competence

### (i) The High Court

The jurisdiction of the High Court to try crimes committed within its territorial jurisdiction is almost universal. It may be excluded where jurisdiction is reserved by statute to some other court, but this must be done expressly or by necessary implication[23]. The High Court exercises exclusive jurisdiction in cases of treason, murder, rape, deforcement of court messengers, breach of duty by magistrates and in any other case where exclusive jurisdiction is conferred on the court by statute[24].

Trials before the High Court are conducted according to the rules of solemn procedure before a judge and a jury. The High Court has no summary trial jurisdiction. Judges in the High Court enjoy a full range of sentencing powers. The maximum penalty that may be imposed in the High Court (where this is permitted) is life imprisonment. The death penalty is only available in certain cases of treason and piracy, and is effectively obsolete.

### (ii) The sheriff court

Like the High Court, the competence of the sheriff court is virtually universal[25]. The jurisdiction of the sheriff court may be excluded - as, for example, in the case of those offences reserved to the exclusive jurisdiction of the High Court- but otherwise any statutory or common law crime may be tried in the sheriff court.

Trials before the sheriff court may be conducted according to the rules of solemn or summary procedure. In solemn proceedings the sheriff sits with a jury and the maximum penalty he or she may impose is a sentence of three years' imprisonment[26]. If the sheriff considers his sentencing powers to be inadequate in a particular case he may remit that case to the High Court for sentence[27].

In summary proceedings the sheriff sits alone. Normally, the maximum punishment which the sheriff may impose in summary proceedings for a common law offence is three months' imprisonment, or a fine of five thousand pounds[28]. The penalties applicable in the case of statutory offences depend on the terms of the provision creating the offence.

---

[23]*Robert Rowet* (1843) 1 Broun 540; *George Duncan* (1864) 4 Irvine 474.

[24]See, for example, Official Secrets Act 1911, s.10(3).

[25]*McPherson v Boyd* 1907 S.C. (J.) 42.

[26]1975 Act, s.2 .

[27]1975 Act, s.104.

[28]1975 Act, ss.289(a), 289B(6) and Criminal Justice Act 1991, s.17(2)e (1993 figure).

*(iii) The district court*

The district court was established by the District Courts (Scotland) Act 1975 and replaced the existing inferior courts (justice of the peace courts, burgh courts and police courts). The jurisdiction and powers of those courts were, however, inherited by the district court[29].

District courts are presided over either by lay justices or by legally qualified judges known as stipendiary magistrates[30]. When the district court is presided over by a stipendiary magistrate, it has the same criminal jurisdiction as the sheriff court in summary proceedings[31]. When the district court is presided over by lay justices is has a more limited competence and it usually deals with minor assaults, thefts and breaches of the peace. A large number of offences are expressly excluded from the jurisdiction of the district court by section 285 of the 1975 Act. These include offences reserved to the jurisdiction of other courts and serious examples of offences of a type which the district court is competent to try, such as theft when committed by housebreaking or where the value of the property stolen exceeds five hundred pounds[32].

Trials in the District court are always conducted according to summary procedure. Where the court is presided over by one or more lay justices, the court is assisted by a legally qualified clerk.

The powers of the justices in terms of sentencing are limited. Section 284 of the 1975 Act provides that generally the district court may not impose a sentence of imprisonment of more than sixty days, nor may it impose a fine exceeding five hundred pounds, nor may it make a compensation order in excess of that sum[33].

### 2.3.3. Personnel

With the exception of district court justices, all criminal judges in Scotland are professionally qualified.

*(i) The High Court*

In practice judges of the High Court are appointed from the Faculty of Advocates (the Scottish bar) although in strictly legal terms eligibility for appointment has never been restricted to advocates[34]. Section 35 and Schedule 4 of the Law Reform (Miscellaneous Provisions) (Scotland) Act 1990 have extended the categories of eligibility for appointment to the High Court to include sheriffs of not less than five years' standing and solicitors

---

[29]District Courts (Scotland) Act 1975, s.3.
[30]District Courts (Scotland) Act 1975, s.5.
[31]*Ibid.*, s.3(2).
[32]1975 Act, section 285 (a) (iii).
[33]1980 Act, s.59(3)(b).
[34]Act of Union 1706-1707, Article 19.

who have held, for a period of five years, the right of audience in the High Court and the Court of Session (the supreme civil court in Scotland). Appointments to the High Court bench are made by the Crown on the advice of the Secretary of State for Scotland who, by convention, forwards to the Crown nominations submitted to him by the Lord Advocate[35]. All appointments to the High Court are, therefore, made in effect by the Government of the day, although there is in practice little evidence that political considerations influence such appointments. It would, however, be right to say that there are no constitutional safeguards against this happening.

According to the Claim of Right of 1689[36] a judge of the High Court can only be removed for misconduct. There is no recognised procedure for such removal and there is no instance in modern times of a judge of the High Court being removed for misconduct.

### (ii) The sheriff court

Sheriffs must all be advocates or solicitors of at least ten years' standing before appointment to the bench[37]. They enjoy significant security of office, although rather less than that enjoyed by judges of the High Court. A sheriff may only be removed from office following an inquiry conducted by the holders of the two most senior judicial positions in Scotland - the Lord President of the Court of Session and the Lord Justice-Clerk - which has found that the sheriff is unfit to hold office by reason of inability, neglect of duty or misbehaviour. In order to remove the sheriff the Secretary of State for Scotland must make an order removing him from office and this must be laid before Parliament[38].

### (iii) The district court

District Court justices are appointed by the Secretary of State for Scotland and may be removed by the Secretary of State[39]. Stipendiary magistrates are appointed by the local authority, subject to the approval of the Secretary of State[40]. A stipendiary magistrate enjoys the same security of office as a sheriff[41].

---

[35]*Constitutional and Administrative Law* by E.C.S. Wade and A.W. Bradley, 10th ed. by A.W.Bradley, Longman, London, 1985. Hereafter,'Wade and Bradley'.

[36]That is, the Scottish equivalent of the English Bill of Rights of 1689.

[37]Sheriff Courts (Scotland) Act 1971, s.29.

[38]Sheriff Courts (Scotland) Act 1971, s.12 This procedure was last used in 1977 in the case of Sheriff Peter Thompson who was held to have abused his judicial position to promote his political interests. See WADE and BRADLEY, p.335 and *House of Commons Debates*, 25 Nov. 1977, col.922 (Written Answers), 30 Nov. 1977, col. 245 (Written Answers) and 6 Dec. 1977, co.1288.

[39]District Courts (Scotland) Act 1975, s.9(2).

[40]District Courts (Scotland) Act 1975, s.5(3).

[41]*Ibid.*, s.5(8).

## 3. Parties to criminal proceedings

### 3.1. THE PROSECUTOR

The position of the public prosecutor in the Scottish system of criminal procedure is a complex one. In certain ways he is a party to the proceedings, but his involvement in the criminal process is not merely as a party. Rather, he is *master* of those proceedings. In Scottish terminology, he is "master of the instance". The attributes of the public prosecutor as master of the instance are discussed later[42].

The prosecutor is not a "party" to criminal proceedings in the sense of having an individual or personal interest in their outcome. The public prosecutor, in bringing criminal proceedings, acts in the public interest (and even a private prosecutor does not act wholly on behalf of him- or her- self). However, a number of considerations indicate that in some senses the prosecutor must be regarded as a party to criminal proceedings. In the first place, there can be no proceedings unless these are initiated by a prosecutor. Secondly, at least in the case of summary proceedings, prosecutions are conducted in the name of the procurator fiscal himself. Thirdly, a combination of the adversarial nature of the Scottish trial, and the particular powers of the public prosecutor, demonstrate that while he acts in the public interest, in no sense does he occupy a "neutral" position.

### 3.2. THE DEFENCE

It is convenient here to distinguish between the personal position of the accused and the facilities afforded him, whether at the stage of investigation or during the trial, to protect his interests through adequate legal advice.

### 3.2.1. The position of the accused

The accused enjoys significant rights in the criminal process, both at the pre-trial and trial stages, all of which reflect the underlying notion that the accused is not obliged to cooperate in any way with the investigation or prosecution of charges brought against him. While he is undoubtedly an *object* of the proceedings, he can refuse the role of active participant in those proceedings. Thus at the pre-trial stage the suspect is not obliged to answer any questions put to him by the police. While a suspect can be compelled to submit to fingerprinting and similar procedures once he has been arrested and charged[43], such procedures cannot be adopted before this stage without a warrant from the court, except, perhaps, in cases of urgency[44].

---

[42]See below, section 5.2.
[43]See below.
[44]*Hay v H.M.Advocate* 1968 SLT 202.

At the trial stage, while the accused is entitled to lead evidence on his behalf and question the witnesses produced by the prosecution, he is not obliged to be a witness himself. If he chooses to do so he may be exposed to cross-examination by the prosecutor, but even here the accused enjoys safeguards regarding such matters as his character and previous convictions.

With respect to access to legal advice, it is convenient here to distinguish between the pre-trial and the trial stages.

### (i) Pre-trial access to legal advice

Section 19(1) of the 1975 Act provides that any person arrested on any criminal charge, is entitled, immediately upon arrest, to inform a solicitor that his professional assistance is required. Under section 19(3) of the 1975 Act the solicitor has the right to a private interview with his client before he appears before the court for examination (which must normally take place the following day). He also has the right to be present at such examination. The arrested person must be told of the rights under section 19(1) and 19(3)[45].

It is important to note, however, that while the fact of arrest must be immediately intimated to the solicitor, access is only guaranteed prior to appearance before the court. It follows that neither the suspect, nor the solicitor, has the right to demand the presence of the solicitor while the suspect is being questioned by the police.

Under section 3(1)(a) of the 1980 Act a person who has been arrested and who is in custody is entitled to notify a person "reasonably named" by him that he is in custody and to notify him of the place where he is being held. Such intimation must be made "without delay", unless "some delay is necessary in the interest of the investigation or the prevention of crime or the apprehension of offenders" in which case such intimation may be delayed, although for no longer than is "necessary". This right is additional to, and is not intended to replace, the right of access to legal advice.

The above rights apply where the suspect has been *arrested*. The 1980 Act introduced new statutory powers of *detention* for the purpose of investigation[46]. Section 2 of the 1980 Act gives a constable the power to detain a person at a police station for not more than six hours for the purpose of facilitating the carrying out of investigations. A person detained under section 2 is entitled to notify his solicitor and one other person reasonably named by him of the fact that he has been detained and of the place where he is being detained. Again, there is no guarantee of immediate access to legal advice since intimation either to a solicitor or to a person reasonably named may be delayed where this is necessary in the interest of the investigation or the prevention of crime or the apprehension of offenders.

---

[45]1975 Act, s.19(1)(b). Section 305 of the 1975 Act contains provisions similar to s.19 for arrest in summary proceedings.

[46]These are discussed below, section 5.1.

## (ii) Legal representation at trial

An accused person may, if he so chooses, conduct his own defence and he is not obliged to accept legal representation if he does not wish to do so[47]. It is not clear whether Scots law recognises the absolute right of an accused person to be represented by legal assistance of his own choosing. Clearly no court is entitled to deny a hearing to the accused on the ground that it does not approve his choice of adviser. It also appears that to convict an accused in the absence of his advisers, when this is due to no fault on the part of the accused, may justify quashing the conviction[48]. But it will not always do so, particularly where it appears that, despite the absence of counsel, the accused has suffered no prejudice[49].

Criminal legal aid in Scotland is governed by Part IV of the Legal Aid (Scotland) Act 1986, and regulations made under section 21 of that Act. Legal aid is available in the High Court, the sheriff court and the district court. It normally consists of representation by a solicitor, or, where necessary[50], by solicitor and advocate.

Subject to financial limits and other regulations, legal aid is available to every accused person during the preliminary stages of criminal proceedings (except in the case of an accused in summary proceedings if he is not in custody)[51].

Legal aid in solemn proceedings is granted by the court where it is satisfied after consideration of the accused's financial circumstances that the expenses of the case cannot be met without undue hardship to him or his dependants[52].

In summary proceedings, legal aid is not granted by the court, but by a body known as the Scottish Legal Aid Board. Legal aid is granted in summary proceedings if the Board is satisfied, after consideration of the financial circumstances of the accused person, that the expenses of the case cannot be met without undue hardship to him or his dependants and that in all the circumstances of the case it is in the interests of justice that legal aid should be made available[53].

Legal aid is available for appeal against conviction or sentence, or both (and also in connection with a prosecutor's appeal in summary proceedings) under section 25 of the 1986 Act. Legal aid for appeals is administered by the Legal Aid Board, and is available if the Board is satisfied that there are

---

[47]Cfr. *Manuel v H.M.Advocate* 1958 JC 41. Cfr. *Montgomery v H.M.Advocate* 1987 SCCR 264.

[48]*Fraser v MacKinnon* 1981 SCCR 91; *Benson v Tudhope* 1986 SCCR 422.

[49]*Ralston v H.M.Advocate* 1988 SCCR 590.

[50]For example, for trial in the High Court if the accused's solicitor does not have rights of audience.

[51]Legal Aid (Scotland) Act 1986, ss.21(3) and 22 (1)(c).

[52]*Ibid.*, s.23.

[53]*Ibid.*, s.24(1).

substantial grounds for making the appeal and that it is reasonable, in the circumstances, that legal aid should be made available to the applicant[54]. Where the applicant has not already been awarded legal aid under section 23 or 24 of the Act, legal aid for an appeal is subject to the same financial test as is applicable under those sections.

### 3.3. THE VICTIM

Unless he or she is in the position of being a prosecutor, the victim has no *locus standi* in Scottish criminal proceedings. Although the court has the power under section 58 of the 1980 Act to order a convicted person to pay compensation to the victim for any personal injury, loss or damage caused by his offence, the victim is not a party even to this part of the proceedings and has no right to be represented in respect of entitlement to compensation or *quantum*. However, the victim may, in certain cases, bring a private prosecution and thus become a party to the proceedings[55].

## 4. General principles concerning criminal procedure

### 4.1. BASIC PRINCIPLES

The following discussion identifies what might be described as the "basic principles" of Scottish criminal procedure.

#### 4.1.1. The public prosecutor as "master of the instance"

In Scottish criminal procedure the public prosecutor is "master of the instance". This means that it is for him to decide when and against whom to initiate criminal proceedings and upon what charges. Unless the mode of trial for a particular offence is fixed by statute, or the offence is one which is reserved to the exclusive jurisdiction of the High Court, the public prosecutor determines the mode of trial, and the court in which proceedings are to be taken. It is for the public prosecutor (and not the court) to decide what pleas of guilt to accept and it is for him to decide when to withdraw or abandon proceedings. At the end of the trial, even if a verdict of guilty has been returned, the court cannot impose any sentence on the accused unless the prosecutor moves the court to pronounce sentence[56].

---

[54]*Ibid.*, s.25(3).
[55]See section 8, *infra.*
[56]*Noon v.H.M.Advocate*, 1960 *JC* 52.

## 4.1.2. Distinction between solemn and summary procedure

Central to many aspects of the criminal process is the distinction between "solemn" and "summary" criminal proceedings. While the distinction may in some respects be irrelevant - the rules of evidence are the same in both types of proceeding; the presumption of innocence applies with equal force in both types of proceeding; the powers of arrest, detention, search, etc. are not affected by the form of procedure - nevertheless the distinction is fundamental.

In the first place, the mode of trial is quite different. In solemn proceedings trial takes place before a judge and jury whereas in summary proceedings trial takes place before a judge sitting alone. Secondly, the punitive powers of the court are significantly less in summary proceedings than in solemn proceedings. Thirdly, pre-trial procedures differ between the two forms of procedure. In solemn proceedings, for example, the arrest of the accused will be followed by judicial examination; in summary proceedings there is no such pre-trial judicial examination. Finally, the rules governing appeals differ fundamentally as between the two forms of procedure. In particular, the prosecutor may appeal against an acquittal in summary proceedings[57]. No appeal is possible against an acquittal in solemn proceedings.

## 4.1.3. The presumption of innocence and the burden of proof

The presumption of innocence is fundamental to the whole system of criminal prosecution and applies to every person charged with a criminal offence[58]. In general it cannot be overcome except by proof beyond reasonable doubt of all facts required to establish the crime charged. However, in the case of certain offences the proof of certain facts by the prosecution may result in conviction unless the accused establishes his innocence, usually on a balance of probabilities[59].

## 4.1.4. The principles of "fairness" and "balance"

It is frequently said that "fairness to the accused" is a fundamental part of the Scottish criminal justice system. This "principle" has been most frequently discussed in relation to extra-judicial confessions and statements to the police where it is used as a test of the admissibility of such statements in evidence. In *Miln v Cullen*[60] the court stated that fairness was not a "unilateral consideration", but rather it was one aspect of a balance between the interests of

---

[57]1975 Act, s.442.
[58]*Slater v H.M.Advocate* 1928 JC 94.
[59]See, for example, the Incest and Related Offences (Scotland) Act 1986.
[60]1967 JC 21.

the accused and the public interest: "Fairness to the public is also a legitimate consideration"[61].

According to this view, one of the functions of the court in the criminal process is to seek to provide a proper balance; "to secure that the rights of individuals are properly preserved, while not hamstringing the police in their investigation of crime with a series of academic vetoes which ignore the realities and practicalities of the situation and discount completely the public interest"[62].

There is, however, something of a false dichotomy here since it assumes that the public do not have an interest in the protection of the suspect or the accused from improper or over-zealous police (or prosecutorial) conduct.

### 4.2. PRINCIPLES GOVERNING THE OPENING OF CRIMINAL PROCEEDINGS

#### 4.2.1. The "ex officio" principle

As we have already noted, whether or not to initiate criminal proceedings is a matter for the discretion of the public prosecutor. An Act of the Scottish Parliament of 1587[63] gave the "King's Advocate" authority to prosecute irrespective of the wishes of the injured party, an authority which he continues to exercise today.

#### 4.2.2. Principles of "legality" and "opportunity"

There is no obligation on the public prosecutor to initiate criminal proceedings, even in the presence of clear proof that an offence has been committed. Indeed, one of the most important duties of a prosecutor is to consider whether, in the circumstances of a case, it is in the public interest that a criminal charge should be brought, and if brought proceeded with[64]. The public prosecutor's discretion in this area is virtually, but not entirely, unfettered. It is subject to the over-riding power of the court to refuse to allow a prosecution to proceed if it considers it to be oppressive, as, for example, where the prosecution is "stale" or has been affected by pre-trial publicity[65]. It may also be indirectly controlled by an individual making an application to bring a private prosecution which, at least in theory, could involve the High Court compelling the public prosecutor to proceed.

The public prosecutor may also find himself barred from proceeding

---

[61]*Ibid.*

[62]*Ibid.* (Lord Wheatley).

[63]Act 1587, cap.77.

[64]See RENTON and BROWN, paras. 3-01 *et seq.* for a consideration of the factors which the prosecutor should take into account.

[65]*H.M.Advocate v Stewart* 1980 JC 84; *Stuurman v H.M.Advocate* 1980 JC 111; *H.M.Advocate v O'Neil* 1992 SCCR 130.

with a case if he has previously renounced the right to prosecute. This may happen either as regards proceedings against a particular offender for some particular offence[66] or, more generally, in respect of all potential offenders for a particular type of offence[67]. In either case he must have unequivocally relinquished the right to prosecute. This may be done by communicating his decision to the offender or his legal representatives, or to any other person who might normally be expected to communicate the decision to him. It may also be done by a general public statement.

It follows from the above that Scots law recognises the *"ex officio"* principle as governing criminal procedure, and that so far as concerns the distinction between *la légalité des poursuites* and *l'opportunité des poursuites* it unquestionably favours the latter.

## 4.2.3. Accusatorial and inquisitorial procedure

So far as concerns the trial stage, Scottish criminal proceedings follow strictly the accusatorial model. Excessive involvement by the judge in the examination of witnesses has been condemned by the High Court on more than one occasion. The function of the judge during the trial is to act as a "referee". The judge should not take over the role of examiner or cross-examiner. He is entitled to ask questions, but in doing so his function is limited to clearing up ambiguities that are not being cleared up by counsel. He is entitled to ask such questions as he might consider to be relevant and important for the proper determination of the case, but that right must be exercised with discretion, and only when the occasion requires it[68].

A further aspect of the accusatorial nature of trial proceedings is that the calling of witnesses is the responsibility of the prosecutor and the defence. The court has no power to call witnesses *ex officio*.

At the pre-trial stage there is, in solemn procedure, a form of judicial examination conducted before the sheriff. Historically this procedure was of a quasi-inquisitorial nature, but any real vestige of the inquisitorial character of the proceeding has now been lost, and in modern procedure pre-trial judicial examination is conducted by the prosecutor before the sheriff.

### 4.3. PRINCIPLES GOVERNING THE TAKING OF EVIDENCE

Although elaborate rules of evidence are gradually being abandoned in civil proceedings, Scottish criminal procedure retains a substantial, and complex, body of rules governing the taking of evidence. In the light of these rules it

---

[66]*Thom v H.M.Advocate* 1976 SLT 49; *H.M.Advocate v Waddell and Another* 1976 SLT (Notes) 61; *H.M.Advocate v Stewart* 1980 JC 84

[67]*Lockhart v Deighan* 1985 SCCR 204; *Benton v Cardle* 1987 SCCR 738.

[68]*Livingston v H.M.Advocate* Criminal Appeal Court, March 1974, Crown Office Circular A7/74; 1982 SCCR 100; *Elliot v Tudhope* 1987 SCCR85.

is possible to argue that the leading of evidence in a criminal trial does not involve a search for the "objective truth". The trial is concerned rather with those facts and circumstances which can be established according to the rules of evidence. These include the rules governing the competence and compellability of witnesses, the issues of relevance and sufficiency of evidence, the requirement of corroboration and the various exclusionary rules relating to hearsay and unfairly obtained evidence.

### 4.4. PRINCIPLES GOVERNING THE TRIAL

Criminal trials, whether on indictment or in summary proceedings, are held in public. Proceedings are oral, and in general the pre-trial statements of witnesses are not admissible as evidence. Witnesses are normally examined in open court, but it may be that a court has the power at common law to sit in private if justice cannot otherwise be done, or if publicity is not in the public interest. Where a court allows a name or other matter to be withheld from the public in proceedings before the court, the court may prohibit the publication of that name or matter in connection with the proceedings[69]. The power is typically used to protect the identity of witnesses, although it may also from time to time be used to protect the identity of the victim. To publish information which is the subject of a court prohibition constitutes contempt of court and is punishable with up to two years' imprisonment[70].

The televising or radio broadcasting of proceedings in court is not permitted, and it is not permitted to use a tape recorder to record proceedings in court except with the leave of the court, nor is it permitted to publish a recording of legal proceedings obtained in this way.

## 5. Coercive measures

In this section we will discuss (1), arrest and detention, (2) search and seizure, (3) the questioning of suspects and (4) other forms of interference with the liberty and privacy of the suspect.

### 5.1. ARREST AND DETENTION

The terms "arrest" and "detention" mean quite different thing in Scots law, both in terms of the circumstances when these two types of coercive measures may be adopted, and also in terms of the steps which may lawfully be taken following the exercise of these powers.

At common law there existed no power on the part of the police to apprehend or detain a person short of arrest, and the rule was that arrest was not permissible unless the police were in a position to proceed forthwith to

---

[69]Contempt of Court Act 1981, s.11.
[70]Contempt of Court Act 1981, s.11, s.15(2).

the stage of charging the suspect with the crime for which he or she had been arrested.

Certain statutes did confer on the police some limited powers of detention for particular purposes, but in general a person was either arrested or he was not. There was no "half-way house"[71]. The 1980 Act brought about a radical departure from this position by introducing certain general police powers to detain suspected persons, without arresting them or charging them, for the purpose of investigation. It is necessary, therefore, to discuss these two procedures separately.

### 5.1.1. Arrest

Arrest may be employed for a variety of purposes. Strictly speaking, as an initial step in criminal procedure, arrest is used to secure the attendance of a suspect or accused person before a court. It may also be used to ensure the attendance of persons required as witnesses. Arrest may be necessary after trial in order to secure compliance with the order or judgment of the court. The police also enjoy powers of arrest in order to preserve the public peace. In this section we are concerned only with the powers of arrest enjoyed by the police (and others, including, in certain circumstances, the ordinary citizen) as an initial step in the criminal process.

Such powers of arrest derive from a wide variety of sources. It is convenient to distinguish between powers of arrest exercised under a warrant issued by a court, and powers of arrest without warrant. In the latter case, a further distinction may be drawn between common law powers of arrest and statutory powers of arrest.

#### (i) Arrest under a warrant
While arrest under a warrant is a common early step in solemn proceedings, it is less common in summary proceedings where arrest should not be used unless the circumstances of the case justify deprivation of liberty. Any judge, sheriff or justice may issue a warrant for arrest, but in practice application is usually made by the procurator fiscal to the sheriff. Once granted, the warrant authorises officers of the law (in practice the police) to apprehend the accused, which should be done as soon as possible.

An officer is not entitled to use force to enter premises to execute a warrant unless he has first stated his identity and the purpose of his visit and has asked for and been refused entry[72].

---

[71]*Swankie v Milne* 1973 JC 1.
[72]Renton and Brown, para. 5-27.

## (ii) Arrest without warrant

A police officer undoubtedly enjoys a general common law power of arrest without warrant, which may be exercised in respect of common law crimes or statutory crimes. The great difficulty rests in defining the limits of this power. The first thing that can be said is that the exercise of this power, since it clearly interferes with the liberty of the subject, must, if required, be justified. Regard must be had to all the circumstances surrounding the arrest, the most important of which is the seriousness of the offence. Indeed, in some instances the seriousness of the offence will, of itself, justify an arrest without warrant. If, for example, a police officer comes across someone in the act of committing an armed robbery, or a rape, he would clearly be entitled to arrest without a warrant. But in less serious crimes regard must be had to the presence or absence of circumstances which would point to immediate arrest as opposed to some other procedure. Is the accused likely to abscond, or to destroy evidence, or to tamper with witnesses? Is he or she likely to repeat the offence or commit further offences? In weighing up these considerations it is relevant to have regard to the lapse of time between the commission of the offence and the arrest. If there is a significant delay between the commission of the offence, and arrest, then it is less easy to justify arrest without warrant, particularly if, in the period of delay it would have been possible to obtain a warrant for arrest.

A private citizen may also arrest without warrant, but this power is limited in two respects. It is limited to arrest for serious crimes and may only be exercised by persons who have witnessed the crime. Secondly, the purpose of such private arrest is limited to handing the arrested person over to the police, which must be done as soon as possible.

One of the most significant developments in criminal procedure over the past 15 to 20 years has been the proliferation of statutory powers of arrest without warrant. It would not be possible to go into all of these powers in detail here. Certain broad categories of power may, however, be identified: (a) Powers of arrest exerciseable only when the person is found, or seen, committing a specified offence; (b) Powers of arrest exerciseable where there is reasonable suspicion that a person has committed or is committing a specified offence; (c) Powers of arrest exerciseable where the name and address of the person cannot be ascertained and / or he is likely to abscond.

## 5.1.2. Detention

The distinction between arrest and detention tends to suggest that there is only one form of detention. In fact the police enjoy a wide variety of powers of detention. There are, first of all, what might be described as "street detentions" which confer the power to detain for questioning, search, production of documents, etc., but which do not confer any power to take the detained person into custody. Secondly, there is the power to detain, analogous to the power of arrest, which does permit the police to take the person detained into custody. Finally, there is the power to detain without charge, but subsequent to arrest, as, for example, under section 14 of the Prevention of Terrorism (Temporary Provisions) Act 1989. The first two types of detention depart from the general rules of the common law by permitting interference with the liberty of the subject short of arrest. The third form derogates from the common law rule that arrest must be accompanied by charge.

### (i) "Street" detention

Although powers of this kind may be exercised under a number of statutes, the most important, general, power of this nature is conferred by section 1 of the Criminal Justice Act 1980. Under this section a constable who has reasonable grounds for suspecting that a person has committed an offence or is committing an offence may require that person to give his name and address and may ask him for an explanation of the circumstances which have given rise to the constable's suspicion. The constable may also require other persons whom he believes have information relating to the offence to give their names and addresses[73]. A person detained under this section must be told why he is being detained and that it is an offence not to comply with the police officer's requirements.

### (ii) Detention in custody

Where a police officer has reasonable grounds for suspecting that a person has committed or is committing an offence punishable by imprisonment, he may, for the purpose of facilitating the carrying out of investigations into the offence, and as to whether criminal proceedings should be instigated against the person, detain and take him as quickly as is reasonably practicable to a police station or other premises and detain him there[74].

Detention in custody must end not later than six hours after it begins or, if earlier, when the person is arrested or where the ground for detention no longer exist. If a person has been detained for six hours he must be informed, immediately, that the period of detention has expired. At this point the person detained is at liberty to leave, and may not be re-detained under this provision on the same ground, or on any other ground arising out of the circumstances which led to his initial detention. There is nothing, however, to prevent him being arrested or, for that matter, detained on other grounds, provided that the procedures under section 2 are complied with. At the time when the police officer detains a suspect, he must inform him of his suspicion, of the general nature of the offence which he suspects has been or is being committed and of the reason for the detention[75].

There are other procedural safeguards attached to detention. In particu-

---

[73]1980 Act, s.1(1)(b).
[74]1980 Act, s.2.
[75]1980 Act, s.2(4).

lar, a record must be kept of significant matters such as the time and place where detention began, the premises to which he was taken and his time of arrival there, the general nature of the suspected offence, the time when the suspect left the police station or other place to which he was taken, or, if he is arrested rather than being set at liberty, the time at which he was arrested[76].

## 5.2. SEARCH AND SEIZURE

In this section we will consider the powers of the police to search for and seize evidence from premises and also from the person of the suspect.

### 5.2.1. Personal search

#### (i) Search prior to arrest
At common law, personal search prior to arrest is not normally permitted. In particular, it is not permissible to search a person in order to find evidence on which to arrest him[77]. There are, however, three exceptions to this rule:

#### A. Statutory powers of search
A large number of statutes permit personal search without a warrant and without arrest. For example, a person who has been detained under section 2(1) of the of the Criminal Justice (Scotland) Act 1980 may be searched in the same way as if he had been arrested[78]. Section 4 of the 1980 Act permits a constable to search a person if he has reasonable grounds for suspecting that he is carrying an offensive weapon in contravention of section 1 of the Prevention of Crime Act 1953 (carrying an offensive weapon in public). Another commonly encountered power of search is that contained in section 23 of the Misuse of Drugs Act 1971, which permits a constable to search a person suspected of being in possession of a controlled drug.

#### B. Personal search under warrant
In exceptional circumstances, personal search prior to arrest may be authorised by a warrant granted by the court. In *Hay v H.M. Advocate*[79] a warrant was granted to take dental impressions from a suspect in a murder case in order to compare those impressions with teeth marks found on the body of the deceased.

---

[76]*Ibid.*
[77]*Jackson v Stevenson* (1897) 2 Adam 255.
[78]1980 Act, s.2(5)(b) .
[79]1968 SLT 334;

## C. Personal search in cases of urgency

It appears also that the taking of evidence from the person of a suspect may be permissible under the doctrine of urgency, that is, where it is necessary to take the evidence in order to preserve it[80].

### (ii) Search following arrest and detention

Once a person has been arrested (with or without a warrant) or detained under section 2(1) of the 1980 Act, his fingerprints and palm prints may be taken, as may other prints and impressions of any external part of the body[81]. Provided he obtains the authority of a officer of at least the rank of inspector, a constable may also take samples of hair, nail scrapings and samples of blood or other body fluid, by means of a swab, from any external part of the body[82]. An arrested person may also be placed on an identification parade. There is no general common law or statutory power to engage in any more intrusive form of search, and the taking of body samples such as blood, saliva or semen by more intrusive means requires a warrant[83].

### 5.2.2. Search of premises

Police officers cannot search premises for the evidence of crime unless they do so with the consent of the occupier (or other person having authority to consent) or under a warrant or some lawful power to search without warrant.

### (i) Search under warrant

Search warrants should be specific, as regards the premises and the purpose and limits of the search. As a general principle warrants which are indefinite and over-general are illegal[84]. However, the illegality of a search warrant is not necessarily fatal to the admission of evidence obtained under that warrant[85]. While searching under a warrant the police cannot actively search for evidence beyond the limits of the warrant. But if they happen to find evidence of a "plainly incriminating character" or even of a "very suspicious nature" they may seize that evidence. It does not matter that there is no connection between the "suspicious" material and the offence originally under investigation[86].

---

[80]*Ibid.* See also, *Bell v Hogg* 1967 JC 49 and *Cairns v Keane* 1983 SCCR 277.

[81]Prisoners and Criminal Proceedings (Scotland) Act 1993, s.28(1) and (2).

[82]*Ibid.*, s.28(4).

[83]*H.M.Advocate v Milford* 1973 SLT 12; *Wilson v Milne* 1975 SLT (Notes) 26.

[84]*Nelson v Black and Morrison* (1866) 4 M 328.

[85]*Lawrie v Muir* 1950 JC 19.

[86]*H.M.Advocate v Hepper* 1958 JC 39.

## (ii) Search without warrant
### A. Search following arrest
Where a person is arrested in his or her home it may be competent to search the house for stolen property, or other evidence of guilt.

### B. Search in cases of urgency
It appears that the police have the power to search premises without a warrant where this is justified by the urgency of the case. In *H.M.Advocate v McGuigan*[87] the police arrested and charged the accused with murder. A little over an hour after charging the accused the police went to his home, without a warrant, and searched it. The court held that they were entitled to do so without first having obtained a warrant, relying on the doctrine of urgency. It is important to note in this context that the court emphasised the gravity of the offence. Arguably, the search of premises without a warrant might not be acceptable in the case of less serious offences.

## (iii) Statutory powers of search
Various statutes confer on the police a power to search premises without a warrant. Section 60 of the Civic Government (Scotland) Act 1982, for example, provides that if a constable has reasonable grounds to suspect that a person is in possession of any stolen property, he may without warrant enter and search any vehicle or vessel in which he suspects that the thing may be found.

### 5.3. QUESTIONING OF SUSPECTS

The starting point for a consideration of the police powers of interrogation is the so-called "right to silence". This is a convenient, if rather misleading, shorthand for a number of well-established propositions. At common law there is no duty on any person to answer questions put to them by the police[88]. Although giving false information in response to police questions does not constitute the offence of obstructing a police officer in the execution of his duty[89] it may amount to an attempt to pervert the course of justice[90].

The principle that a person is not under a duty to answer questions put to him by the police is reinforced by the rule that before asking a suspect any questions the police officer should caution him, telling him that he is not obliged to say anything, and that anything he does say will be taken down and may be given in evidence.

A minor exception to the rule that a person need not answer questions

---

[87] 1936 JC 16.

[88] *Twycross v Farrell* 1973 SLT (Notes) 85.

[89] *Curlett v McKechnie* 1938 JC 176.

[90] *Dean v Stewart* 1980 SLT (Notes) 85.

put to him by the police is to be found in sections 1 and 2 of the 1980 Act which do require a person detained under those sections to provide his name and address to the police.

The admissibility in evidence of statements made while in police custody is discussed below.

5.4. OTHER FORMS OF INTERFERENCE WITH THE RIGHT TO PRIVACY

Scots law does not recognise any general right to privacy such as is provided for under article 8 of the European Convention on Human Rights. So, for example, objection cannot be taken to police surveillance which does not involve a trespass to property or similar damage.

However, following the decision of the European Court of Human Rights in the case of *Malone v United Kingdom*[91] Parliament enacted the Interception of Communications Act 1985. Under section 1 of that Act it is an offence to intercept a communication in the course of its transmission by post or by means of the public telecommunication system, unless that interception takes place under a warrant issued by the Secretary of State, or is otherwise authorised by the Act (e.g. because it takes place in connection with the provision of postal or telecommunications services). A warrant may only be issued if the Secretary of State is satisfied that it is necessary in the interests of national security, for the purpose of preventing or detecting serious crime or for the purpose of safe-guarding the economic well-being of the United Kingdom. Any person who believes that communications sent to or by him have been intercepted in the course of transmission may apply to a tribunal established under the act for an investigation of the suspected interception. If the tribunal finds that the rules governing the issue of warrants and the interception of communications have been violated, it notifies the applicant of that conclusion, makes a report to the Prime Minister, and, if it thinks fit it may, *inter alia*, direct the destruction of copies of the intercepted material and direct the secretary of state to pay compensation to the applicant[92].

# 6. The ordinary course of criminal proceedings

Since the distinction between solemn and summary proceedings is central to the Scottish system, and since in some important respects the course of proceedings differs according to the type of procedure adopted, an outline of both procedures is given beginning with solemn procedure. The discussion of summary procedure may then be limited to the ways in which it differs from solemn procedure.

---

[91]MALONE v. United Kingdom, European Court of Human Rights,2 August 1984, *Publ.E.H.R.R.* Series A, vol. 82.

[92]Interception of Communications Act 1985, s.7

## 6.1. SOLEMN PROCEDURE

### 6.1.1. Investigation, arrest and charge

As we have already noted, investigation of offences is carried out by the police under the general supervision of the procurator fiscal. Once sufficient evidence has been gathered to permit the suspect to be arrested the prosecutor presents a petition to the court (usually the sheriff court) for a warrant to arrest. Following his arrest, the accused is entitled to have intimation of this fact sent to his solicitor, and to have any other person reasonably named by him informed of the fact of arrest. The accused is entitled to have a private interview with his solicitor before he appears for judicial examination.

### 6.1.2. Judicial examination

Following charge the accused must be brought before the sheriff for examination, normally within 24 hours, although the sheriff may delay examination for up to 48 hours to enable attendance of the accused's solicitor. At judicial examination the accused may, if he so desires, make any declaration or statement. He may be questioned by the prosecutor with a view to eliciting any denial, explanation, justification or comment which he may have as regards (a) the matters averred in the charge, (b) the alleged making by the accused of any statement, admission or confession to the charge, and (c) what is said in any declaration emitted in regard to the charge by the accused at the examination.

There is no obligation on the accused to make any statement or declaration at this stage, and frequently the matter is disposed of by the accused's solicitor simply stating "No plea: no declaration". In this case the prosecutor will apply for the accused to be committed for further examination or for trial.

### 6.1.3. Bail

Applications for bail are frequently dealt with at this stage. All crimes and offences are bailable except murder and treason, and even a person accused of these offences may be granted bail at the discretion of the Lord Advocate or a bench of the High Court. An accused person does not have a general right to bail, but under the Bail (Scotland) Act 1980 bail may not generally be made conditional on the pledge or deposit of money. Bail may be granted on conditions which are designed to ensure that the accused attends court at all appointed times, does not commit an offence when on bail, does not interfere with witnesses and makes himself available for reports and inquiries to be made to assist the court in dealing with him for the offence for which he is charged.

## 6.1.4. Indictment

Following committal for trial the indictment is prepared and served on the accused. It must be served within 80 days of committal for trial. If it is not, the accused must be liberated, unless the period of service is extended by a High Court judge[93]. There must be at least 29 days' clear between the service of the indictment and the date fixed for trial[94].

## 6.1.5. Preliminary diet

Under section 76 of the 1975 Act a pre-trial hearing, known as a "preliminary diet", may be held in order to deal with matters such as pleas in bar of trial (such as the accused's unfitness to stand trial or prejudicial pre-trial publicity), objections to the form or content of the indictment, and applications for separation (or conjunction) of trials where there are more than one accused.

## 6.1.6. Trial

The trial must normally commence within 110 days of the accused being committed for trial if he is held in custody. This period may be extended by the court on the application of the prosecutor or the accused[95]. Failure by the prosecutor to observe this deadline will result in the accused being set free, and no further proceedings may be brought against him or her in respect of the charges in that indictment.

On the date fixed for trial the accused is brought in to court to answer to the indictment. If he pleads "not guilty" a jury is selected. A plea of guilty may be accepted, but it is for the prosecutor, rather than the court, to determine whether or not a plea of guilty, whether general, or to part only of the charge, is acceptable.   Trial takes place before a judge and jury of 15 persons chosen at random from names on the electoral role. There should be no general questioning, either by the judge or on behalf of the prosecutor or the accused, of persons cited for possible jury service to ascertain whether any of them could or should be excused from jury service in a particular trial[96]. However, the prosecutor and the defence each have the right to three peremptory challenges[97], and they may challenge any number of potential jurors on cause shown.

There are no opening speeches as in English procedure. Evidence is led

---

[93]1975 Act, s.101(2).

[94]1975 Act, s.75.

[95]1975 Act, s.101.

[96]*M v H.M.Advocate* 1974 SLT (Notes) 25.

[97]1975 Act, s.130. The right of peremptory challenged has been abolished in English procedure: Criminal Justice Act 1988, s.118.

first by the prosecutor. The defence have the right to cross-examine witnesses led on behalf of the Crown. At the close of the prosecution evidence the defence may ask the court to dismiss the charge on the ground that there is no case to answer. If this is not successful, and before any defence evidence is led, the Clerk of the court reads the record of the proceedings at judicial examination. Following this the defence evidence is led.

At the close of evidence both sides make their closing speeches to the jury. The judge then directs the jury on the law and will summarise the salient points of the evidence. There is no lengthy "summing up" of the evidence such as is encountered in English practice. The jury then retire to consider their verdict in private and there should be no further communication with the jury on matters relevant to the trial, except through the court.

The jury may return one of three verdicts in Scottish proceedings, all of them by a simple majority: guilty, not guilty, not proven. The effect of a "not proven" verdict is the same as that of not guilty, namely acquittal. In order, therefore, to convict the accused on any charge, there must be at least eight persons in favour of a guilty verdict. Seven persons in favour of guilt, seven in favour of not proven and one in favour of not guilty is still a verdict of acquittal.

In the case of conviction, no sentence of any kind may be imposed unless this is requested by the prosecutor, so that a verdict of guilty does not automatically lead to the imposition of a penalty[98]. Sentence may, and in some cases must, be postponed for the court to consider social inquiry, background and other reports on the accused.

If the trial has taken place in the sheriff court, and the sheriff considers that the appropriate sentence is beyond his powers, he may remit the case to the High Court for sentence.

### 6.2. SUMMARY PROCEDURE

In summary procedure it is unlikely that the accused will be arrested and held in custody. If arrested it is likely that he will be released on bail. It is also common for summary proceedings to begin not with the arrest of the accused, but by serving on him a summons to appear at the court on the appointed day. There is no pre-trial judicial examination in summary proceedings.

The trial stage follows a pattern broadly similar to that in solemn proceedings except, of course, that there is no jury and therefore no charge to the jury by the court. The verdict is returned by the presiding judge (sheriff or justice) and again, no sentence may competently be imposed

---

[98] *Noon v H.M.Advocate* 1960 JC 52.

unless requested by the prosecutor. As in solemn proceedings, the sentencing stage may be delayed so that the court may consider social enquiry or other reports on the convicted person.

## 7. Evidence

The basic rule in a Scottish criminal trial is that all evidence is admissible, provided that it is relevant, and is not excluded by one or other of the various exclusionary rules of the law of evidence. However, it is also a basic rule of Scottish criminal procedure (to which there are many exceptions today) that a conviction cannot be obtained on the basis of one item of evidence establishing the guilt of the accused. That item of evidence must be supported by another piece of evidence, from an independent source, so that together they point to the guilt of the accused beyond reasonable doubt. There is, in other words, a general rule requiring corroboration.

It would not be possible in the space available to describe these rules in detail. What follows therefore, is a summary of some of the more important evidentiary rules in Scottish criminal proceedings.

### 7.1. WITNESSES

It is important to draw a distinction between who may lawfully give evidence (competence) and who may lawfully be compelled to give evidence (compellability). The following cases illustrate this distinction:

### 7.1.1. Competence

Certain persons may not be competent to give evidence because, for example, of their mental condition, youth or other condition or status.

### (i) Mental disability

There is no general rule that a person who is mentally ill, or who suffers from mental incapacity or handicap is no competent as a witness. What matters in every case is whether or not the individual can understand the difference between truth and falsity, appreciates the duty of telling the truth and can give his or her testimony in a coherent fashion[99]. Whether an individual has this capacity is a matter of degree, depending upon his or her condition and the circumstances of the case: "the man who is convinced that he is the reincarnation of John the Baptist may be a perfectly good witness to an assault in a bus station"[100].

---

[99]Cfr. D. FIELD, *The Law of Evidence in Scotland*, W. Green & Son Ltd., Edinburgh 1988, p.227.
[100]*Ibid.*

## (ii) Children

As with the case of those who are mentally ill or suffering from mental disability, there is no general rule that children of tender years cannot be admitted as witnesses. Before permitting a child to give evidence the judge should satisfy himself that the child knows the difference between what is true and what is false and that the child understands the duty of telling the truth. He should also admonish the child to tell the truth[101]. Sections 56 to 59 of the Law Reform (Miscellaneous Provisions) (Scotland) Act 1990 contain special provisions relating to the giving of evidence by children, and in particular provide that in certain circumstances the evidence of a child may be given by means of a live television link.

### 7.1.2. Compellability

The general principle is that is all witnesses who are competent are also compellable. But to this general rule there are certain important exceptions.

## (i) The accused

Prior to 1898 the accused was not, in general, a competent witness at his own trial. With the passing of the Criminal Evidence Act 1898 the accused became a competent witness at his trial, and under the 1975 Act the accused is a competent witness for the defence at every stage of the trial, whether he is tried alone or with a co-accused[102]. He cannot be compelled to give evidence, and the prosecution should not comment on his failure to do so[103]. However, adverse comment by the prosecutor is not necessarily fatal to a subsequent conviction, but the presiding judge should instruct the jury to disregard any such observation[104].

## (ii) The accused's spouse

The spouse of a person charged with an offence may be called as a witness by that person, by a co-accused or by the prosecutor[105]. A spouse is, therefore a competent witness for all parties. Since the case of *Hunter v H.M.Advocate*[106] he or she is also a compellable witness for the accused. The spouse of an accused person cannot be compelled to testify by a co-accused, and is only a compellable witness for the prosecution if he or she is the victim of the crime with which the accused is charged[107].

---

[101]*Rees v Lowe* 1989 SCCR 664.
[102]1975 Act, ss. 141 and 346.
[103]1975 Act, s.141(1)(b) and s.346(1)(b).
[104]*Upton v H.M.Advocate* 1986 SCCR 188; *Ross v Boyd* (1903) 4 Adam 184.
[105]1975 Act, ss.143 and 348.
[106]1984 SLT 434.
[107]1975 Act, ss.143(2)(a) and 348(2)(a).

## 7.2. EXCLUSIONARY RULES

The most important exclusionary rules relate to (1) hearsay, (2) unfairly or unlawfully obtained confessions, (3) other evidence unlawfully or unfairly obtained, and (4) evidence relating to the character or previous convictions of the accused.

### 7.2.1. Hearsay evidence

Although there are many exceptions, the basic rule is that hearsay evidence is not admissible. The rule against hearsay is based on the proposition that the evidence given by a witness in court must be an account of facts perceived by the witness with his own senses. It should not consist of an account of facts or opinions related to him by a third party. Hearsay is, therefore, excluded because it is not the "best evidence" of what allegedly occurred, nor can its truthfulness or accuracy be tested by cross examination[108].

### 7.2.2. Unfairly or unlawfully obtained confessions

The basic rule governing the admissibility of an extra-judicial statement or confession is that of 'fairness'. A suspect's self-incriminating answers to police questioning will be admissible in evidence unless it can be shown that they were extracted from him by unfair means[109]. A judge will normally only be justified in withholding the evidence of a confession from the jury if, having heard all the evidence relating to its admissibility, he is satisfied that no reasonable jury could hold on that evidence that the answers had been fairly obtained[110]. Unfairness will include (but is not limited to) deception, questioning tainted with an element of bullying or pressure designed to break the will of the suspect or force a confession out of him[111]. Regard must be had to all the circumstances, including such factors as the mental or physical state of the suspect, or the fact that he is very young or of limited intelligence. Failure to caution the suspect may render a statement inadmissible[112], but this is by no means automatic and probably the better view is that the fact that the police had failed to caution the suspect is a factor affecting the question of fairness[113].

---

[108]Cfr. *Teper v R.* [1952] AC 480.

[109]*Lord Advocate's Reference (No.1 of 1983)* 1984 SCCR 62.

[110]*Ibid.*

[111]*Ibid.*, and see also *Jones v Milne* 1975 JC 16.

[112]*Tonge and Others v H.M.Advocate* 1982 S.C.C.R 313.

[113]*Pennycuick v Lees* 1992 SCCR 160. See also *Custerson v Westwater* 1987 SCCR 389 and *McClory v Innes* 1992 SCCR 319.

### 7.2.3. Other evidence unlawfully or unfairly obtained

"An irregularity in the obtaining of evidence does not necessarily make that evidence inadmissible"[114]. But such irregularities will render the evidence inadmissible unless they can be excused, and they are not lightly to be condoned. All the circumstances must be taken into account, and in the end the test will include, if it does not in fact reduce to, the issue of fairness[115].

### 7.2.4. Evidence relating to the character or previous convictions of the accused

Section 141(1)(f) of the 1975 Act provides that, subject to certain exceptions, an accused who gives evidence on his own behalf shall not be asked, and if asked shall not be obliged to answer, any question tending to show that he has committed, or been convicted of, or been charged with, any offence other than that with which he is then charged, or is of bad character.

The most important exceptions to this rule are where the accused puts his own character in issue by seeking to establish in evidence that he is of good character[116], and where the nature and conduct of the defence has been such as to involve imputations on the character of the prosecutor or of witnesses for the prosecution[117].

### 7.3. CORROBORATION

In general, a person cannot be convicted of a crime unless there is evidence from at least two independent sources implicating the accused with the commission of the crime charged. "The question is not whether each of the several circumstances points by itself to guilt ... but whether taken together they are capable of supporting the inference of guilt beyond reasonable doubt"[118].

The requirement of corroboration is relaxed where an offender commits a series or sequence of offences which are so closely linked in time and manner as to demonstrate a course of conduct. In this situation, each offence need only be proved by one witness, each offence corroborating, and deriving corroboration from, the others[119].

---

[114]*H.M.Advocate v McGuigan* 1936 JC 16.

[115]*Lawrie v Muir* 1950 JC 19.

[116]1975 Act s.141 / 346 (1)(f)(ii).

[117]*Ibid.* See, generally, *Leggate v H.M.Advocate* 1988 SLT 665.

[118]Renton and Brown, para. 18-52.

[119]*Moorov v H.M.Advocate* 1930 JC 68.

## 8. Special forms of procedure

### 8.1. PRIVATE PROSECUTION

As we have already noted, the prosecution of crime in Scotland is generally regarded as a public function. That power gradually evolved into an effective monopoly over proceedings on indictment[120] although the right to bring a private prosecution was not formally abolished. Its continued existence has been recognised on several occasions this century[121].

An individual who wishes to bring a private prosecution on indictment may do so only in the High Court. The first stage is to apply to the Lord Advocate for his concurrence in the prosecution. If he does not concur, he must give reasons for not doing so[122], and the applicant may then apply to the High Court for permission to proceed with or without the Lord Advocate's concurrence[123]. The court will not normally interfere with the discretion of the Lord Advocate. Although technically the court could order him to concur, the accepted modern view is that it will not do so, but rather it will authorise the prosecution to proceed without his concurrence[124].

Technically, the right to bring a private prosecution is not restricted to the victim, but since a private prosecutor must satisfy the court that he has at least suffered a personal wrong through the commission of the alleged offence this necessarily limits the range of potential private prosecutors in any given case. Even if the private prosecutor can establish this element of personal wrong, it does not necessarily follow that he or she will be permitted to bring a private prosecution.

In modern practice it is probably the case that an application to the court will be refused if the offence in question falls into a (somewhat ill-defined) category of "public" offences which includes such offences as perjury or perverting the course of justice[125]. As the court pointed out in *Meehan v Inglis*[126], it would require a very special case to justify departure from the general rule that prosecution is the function of the Lord Advocate,

---

[120]Although in practice private prosecutions in summary proceedings are not uncommon.

[121]*J. & P. Coats Ltd. v Brown* 1909 S.C. (J.) 29; *McBain v Crichton* 1961 JC 25; *Trapp v M.; Trapp v Y.* 1971 SLT (Notes) 30; *Trapp v G.* 1972SLT (Notes) 46; *Meehan v Inglis and Others* 1974 SLT (Notes) 61; *Meehan v Carmichael and Others* (1976) SCCR (Supplement) 109; *H. v Sweeney and Others* 1983 SLT 48; *McDonald v Lord Advocate* 1988 SCCR 239.

[122]*Meehan v Inglis and Others*, above; *McDonald v Lord Advocate*, above.

[123]*J. & P. Coats Ltd. v Brown*, above.

[124]*Ibid.*

[125]*Trapp*, above; *Meehan*, above; *McDonald*, above.

[126]Above.

and the broad considerations of public interest and public policy must normally outweigh the private interest which an individual may have in pursuing a prosecution.

## 8.2. PLEA-BARGAINING

As we have already noted, the public prosecutor has an absolute discretion to accept or reject any plea which might be entered by the accused at his trial. In particular, the court has no power to dictate the prosecutor's reaction to any plea. If, for example, the prosecutor does not wish to accept a plea of guilty then a plea of not guilty must be entered, and the court cannot refuse[127]. A similar discretion operates at the pre-trial stage, which, combined with the absence of judicial controls over pleas at the trial stage, means that the prosecutor has complete freedom to enter into plea bargains with the defence. The only effective control in this respect is, as we have seen, that if the prosecutor unequivocally and unconditionally undertakes not to prosecute an offender on a particular charge, he bars himself from proceeding at any future date on that charge.

## 8.3. FIXED PENALTIES

The fixed penalty system, as an alternative to prosecution, was first introduced in relation to road traffic offences (and for such offences is now contained in Part III of the Road Traffic Offenders Act 1988). That system has been extended to other offences by 56 of the Criminal Justice (Scotland) Act 1987. Under that section, where the procurator fiscal receives a report that an offence which could competently be tried before a district court has been committed, he may make a conditional offer of a fixed penalty as an alternative to prosecuting the alleged offender. If the latter accepts the conditional offer by making payment of the penalty (or its first instalment) any liability to conviction is discharged. The fiscal is not obliged to make such an offer, but once an offer has been made and accepted no proceedings can be taken.

## 8.4. CHILDREN AND YOUNG OFFENDERS

No child under eight years can be guilty of any offence[128]. A child over the age of eight who is alleged to have committed an offence may be dealt with by way of prosecution under the 1975 Act, or under the procedures contained in Part III of the Social Work (Scotland) Act 1968.

---

[127]*Strathern v Sloan* 1937 JC 76.
[128]1975 Act, ss. 170 and 369.

## 8.4.1. *Prosecution of children*

No child[129] may be prosecuted for any offence except on the instructions of the Lord Advocate, or at his instance[130]. A child may only be prosecuted before the High Court or the sheriff court[131]. If the child is prosecuted under solemn procedure the proceedings follow the normal pattern. If the child is prosecuted under summary procedure in the sheriff court, certain special procedures apply. Thus the sheriff must sit in a different building or room from that in which he normally sits, or, if this is not possible, he must sit on a different day from those on which other courts in the same building are doing criminal business[132]. The Act of Adjournal (Consolidation) 1988[133] sets out the procedures which must be followed by the sheriff during the conduct of the hearing of the case against the child, procedures which are, in the main, intended to safeguard the interests of the child.

No newspaper report of any proceedings in a court shall reveal the name, address or school, or include any particulars calculated to lead to the identification, of any person under the age of 16 years concerned in the proceedings, whether that person be involved as an accused person or as a witness[134].

## 8.4.2. *Proceedings under Part II of the Social Work (Scotland) Act 1988*

Part III of the Social Work (Scotland) Act 1968 established a framework for dealing with young persons in need of "compulsory measures of care". Section 32(1) of the 1968 Act provides that a child may be in need of compulsory measures of care if, *inter alia*, the child has committed an offence. The responsibility for determining whether a child is in need of such measures rests with a body known as a "children's hearing"[135]. Responsibility for referring the child's case to the children's hearing rests with a local authority officer known as the reporter.

The reporter may receive information from any person or source that a child may be in need of compulsory measures of care (including the police who have a duty to report alleged offences involving children to the reporter). On receiving such information the reporter conducts an initial investigation and decides whether or not any further action is required. If he decides that no further action is required he may inform the child and his parents and the person who brought the case to his notice, or any of those

---

[129]Generally, a person under the age of 16: Social Work (Scotland) Act 1968, s.30(1).
[130]Social Work (Scotland) Act 1968, s.31.
[131]*Ibid.*
[132]1975 Act, s.366.
[133]S.I. 1988 No.110.
[134]1975 Act, s.169.
[135]Social Work (Scotland) Act 1968, ss. 33 *et seq.*

persons. He may, as an alternative course of action, refer the case to the local authority so that they may, through their social work department, make arrangements for the advice, guidance and assistance of the child and his family. Where it appears to the reporter that the child is in need of compulsory measures of care, he refers the matter to the children's hearing.

The children's hearing consists of a chairman and two other members (including at least one man and one woman). Hearings are held in private in accommodation which must be dissociated from criminal courts and police stations. Where a child is notified that his case has been referred to a children's hearing he is obliged to attend that hearing. The child's parent has a right to attend, and is required to attend unless the hearing are satisfied that it would be unreasonable to require such attendance, or that such attendance would be unnecessary for the consideration of the case.

If there is a risk of conflict between the interests of the child and those of the parent, it is the duty of the chairman of the hearing to ensure that the interests of the child are safeguarded, and this may be done by the appointment of a person to safeguard the child's interests.

At the hearing, the chairman explains the grounds on which the case has been referred to the hearing, and asks if the child and his parent accept those grounds. If the grounds are accepted in whole, or in part, the hearing may proceed to deal with the child's case in its entirety or in respect of the grounds of referral that have been accepted. Where the grounds for referral are not accepted, the hearing then refers the case to a sheriff whose function it is to determine whether such grounds of referral as have not been accepted are established. The hearings before the sheriff, which must take place within 28 days of the referral, are held in private. They are not criminal hearings but civil proceedings to which the ordinary rules of civil, as opposed to criminal, evidence apply.

Where the sheriff is satisfied that any of the grounds of referral remitted to him have been established he returns the case to the reporter to make arrangements for a children's hearing to consider and determine the case. Where he decides that none of the grounds of referral has been established, the application is dismissed and the referral to the children's hearing is discharged in respect of those grounds.

Where the children's hearing considers and disposes of a case, whether without or after referral to the sheriff, its responsibility is to determine whether the child is in need of compulsory measures of care. If the hearing decides that such measures are needed they make what is known as a "supervision requirement". This may require the child to submit to supervision in accordance with conditions laid down by the hearing. These may include conditions as to the place where the child is to live (other than a residential establishment). In more serious cases, where it is thought appropriate in the interests of the child, the hearing has the power to require the child to reside in a residential establishment.

No child may be subject to a supervision requirement of any kind for any time longer than is necessary in his interests, and no supervision requirement may remain in force for more than twelve months. Supervision requirements are subject to review, and where a local authority think that in the interests of the child a requirement should be varied or brought to an end, they are required to refer the case to the reporter for review. The matter is then brought before the hearing who may continue the requirement, vary it or terminate it.

Decisions of the children's hearing, whether on initial referral or on review, may be made the subject of appeal to the sheriff, and the child, its parent and the reporter all have the right to appeal to the Court of Session on points of law in respect of any irregularity in the case. The one matter which cannot be appealed to the Court of Session is the decision of the hearing to impose a supervision order where the ground of appeal is that the treatment prescribed is inappropriate for the child.

## 8.5. MENTAL ABNORMALITY

It is important to distinguish between mental abnormality as it affects criminal responsibility, and mental abnormality as it affects fitness to be tried.

### 8.5.1. Mental abnormality at the time of the offence

Scots law distinguishes between the plea of "insanity" and the plea of "diminished responsibility". The former is a general plea, applicable in the case of any offence, and if established is a complete defence to the charge. The latter, in modern practice, is only available as a defence to a charge of murder, and it is a "partial" defence only, which reduces the offence from murder to culpable homicide.

Only the plea of insanity raises special procedural issues. As one of the "special defences", a plea of insanity at the time of the offence must be lodged with the clerk of the trial court and notified to the prosecutor (and any co-accused) by the defence not less than ten days before the trial date. It is possible, however, to lead a special defence even if it has not been properly notified if the accused satisfies the court that there was good reason for the failure to observe the notice requirements[136].

### 8.5.2. Insanity as a bar to trial

An accused may not be tried if his condition is such that he is unable, either from mental or physical defect, or a combination of these, to tell his legal advisers what his defence is and instruct him so that he can appear and defend him. A similar situation arises if his condition is such that he does not

---

[136]1975 Act, s.82.

understand the proceedings in court and cannot intelligibly follow his trial[137].

The question of fitness to plead may be raised by the defence, the prosecutor or the judge himself. If it is raised by the accused, then it must ordinarily be notified to the prosecutor not less than ten days in advance of the trial[138].

Normally, the question of fitness for trial is dealt with at a preliminary hearing, but it may also be determined by the jury at the trial[139].

### 8.6. TRIAL IN ABSENTIA

Trial *in absentia* is not normally permitted under solemn procedure. However, if the accused's conduct during his trial is such that a proper trial cannot be conducted, the court may order the accused to be removed from the court for so long as his conduct makes it necessary, and the trial may proceed in his absence. However, if the accused is not legally represented, the court must appoint a solicitor (or in the High Court an advocate) to represent his interests while the accused is not present in court.

In summary proceedings, trial may be conducted in the absence of the accused if, having been properly summoned to appear, the accused does not do so. If he is charged with an offence for which a sentence of imprisonment cannot be imposed, or if trial in absence is otherwise permitted by statute, a plea of guilty may be tendered on his behalf by a solicitor or other authorised person, or a full trial may be conducted[140].

### 8.7. LORD ADVOCATE'S REFERENCE

Section 263A of the 1975 Act confers what might be described as an "advisory" jurisdiction on the High Court. That section provides that where a person tried on indictment is acquitted of a charge, the Lord Advocate may refer a point of law which has arisen in relation to that charge to the High Court for their opinion. The acquitted person is entitled to be represented in these proceedings, but the opinion of the High Court has no effect on the acquittal at the trial.

---

[137]See *H.M.Advocate v Wilson* 1942 JC 75; *H.M.Advocate v Brown* 1907 S.C. (J.) 67.
[138]1975 Act, ss. 76 and 108.
[139]*H.M.Advocate v Brown*, above.
[140]1975 Act s.338.

# 9. Remedies

It is possible here to distinguish between ordinary remedies of appeal and review on the one hand, and extraordinary remedies on the other. As always, the distinction between solemn and summary proceedings must be born in mind.

## 9.1. ORDINARY REMEDIES

### 9.1.1. Appeal in solemn proceedings

In solemn proceedings, the accused may appeal to the High Court against conviction, or sentence, or both. The prosecutor cannot appeal against an acquittal. It is competent to appeal against conviction even where that conviction results from a guilty plea[141].

The only ground on which appeal is permitted is that there has been a miscarriage of justice in the proceedings in which he was convicted. A simple miscarriage of justice will not necessarily result in a successful appeal. The High Court has a discretion not to allow the appeal if it does not consider that the miscarriage is sufficiently serious to warrant setting aside the verdict[142]. There are, however, cases where the court will be compelled to set aside the verdict, as, for example, where it is satisfied that it is perverse or not supported by the evidence[143].

In disposing of an appeal against conviction the High Court may affirm the verdict of the jury, set aside the verdict of the jury and quash the conviction, set aside the verdict and substitute an amended verdict (provided that it is one which could have been returned on the indictment presented to the trial court) or set aside the verdict and grant authority for a new trial[144]. If the Court grants authority for a new trial the public prosecutor is free to re-indict the accused with all of the charges which appeared in the original indictment, including charges of which the accused was acquitted by the jury in the first trial[145]. In deciding whether or not to authorise a new trial, the Court must have regard to why the conviction was quashed. The court is more likely to grant authority to bring a new prosecution where it is not suggested that there was insufficient evidence to warrant the conviction, or any fault on the part of the prosecutor, and the sole reason for setting aside the verdict is a misdirection by the trial judge[146].

---

[141]*Boyle v H.M.Advocate* 1976 JC 32.

[142]*McCuaig v H.M.Advocate* 1982 SLT 420.

[143]*McAvoy v H.M.Advocate* 1982 SCCR 263.

[144]1975 Act, s.254(1).

[145]*H M Advocate v Boyle* 1992 SCCR 939.

[146]*Mackenzie v H.M.Advocate* 1982 SCCR499; *Kennedy v H.M.Advocate* 1990 SCCR 417.

In disposing of an appeal against sentence the High Court may affirm the sentence or quash the sentence of the trial court and impose another sentence which may be more or less severe[147].

### 9.1.2. Appeal and review in summary proceedings

A distinctive feature of summary proceedings is that avenues of appeal and review are open not only to the accused but also to the prosecutor.

### (i) Appeal by the accused
#### A. Grounds and methods of appeal
Under section 442 of the 1975 Act, the accused may appeal to the High Court against conviction, sentence, or conviction and sentence on the ground that there has been a miscarriage of justice in the proceedings. The method of appeal against conviction or conviction and sentence is by "stated case". The method of appealing against sentence alone is by note of appeal against sentence.

#### B. Appeal by stated case
In a stated case the trial judge states the facts as found by him and, depending upon the point raised by the appellant in his appeal, will pose certain questions to the High Court, such as, "On the facts stated, was I entitled to find the appellant guilty of theft", "On the facts stated, was there sufficient evidence to entitle me to make finding-in-fact No.10"? The stated case will normally be accompanied by a note by the trial judge explaining, for example, his views of the evidence, the demeanour and credibility of witnesses, and so on.

In disposing of an appeal by stated case the High Court may: remit the cause to the lower court with their opinion and any direction thereon; affirm the verdict of the inferior court; set aside the verdict of the inferior court and either quash the conviction or substitute therefor an amended verdict of guilty (provided that this is one which could have been returned on the complaint before the inferior court); set aside the verdict of the inferior court and grant authority to bring a new prosecution[148].

#### C. Note of appeal against sentence
In disposing of a note of appeal against sentence, the Court may affirm the sentence, or, having regard to all the circumstances, including additional evidence laid before the appeal court, quash the sentence and substitute another, whether more or less severe[149].

---

[147]1975 Act, s.254(3).
[148]1975 Act, s.452A.
[149]1975 Act, s.453C.

## D. Suspension

An alternative method of appeal open only to the accused is "suspension". "Suspension is the appropriate mode of bringing under review of the High Court an illegal or irregular warrant, conviction or judgment of an inferior court"[150]. At common law, suspension is possible on a variety of grounds and in disposing of an appeal by way of suspension, the High Court may: pass the bill and suspend the sentence, order, etc.; repel the reasons of suspension and refuse the bill; amend any conviction or sentence; remit the case to the inferior court with instructions to proceed if necessary.

It is possible to make an application for suspension on the ground of miscarriage of justice under section 453A of the 1975 Act, and in this case the Court has the same powers as it enjoys when dealing with an appeal against conviction by way of stated case.

### (ii) Appeal by the prosecutor

The prosecutor may appeal, on a point of law, against an acquittal or sentence passed in summary proceedings[151].

The appropriate method of appeal is by stated case, and the only ground of appeal is that there has been a miscarriage of justice. Fresh evidence may not be introduced on appeal at the instance of the prosecutor. Where an appeal against acquittal is sustained, the High Court may: convict and sentence the accused; remit the case to the inferior court with instructions to convict and sentence the accused; remit the case to the inferior court with their opinion thereon.

The prosecutor cannot appeal by way of suspension, but an alternative and equivalent method of appeal, known as advocation, is open to him. (Technically, advocation is also open to the accused, but this is only in exceptional circumstances and in practice advocation is regarded as a prosecutor's remedy, equivalent to the accused's right to bring a suspension.)

### 9.2. EXTRAORDINARY REMEDIES

### 9.2.1. The nobile officium of the High Court

An important feature of the common law powers of the High Court of Justiciary is the power "of interfering in extraordinary circumstances, for the purpose of preventing injustice or oppression"[152]. This power, which is commonly known as the *nobile officium* of the High Court cannot be exercised by a High Court judge sitting alone but only by a quorum of the High

---

[150]*A Treatise on the Law of Review in Criminal Cases, etc.* by the Hon. H.J. Moncrieff, Edinburgh 1877, pp.169-170.

[151]1975 Act, s.442.

[152]MONCRIEFF, *op. cit.*, p.264. See also, RENTON and BROWN, para.2-06.

Court (three judges)[153].

An application to the High Court for the exercise of this "equitable" jurisdiction may be made by an accused or convicted person, the prosecutor or other aggrieved party. It is typically invoked in order to redress or avoid an injustice arising from a *lacuna* or oversight in statutory provisions[154], but is available for the redress of any exceptional and unforeseeable injustice or hardship in criminal procedure[155].

### 9.2.2. The Royal prerogative of mercy

A person convicted of an offence may apply to the Monarch for the exercise of the Royal Prerogative of mercy. In practice this involves a petition to the Secretary of State for Scotland. If the Secretary of State decides to recommend the exercise of the prerogative of mercy, this may result in a "Free Pardon" or a conditional pardon. It has been held by the Court of Appeal in England that the effect of a "free pardon" is to release the convicted person from all the pains and penalties consequent upon conviction, but that it does not have the effect of quashing the conviction[156]. However, the effect of a pardon in modern Scots law has not been authoritatively determined, and it may well be that this would depend on the precise terms of the pardon[157]. Decisions taken by the Secretary of State in the exercise of the prerogative of mercy are not subject to review in the courts[158].

## 10. Other questions

### 10.1. STATUTES OF LIMITATION

There is no general statutory limitation period for crime, and in the case of *Sugden v H.M.Advocate*[159] the High Court held that at common law crimes do not prescribe. There is, therefore, no fixed period the elapse of which will automatically bar the prosecution of a common law offence.

However, as regards summary statutory offences, the statute creating the offence may contain a specific time bar beyond which proceedings cannot be commenced, and under section 331 of the 1975 Act summary proceedings for the prosecution of a statutory offence must be brought within six months of the date of the offence, unless the statute in question specifies some other

---

[153]*H.M.Advocate v Lowson* (1909) 2 SLT 329.
[154]See, for example, *Lloyds and Scottish Finance Ltd. v H .M.Advocate* 1974 SLT 3.
[155]*Boyle, Petitioner* 1992 SCCR 949.
[156]*R v Foster* [1984] 2 *All ER* 679.
[157]See Christopher GANE, 'The Effect of a Pardon in Scots Law' 1980 *J.R.* 18.
[158]*Cfr. Moore v Secretary of State for Scotland* 1985 SLT 38
[159]1934 JC 103.

period.

In any event, although there is no prescriptive period for common law crimes, the court has the power, in both solemn and summary proceedings, to refuse to allow a prosecution to proceed if it would be unfair to do so in view of the passage of time since the discovery of the offence. Thus in *Stewart v H.M.Advocate*[160] the High Court upheld a plea in bar of trial where the charge, one of corruption by taking bribes, related to conduct over 14 years previously. In such cases the test is whether the delay is such as to have caused grave prejudice to the accused. The Court will not readily dismiss charges on the ground of delay, but it is more inclined to do so where the delay can be attributed to fault on the part of the prosecutor[161].

## 11. Select bibliography

### Textbooks and Works of Reference

FIELD, D., *The Law of Evidence in Scotland*, Edinburgh, W. Green & Son Ltd. (1988)

GANE, C.H.W. and STODDART, C.N., *A Casebook on Scottish Criminal Law*, (2nd ed.), Edinburgh, W. Green & Son Ltd. (1988)

GANE, C.H.W. and STODDART, C.N., *Criminal Procedure in Scotland: Cases and Materials*, Edinburgh, W. Green & Son Ltd. (1983)

GORDON, G.H., Q.C., LL.D. assisted by MACLEAN, J. and GANE, C.H.W., *Renton and Brown's Criminal Procedure*, (5th edition), Edinburgh, W. Green & Son Ltd. (1983)

HUME, Baron David, *Commentaries on the Law of Scotland Respecting Crimes* (2 Vols.) (4th.ed) (1844).

SMITH, T.B., *A Short Commentary on the Law of Scotland*, Edinburgh, W. Green & Son Ltd. (1963)

WALKER, A.G. and WALKER, N.M.L., *The Law of Evidence in Scotland*, Edinburgh, William Hodge & Co. Ltd. (1964)

### Law Reports and Journals

Decisions of the Scottish Courts are reported in the following series of law reports:

*The Scots Law Times* ("SLT"), published by W. Green & Son Ltd., Edinburgh

*Scottish Criminal Case Reports* ("SCCR") (edited by Sheriff G. H. Gordon),

---

[160]1980 JC 84.

[161]*Hamilton v H.M.Advocate* 1989 SCCR 42.

published by the Law Society of Scotland, Edinburgh
*Justiciary Cases* ("JC") published as part of the Session Cases reports by the Scottish Council for Law Reporting, Edinburgh.

Articles on Scottish criminal law and procedure, and commentaries on judicial decisions, legislation etc. are published in the following journals:
*Criminal Law Review*, published by Sweet and Maxwell Ltd., London.
*Scots Law Times*
*Juridical Review* ("JR") the Law Journal of the Scottish Universities, published by W. Green & Son Ltd., Edinburgh
*SCOLAG Bulletin*, published by the Scottish Legal Action Group, Dundee.

# Chapter 13 - Spain

Enrique **RUIZ VADILLO**
President of the Criminal Chamber
Supreme Court, Spain
Permanent member of the Commission on Codification

## 1. Sources

### 1.1. THE CONSTITUTION

The Spanish Constitution was approved by the *Cortes,* in plenary sessions of the Congress and the Senate on 31 October 1978. It was thereafter ratified by the Spanish people in a Referendum held on 6 December 1978 and given Royal approval on 27 December 1978.

The Constitution contains various provisions which have a special impact on criminal procedure. Constitutional norms are qualitatively different from other norms because they embody fundamental values which form the basis of our political society, and shape the whole of the legal order. Constitutional provisions have immediate and direct effect in the Spanish legal order. Violations of fundamental rights can give rise to a special remedy in Spain, the *amparo* (infra, 9.3.). For this reason, the Constitution remains the fundamental norm, even though all constitutional rights have been incorporated in legislation.

The basic constitutional principles relevant to criminal procedure are: the right to personal freedom (art.17), the inviolability of the home and the secrecy of postal, telephonic and telegraphic communications (art.18), the right to judicial protection (art.24(1)), the right to a fair trial (art.24(2)), the legality principle (art.25(1)). The Constitution also provides that sanctions involving the deprivation of liberty shall be directed towards the rehabilitation of the offender and his return to society (art.25(2)).

### 1.2. THE CODE OF CRIMINAL PROCEDURE (*LEY DE ENJUICIAMIENTO CRIMINAL*)

The Code of Criminal Procedure (*Ley de Enjuiciamiento Criminal*) (hereafter CCP), was approved by a Royal Decree of 14 September 1882. Its preamble bears the signature of a great jurist of the time, Don Manuel Alonso Martinez. It retains its qualities of a literary and juristic work of exceptional value, and most of its principles, except for some minor and very specific points, are still fully valid in contemporary democratic society based on the rule of law, despite the fact that the courts have set aside a number of provisions, by virtue of the new constitution.

The CCP has been the subject of numerous and sometimes important reforms, some of which preceded, others followed the Constitution. For example, the *Ley Orgánica 14/83* of 12 December 1983 has incorporated some the fundamental rights and freedoms, set out in the Constitution (arts.17 and 24, supra, 1.1.) into the CCP. *Law No.53/1978* of 4 December 1978 introduced adversarial elements in the pre-trial investigations.

The most important reform was the *Ley Orgánica 7/88* of 28 December 1988, which was promulgated with the purpose of adapting the existing criminal procedure system to the Constitution.

## 1.3. OTHER STATUTES

### 1.3.1. The Law on the Organisation of the Judiciary (Ley Orgánica del Poder Judicial)

The Law on the Organisation of the Judiciary (Law No.6/85 ) was promulgated on 1 July 1985. Important statutes which followed are: *Ley Orgánica 7/88* creating the single-judge criminal courts of first instance (*Juzgados de lo Penal*), thus giving effect to a decision of the Constitutional Court rendered on 12 July 1988, on the question of the objective impartiality of trial judges, and *Ley 38/1988* of 28 December 1988 on judicial demarcation and establishment, which was implemented by Royal Decree No.122/1989 of 3 February 1989.

### 1.3.2. Law on the jury (Ley del Jurado)

Article 125 of the Constitution grants citizens the right to prosecute crimes (*actio popularis*) and to participate in the administration of justice through the institution of the jury, in the manner recognised by the law and with respect to those criminal proceedings which the law determines, as well as in the common law and traditional courts. In this respect, mention must be made of the *Tribunal de las Aguas* of Valencia.

Despite this constitutional provision, the jury has not yet taken root in Spain, probably because of the grave difficulties which the administration of justice faces today. The judicial system is facing a crisis, due to the growing volume of cases and an intense and extensive "legalisation" of everyday life, as a result of the emphasis placed on Law and Justice by the Constitution. The establishment of the jury would increase such difficulties. However, it is to be hoped that its creation as a matter of law will quickly be translated into practice. Through this medium the People can take an active part in the administration of criminal justice and it is absolutely certain that this is a way to achieve a better understanding of the difficulties involved in judging others. In this manner they will also achieve a better understanding of the reports of the more notorious trials such as murders, rapes, major fraud cases, etc., where one of the principal problems precisely is that of the evaluation of the evidence.

### 1.3.3. Miscellaneous statutes

There are a number of important statutes that are worth mentioning, but that cannot be further discussed within the scope of this chapter. They are: the Laws of 18 June 1870 and 8/88 of 14 February 1988 in relation to pardons; the Law of 17 March 1907 on conditional sentences; the Law of 9 February 1912 concerning Deputies and Senators and the rules governing criminal proceedings against members of Parliament; the Law of 17 July 1948 on conflicts of jurisdiction; the Decree of 21 November 1952 concerning the trial of minor offences (*faltas*); Law No.1/1979 of 26 September 1979, concerning the execution of custodial sentences; Law No.6/1984 of 24 May 1984 concerning *Habeas Corpus;* Law No.4/1988 of 25 May 1988 on terrorism (amending the CCP).

In the field of military law, the *Ley Procesal Militar*, approved by Law No. 2/1989 of 13 April 1989 should be mentioned. This law basically governs military criminal procedure although it also contains rules relating to proceedings which are by nature not properly penal, such as disciplinary proceedings, which are obviously concerned with the application of sanctions and of great importance in the military context.

In addition, the following statutes are worth mentioning: the Law on the Constitutional Court of 3 October 1979, modified by Law No.4/1984 of 7 July 1984 which regulates the functioning of the Constitutional Court, the General Statute of the Legal Profession (*Estatuto General de la Abogacia*) approved by Royal Decree 2090/1982, and the General Statute relating to the office of the Public Prosecutor (*Estatuto Orgánico del Ministerio Fiscal*) which was approved by Royal Decree 2046/1982 of 30 July 1982.

## 2. Structure of the criminal justice system

### 2.1. INVESTIGATING AUTHORITIES

Spanish police is divided into two national forces: the National Police (*Policía Nacional)* which operates in cities and larger towns, and the *Guardia Civil*, which operates in smaller towns and rural areas. Both forces are generally answerable to *Director de la Seguridad del Estado*.

All police officers are part of the "judicial police" (*policía judicial*). Article 126 of the Constitution provides that in the exercise of their functions of investigating crime and discovering and securing offenders, the judicial police are subordinate to the judges, the courts and the public prosecutor.

The composition, powers and duties of the judicial police are set out at greater length in articles 282 *et seq.* of the CCP.

A distinction must be made between two types of offences: public and private crimes. Public crimes (*delitos publicos*) can be prosecuted without a formal complaint of the victim. Private crimes (*delitos privatos*), however, may only be prosecuted at the instance of the victim. The judicial police must investigate all public crimes committed within their jurisdiction, and carry out such investigations (*diligencias*) as are necessary to establish these crimes and to discover the offenders; they must collect all objects and items of evidence concerning the crime where there is a danger of the latter disappearing, and they must place these at the disposal of the judicial authorities. The same obligations exist with respect to private crimes, but only if the victim requests them to act (art.282 CPP).

Members of the judicial police are auxiliaries of the criminal courts and the public prosecutor. They are obliged to follow the instructions issued to them by these authorities in respect of the investigation of crimes and the pursuit of offenders (art.283 CPP).

As soon as the officers of the judicial police become aware of a public crime, or are required by the victim to investigate a private crime, they must notify the investigating judge or the public prosecutor. They are obliged to do so immediately, if they can do so without interrupting preventive investigations (*diligencias de prevención*), otherwise, they must notify the crime as soon as they have finished such investigations (art.284 CPP).

When the investigating judge (*juez de instrucción*) or municipal judge (*el municipal*) have started a preliminary judicial investigation (*el sumario*), all preventive police investigations must cease, and police officers must immediately hand over the case to the judge, along with the objects relating to the offence which they may have seized, and place any arrested persons at his disposition.

## 2.2. PROSECUTING AUTHORITIES

### 2.2.1 The public prosecutor (ministerio fiscal)

The task of the public prosecutor is defined by the Constitution. According to art.124, the *Ministerio Fiscal* must promote justice in defence of the rule of law, of the rights of citizens and of the public interest as safeguarded by the law, he must watch over the independence of the courts and secure before them the protection of the public interest. In the exercise of these functions the public prosecutor may act *ex officio* or at the request of interested parties. The function of the public prosecutor is regulated by the General Statute relating to the office of the Public Prosecutor (*Estatuto Orgánico del Ministerio Fiscal*), *supra*, 1.3.3.

### 2.2.2. Private prosecutors

The *ministerio fiscal* does not have a monopoly over criminal prosecution in Spain. The victim of the crime and, subject to certain exceptions, any member of the general public, may initiate criminal proceedings. See *infra*, par.3.2.2.

## 2.3. THE JUDICIARY

### 2.3.1. The classification of offences

As in most countries, the classification of offences has a direct bearing on the competence of the criminal courts in Spain. The Penal Code distinguishes between two categories of offences, *delitos*, which are the serious crimes, and *faltas*, which are the petty offences. *Delitos* are defined in Book II of the Penal Code, *faltas* in Book III. As far as the competence of the courts is concerned, there is a further distinction between more serious *delitos*, which carry a penalty more than six years in prison and less serious *delitos*, which carry a penalty of six years or less, or a lesser penalty.

### 2.3.2. Courts during the pre-trial stage

As in many countries on the continent, criminal proceedings in Spain consist of a pre-trial stage and a trial proper. The pre-trial judicial investigation of *delitos* is carried out by the investigating judge (*juez de instrucción*) of the region in which the crime was committed.

The central investigating judge (*juez central de instrucción*) is competent in respect of those *delitos* which are within the competence of the National Court of Justice, the *Audiencia nacional* (see below, 2.3.3.).

There is no preliminary judicial investigation in the case of *faltas*. Court proceedings are confined to the oral hearing.

### 2.3.3. Courts in the trial stage

*Faltas* are judged by the investigating judge (*juez de instrucción)*, except for cases of minor importance which are dealt with by the justices of the peace of the place in which the offence was committed (art.14 para.1 CPP).

Less serious *delitos*, *i.e. delitos* carrying a penalty of 6 years' imprisonment or less, or a patrimonial sanction, are likewise judged by the investigating judge.

Serious *delitos*, *i.e.* those carrying a penalty of over 6 years' imprisonment, are judged by the provincial court of justice, the *Audiencia provincial*, which is a court composed of three judges, created in 1988 (*Ley Orgánica* 4/1988 of 25 May 1988 and *Ley Orgánica* 7/1988).

A number of serious *delitos*, are judged, not by the Provincial Court of Justice, but by the National Court of Justice, the *Audiencia nacional*, which was created by legislative decree No.1/77 of 4 January 1977. The jurisdiction of this court extends to organised crime, business crime, drug offences, offences whose effects reach beyond the territory of a single province and terrorism. The reason for conferring this competence to the national court was to establish a single judicial organ to hear such cases, in order to ensure consistency. This special procedure has been criticized ever since its creation: some experts on criminal procedure doubted whether the National Criminal Court was compatible with the Constitution, and raised doubts in respect of the Criminal Chamber as a judicial organ deciding matters of terrorist offences. But today, given the nature and composition of the court, it appears that its compatibility with the Constitution is clear.

## 3. Parties to criminal proceedings

### 3.1. THE PROSECUTORS (*THE ACCUSADORES*)

The public prosecutor, the *ministerio fiscal* does not have the monopoly of prosecutions in Spain. Both the victim and the general public are entitled to bring penal prosecutions before the courts (*infra*, 3.2.2.). At the hearing, all the *accusadores* have the same rights and facilities.

### 3.2.1. The public prosecutor (*ministerio fiscal*)

The *ministerio fiscal* is the active party to the proceedings. He is bound by the principles of legality and impartiality (Constitution, art 124 and *Estatuto Orgánico del Ministerio Fiscal)*. He is impartial in the sense that he defends the public interest, with the purpose of establishing the objective truth. Spanish criminal procedure adheres to the principle of legality of the prosecutions: the public prosecutor is obliged to prosecute all crimes which are reported to him. However, this obligation only extends to *delitos publicos*, which constitute the great majority of the offences. Private crimes (*delitos privados)* such as defamation, can only be prosecuted by the victim (art.105 CPP). But even in respect of public crimes, the public prosecutor is only obliged to prosecute if the facts that have been denounced to him constitute a criminal offence and if one or more persons are suspected of having committed this offence.

### 3.2.2. Private prosecution

*(i) prosecution by the victims of the offence (perjudicados)*
Those who have been injured or prejudiced by the crime are entitled to bring penal prosecutions alongside the public prosecutor.

Some offences can only be prosecuted if there has been a formal complaint (*querella)* by the victim. These are the private offences referred to above. The public prosecutor does not intervene in such proceedings (art.104).

Foreigners may exercise the *querella* in respect of offences committed against them and their property (art.270 CPP).

*(ii) prosecution by the general public: the actio popularis*
*Delitos publicos* may be prosecuted by any Spanish citizen (art.101 and 270 CPP). Any citizen can participate to the proceedings as an active party either alongside the public prosecutor, if the latter has decided to prosecute the case, or independently, if the public prosecutor has decided not to prosecute, for example because he believes that the evidence is not sufficient. The same rule applies in respect of 'semi-public' offences (*e.g.* rape), *i.e.* offences which can only be prosecuted if there is a formal complaint of the victim.

Even persons who have not been injured or prejudiced by the crime may exercise the *actio popularis* (art.125 of the Constitution and art.101 CPP). The differences between the private prosecution by the victim and the *actio popularis* are minimal: e.g., *perjudicados* are entitled to legal aid if they are indigent (arts.119 and 788(4) CPP).

### 3.2. THE ACCUSED

The accused is the passive party in the criminal proceedings, against whom the prosecution is directed. He is a necessary party to those proceedings, unlike, for example, the private prosecutor (see above).

Whereas, until 1978, the rights of the accused during the pre-trial stage were rather restricted, the accused now has procedural rights from a very early stage in the proceedings. These rights differ according to the stage of the proceedings and, concomitantly, the accused is referred to by different names in the various stages.

An *inculpado* is a suspect, *i.e.* a person to whom an offence has been "imputed" (*persona a quien se impute un acto punibile* (art.118 CCP)). He has certain procedural rights such as the right to be assisted by counsel, the right to be informed of the charges against him, and he right to effective judicial protection. A *procesado* is a suspect in respect of whom a formal accusation (*auto de procesamiento*) has been formulated. An *accusado* is a suspect who has been committed for trial.

### 3.3. THE VICTIM

#### *3.3.1. Private prosecution*

The victim has the right to initiate criminal proceedings and to prosecute the accused alongside the public prosecutor. Some offences, the so-called private crimes, can only be prosecuted by the victim (see *supra*, 2.1. and 3.2.2.)

#### *3.3.2. Civil claims*

In Spanish criminal procedure it is the general rule, almost without exception in practice, that both the penal and the civil action are brought by the public prosecutor, unless the victim has expressly renounced its civil claims (art.108) or wishes to bring the civil claims before the civil courts. Accordingly, the civil claim for restitution of property, for reparation of the damages and the indemnification of financial loss is normally brought by the public prosecutor. However, the victim may play a more active role in the proceedings if he wants to bring other charges against the accused, if he wants a higher indemnification or if he wishes to be formally present in the proceedings.

### 3.4. THE CIVILLY RESPONSIBLE PARTY

As in other continental systems, Spanish criminal procedure allows the civilly responsible party to participate in the criminal proceeding. See art.22 of the Penal Code.

## 4. General principles

### 4.1. PRINCIPLES GOVERNING THE OPENING OF THE PROCEEDINGS

#### *4.1.1. The legality principle*

Public crimes must be prosecuted *ex officio*: the public prosecutor has no discretion as to whether or not to prosecute (art.105 CPP).

#### *4.1.2. The ex officio principle combined with the actio popularis*

The public prosecutor does not have a monopoly on prosecution: the victim of the offence, and any Spanish citizen, can bring a *querella* and act as a prosecutor during the criminal proceedings (see further supra, 3.2.2.).

### 4.2. PRINCIPLES GOVERNING THE TAKING OF EVIDENCE

#### *4.2.1. The presumption of innocence*

The right to be silent is explicitly recognized by the Constitution (art.24).

#### *4.2.2. The privilege against self-incrimination*

The right to be silent is also explicitly recognized by the Constitution (art.24).

#### *4.2.3. The principle of the free evaluation of the evidence*

According to art.741 CPP, the court freely appreciates the evidence that is put before it. It freely (*del libre arbitrio*) decides about the crime (*la calificación del delito*) and the penalty.

## 4.3. PRINCIPLES GOVERNING THE TRIAL

### 4.3.1. The three stages of the proceedings

The criminal trial in Spain is conducted in three stages, the pre-trial investigations, the intermediate proceedings, and the trial proper.

Since the reform of 4 December 1978, pre-trial investigations have become more adversarial: the accused now has access to the investigation *dossier* and has the right to intervene in the proceedings.

The proceedings during the trial proper are characterised by the principles of concentration (art.744), orality and publicity (art.681).

### 4.3.2. The principle of immediacy

All evidence must be produced in court, during the public hearing For example, witnesses who have made statements during the pre-trial proceedings, must be heard again at the trial, except when they are unable to attend (art.730).

## 5. Coercive measures

### 5.1. ARREST AND DETENTION ON REMAND

### 5.1.1. Arrest (detención)

Art.489 of the CCP sets out the principle that no Spaniard nor foreigner may be detained except in the cases and in the forms provided for by law[1].

The CCP distinguishes between situations where a private citizen can proceed to an arrest (arts.490 and 491) and when the authorities or a police officer have the duty to arrest (art.492).

In principle, a person cannot be arrested for minor offences (*simples faltas*) (art.495).

Arrest must be brought immediately to the attention of a judicial authority, and always within 24 hours (art.496). The latter must within 72 hours either turn the arrest into detention on remand or declare it without effect (art.497). This is done by means of an order (*auto*) which is communicated to public prosecutor and notified to the private prosecutor if there is one (*supra*, 3.2.2.), and to the accused. The accused may request, orally or in writing, that the order should be repealed (*reposición*) (art.501 CPP).

---

[1] Cfr. art.17 and 55 *et seq.* of the Constitution and various international conventions.

## 5.2.2. Detention on remand (prisión provisional)

Detention on remand can only be ordered by judicial authorities, under the conditions laid down in art.503 CPP. The offence for which it is ordered must an offence bearing the characteristics of a *delito*, and carry a sentence of more than six years' imprisonment. Offences carrying a lesser sentence can only give rise to detention on remand if the judge considers such detention to be necessary by reason of the antecedents of the suspect, the circumstances of the crime, the social alarm caused by the offence or the frequency with which similar offences are committed. This measure may be reviewed at any time.

Detention on remand is limited in time. It may only continue for so long as the reasons which provoked it subsist (art.528). It cannot exceed a certain time limit, depending on the seriousness of the offence: three months if the offence carries *arresto major* (i.e. imprisonment between one month and one day and six months), one year if the offence carries *prisión menor* (between six months and 1 day and six years), and to two years in case of a higher penalty. In the two last cases, the time limits can be extended up to two or four years respectively by means of a motivated judicial decision taken after a hearing to which the accused and the public prosecutor are present (art.504, par.4).

Once the accused has been sentenced, detention on remand may be continued up to the limit of the mid-point of the sentence imposed when the latter is appealed against (art.504, par.5). The period served during arrest and detention are deduced from the time that is to be served pursuant to the sentence.

Provisional release may be secured with or without bail (art.530). The nature and the amount of the bail are determined taking into account the nature of the offence, the social situation and antecedents of the accused and any other circumstances which may influence his interest in putting himself beyond the reach of justice (art.531).

According to art.121 of the Constitution, persons who have suffered damage as a result of a judicial error are entitled to compensation. This article is further implemented by Law on the Organisation of the Judiciary (art.294(1)), which grants a right to compensation to persons who, after having been detained on remand, are either acquitted because the fact they were charged with did not constitute a punishable act, or discharged by an unconditional stay of proceedings *(sobreseimiento libre* (see further *infra*, 6.2.), provided always that they have suffered prejudice.

### 5.2. SEARCH AND SEIZURE

According to art.18(2) of the Constitution, the home is inviolable. No entry or search can be carried out therein without the consent of the owner or a judicial order, except in the case of *flagrante delicto*. The rules with respect to search and seizure are further developed in the CCP. Arts.545 to 567 relate to entry, arts.568 to 578 to searches.

Only the judge who is seized of the case can authorise these measures, except in a number of circumstances, namely (a) when the suspect is caught while committing the offence; (b) within the framework of the anti-terrorist legislation[2]; (c) when there is a state of emergency or under martial law; (d) when detention on remand has been ordered or (e) when, as part of a police pursuit the suspect hides or takes refuge in any house.

The CCP establishes the conditions for search and seizure and the manner in which to carry them out. The Law on the Organisation of the Judiciary (art.281(1)) provides that searches must be carried out in the presence of the *Secretario Judicial*, the clerk of the investigating judge. He is the judicial officer who is competent to give full faith to the effects of the judicial actions.

## 5.3. INTERFERENCE WITH THE RIGHT TO PRIVACY

Article 18(3) of the Constitution guarantees the secrecy of communications, especially postal, telegraphic and telephonic communications. Any interference with these rights must be decided by a judge. Arts. 579 *et seq.* CCP regulate the seizure of correspondence, the monitoring of telegraphic and telephone communications. In the future, it may be necessary to develop rules in respect of the surveillance of computer data.

According to art.579, the following rules apply: (1) The judge may authorise the interception of private correspondence emanating from or addressed to the suspect, whether postal or telegraphic, and may permit it to be opened and examined if there are indications that by these means an offence may be discovered or further evidence or some important circumstance of the case may be obtained; (2) similarly, the judge may, under the same circumstances, and by a reasoned decision, authorise the interception of the suspect's telephonic communications; (3) in the same manner, the judge may authorise, by a reasoned decision, for a period of up to three months, which may be extended by periods of a similar length, the surveillance of postal, telegraphic or telephonic communications of persons suspected of crime, or of communications that will be used for the realisation of their criminal purposes.

In case of urgency, when the investigations are carried out to discover crimes related to action undertaken by armed groups or terrorists or rebels, the measures contemplated in the afore-mentioned par.3 of art.579 can be authorised by the Minister of the Interior or the Director of State Security. This decision, together with the reasons for it, must be immediately com-

---

[2]Art.553 CPP as amended by the LO 4/1988 of 25 May 1988.

municated, in writing, to the competent judge. The latter may, by reasoned order, revoke or confirm the decision, within 72 hours of the time when the surveillance was ordered to be carried out (art.579(4)).

## 6. The ordinary course of criminal proceedings

### 6.1. THE PRELIMINARY INVESTIGATION

The preliminary investigation starts after either a denunciation (*denuncia*), *i.e.* the reporting of an offence by anyone who has witnessed the commission of a public offence to the nearest judge or public prosecutor (art.259 CPP) or by a complaint (*querella*), *i.e.* the formal complaint which any Spanish citizen may formulate whether or not he is the victim of the offence (see *supra*, 3.2.2.). It may take the form of either an abbreviated investigation, or of a judicial investigation.

### 6.1.1. The abbreviated investigation (proceso abreviado)

The abbreviated investigation is conducted by the public prosecutor, with the help of the judicial police.

### 6.1.2. The preliminary judicial investigation (sumario)

The preliminary judicial investigation is conducted by the investigating judge, the *juez de instrucción*. It is only used for relatively serious offences (*delitos*), not for petty crimes (*faltas*). Its purpose is to prepare the trial, i.e. to collect all the information with respect to the offence, in order to allow for the exact *calificación*, i.e. the formulation of the charge, and to determine the guilt of the accused (see art.299 *et seq*. CCP).

The investigating judge conducts the *sumario* under the supervision of the public prosecutor (art.306 CPP). He composes the investigation *dossier* and by putting in the evidence produced by the public prosecutor and by the other parties. He may also include evidence he has produced himself *ex officio*, but only if such evidence is relevant (art.315).

The preliminary judicial investigation is a preparation or the trial, not a substitute for it. Accordingly, the investigation *dossier* does not, in itself, constitute the evidence which will be laid before the trial judge. Spanish criminal procedure applies the principle of immediacy, according to which all evidence must be produced at the public trial, during the hearing. Only in exceptional cases, *i.e.* when it is impossible or very difficult to reproduce investigations of the *sumario* during in the hearing, may the elements contained in the *dossier* be treated as evidence, subject to the conditions laid down in the CCP. For example, when witnesses who have testified during the *sumario*, cannot be heard again during the trial, *e.g.* because they have deceased, their statements during the *sumario* may be used as evidence during the trial. This is justified by the fact that the criminal trial pursues the historical or material truth and it is not possible to exclude essential pieces of information from the trial. Art.720 even allows witnesses to make a "recognition" (*reconocimiento*) in a determined place, outside of that in which the *audiencia* is being held. See also arts.718 and 719 CPP.

During the *sumario*, the accused has access to the investigation *dossier* (art.301) and is entitled to ask specific investigations from the investigating judge. If the judge refuses to order such an investigation, the accused may appeal against this refusal (art.311).

Once the *sumario* is finished, the investigating judge transmits the *dossier* to the court which is competent to hear the case (art.622).

## 6.2. THE INTERMEDIATE PROCEEDINGS

Prior to the hearing, the court to which the case has been referred renders a decision about whether or not the case shall be continued. These committal proceedings, called "intermediate proceedings", are held *in camera*, in the presence of the parties.

The public prosecutor, and, if there is one, the private prosecutor, make their written submissions to the court. In these submissions, the *escrito de caleficacion*, the following elements are included: the offences resulting from the investigation *dossier*, the charge, the participation of the accused in the offences thus charged, the circumstances that may affect his responsibility and the penalty that he may incur (art.650). The accused must answer these submissions, also in writing, and may make alternative submissions. Both parties must indicate the evidence they intend to adduce during the hearing, by presenting the list of witnesses and experts they wish to call.

The court may either send the case back to the investigating judge for further investigations (art.631), or close the *sumario,* in which case it can either decide to open the public hearing, or to dispose of the case by way of *sobreseimiento* (art.632). A *sobreseimiento* is a dismissal of the case, either unconditional or provisional. An unconditional dismissal (*sobreseimiento libre*) is equivalent to an acquittal[3]. A provisional *sobreseimiento* means that the case is shelved pending the discovery of further evidence (arts.634 *et seq.*).

## 6.3. THE TRIAL

The oral hearing is the very centre of the criminal proceeding in which the fundamental principles of orality, publicity, equality, immediacy and

---

[3]An order for *sobreseimiento libre* will be issued: 1. When there are no rational indications that the detained person committed the offence; 2. When the acts in question do no amount to a *delito;* and 3. When the accused appear free from criminal responsibility whether as authors, accomplices or accomplices after the fact (art.637).

contradiction are fully applicable. The accused must be present during the trial: trials *in absentia*, save for minor offences, are not possible in Spain.

During the trial, the evidence is produced by the parties, and also collected by the court if this is considered necessary to discover the truth.

The statements of the accused are received (arts.688 *et seq.*). The accused is not obliged to tell the truth. Thereafter, the witnesses are examined, first by the party who called them, second by the other parties, and exceptionally by the judge. Confrontations are possible although not very frequent in practice. Unlike the accused, witnesses are obliged to tell the truth (arts.701 *et seq.*).

There are no special rules in the code with respect to statements of victims and those who have been prejudiced by the crime. It is generally accepted that they can be heard as witnesses, and that they are under the obligation to tell the truth, failing which they can be punished.

The experts are heard (art.723-725), and the documentary evidence and other evidentiary items are presented to the court (art.726-727).

Once the evidence has been presented, the parties may modify their initial submissions, presented during the intermediate proceedings (arts.650, 653, 733, 793(6)). If the court considers that, on the basis of the evidence produced during the hearing, there has been an obvious mistake in the *calificacion*, it can read to the parties what is known as a "*tesis*", inviting them to reflect on and to modify their positions.

Then follows the deliberation of the judges, and the pronunciation of the judgment.

## 7. Evidence

According to case-law, evidence cannot be restricted to the evidence which is produced during the oral hearing. Evidence can also been obtained during the pre-trial investigations, such as, for example, the confession of the accused, or evidence obtained from correspondence, which may be produced at the hearing as documentary evidence by the route provided in art.730 CCP.

In order to be admissible, the evidence must fulfil the following conditions:

(a) It must have been obtained without violation of the fundamental rights of the individual and it may not be tainted by irregularities. In other words, it must have been obtained in conformity with the fundamental guarantees contained in the Constitution (see art.10 and 24, and also art.14(2) of the International Covenant on Civil and Political Rights). For example, a statement obtained by means of torture is absolutely invalid, as also would be the irregular seizure of items of real evidence. However, this does not imply that the offence could not be proved by other means.

In this connection, it has been held by the Supreme Court[4] that as a consequence of this extraneous category of *retención* created by the police, a confession provided by the accused before the instructing judge is deprived of all probative weight for the purpose of overcoming the presumption of innocence.

(b) It must be capable of being contradicted. The principle of contradiction is one of the basic principles of legal procedure, and of criminal procedure in particular. Evidence which cannot be contradicted is legally non existent.

## 8. Special forms of procedure

### 8.1. PROCEEDINGS AGAINST MEMBERS OF PARLIAMENT

Proceedings against deputies and senators are governed by the Law of 9 February 1912 and by articles 750 to 756 CCP, by the By-laws of the House of Commons (*Reglamento del Congreso de los Diputados*) of 24 February 1982 (arts.10 and 14), of the Senate of 26 May 1982 (articles 21 and 22), and by article 71 of the Constitution. Members of parliament cannot be prosecuted without the authorization of the chamber to which they belong.

### 8.2. TRIAL *IN ABSENTIA*

Except in certain very exceptional cases, there is no place for trials *in absentia* in the Spanish criminal justice system (see arts.791(4), 789(4) and 793 CPP).

## 9. Remedies

### 9.1. APPEAL

Appeal lies only against judgments of justices of the peace and of the investigating judge[5]. There is no possibility of lodging an appeal against judgments of the Audiencia Provincial or the Audiencia Nacional. These judgments are only open to cassation.

Decisions of justices of the peace can be appealed before the investigating judge. Judgments of the investigating judge can be appealed before the Audiencia Provincial, or, if it is a judgment of the central investigating judge, before the Audiencia Nacional.

---

[4]Decisions of 3 October 1987, 10 November 1982, 4 October 1984 and 4 April 1987.

[5]The investigating judge does not only act as an investigating magistrate, but also sits as a trial judge, in cases relating to less serious offences, see supra, 2.3.

This system of review is heavily criticized, because judgments relating to the most serious crimes are not subject to appeal, whereas convictions concerning less serious crimes and offences are susceptible to appeal.

### 9.2. *CASSATION*

An application for cassation may be filed before the Criminal Chamber of the Supreme Court against the judgments (and exceptionally against other judicial orders) handed down by the Audiencia Provincial and the Audiencia Nacional,

Cassation is an extraordinary remedy. It can only be used on certain grounds which are expressly laid down in the CCP, namely for violation of the law and breach of procedural rules (see arts.849 *et seq.*). Quite obviously, cassation is also possible for breaches of the Constitution which is the higher norm in the Spanish legal order (Law on the Organisation of the Judiciary, art.5(4)).

### 9.3. *AMPARO*

The Constitutional Court has jurisdiction over the whole of the Spanish territory and is competent to hear, amongst other things, applications for constitutional review for violation of the rights and freedoms referred to in art.14 of the Constitution (art.53(2) and art.161(1)b)). All citizens have the right to apply to the constitutional court by means of the remedy of *amparo*, which has been characterised as the "final appeal" (*el último recurso*), which can only be used after exhausting all other existing remedies.

### 9.4. *CASSATION* TO REVISE A FINAL JUDGMENT *(REVISION)*

*Revision* is a remedy that can be used to attack final judgments of conviction, not those of acquittal (art.954.). This remedy is available to persons who have either been the victim of judicial errors or mistakes in the procedure or who can produce new evidence, which was unknown on the moment of the judgment, and which proves their innocence.

## 10. Select Bibliography

*Textbooks*

FAIREN GUILEN, V., *Estudios de derecho procesal civil, penal y consitucional*, Editoriales de derecho reunidos, Madrid, 1983, 466p.
GOMEZ ORBANEJA, E. and HERCE QUEMADA, V., *Derecho procesal penal*, 10th ed., Artes graficas y ediciones, Madrid, 1984, 422p.
MARTIN GONZALEZ, F., *Procedimientos civiles y penales. Formularios de juzgados de la instancia e instruccion*, 3rd.ed, Hesperia, Madrid, 1985, 542p.

SAINZ DE ROBLES, F.C., "La reforma del proceso penal (algunas observaciones)", VIII *Estudios penales y criminologicos*, 181-216.

## *Periodicals*

Annuario de derecho penal y ciencias penales
Justicia
Poder Judicial
Revista de derecho procesal iberoamericana
Revista general de legislacion y jurisprudencia

# Subject Index

Accessory prosecution 158
    *See also* Private prosecution, *Partie civile*
*Accusador* 388
    *See also* Private prosecutor
Accusatorial
    *See* Adversarial
Accused 14-16, 58, 115, 169, 190-192, 230, 267, 290, 320, 350, 389
*Actio popularis* 385, 389, 390
Adversarial 33, 34, 41, 82, 229, 239, 262, 349, 384, 391
Advocate
    *See* Defence counsel
*Agents provocateurs* 53, 128
    *See also* Informers, Undercover agents
Amnesty 118, 236, 249
*Amparo* 383, 398
Anonymous witnesses 41, 285, 292, 298, 309, 310, 311
Appeal 46, 71, 100-102, 134, 160, 181, 216, 256, 277, 314, 333, 377-379, 398
*Archiviazione* 246
    *See also* Sepot
Arrest 9, 24-26, 63, 64, 85-88, 120, 121, 150, 175, 176, 197-199, 217, 220,
        241-243, 271-272, 290, 300, 326, 332, 340, 350, 353, 356-361, 364,
        391, 392
*Assistente* 319-321, 328, 334, 337
Assize court 10, 11, 14, 16, 32-34, 37-38, 45-47, 113-115, 120, 126-128, 132,
        133, 227, 228, 229, 275
    *See also* Jury, Lay judges
*Autrefois acquit, autrefois convict* 82, 91
    *See also* Ne bis in idem
Bail 25, 65, 73, 81, 82, 91, 150, 176, 189, 202, 242, 271, 302, 326, 341, 392
Bank secrecy 36, 250
Binding over 88, 216
Blood sample 89, 304, 312
Blood tests 58, 66, 108, 152
Book of evidence 195, 202, 203
Breath testing 89
Breathalyzer 66, 298, 311
Burden of proof 21, 82, 118, 142-145, 193, 238, 353
Case stated 100, 218
Cassation 46, 134, 160, 181, 256, 277, 315, 335, 398
Cassation to revise a final judgment (revision) 48, 134, 257, 335
    *See also* Revising a final judgment
*Chambre d'accusation*
    *See* Court of indictment
*Chambre des mises en accusation*
    *See* Court of indictment
*Chambre du conseil*
    *See* Judicial council
Chief constable 75, 76, 344
Children 18, 40, 55, 70, 98, 99, 112, 171, 180, 215, 225, 313, 368, 373, 374, 375
    *See also* Juveniles
Children's court
    *See* Juvenile court
*Citation directe* 17, 31, 115, 125
Civil party
    *See Partie civile*
Civil servants 5, 111, 128, 264, 344
Civilly responsible party 18, 46, 47, 114, 170, 179, 233, 390

*Patteggiamento*  226, 230, 235, 236, 252-256
    *See also* Plea bargaining, *Transaction*
Penal order  125, 130, 131, 158, 230, 235, 254, 276, 277
Perjury  36, 48, 68, 93, 128, 161, 169, 249, 371
Petty offences  32, 43, 56, 130, 142, 158, 165, 167, 178, 181, 189, 214, 323, 331,
        332, 333, 337, 387, 391, 394, 396
Piracy  166, 215, 345, 346
Plea bargaining  42, 98, 131, 132, 145, 156, 157, 181, 213, 226, 236, 276, 295
    *See also Patteggiamento*
Plea of guilty  40, 42, 55, 61, 92, 98, 194, 204, 205, 213, 215, 376
Police
    *See* Investigating authorities
    *See also Officier de police judiciaire,* Judicial police
Police and Criminal Evidence Act  73, 75, 85, 86, 88-90, 95
Political crimes  2, 11, 142, 156, 223, 224, 259
Pre-trial stage  29-32, 124, 125, 177, 195, 305-307
Pregnant women  241
Preliminary judicial investigation  31, 125, 147, 177, 227, 268, 305, 328, 394
Press crimes  2, 11
Presumption of innocence  15, 21, 58, 62, 82, 85, 116-118, 145, 148, 163, 173,
        190, 193, 195, 204, 206, 224, 230, 241, 242, 296-297, 320, 321,
        353, 390, 397
*Prima facie* case  30, 32, 96, 177, 253
Principle of acceleration  60, 146, 171, 294
    *See also* Expedition, Reasonable time, Undue delay
Principle of immediacy  62, 147, 239, 297, 391
Principle of legality  2, 55, 61, 146, 159, 172, 224, 236, 322, 323, 384, 388, 390
Principle of "nemo tenetur"  297
    *See also* Right to silence
Principle of "opportunity"  20, 61, 55, 117, 141, 146, 270, 295, 323
    *See also* Sepot, Prosecutorial discretion
Principle of orality  23, 62, 119, 148, 175, 239, 298
Private crimes  322, 386, 388
Private prosecution  16, 44, 59, 60, 97, 130, 144, 157, 158, 170, 232, 233, 276,
        292, 322, 352, 371, 372, 389, 390
    *See also Partie civile*
Private prosecutor  144, 157, 158, 349, 371, 372, 389, 392, 395
Privilege against self-incrimination
    *See* Right to silence
*Pro deo* advocates  16
    *See also* Legal aid
Proceeds of crime  151, 195, 306, 308
    *See also* Criminal financial investigation
*Procès-verbal*  6, 20, 21, 22, 23, 30, 31, 34, 35, 37-39, 41, 43, 109, 119, 125,
        129, 130, 275
Professional secrecy  27, 36, 68, 122, 127, 128, 155, 232, 249, 259, 273, 304
    *See also* Legal privilege
Prosecution authorities  6, 7, 54-56, 75, 80, 111, 114, 141, 142, 163, 168, 188,
        190, 227, 229, 264, 266, 287, 290, 318, 319, 344, 349, 386
Prosecution *dossier*  235, 239, 246-248, 252
Prosecutorial discretion  42, 96, 97, 141, 156, 194, 264, 275, 276
    *See also* Principle of "opportunity", *Sepot*
Pseudo-legislation  284
Proof beyond reasonable doubt  12, 21, 62, 82, 95, 193, 214, 297, 353, 367
Public interest immunity  84, 210, 250
Public order  23, 26, 77, 88, 90, 119, 164
Public prosecutor
    *See* Prosecuting authorities
    *See also Ministère public, Parquet*
*Querela*  232, 236, 255
*Querella*  388, 390, 394

Racism 18
Radio 62, 174, 356
Reasonable time 65, 171, 201, 233, 239, 278, 282, 293, 316
    *See also* Expedition, Principle of acceleration, Statutes of Limitation, Undue delay
Remedies 45-48, 70-72, 100-102, 133-135, 160-161, 181, 216-219, 255-258, 277, 313-315, 333, 337-380, 397-398
    *See also* Amparo, Appeal, Case stated, Cassation, Cassation to revise a final judgment, Constitutional complaint, Habeas corpus, *Nobile officium*, Opposition, Revision,
*Res judicata* 182, 219
    *See also* Ne bis in idem
Restitution 123, 233, 273, 390
Restriction order 25, 99, 126, 271
Retrial 48, 71, 78, 101, 161, 258, 277, 315
Revising a final judgment 71, 134, 160, 219
    *See also* Cassation to revise a final judgment (revision)
Revision
    *See* Cassation to revise a final judgment
    *See also* Revising a final judgment
Right of individual application 1-3, 52, 75, 161, 258, 315, 343
Right to a fair trial 1, 19, 163, 269, 383
Right to be assisted by counsel 58, 155, 169, 224, 232, 233, 267, 291, 389
Right to be present 14, 16, 169, 231, 237, 269, 275, 291, 298, 312, 350
Right to be silent
    *See* Right to silence
Right to privacy 26, 28, 40, 66, 91, 106, 123, 152, 163, 177, 200, 212, 231, 244, 273, 304, 363, 393
Right to silence 15, 21, 22, 36, 40, 67, 75, 82, 83, 154, 190, 209, 210, 230, 321, 330, 331, 362, 363, 390, 391
Royal Commission on Criminal Justice 74, 80-84, 104
Search and seizure 26, 40, 51, 65, 88, 122, 151, 176, 199, 243, 272, 297, 303, 327, 360, 392
Self incrimination
    *See* Right to silence
Semi-public crimes 322, 389
*Sepot* 17, 31, 42, 43, 125, 175
    *See also* Archiviazione, *Nolle prosequi*, Omission to prosecute, Prosecutorial discretion
Special verdict 196, 207
Statutes of limitation 42, 45, 48, 72, 103, 135, 162, 277, 316, 337, 380
    *See also* Reasonable time
Stop 66, 73, 88, 89, 270
*Strafbefehl*
    *See* Penal order
Substantive truth
    *See* Material truth
*Sumario*
    *See* Preliminary judicial investigation
Summary proceedings 43, 69, 97, 130, 158, 181, 214, 252, 332, 333
    *See also* Extra summary-proceedings
Summary trial 79, 80, 214-216, 235, 252, 253, 254, 255, 346
Summing up 207, 366
*Tantum devolutum quantum appelatum* 47, 256
Tape recordings 69, 85, 155
Tax evasion 55, 117, 181
Tax matters 131, 231
Telefax 304
Telephone 28, 29, 40, 58, 61, 66, 91, 106, 121, 123, 124, 153, 200, 231, 244, 271, 273, 282, 299, 304, 327, 393
Telephone-tapping 58, 106, 124, 231, 282, 299, 305, 327
Television 62, 240, 356, 368

Terrorism  79, 114, 121, 141, 143, 152, 166, 177, 223, 359, 385, 387
*Transaction*  20, 31, 32, 42, 43, 98, 131, 132, 181, 295
  *See also* Oblazione
Trial by jury
  *See* Jury
Trial *in absentia*  45, 69, 99, 133, 159, 180, 277, 312, 336, 376, 397
  *See also Opposition,* Right to be present
Unconstitutionally obtained evidence  212, 214
Undercover agents  36, 153, 284
  *See also Agents provocateurs,* Informers
Undue delay  158, 194, 293
  *See also* Expedition, Principle of acceleration, Reasonable Time, Statutes of Limitation
Verification  25, 109, 226, 253
Victim  16-18, 30, 31, 43, 44, 59-60, 68, 81, 93, 96, 115-117, 125, 144, 157, 158, 170-171, 187, 192, 208, 232, 233, 236, 246, 270, 291, 292, 321, 337, 352, 371, 388-390, 394
  *See also Assistente, Partie civile,* Private Prosecutor
Video  85
Waiver  70, 231, 294, 295
War crimes  48, 283
Witness  33, 36, 40, 41, 48, 68, 85, 92, 93, 126, 127, 128, 140, 154, 155, 180, 191, 205, 206, 209, 211, 249, 250, 297, 309, 310, 330, 367, 368, 373, 394, 396
  *See also* Anonymous witnesses
Written proceedings  62, 299
*Zwischenverfahren*
  *See* Intermediate proceedings

# Case Index European Court of Human Rights

Abdoella v.The Netherlands 282, 293
Ben Yaacoub v.Belgium 13
Brogan v.United Kingdom 282
Bunkate v.The Netherlands 282, 294
Can v.Austria 15
Cardot v.France 36
Colozza v.Italy 312
De Cubber v.Belgium 13, 282, 289
De Jong et al. v.The Netherlands 281
Engel et al v.The Netherlands 281, 282
Hauschildt v.Denmark 52, 58, 282, 289
Huvig and Kruslin v.France 28, 29, 106, 124, 282, 305
Klass v.Germany 28
Kostovski v.The Netherlands 282, 298, 310
Lamy v.Belgium 3, 4, 15
Luedicke, Belkacem and Koc v.Germany 15, 139, 161
Malone v.United Kingdom 28, 91, 363
Ozturk v.Germany 161, 280
Piersack v.Belgium 13
Salabiaku v.France 296
Soering v.United Kingdom 282
Unterpertinger v.Austria 282
X and Y v.The Netherlands 281